The Collected Work

JOHN DEWEY

THE MIDDLE WORKS, 1899-1924

Volume 4: 1907—1909

Edited by Jo Ann Boydston
Associate Textual Editor, Barbara Levine
With an Introduction by Lewis E. Hahn

Carbondale
SOUTHERN ILLINOIS UNIVERSITY PRESS

The Collected Works of John Dewey

CENTER FOR EDITIONS OF
AMERICAN AUTHORS
AN APPROVED TEXT
MODERN LANGUAGE
ASSOCIATION OF AMERICA
®

Editorial expenses for this edition have been met in part by grants
from the National Endowment for the Humanities. Publication
expenses have been met in part by grants from the John Dewey
Foundation and from Mr. Corliss Lamont.

ISBN-10: 0-8093-0776-6 (cloth: alk. paper)
ISBN-13: 978-0-8093-0776-0 (cloth: alk. paper)
ISBN-10: 0-8093-2799-6 (pbk.: alk. paper)
ISBN-13: 978-0-8093-2799-7 (pbk.: alk. paper)

The Library of Congress has cataloged the original issue of this book
as follows:
Dewey, John, 1859–1952.
The middle works, 1899–1924.
Bibliography: p.
Includes indexes.
CONTENTS: v. 1. 1899–1901.—v. 2. 1902–1903.—v. 3. 1903–1906.—
v. 4. 1907–1909.
1. Dewey, John, 1859–1952. 2. Education—Philosophy.
LB875.D34 1976 370.1'092'4 76-7231
ISBN 0-8093-0776-6 (v. 4)

The Middle Works, 1899–1924

Advisory Board

Lewis E. Hahn, *Chairman, Southern Illinois University*
Joe R. Burnett, *University of Illinois*
S. Morris Eames, *Southern Illinois University*
William R. McKenzie, *Southern Illinois University*
Vernon A. Sternberg, *Southern Illinois University Press*

Textual Consultant

Fredson Bowers, *University of Virginia, Emeritus*

CONTENTS

INTRODUCTION

By Lewis E. Hahn

"I have piped my own song," Dewey wrote, probably in late 1908 or early 1909, by way of preface to some critical comments on "Knowledge and Existence,"[1] "and few have listened, and fewer yet have found a melodic theme. There seems to be little belief in the need of any new musical mode."

In spite of the fact that, as Dewey saw it, few seemed to feel the need for a new philosophy, during 1907, 1908, and 1909 he continued to work at developing the new pragmatic philosophy, defending it from attacks, launching vigorous counterattacks, and trying to show that the difficulties in its alternatives were too great for one to risk not considering the new view. These were, moreover, very productive years for Dewey. In addition to numerous lectures and speaking engagements and participation in professional meetings, he published fifteen or so substantial articles, almost as many shorter things, a syllabus on *The Pragmatic Movement of Contemporary Thought*, a monograph on *Moral Principles in Education*, and, with J. H. Tufts, the first edition of a very popular textbook, *Ethics*. The subject-matter of the articles ranged over metaphysics and theory of knowledge, philosophic method, instrumental logic, ethics, religion, education, and contemporary philosophy, with emphasis on central themes of pragmatism with respect to the nature of the world and the practical character of reality, the nature and function of ideas, experience, the proper function of moral theory, knowledge, truth, method, and education.

It is worthy of note that Dewey piped his pragmatic philosophic song not exclusively for philosophers but also for general audiences and various other professional groups. Two of his most important essays in this volume ("The Influence of Darwinism on Philosophy" and "Intelligence and

1. John Dewey Papers, Special Collections, Morris Library, Southern Illinois University at Carbondale.

Morals") were given originally as lectures in general series
at Columbia. Two others were presented at meetings of
the National Negro Conference and the Northern Illinois
Teachers' Association. Some were published in such journals
as the *Popular Science Monthly*, the *Progressive Journal of
Education, School Science and Mathematics*, the *Columbia
University Quarterly*, the *Educational Review*, the *Political
Science Quarterly*, and the *Hibbert Journal*.[2] Seven appeared
in the *Journal of Philosophy, Psychology and Scientific
Methods*, four in the *Philosophical Review*, and one in *Mind*.

Dewey found himself in quite a different philosophical
atmosphere at Columbia from that he had enjoyed at the
University of Chicago. In Chicago he was the leader of a
group of pragmatic colleagues, and the graduate students
were all well versed in the general pragmatic position.[3] At
Columbia his colleagues represented diverse philosophical
outlooks. There, for example, he had the challenge and the
stimulus of direct contact with the Aristotelian realism of
Frederick J. E. Woodbridge and the monistic realism of
William Pepperell Montague, and no one of his new colleagues was as close to his general position as was almost
every one of his former Chicago colleagues. The graduate
students at Columbia in the early years, moreover, as Jane M.
Dewey tells us,[4] included many for whom his point of view
was quite foreign. So he had to rethink his philosophic ideas
and restate them for an audience made up primarily of non-
pragmatists. The relatively close-knit group at Chicago perhaps encouraged use of a technical vocabulary which was, of
course, familiar enough to the initiated. Dewey feared, how-

2. Some of these are written in relatively simple, nontechnical
   language anticipatory of his later *How We Think* (Boston: D. C.
   Heath and Co., 1910); *Democracy and Education* (New York:
   Macmillan Co., 1916); *Human Nature and Conduct* (New York:
   Henry Holt and Co., 1922); and *Reconstruction in Philosophy*
   (New York: Henry Holt and Co., 1920).
3. Indeed, as he wrote in a letter to William James in December
   1903, even some of his undergraduates got hold of the pragmatic
   outlook and made it a working method. R. B. Perry, *The Thought
   and Character of William James* (Boston: Little, Brown and Co.,
   1935), 2:525.
4. "Biography of John Dewey," ed. Jane Dewey, in *The Philosophy
   of John Dewey*, ed. Paul Schilpp (Evanston: Northwestern
   University, 1939), p. 13.

ever, as he tells us in "Experience, Knowledge and Value,"[5] that at times he tended to be overly technical, and the new situation at Columbia encouraged him to make special efforts to express his ideas in relatively straightforward, nontechnical language. In his final years at Chicago, moreover, he had heavy administrative duties, but at Columbia he tried to concentrate on his research and teaching, including thesis supervision. He did take an occasional two-year turn as executive head of the department, one of them starting 1 July 1909,[6] but for the most part he left administrative responsibilities to others. The titles of his courses were much the same as at Chicago, but the contents varied from time to time in accordance with changes in his thinking and interests. They included courses on the Logic of Experience, Theories of Experience, Analysis of Experience, Types of Logical Theory, Advanced Logic, the Logic of Ethics, Psychological Ethics, and Moral and Political Philosophy.[7] As a means of increasing his salary, his appointment at Columbia called for two hours a week at Teachers College,[8] and occasionally he taught or lectured at other colleges and universities. For example, during the fall semester of the academic year 1906–7 he made weekly trips to The Johns Hopkins University to teach a graduate course in Greek Philosophy.[9]

Several major themes of Dewey's pragmatic philosophic song come out fairly clearly in the first four essays of this volume, all of which were included in *The Influence of Darwin on Philosophy*: for example, change rather than permanence as the touchstone of the real; concern with specific, diverse problems rather than with absolute origins and the world at large; a naturalistic experimental approach from the genetic standpoint in place of the traditional supernatural outlook; knowledge as an affair of the sentient organism interacting with its environment as opposed to a knowing subject seeking to know an alien external world as object;

5. *Philosophy of Dewey*, p. 523n.
6. George Dykhuizen, *The Life and Mind of John Dewey* (Carbondale: Southern Illinois University Press, 1973), p. 119.
7. Dykhuizen, *Life of Dewey*, p. 123.
8. "Biography of Dewey," p. 34.
9. The John Dewey Papers include two folders of notes for this course.

truth as successful working or the adequate fulfillment of
the function of intelligence as contrasted with orthodox correspondence or coherence theories; intelligence as an organ
of adjustment in difficult situations (the method of reflective
or scientific inquiry with its familiar stress on problems, hypotheses, and verification) as over against the intellectualist's
advocacy of pure, nonpractical theory; replacing the quest for
the final good by discrimination of multiple and present
goods, noting their conditions and obstacles, and devising
means of realizing them or making them more secure; the
need to set aside certain of the traditional questions of philosophy and turn to concrete, actual problems of men; philosophy as love of that wisdom which is the source of secure
and social good; and a critique of British Empiricism, Neo-
Kantian Idealism, and certain forms of Realism.

Thus "The Influence of Darwinism on Philosophy" is not
simply a report on Darwinism but a plea for the new pragmatic outlook with its emphasis on the changing, the multiple
and heterogeneous, and the specific. Whereas for two thousand years in field after field permanence and perfection had
been equated and the ruling conceptions on the philosophy of
nature and knowledge had rested on the superiority of the
fixed and final, Darwin's account of the coming to be and
passing away of species, the very epitome of the fixed and
final, led to the suspicion that the fixed and permanent, far
from being signs of perfection, are expressions of the dead
and outmoded. As Dewey put it:

The influence of Darwin upon philosophy resides in his having
conquered the phenomena of life for the principle of transition,
and thereby freed the new logic for application to mind and
morals and life. When he said of species what Galileo had said
of the earth, *e pur si muove*, he emancipated, once for all, genetic
and experimental ideas as an organon of asking questions and
looking for explanations (pp. 7–8).

For Dewey and the pragmatists, accordingly, nature is "an
indefinite congeries of changes" (p. 47), and the method of
inquiry is concerned, not with relating things to the fixed
and unchanging, but with tracing patterns of changes. The
emphasis on the changing and the ways of dealing with
changes receive, of course, more elaborate treatment in

Dewey's later *Experience and Nature* and *The Quest for Certainty.*

But in 1909 he was already convinced that the pragmatic philosopher must "forswear inquiry after absolute origins and absolute finalities in order to explore specific values and the specific conditions that generate them" (p. 10). As he saw it, what is needed is not some elaborate and imposing system but rather a tentative, piecemeal reconstruction of stock notions.

Eaton, the pragmatic spokesman in "Nature and Its Good: A Conversation," argues that we do not need an absolute to enable us to "distinguish between, say, the good of kindness and the evil of slander" (p. 20), nor do we need reliance on an absolute or supernatural power to recognize values and attempt to make them more secure. For this task the experimental method of science with its concern for conditions and consequences is what is requisite, and "the recognition that natural energy can be systematically applied, through experimental observation, to the satisfaction and multiplication of concrete wants is doubtless the greatest single discovery ever imported into the life of man—save perhaps the discovery of language" (p. 38). Neither theology nor the system of the absolute idealist can match this method. Nor is Herbert Spencer's attempted justification of values in terms of an unknowable absolute any better. Spencer's designation of his absolute unknowable energy as "God" Dewey characterizes as a "faded piece of metaphysical goods" (p. 12).

If there was any part of the pragmatic song which struck a particularly discordant note for his hearers, it was probably the account of truth. It seemed to many of his critics that what he called intellectualism, far from being fallacious, was plain common sense.[10] They held that an idea is true if the object of one's thought is as one thinks it, and Dewey's account of truth and knowing within the context of the steps in a complete act of reflective inquiry seemed to them plainly wrong. To speak of ideas as plans of action, hypotheses, which are made true or verified by working out

10. See, for example, James Bissett Pratt, "Truth and Ideas," *Journal of Philosophy, Psychology and Scientific Methods* 5 (1908): 124.

as planned, by leading truly, seemed to them to deny the eternal character of truth. An idea is true whether we know it or not, and it works because it is true; it is not true because it works. But, asked Dewey, how do we know this without putting the idea to work? For the experimentalist "the effective working of an idea and its truth are one and the same thing—this working being neither the cause nor the evidence of truth but its nature" (pp. 68–69).

Dewey uses the example of a man under peculiarly precarious circumstances who has been rescued from drowning. "A by-stander remarks that now he is a saved man." And he has the intellectualist reply: " 'Yes, . . . but he was a saved man all the time, and the process of rescuing, while it gives evidence of that fact, does not constitute it.' " If this be regarded as more than a misleading tautology which characterizes the entire process in terms of its issue, "as revealing the earlier condition of affairs, apart from the active process by which it was carried to a happy conclusion," Dewey declares that "such a statement would be monstrously false; and would declare its falsity in the fact that, if acted upon, the man would have been left to drown. In like fashion," he adds, "to say, *after the event,* that a given idea was true all the time, is to lose sight of what makes an idea an idea, its hypothetical character; and thereby deliberately to transform it into brute dogma" beyond any canon of verification (p. 69).

Although Dewey includes both realists and Neo-Kantian idealists among the intellectualists who insist on correspondence between ideas and an antecedent reality, "The Intellectualist Criterion for Truth" is largely a critique of F. H. Bradley's chapter on "Thought and Reality" in *Appearance and Reality* and of a position he himself had held in the *Psychology* some twenty years earlier. He complains that the idealists use truth in at least three ways, the first of which he finds intelligible and the other two confusing and unnecessary: (1) as something which characterizes ideas as intellectual statements, (2) as a certain kind of reality which serves as the criterion of ideas, and (3) as Absolute Truth, the criterion for the criterion (p. 65).

The persistent misinterpretations of his view of truth

led Dewey to devote a paper read to the Smith College Philosophy Club in the spring of 1909, "A Short Catechism concerning Truth,"[11] to answering nine common objections to it, objections raised by an inquiring pupil on the basis of Professor Purus Intellectus's exposition of the view. In response to the charge that his view is subjectivistic, Dewey maintains that he holds to "existences independent of ideas, existences prior to, synchronous with, and subsequent to ideas" and that, "according to pragmatism, ideas . . . are attitudes of response taken toward extra-ideal, extra-mental things."[12]

But, the pupil continues, if Dewey holds "that truth is an *experienced* relation, instead of a relation between experience and what transcends it,"[13] does not that make the whole affair intra-mental? Not at all, Dewey answers. Although pragmatism is bound to deny transcendence of "that which lies inherently and essentially beyond experience," this does not convict him of subjectivism unless experience means only mental states; and "the pragmatist has insisted that experience is a matter of functions and habits, of active adjustments and re-adjustments, of co-ordinations and activities, rather than of states of consciousness."[14] "The critic appears to hold the Humian doctrine that experience is made up of states of mind, of sensations and ideas,"[15] and the critic, according to Dewey (warming to one of his favorite themes, the criticism of British Empiricism) may have problems enough in deciding how, on *his* basis, he escapes subjective idealism. But to criticize the pragmatist "by reading into him exactly the notion of experience that he denies and replaces, may be psychological and unregenerately 'pragmatic,' but it is hardly 'intellectual'."[16]

This is by no means Dewey's first attempt to make clear the pragmatic notion of experience, nor was it the last. Although late in life he reluctantly concluded that he might

11. "A Short Catechism concerning Truth," *The Influence of Darwin on Philosophy* (New York: Henry Holt and Co., 1910), pp. 154–68.
12. Ibid., p. 155.
13. Ibid., p. 156.
14. Ibid., p. 157.
15. Ibid., p. 157.
16. Ibid., p. 157.

have done better to use another term than experience, it is a central concept in his mature philosophy, and his efforts to clarify it constitute a theme with many variations, finding expression in such important works as *Art as Experience, Experience and Education*, and his Carus Lectures, *Experience and Nature*.

One might comment in similar fashion about the account of reflective inquiry assumed in this group of papers. This is a theme whose variations go back to his *Psychology* (1887) and recur throughout his career. It finds clear expression, for example, in the *Studies in Logical Theory* (1903). It was to find its simplest articulation in *How We Think* (1910, 1933) and its fullest, most sophisticated formulation in *Logic: The Theory of Inquiry* (1938).

It is ironic but understandable that Dewey, whose greatest contribution may well be his insistence on the role of intelligence in human affairs, should be charged with anti-intellectualism. Intellectualism was the name he and the other pragmatists gave to the theory of knowledge and truth they opposed, and this naturally led many to think he was opposed to intellect. But the difference between him and the intellectualists is not primarily that he is opposed to intellect and they are for it but rather that he has a different notion of the role and function of intellect. For him intellect, or intelligence, has a reconstructive role. It is not simply a mirror of the antecedently real but a means of resolving problematic situations, solving difficulties.

He was convinced of the need to set aside certain of the traditional questions of philosophy, for example, that of design *versus* chance as the cause of nature and life as a whole, and of the need to turn to applying intelligence to the concrete problems of men. Intellectual progress, he argued, may come not through solving certain of these traditional questions but rather through abandonment of both the questions and the alternatives they provide. Instead of solving them, we get over them and attend to new and more important questions. One of Darwin's greatest contributions came in this connection. In Dewey's words: "Doubtless the greatest dissolvent in contemporary thought of old questions, the greatest precipitant of new methods, new intentions, new

problems, is the one effected by the scientific revolution that
found its climax in the *Origin of Species*" (p. 14).
And what are these new tasks for philosophy? Dewey
answers: "If insight into specific conditions of value and
into specific consequences of ideas is possible, philosophy
must in time become a method of locating and interpreting
the more serious of the conflicts that occur in life, and a
method of projecting ways for dealing with them: a method
of moral and political diagnosis and prognosis" (p. 13). This
is an anticipation of his stand in "The Need for a Recovery
of Philosophy," where he maintains that philosophy must
cease to be "a device for dealing with the problems of philosophers" and become "a method, cultivated by philosophers, for dealing with the problems of men."[17] *Reconstruction in Philosophy* and *Democracy and Education* also stress
the social function of philosophy.

If philosophy be conceived as "a love of that wisdom
which is the source of secure and social good" (p. 32), some
such social function would seem appropriate for it; and the
moral side of philosophy, viewing future possibilities with
reference to attaining the better and averting the worse, is a
continuing emphasis of Dewey's in *Experience and Nature*
and *The Quest for Certainty*.

When Dewey gave his lecture on Ethics[18] in a series on
Science, Philosophy, and Art at Columbia University in the
spring of 1909, President Nicholas Murray Butler had already lectured on Philosophy and Frederick J. E. Woodbridge
on Metaphysics. He gives in this lecture a condensed version
of his contribution to the Dewey and Tufts *Ethics*. His history of Greek philosophy as background for contemporary
moral theory illustrates his tendency to go back to the
Greeks, a tendency also exemplified in *Reconstruction in
Philosophy* and *The Quest for Certainty*. As in *Ethics* he uses
utilitarianism and Kantian ethics to contrast with the pragmatic view with its emphasis on the application of the
method of critical inquiry to the many problems within contemporary life.

17. "The Need for a Recovery of Philosophy," *Creative Intelligence*
(New York: Henry Holt and Co., 1917), p. 65.
18. Included in the present volume as "Intelligence and Morals."

There are five characters in "Nature and Its Good: A Conversation," each representing a different outlook. In addition to Eaton the pragmatist, there are Moore the absolute idealist with his emphasis on transcendent values, Arthur the Aristotelian who represents a view very like Woodbridge's, Grimes the economic determinist, and Stair the mystic advocate of feeling. Eaton defines philosophy as "a catholic and farsighted theory of the adjustment of the conflicting factors of life" (p. 30), the application of the method of intelligence to problems of adjustments at various levels.

"The Control of Ideas by Facts," "The Logical Character of Ideas," and "What Pragmatism Means by Practical" were included in the *Essays in Experimental Logic*, and they with "Does Reality Possess Practical Character?" form our next group for discussion. Various of the main themes of Dewey's pragmatic song come out clearly in them also, but the dominant one is the method of reflective inquiry with its stress on problems, hypotheses, and the resolution of difficulties. When Dewey seeks to clarify the meaning of any term, say, "idea," "fact," or "existence," he tries to indicate its function in a complete act of reflective thinking.

This is well illustrated in "The Control of Ideas by Facts," an essay which also shows the formidable polemicist at his best. He insists that his pragmatic view has never denied the prima facie working distinction between "ideas" and "facts," or the necessity of a control of meaning by facts. But what is one to understand by this? It may be noted, he avers, that it was "precisely the lack of an adequate and generally accepted theory of the nature of fact and idea, and of the kind of agreement or correspondence between them which constitutes the truth of the idea, that led to the development of a functional theory of logic" (p. 78).

If we take as a typical case of problem solving the illustration of a man lost in the woods, the problem "is to find a correct idea of the way home—a practical idea or plan of action which will lead to success, or the realization of the purpose to get home" (pp. 82–83). The critics of the experimental view, however, "make the point that this practical idea, the truth of which is evidenced in the successful meeting of a need, is dependent for its success upon a purely presentative idea, that of the existent environment, whose validity has nothing to do with success but depends on agreement with the given state of affairs. It is said that what makes a man's idea of his environment true is its agreement with the actual environment" (p. 128), and similarly with other true ideas. Dewey, moreover, indicates his willingness to accept this formula, but, he adds, "it was long my misfortune not to be possessed offhand of those perfectly clear notions of just what is meant in this formula by the terms 'idea,' 'existence' and 'agreement' which are possessed by other writers on epistemology; and when I analyzed these notions I found the distinction between the practical idea and the theoretical not fixed nor final, and I found a somewhat startling similarity between the notions of 'success' and 'agreement' " (p. 83).

Dewey goes on to explain what the environment is of which an idea is to be formed, and the definition assigned to it turns out to be as tentative and experimental as that assigned to the idea. "It is the *practical* facts of being lost and desiring to be found which constitute the limits and the content of the 'environment' " (p. 84). And if the individual is to test the agreement of his idea and the environment, "with what reality is he to compare it? Not with the presented reality, for *that* reality is the reality of himself lost; not with the complete reality, for at this stage of proceedings he has only the idea to stand for the complete theory. What kind of comparison is possible or desirable then, save to treat the mental layout of the whole situation as a working hypothesis, as a plan of action, and proceed to *act* upon it, to use it as a director and controller of one's divagations instead of stumbling blindly around until one is either exhausted or accidentally gets out? Now suppose one uses the idea—that is to say, the present facts projected into a whole in the light of absent facts—as a guide of action. Suppose, by means of its specifications, one works one's way along until one comes upon familiar ground—finds one's self. *Now*, one may say, my idea was right, it was in accord with facts; it agrees with reality. That is, acted upon sincerely, it has led to the desired conclusion; it has, *through action*, worked out the state of things which it contemplated or intended. The agreement,

correspondence, is between purpose, plan, and its own execution, fulfillment. . . . Just how does such agreement differ
from success?" (p. 84).

As is perhaps obvious from the above discussion the
themes of truth as successful working or verified prediction
and knowledge as an affair of the sentient organism interacting with its environment also figure prominently in this
essay, and Dewey makes the point that knowledge involves
taking one thing as a sign of another.

Dewey's statement found a measure of support from
Roy Wood Sellars, who affirmed his fundamental agreement
with Dewey's logical position and praised genetic analysis
while noting some ambiguities in the statement and raising
enough questions to win the praise of such critics of pragmatism as J. B. Pratt.[19]

"The Logical Character of Ideas" emphasizes essentially
the same themes as "The Control of Ideas by Facts." Dewey
blasts the traditional dualism of things and consciousness
and treats of the logical function of ideas in reflective inquiry, crediting his former colleague G. H. Mead with a be-
havioral interpretation of symbols.

Perhaps the most noteworthy feature of "What Pragmatism Means by Practical" and "Does Reality Possess Practical Character?," the first described by Dewey as an account
of the pragmatic movement, based on James's *Pragmatism*,[20]
and the second written for *Essays, Philosophical and Psychological*, a volume in honor of James by his colleagues at
Columbia University, is that they offer an interpretation by
Dewey of James and of the doctrine they shared.[21] Although
their basic agreement outweighed their differences and each
held the other in very high regard, Dewey was troubled by
some of James's language—for example, his use of "satisfaction"—and he had some misgivings about his "will" or "right"

19. Roy Wood Sellars, "Professor Dewey's View of Agreement,"
    Journal of Philosophy, Psychology and Scientific Methods 4
    (1907): 432–35; Pratt, "Truth and Ideas," ibid. 5 (1908): 122–
    31.
20. Dewey to William James, 28 November 1907, in Perry, *Thought
    of James*, 2:528.
21. Cf. "The Development of American Pragmatism," in *Studies in
    the History of Ideas*, II (New York: Columbia University Press,
    1925), Supplement, 353–77.

to believe. For his part James sometimes thought that
Dewey's primary appeal was "to those who like their philosophy difficult and technical, and will respect nothing that
is not obscure,"[22] but he followed Dewey's advice in certain
of his formulations.[23]

In writing "What Pragmatism Means by Practical"
Dewey became aware of some points of possible divergence
between Schiller, James, and himself, and he thought that
some misunderstandings among their critics might be cleared
away if their points of respective agreement and possible
disagreement were brought out.[24] James tended to play down
the differences and to treat the different versions as com-
plementary.

In the essay itself, following what he takes to be James's
example, Dewey regards pragmatism as primarily a method
and treats the account of the pragmatic attitude, ideas and
their truth, and reality "somewhat incidentally so far as
the discussion of them serves to exemplify or enforce the
method" (p. 99). This method has been applied to a host of
different things from philosophic controversies to beliefs,
truths, ideas, and objects, in connection with numerous problems in many diverse situations; and yet, he adds, when we
consider these different subjects separately, we find that
James, "with his never-failing instinct for the concrete" (p.
101), has provided the necessary formula for each. Nevertheless, Dewey's explanation of "the unsatisfactory condition
of contemporary pragmatic discussion is that in composing
these 'different points of view' into a single pictorial whole,
the distinct type of consequence and hence the meaning of
'practical' appropriate to each has not been sufficiently
emphasized" (p. 101), with the consequence that some misunderstanding of the pragmatic movement has resulted. Accordingly, he endeavors "to elucidate from the standpoint of
pragmatic method the importance of enforcing these distinctions" (p. 104). For example, whereas "the meaning of an
object is the changes it requires in our attitude, the meaning

22. James to F. C. S. Schiller, 27 May 1907, in Perry, *Thought of
James*, 2:508.
23. See, for example, Perry, *Thought of James*, 2:531–32.
24. Dewey to James, 28 November 1907, in Perry, *Thought of
James*, 2:528–29.

of an idea is the changes it, as our attitude, effects in objects" (p. 103), or the practical factor in connection with a belief may be whether its consequences are good, bad, or indifferent, "in which latter case belief is idle, the controversy a vain and conventional, or verbal, one" (p. 103).

As for the book *Pragmatism* itself, Dewey says that it "is more likely to take place as a philosophical classic than any other writing of our day," though a critic who attempts to appraise it "would probably give one more illustration of the sterility of criticism compared with the productiveness of creative genius" (p. 115). And even those who dislike pragmatism, he continues, can hardly fail to find much of profit in the exhibition of James's "instinct for concrete facts, the breadth of his sympathies, and his illuminating insights. Unreserved frankness, lucid imagination, varied contacts with life digested into summary and trenchant conclusions, keen perceptions of human nature in the concrete, a constant sense of the subordination of philosophy to life, capacity to put things into an English which projects ideas as if bodily into space till they are solid things to walk around and survey from different sides—these things are not so common in philosophy that they may not smell sweet even by the name of pragmatism" (p. 115).

The theme of Dewey's pragmatic song focused on in "Does Reality Possess Practical Character?" is that of knowledge as an affair of the sentient organism interacting with its environment and, hopefully, making a difference in it; but, of course, various other themes also find a place in it. For example, with reference to change rather than permanence as the touchstone of the real and the conception of philosophy as being concerned with the affairs of men, Dewey speaks of the "danger that the philosophy which tries to escape the form of generation by taking refuge under the form of eternity will only come under the form of a by-gone generation" (p. 142) and says that it is better "for philosophy to err in active participation in the living struggles and issues of its own age and times than to maintain an immune monastic impeccability, without relevancy and bearing in the generating ideas of its contemporary present" (p. 142). He also touches on the problem of reconciling the scientific view of the universe with the claims of the moral life (p. 131), a topic treated at length in *The Quest for Certainty* and described by him in "Experience, Knowledge and Value" as one of the two issues which have controlled the main course of modern thought.[25]

But knowledge as interaction with the environment and intelligence as an organ of adjustment in difficult situations are the focus of "Does Reality Possess Practical Character?" Dewey complains that in current philosophy "everything of a practical nature is regarded as 'merely' personal, and the 'merely' has the force of denying legitimate standing in the court of cosmic jurisdiction" (p. 126), or characterizing as invidiously subjective. The practical function of knowledge, moreover, seems to be the sticking point; but, Dewey asks, "if one believes that the world itself is in transformation, why should the notion that knowledge is the most important mode of its modification and the only organ of its guidance be *a priori* obnoxious?" (p. 127).

Unless one has fallen prey to that "species of confirmed intellectual lock-jaw called epistemology" (p. 138n), the evidence for the practical character of reality and for intelligence as the most efficacious expression of that character is overwhelmingly obvious. "The parts and members of the organism," Dewey contends, "are certainly not there primarily for pure intellection or for theoretic contemplation. The brain, the last physical organ of thought, is a part of the same practical machinery for bringing about adaptation of the environment to the life requirements of the organism, to which belong legs and hand and eye" (p. 132).

The function of consciousness, awareness, attention, is not to copy "reality at large, a metaphysical heaven to be mimeographed at many removes upon a badly constructed mental carbon paper which yields at best only fragmentary, blurred, and erroneous copies" (p. 136), but rather to signalize some crisis or obstacle in an existent situation and thus to help set up a relation between organism and environment which will facilitate ample and effective functioning. Thus the issue is not "ideally necessary but actually impossible

25. *Philosophy of John Dewey*, p. 523.

copying, *versus* an improper but unavoidable modification of reality through organic inhibitions and stimulations" but rather "the right, the economical, the effective, and . . . the useful and satisfactory reaction *versus* the wasteful, the enslaving, the misleading, and the confusing reaction" (p. 134).

The intellectualist critics of this view oppose it, however, because they "assume that to hold that knowledge makes a difference in existences is equivalent to holding that it makes a difference in the object *to be* known, thus defeating its own purpose; witless that the reality which is the appropriate object of knowledge in a given case may be precisely a reality in which knowing has succeeded in making the needed difference" (p. 128). This, however, is an unwarranted assumption, for, as Dewey sees it, "It is practically all one to say that the norm of honorable knowing is to make no difference in *its* object, and that its aim is to attain and buttress a specific kind of difference in reality" (p. 136).

As might have been expected, this vigorous polemical essay stirred up a host of able critics such as E. B. McGilvary, and we shall touch on some of this criticism later.

Two other items dealing with pragmatism might be mentioned here: namely, the syllabus on *The Pragmatic Movement of Contemporary Thought* and "The Bearings of Pragmatism upon Education." The former was intended primarily for his classes but was evidently given wider circulation inasmuch as the copy from Harvard College Library used in preparing the present edition was apparently one sent to George H. Palmer. It is of interest primarily in indicating something of Dewey's way of presenting pragmatism to his Columbia classes, but it touches, to be sure, on various of the themes of his pragmatic song. On its positive side, he notes, the view "grows out of the development of experimental methods and of genetic and evolutionary conceptions in science" (p. 253). In the section on application of the view to religion, he indicates that "James's method, while empirical, [is] not specially pragmatic" (p. 257), and in the section on application to philosophy, he hints at what the pragmatic metaphysics, if any, will be like. It cannot be a metaphysics in the old sense because, "being itself a mode of knowledge, all its theories must be recognized to be only working hypotheses and experimental in quality" (p. 257).

"The Bearings of Pragmatism upon Education" is a simple, elementary account of the implications of pragmatism for education and an interesting anticipation of *Democracy and Education*. There is an outline of some of the main pragmatic themes, with emphasis on intelligence as an organ of adjustment in difficult situations, in contrast to the transcendental theory of pure rationalism and the Lockean empiricism. This is followed by an account of the implications of pragmatism for educational method, with emphasis on learning by doing. "In an educational scheme which should embody practically the pragmatic conception of thought, intellectual instruction would have then the following traits: (a) It would grow—all of it—out of the needs and opportunities of activities engaged in by the students themselves. . . . (b) Information would not be amassed and accumulated and driven into pupils as an end in itself, but would cluster about the development of activities. . . . (c) Instruction carried on upon this basis would teach the mind that all ideas, truths, theories, etc., are of the nature of *working hypotheses*" (pp. 187–88). The stress should be on "the *experimental* habit of mind, that which regards ideas and principles as tentative methods of solving problems and organizing data" (p. 188).

As to the course of study, it might well be organized about the occupations, "training in typical and continuous lines of activity, which are of social value for everybody" (p. 190). Occupational activities would include a broad and liberal scheme of knowledge, science, history, social studies, and fine arts. "Finally, such an education would change the morale of the school. Since the activities of the latter would be continuous with the interests and activities of men and women at large, the school would lose the special code of ethics and moral training, which must characterize it as long as it is isolated. It would take up into itself the moral aims and forces of social sympathy, cooperation and progress" (pp. 190–91).

Pragmatism was newer than perhaps anyone realized

at the time, and the newcomer had to defend itself against the protagonists of older established views and alternative new possibilities. Dewey, moreover, tried to describe his new instrumental version of it in everyday terms, redefining some of them to make them more suitable for his purposes. At other times he perhaps thought that the terms needed no redefinition in spite of the changed context in which he was using them. At any rate, the combination of a new philosophy and special meanings for familiar language created no end of questions for him, and he labored to answer questions about his position, restate it in what he hoped was clearer fashion, and defend it from attack. Sometimes he carried on for years a running debate with another philosopher, and one such exchange was that between him and Evander Bradley McGilvary, a witty, sharp, and tenacious critic. The next three items discussed are Dewey's responses to three sets of criticism by McGilvary.

"Pure Experience and Reality: A Disclaimer" is Dewey's reply to McGilvary's "Pure Experience and Reality," which in turn criticizes Dewey's "Reality as Experience" and *Studies in Logical Theory*. McGilvary charges that Dewey's view is contrary to scientific knowledge of the past in de-realizing the past. "If the reality of anything is the reality it has as experienced and only when experienced, then it would seem that the sciences which deal with objects purporting to have existed before any verifiable experience do not have to do with reality . . ." (p. 295). According to McGilvary, the truth contained in Dewey's position is: "No thinker, no thought-object; no experience somewhere and somewhen, no meaningful reality anywhere and anytime" (p. 303). He adds immediately, however, "But it is one thing to say, No experience; no reality, and it is another thing to say, No *contemporaneous* experience, no reality" (p. 303). McGilvary then says: "The real trouble with this pragmatic variety of empiricism is that it is so much engaged in the business of the interpretation of the place of *reflective knowledge, or thought,* in the control of experience, that it ignores the right of the *object* to the place it claims,—a place in time prior to the date of the experience" (pp. 304–5).

Dewey's response is quite brief, maintaining that Mc-

Gilvary has misconceived his position in extreme fashion. He declares that he has never held that the " 'reality of anything is the reality it has as experienced and *only when experienced*' " or " 'No *contemporaneous* experience, *no* reality' " (p. 120). What McGilvary calls the truth contained in Dewey's position Dewey asserts is the only truth for which he has contended. "My enjoyment, accordingly, of the ludicrous position in which Professor McGilvary places the 'pure empiricist,' with me as *corpus vile*, is heightened by the fact, that in view of his expressed agreement, I can stand the joke —if he can" (p. 121). Dewey concludes by saying that his critic has attributed to him a traditional view of experience rather than the one he actually holds. Thinkers "who have got habituated to a mode of psychological analysis, which, in the interests of psychology, resolves experience into certain transient acts and states of a person, into sensations and images of a psycho-physical organism, may forget that others employ the term experience in a more vital, concrete, and pregnant sense. Hence, when others talk about experience, it is assumed that this means the psychological abstract which it means to the critic" (p. 124).

McGilvary had the final word in this particular exchange in his "Pure Experience and Reality: A Reassertion," arguing that, on Dewey's own grounds, his interpretation of Dewey's view could not be mistaken.

"Immediate empiricism postulates that things . . . are what they are experienced as. Hence, if one wishes to describe anything *truly*, his task is to tell what it is experienced as being." (*Journal of Philosophy, Psychology and Scientific Methods*, Vol. II, p. 393; italics mine.) Now in my article, I told exactly what Professor Dewey's logical theory was by me experienced as being; hence that article has described his philosophy truly.[26]

Dewey's "A Reply to Professor McGilvary's Questions" is a rejoinder to "Professor Dewey's 'Action of Consciousness',' and he claims that the questions are based on attributing to him the view he is criticizing.

"Objects, Data, and Existences: A Reply to Professor

---

26. Evander Bradley McGilvary, "Pure Experience and Reality: A Reassertion," *Philosophical Review* 16 (1907): 423.

McGilvary" is a response to "The Chicago 'Idea' and Idealism," which is a criticism of *Studies in Logical Theory*. Mc-
Gilvary charges that Dewey is an idealist and a subjective
one at that. Although he concedes that Dewey may not be an
idealist in the new Chicago terminology, he argues that in
terms of current usage he certainly is one. He further maintains that in his neglect of primary data, Dewey, the pro-
ponent of scientific method, holds a position in conflict with
science. McGilvary further claims that we are conscious of
far more than we should be on Dewey's use of "conscious" as
"sign of a problem" and asks for further light on what Dewey
means by "experience."

Dewey's response is one of his stronger dialectical ex-
hibitions. He finds McGilvary's question as to whether he is
an idealist in the current sense of idealism, which McGilvary
describes as "the theory which regards all reality as embraced
within experiences or within experience," to be neither clear
nor unambiguous, but he denies that he is an idealist in any
sense other than McGilvary the realist is. He denies ignoring
the existence of primary data and holds that his critic confuses such noncognitional, nonlogical data with data of a
logical type and puts himself in opposition to science.

Quite commonly, at least in this period, Dewey tends to
hold that his opponents are confused. They refuse to consider
his position on its merits and go on using their meanings for
terms instead of his when talking about his view. Not sur-
prisingly, this results in his appearing to hold a contradictory
position.

Two of his reviews are of special interest, the one on
Studies in Philosophy and Psychology by the former students
of C. E. Garman and the one on Santayana's five-volume *The
Life of Reason*. Garman's former students included J. H.
Tufts and F. J. E. Woodbridge, and almost half of the lengthy
review is devoted to the latter's "The Problem of Consciousness." Some explanation of its length is afforded by the following passage from Dewey's notes on the Problem of Consciousness and of Knowledge:

A philosophic analysis with which one agrees heartily up to
a certain point while beyond that point one begins to wonder, to
suspect divergence and to attempt to define the nature and the

cause of the division arouses more interest than is likely to be found in the cases where one is sympathetic throughout, or where one is in flat disagreement with respect to the fundamental premisses. I find myself in such a situation with respect to Professor Woodbridge's recent discussion of "The Problem of Consciousness."[27]

In the review Dewey characterizes Woodbridge's paper as the most important strictly metaphysical paper in the volume, praises his critique of Kantian idealism, and comments at length on his hypothesis that "consciousness means precisely the possibility of this significance of relationship among things" (p. 225). In the notes referred to above Dewey complains of "a certain ambiguity in the term 'meaning' which . . . is unfortunate for the understanding of the exact import of Professor Woodbridge's position."

The mixture of agreement and disagreement may explain in part the length of the Santayana review. Dewey finds some evidence for interpreting Santayana's view as "pragmatism of a noble and significant type," but he concludes that the bulk of the position is in another direction. Along the first line, *The Life of Reason* may be taken as

representing the only type of philosophy with which it is worth while to engage one's self; a return to the ancient identification of philosophy with morals, with love of wisdom. A survey by intelligence of the past struggles, failures, and successes of intelligence with a view to directing its own further endeavors, emphasizing and safeguarding its achievements, avoiding repetitions of its futile and wasteful excesses, stimulating it to greater patience and courage—this, indeed, is a conception of philosophy fit to rescue it from the slough of disrespect and despondency into which it has fallen in evil days. It is this, I take it, in Mr. Santayana's writing which will permanently count, spite of its signs of hankering after the flesh-pots of "metaphysics" (pp. 232–33).

However accurately this may characterize Santayana's view, Dewey's piping of his own pragmatic song comes through clearly! And even if Santayana turns out not to be a pragmatist after all, Dewey concludes, we are grateful to him "for what he *has* given us: the most adequate contribution America has yet made—always excepting Emerson—to moral philosophy" (p. 241).

27. John Dewey Papers.

In his address to the National Negro Conference Dewey
maintains that although acquired individual characteristics
of heredity are not transmissible, the culture of a society may
be transmitted; and it is the responsibility of society to provide an environment and educational opportunities which
will utilize all of the individual capital that is born into it,
bringing out and making effective superior ability wherever
it is born and without regard to race.

This volume includes a number of significant essays
dealing with education. For example, "Education as a University Study" is an eloquent and well reasoned plea for
the scientific study of education. Dewey pleads for the recognition of education "not merely as a fitting topic for serious
and prolonged study, but the most important of subjects for
such study" (p. 161). He maintains that "it needs no argument to show that the modern university does not exist
simply to rehearse the knowledge of the past; that it exists
precisely because there are so many fields in which, relatively, we have not got very far, but in which it is most
important that we shall get farther; and in which the type
of inquiry and discussion that the university exists to foster
is the sole means of advance" (p. 162). Accordingly, he concludes, "In fine, the scientific study of education should represent the finest self-consciousness of the university of its own
work and destiny—of its mission for itself and for the
society of which it is both minister and organ" (p. 164).

"Religion and Our Schools" is perhaps as timely now
with our current discussions of released time for religious
education as it was in 1908. Dewey's views on supernatural
religion had changed since his earlier years at Michigan. Although twenty years earlier he had maintained in his idealistic phase that "whatever banishes God from the heart of
things, with the same edict excludes the ideal, the ethical,
from the life of man,"[28] by 1908 he regarded supernatural
religion as a false bias (p. 166) and looked forward to the
religion implicit in our still new science and our still newer
democracy (p. 177), to the kind of religion sketched years
later in A Common Faith. Until the practical instrumental-

28. The Early Works of John Dewey, 1882–1898, 1:209.

ities of education have been harmonized with the creed of
life implicit in democracy and in science, a creed which has
to be clarified and developed, religious instruction in the
public schools is out of the question, and "it is better that our
schools should do nothing than that they should do wrong
things" (p. 168). What is sometimes termed, Dewey would
say falsely termed, the separation of church and state, he
identifies as "the necessity of maintaining the integrity of
the state," or the community as a whole, "as against all
divisive ecclesiastical divisions" (p. 169).

Dewey touches on the problem of what knowledge of
religion as an outcome of instruction means today and declares that "as long as religion is conceived as it now is conceived by the great majority of professed religionists, there
is something self-contradictory in speaking of education in
religion in the same sense in which we speak of education in
topics where the method of free inquiry has made its way"
(p. 173). He also takes up the problem of who is to teach
religion and does not "find it feasible or desirable to put upon
the regular teachers the burden of teaching a subject which
has the nature of religion. The alternative plan of parcelling
out pupils among religious teachers drawn from their respective churches and denominations" (pp. 174–75) is even
less satisfactory in that it promotes divisiveness and dis-
credits, if not religion, organized and institutionalized religion, bringing us up against "the multiplication of rival and
competing religious bodies, each with its private inspiration
and outlook" (p. 175). For that matter, Dewey firmly believes that our schools even now, "in bringing together those
of different nationalities, languages, traditions, and creeds,
in assimilating them together upon the basis of what is
common and public in endeavor and achievement, are performing an infinitely significant religious work," for they
"are promoting the social unity out of which in the end
genuine religious unity must grow" (p. 175). Thus, in his
view, in certain respects "schools are more religious in substance and in promise without any of the conventional
badges and machinery of religious instruction than they
could be in cultivating these forms" at the expense of a
sense of social unity (p. 175).

In "History for the Educator" history is considered as an account of the forces and forms of social life, not simply as a record of the past. To study it is "to use information in constructing a vivid picture of how and why men did thus and so; achieved their successes and came to their failures" (pp. 192–93). "The Purpose and Organization of Physics Teaching in Secondary Schools" stresses scientific method and the formation of scientific habits of mind and the importance of the social applications of physical science in modern life.

"The Moral Significance of the Common School Studies" offers an abbreviated version of one portion of the monograph on *Moral Principles in Education*. The two of them are concerned with the moral import of education; and as Sidney Hook indicates in his preface to a new edition of the monograph, moral education is a topic of perennial importance, for the schools have always "been expected to reinforce, supplement, sometimes even to substitute for, the moral education children have acquired at home or church."[29] But can one teach morality? Can one improve character through instruction? If we can teach morality, what are we teaching? And how do we teach it? How may the teaching of, say, art, literature, history, geography, mathematics, and science contribute to moral ends? How is the school related to society, and what significance does this have for moral education? Who is to teach it? What kind of person are we trying to develop? These are the kinds of questions dealt with in these two works.

Dewey is convinced that we can teach morality and improve character if we go at it indirectly. Direct moral instruction is likely to be instruction *about* morals, and its influence, at best, is comparatively slight. It does little to improve conduct or make it better than it otherwise would have been. Accordingly, Dewey's concern in *Moral Principles in Education* is with the "larger field of indirect and vital moral education, the development of character through all the agencies, instrumentalities, and materials of school life" (p. 268). And

29. Sidney Hook, "Preface," in John Dewey, *Moral Principles in Education* (Carbondale: Southern Illinois University Press, Arcturus Paperbacks, 1975), p. vii.

every fact which throws light upon the constitution of society, every power whose training adds to social resourcefulness is moral. "Ultimate moral motives and forces are nothing more or less than social intelligence . . . and social
power . . . at work in the service of social interest and
aims" (p. 285).

Studies "are of moral value in the degree in which they
enable the pupil sympathetically and imaginatively to appreciate the social scene in which he is a partaker; to realize
his own indebtedness to the great stream of human activities
which flow through and about him; the community of purpose with the large world of nature and society and his
consequent obligation to be loyal to his inheritance and sincere in his devotion to the interests which have made him
what he is and given him the opportunities he possesses" (p.
213).

Dewey hopes to develop persons who are thoroughly
efficient and serviceable members of society, ones capable of
taking charge of themselves and leading others, not only able
to adapt to changing circumstances but with power to shape
and direct them. They should be persons who have force of
character, judgment, and emotional responsiveness.

In short, then, just as Emerson found the moral law at
the center of the universe and radiating to the circumference,
so for Dewey moral principles are at the heart of the school
community and society at large and leap out at us from every
situation if only we do not try to teach them directly. Once
we recognize "that moral principles are real in the same
sense in which other forces are real; that they are inherent
in community life, and in the working structure of the individual," then every subject, every method of instruction,
and every incident of school life will prove to be pregnant
with moral possibility (p. 291).

Dewey was to pipe his pragmatic philosophic song for
some forty more years; and whatever may have been his
misgivings about who listened to it or appreciated it, the
new philosophic mode has had a pervasive influence in education, and his theme of turning to the concrete, actual problems of men has won approval both for him and for phi-

losophy on the part of many non-philosophers. In philosophy itself other pipers still provide the music for most of the symposia, but his song has become a part of the repertoire of an increasing number of teachers of philosophy, and the Deweyan mode has changed from something few wished to hear to one of the classic components of standard philosophic programs.

9 September 1975

ESSAYS

THE INFLUENCE OF DARWINISM
ON PHILOSOPHY[1]

I

That the publication of the *Origin of Species* marked
an epoch in the development of the natural sciences is well
known to the layman. That the combination of the very
words origin and species embodied an intellectual revolt and
introduced a new intellectual temper is easily overlooked by
the expert. The conceptions that had reigned in the philosophy of nature and knowledge for two thousand years, the
conceptions that had become the familiar furniture of the
mind, rested on the assumption of the superiority of the
fixed and final; they rested upon treating change and origin
as signs of defect and unreality. In laying hands upon the
sacred ark of absolute permanency, in treating the forms
that had been regarded as types of fixity and perfection as
originating and passing away, the *Origin of Species* introduced a mode of thinking that in the end was bound to transform the logic of knowledge, and hence the treatment of
morals, politics and religion.

No wonder then that the publication of Darwin's book,
a half-century ago, precipitated a crisis. The true nature of
the controversy is easily concealed from us, however, by the
theological clamor that attended it. The vivid and popular
features of the anti-Darwinian row tended to leave the impression that the issue was between science on one side and
theology on the other. Such was not the case—the issue lay

---

1. A lecture in a course of public lectures on "Charles Darwin and
His Influence on Science," given at Columbia University in the
winter and spring of 1909.

[First published in *Popular Science Monthly* 75 (1909): 90–98,
with the title "Darwin's Influence upon Philosophy." Revised
and reprinted in *The Influence of Darwin on Philosophy* (New
York: Henry Holt and Co., 1910), pp. 1–19, with the title "The
Influence of Darwinism on Philosophy."]

primarily within science itself, as Darwin himself early recognized. The theological outcry he discounted from the start,
hardly noticing it save as it bore upon the "feelings of his
female relatives." But for two decades before final publication he contemplated the possibility of being put down by his
scientific peers as a fool or as crazy; and he set, as the measure of his success, the degree in which he should affect three
men of science: Lyell in geology, Hooker in botany and
Huxley in zoology.

Religious considerations lent fervor to the controversy,
but they did not provoke it. Intellectually, religious emotions
are not creative but conservative. They attach themselves
readily to the current view of the world and consecrate it.
They steep and dye intellectual fabrics in the seething vat of
emotions; they do not form their warp and woof. There is
not, I think, an instance of any large idea about the world
being independently generated by religion. Although the
ideas that rose up like armed men against Darwinism owed
their intensity to religious associations, their origin and
meaning are to be sought in science and philosophy, not in
religion.

II

Few words in our language foreshorten intellectual history as much as does the word species. The Greeks, in initiat-
ing the intellectual life of Europe, were impressed by characteristic traits of the life of plants and animals; so impressed
indeed that they made these traits the key to defining nature
and to explaining mind and society. And truly life is so
wonderful that a seemingly successful reading of its mystery
might well lead men to believe that the key to the secrets of
heaven and earth was in their hands. The Greek rendering
of this mystery, the Greek formulation of the aim and standard of knowledge, was in the course of time embodied in the
word species, and it controlled philosophy for two thousand
years. To understand the intellectual face-about expressed
in the phrase "Origin of Species," we must, then, understand
the long dominant idea against which it is a protest.

Consider how men were impressed by the facts of life. Their eyes fell upon certain things slight in bulk, and frail in structure. To every appearance, these perceived things were inert and passive. Suddenly, under certain circumstances, these things—henceforth known as seeds or eggs or germs—begin to change, to change rapidly in size, form and qualities. Rapid and extensive changes occur, however, in many things—as when wood is touched by fire. But the changes in the living thing are orderly; they are cumulative; they tend constantly in one direction; they do not, like other changes, destroy or consume, or pass fruitless into wandering flux; they realize and fulfil. Each successive stage, no matter how unlike its predecessor, preserves its net effect and also prepares the way for a fuller activity on the part of its successor. In living beings, changes do not happen as they seem to happen elsewhere, any which way; the earlier changes are regulated in view of later results. This progressive organization does not cease till there is achieved a true final term, a τελὸs, a completed, perfected end. This final form exercises in turn a plenitude of functions, not the least noteworthy of which is production of germs like those from which it took its own origin, germs capable of the same cycle of self-fulfilling activity.

But the whole miraculous tale is not yet told. The same drama is enacted to the same destiny in countless myriads of individuals so sundered in time, so severed in space, that they have no opportunity for mutual consultation and no means of interaction. As an old writer quaintly said, "things of the same kind go through the same formalities"—celebrate, as it were, the same ceremonial rites.

This formal activity which operates throughout a series of changes and holds them to a single course; which subordinates their aimless flux to its own perfect manifestation; which, leaping the boundaries of space and time, keeps individuals distant in space and remote in time to a uniform type of structure and function: this principle seemed to give insight into the very nature of reality itself. To it Aristotle gave the name, εἶδος. This term the scholastics translated as species.

The force of this term was deepened by its application

to everything in the universe that observes order in flux and
manifests constancy through change. From the casual drift
of daily weather, through the uneven recurrence of seasons
and unequal return of seed time and harvest, up to the ma-
jestic sweep of the heavens—the image of eternity in time
—and from this to the unchanging pure and contemplative
intelligence beyond nature lies one unbroken fulfilment of
ends. Nature, as a whole, is a progressive realization of purpose strictly comparable to the realization of purpose in any
single plant or animal.

The conception of εἶδος, species, a fixed form and final
cause, was the central principle of knowledge as well as of
nature. Upon it rested the logic of science. Change as change
is mere flux and lapse; it insults intelligence. Genuinely to
know is to grasp a permanent end that realizes itself through
changes, holding them thereby within the metes and bounds
of fixed truth. Completely to know is to relate all special
forms to their one single end and good: pure contemplative
intelligence. Since, however, the scene of nature which directly confronts us is in change, nature as directly and
practically experienced does not satisfy the conditions of
knowledge. Human experience is in flux, and hence the instrumentalities of sense-perception and of inference based
upon observation are condemned in advance. Science is compelled to aim at realities lying behind and beyond the processes of nature, and to carry on its search for these realities
by means of rational forms transcending ordinary modes of
perception and inference.

There are, indeed, but two alternative courses. We must
either find the appropriate objects and organs of knowledge
in the mutual interactions of changing things; or else, to
escape the infection of change, we *must* seek them in some
transcendent and supernal region. The human mind, deliberately as it were, exhausted the logic of the changeless, the
final and the transcendent, before it essayed adventure on
the pathless wastes of generation and transformation. We
dispose all too easily of the efforts of the schoolmen to interpret nature and mind in terms of real essences, hidden
forms and occult faculties, forgetful of the seriousness and
dignity of the ideas that lay behind. We dispose of them by

laughing at the famous gentleman who accounted for the fact that opium put people to sleep on the ground it had a dormitive faculty. But the doctrine, held in our own day, that knowledge of the plant that yields the poppy consists in referring the peculiarities of an individual to a type, to a universal form, a doctrine so firmly established that any other method of knowing was conceived to be unphilosophical and unscientific, is a survival of precisely the same logic. This identity of conception in the scholastic and anti-Darwinian theory may well suggest greater sympathy for what has become unfamiliar as well as greater humility regarding the further unfamiliarities that history has in store.

Darwin was not, of course, the first to question the classic philosophy of nature and of knowledge. The beginnings of the revolution are in the physical science of the sixteenth and seventeenth centuries. When Galileo said: "It is my opinion that the Earth is very noble and admirable by reason of so many and so different alterations and generations which are incessantly made therein," he expressed the changed temper that was coming over the world; the transfer of interest from the permanent to the changing. When Descartes said: "The nature of physical things is much more easily conceived when they are beheld coming gradually into existence, than when they are only considered as produced at once in a finished and perfect state," the modern world became self-conscious of the logic that was henceforth to control it, the logic of which Darwin's *Origin of Species* is the latest scientific achievement. Without the methods of Copernicus, Kepler, Galileo and their successors in astronomy, physics and chemistry, Darwin would have been helpless in the organic sciences. But prior to Darwin the impact of the new scientific method upon life, mind and politics, had been arrested, because between these ideal or moral interests and the inorganic world intervened the kingdom of plants and animals. The gates of the garden of life were barred to the new ideas; and only through this garden was there access to mind and politics. The influence of Darwin upon philosophy resides in his having conquered the phenomena of life for the principle of transition, and thereby freed the new logic for application to mind and morals and life. When he said of species what Galileo had said of the earth, *e pur si muove*, he emancipated, once for all, genetic and experimental ideas as an organon of asking questions and looking for explanations.

III

The exact bearings upon philosophy of the new logical outlook are, of course, as yet, uncertain and inchoate. We live in the twilight of intellectual transition. One must add the rashness of the prophet to the stubbornness of the partisan to venture a systematic exposition of the influence upon philosophy of the Darwinian method. At best, we can but inquire as to its general bearing—the effect upon mental temper and complexion, upon that body of half-conscious, half-instinctive intellectual aversions and preferences which determine, after all, our more deliberate intellectual enterprises. In this vague inquiry there happens to exist as a kind of touchstone a problem of long historic currency that has also been much discussed in Darwinian literature. I refer to the old problem of design *versus* chance, mind *versus* matter, as the causal explanation, first or final, of things.

As we have already seen, the classic notion of species carried with it the idea of purpose. In all living forms, a specific type is present directing the earlier stages of growth to the realization of its own perfection. Since this purposive regulative principle is not visible to the senses, it follows that it must be an ideal or rational force. Since, however, the perfect form is gradually approximated through the sensible changes, it also follows that in and through a sensible realm a rational ideal force is working out its own ultimate manifestation. These inferences were extended to nature: (*a*) She does nothing in vain; but all for an ulterior purpose. (*b*) Within natural sensible events there is therefore contained a spiritual causal force, which as spiritual escapes perception, but is apprehended by an enlightened reason. (*c*) The manifestation of this principle brings about a subordination of matter and sense to its own realization, and this ultimate fulfilment is the goal of nature and of man. The design argument thus operated in two directions. Purposefulness accounted for the intelligibility of nature and the possibility of science, while the absolute or cosmic character of this purposefulness gave sanction and worth to the moral and religious endeavors of man. Science was underpinned and morals authorized by one and the same principle, and their mutual agreement was eternally guaranteed.

This philosophy remained, in spite of sceptical and polemic outbursts, the official and the regnant philosophy of Europe for over two thousand years. The expulsion of fixed first and final causes from astronomy, physics and chemistry had indeed given the doctrine something of a shock. But, on the other hand, increased acquaintance with the details of plant and animal life operated as a counterbalance and perhaps even strengthened the argument from design. The marvelous adaptations of organisms to their environment, of organs to the organism, of unlike parts of a complex organ—like the eye—to the organ itself; the foreshadowing by lower forms of the higher; the preparation in earlier stages of growth for organs that only later had their functioning—these things were increasingly recognized with the progress of botany, zoology, paleontology and embryology. Together they added such prestige to the design argument that by the late eighteenth century it was, as approved by the sciences of organic life, the central point of theistic and idealistic philosophy.

The Darwinian principle of natural selection cut straight under this philosophy. If all organic adaptations are due simply to constant variation and the elimination of those variations which are harmful in the struggle for existence that is brought about by excessive reproduction, there is no call for a prior intelligent causal force to plan and preordain them. Hostile critics charged Darwin with materialism and with making chance the cause of the universe.

Some naturalists, like Asa Gray, favored the Darwinian principle and attempted to reconcile it with design. Gray held to what may be called design on the installment plan. If we conceive the "stream of variations" to be itself intended, we may suppose that each successive variation was designed from the first to be selected. In that case, variation, struggle and selection simply define the mechanism of "secondary causes" through which the "first cause" acts; and the doctrine of design is none the worse off because we know more of its *modus operandi*.

Darwin could not accept this mediating proposal. He admits or rather he asserts that it is "impossible to conceive this immense and wonderful universe including man with his capacity of looking far backwards and far into futurity as the result of blind chance or necessity."[2] But nevertheless he holds that since variations are in useless as well as useful directions, and since the latter are sifted out simply by the stress of the conditions of struggle for existence, the design argument as applied to living beings is unjustifiable; and its lack of support there deprives it of scientific value as applied to nature in general. If the variations of the pigeon, which under artificial selection give the pouter pigeon, are not preordained for the sake of the breeder, by what logic do we argue that variations resulting in natural species are predesigned?[3]

IV

So much for some of the more obvious facts of the discussion of design *versus* chance as causal principles of nature and of life as a whole. We brought up this discussion, you recall, as a crucial instance. What does our touchstone indicate as to the bearing of Darwinian ideas upon philosophy? In the first place, the new logic outlaws, flanks, dismisses—what you will—one type of problems and substitutes for it another type. Philosophy forswears inquiry after absolute origins and absolute finalities in order to explore specific values and the specific conditions that generate them.

Darwin concluded that the impossibility of assigning the world to chance as a whole and to design in its parts indicated the insolubility of the question. Two radically differ-

2. *Life and Letters*, Vol. I, p. 282; cf. 285.
3. *Life and Letters*, Vol. II, pp. 146, 170, 245; Vol. I, pp. 283–84. See also the closing portion of his *Variations of Animals and Plants under Domestication*.

ent reasons, however, may be given as to why a problem is insoluble. One reason is that the problem is too high for intelligence; the other is that the question in its very asking makes assumptions that render the question meaningless. The latter alternative is unerringly pointed to in the celebrated case of design *versus* chance. Once admit that the sole verifiable or fruitful object of knowledge is the particular set of changes that generate the object of study, together with the consequences that then flow from it, and no intelligible question can be asked about what, by assumption, lies outside. To assert—as is often asserted—that specific values of particular truth, social bonds and forms of beauty, if they can be shown to be generated by concretely knowable conditions, are meaningless and in vain; to assert that they are justified only when they and their particular causes and effects have all at once been gathered up into some inclusive first cause and some exhaustive final goal, is intellectual atavism. Such argumentation is reversion to the logic that explained the extinction of fire by water through the formal essence of aqueousness and the quenching of thirst by water through the final cause of aqueousness. Whether used in the case of the special event or that of life as a whole, such logic only abstracts some aspect of the existing course of events in order to reduplicate it as a petrified eternal principle by which to explain the very changes of which it is the formalization.

When Henry Sidgwick casually remarked in a letter that as he grew older his interest in what or who made the world was altered into interest in what kind of a world it is anyway, his voicing of a common experience of our own day illustrates also the nature of that intellectual transformation effected by the Darwinian logic. Interest shifts from the wholesale essence back of special changes to the question of how special changes serve and defeat concrete purposes; shifts from an intelligence that shaped things once for all to the particular intelligences which things are even now shaping; shifts from an ultimate goal of good to the direct increments of justice and happiness that intelligent administration of existent conditions may beget and that present carelessness or stupidity will destroy or forego.

In the second place, the classic type of logic inevitably set philosophy upon proving that life *must* have certain qualities and values—no matter how experience presents the matter—because of some remote cause and eventual goal. The duty of wholesale justification inevitably accompanies all thinking that makes the meaning of special occurrences depend upon something that once and for all lies behind them. The habit of derogating from present meanings and uses prevents our looking the facts of experience in the face; it prevents serious acknowledgment of the evils they present and serious concern with the goods they promise but do not as yet fulfil. It turns thought to the business of finding a wholesale transcendent remedy for the one and guarantee for the other. One is reminded of the way many moralists and theologians greeted Herbert Spencer's recognition of an unknowable energy from which welled up the phenomenal physical processes without and the conscious operations within. Merely because Spencer labeled his unknowable energy "God," this faded piece of metaphysical goods was greeted as an important and grateful concession to the reality of the spiritual realm. Were it not for the deep hold of the habit of seeking justification for ideal values in the remote and transcendent, surely this reference of them to an unknowable absolute would be despised in comparison with the demonstrations of experience that knowable energies are daily generating about us precious values.

The displacing of this wholesale type of philosophy will doubtless not arrive by sheer logical disproof, but rather by growing recognition of its futility. Were it a thousand times true that opium produces sleep because of its dormitive energy, yet the inducing of sleep in the tired, and the recovery to waking life of the poisoned, would not be thereby one least step forwarded. And were it a thousand times dialectically demonstrated that life as a whole is regulated by a transcendent principle to a final inclusive goal, none the less truth and error, health and disease, good and evil, hope and fear in the concrete, would remain just what and where they now are. To improve our education, to ameliorate our manners, to advance our politics, we must have recourse to specific conditions of generation.

Finally, the new logic introduces responsibility into the intellectual life. To idealize and rationalize the universe at large is after all a confession of inability to master the courses of things that specifically concern us. As long as mankind suffered from this impotency, it naturally shifted a burden of responsibility that it could not carry over to the more competent shoulders of the transcendent cause. But if insight into specific conditions of value and into specific consequences of ideas is possible, philosophy must in time become a method of locating and interpreting the more serious of the conflicts that occur in life, and a method of projecting ways for dealing with them: a method of moral and political diagnosis and prognosis.

The claim to formulate *a priori* the legislative constitution of the universe is by its nature a claim that may lead to elaborate dialectic developments. But it is also one that removes these very conclusions from subjection to experimental test, for, by definition, these results make no differences in the detailed course of events. But a philosophy that humbles its pretensions to the work of projecting hypotheses for the education and conduct of mind, individual and social, is thereby subjected to test by the way in which the ideas it propounds work out in practice. In having modesty forced upon it, philosophy also acquires responsibility.

Doubtless I seem to have violated the implied promise of my earlier remarks and to have turned both prophet and partisan. But in anticipating the direction of the transformations in philosophy to be wrought by the Darwinian genetic and experimental logic, I do not profess to speak for any save those who yield themselves consciously or unconsciously to this logic. No one can fairly deny that at present there are two effects of the Darwinian mode of thinking. On the one hand, there are making many sincere and vital efforts to revise our traditional philosophic conceptions in accordance with its demands. On the other hand, there is as definitely a recrudescence of absolutistic philosophies; an assertion of a type of philosophic knowing distinct from that of the sciences, one which opens to us another kind of reality from that to which the sciences give access; an appeal through experience to something that essentially goes beyond experience. This reaction affects popular creeds and religious movements as well as technical philosophies. The very conquest of the biological sciences by the new ideas has led many to proclaim an explicit and rigid separation of philosophy from science.

Old ideas give way slowly; for they are more than abstract logical forms and categories. They are habits, predispositions, deeply engrained attitudes of aversion and preference. Moreover, the conviction persists—though history shows it to be a hallucination—that all the questions that the human mind has asked are questions that can be answered in terms of the alternatives that the questions themselves present. But in fact intellectual progress usually occurs through sheer abandonment of questions together with both of the alternatives they assume—an abandonment that results from their decreasing vitality and a change of urgent interest. We do not solve them: we get over them. Old questions are solved by disappearing, evaporating, while new questions corresponding to the changed attitude of endeavor and preference take their place. Doubtless the greatest dissolvent in contemporary thought of old questions, the greatest precipitant of new methods, new intentions, new problems, is the one effected by the scientific revolution that found its climax in the *Origin of Species*.

NATURE AND ITS GOOD:
A CONVERSATION

A group of people are scattered near one another, on the sands of an ocean beach; wraps, baskets, etc., testify to a day's outing. Above the hum of the varied conversations are heard the mock sobs of one of the party.

Various voices. What's the matter, Eaton?

Eaton. Matter enough. I was watching a beautiful wave; its lines were perfect; at its crest, the light glinting through its infinitely varied and delicate curves of foam made a picture more ravishing than any dream. And now it has gone; it will never come back. So I weep.

Grimes. That's right, Eaton; give it to them. Of course well-fed and well-read persons—with their possessions of wealth and of knowledge both gained at the expense of others—finally get bored; then they wax sentimental over their boredom and are worried about "Nature" and its relation to life. Not everybody takes it out that way, of course; some take motor cars and champagne for that tired feeling. But the rest—those who aren't in that class financially, or who consider themselves too refined for that kind of relief—seek a new sensation in speculating why that brute old world out there will not stand for what you call spiritual and ideal values—for short, your egotisms.

The fact is that the whole discussion is only a symptom of the leisure class disease. If you had to work to the limit and beyond to keep soul and body together, and, more than that, to keep alive the soul of your family in its body, you would know the difference between your artificial problems and the genuine problem of life. Your philosophic problems about the relation of "the universe to moral and spiritual

[First published in *Hibbert Journal* 7 (1909): 827–43, with the title "Is Nature Good? A Conversation." Revised and reprinted in *The Influence of Darwin on Philosophy* (New York: Henry Holt and Co., 1910), pp. 20–45, with the title "Nature and Its Good: A Conversation."]

good" exist only in the sentimentalism that generates them. The genuine question is why social arrangements will not permit the amply sufficient body of natural resources to sustain all men and women in security and decent comfort, with a margin for the cultivation of their human instincts of sociability, love of knowledge and of art.

As I read Plato, philosophy began with some sense of its essentially political basis and mission—a recognition that its problems were those of the organization of a just social order. But it soon got lost in dreams of another world; and even those of you philosophers who pride yourselves on being so advanced that you no longer believe in "another world," are still living and thinking with reference to it. You may not call it supernatural; but when you talk about a realm of spiritual or ideal values in general, and ask about its relation to Nature in general, you have only changed the labels on the bottles, not the contents in them. For what makes anything transcendental—that is, in common language, supernatural—is simply and only aloofness from practical affairs —which affairs in their ultimate analysis are the business of making a living.

Eaton. Yes; Grimes has about hit off the point of my little parable—in one of its aspects at least. In matters of daily life you say a man is "off," more or less insane, when he deliberately goes on looking for a certain kind of result from conditions which he has already found to be such that they cannot possibly yield it. If he keeps on looking, and then goes about mourning because stage money won't buy beefsteaks, or because he cannot keep himself warm by burning the sea-sands here, you dismiss him as a fool or a hysteric. If you would condescend to reason with him at all, you would tell him to look for the conditions that will yield the results; to occupy himself with some of the countless goods of life for which, by intelligently directed search, adequate means may be found.

Well, before lunch, Moore was reiterating the old tale. "Modern science has completely transformed our conceptions of Nature. It has stripped the universe bare not only of all the moral values which it wore alike to antique pagan and to our medieval ancestors, but also of any regard, any preference, for such values. They are mere incidents, transitory accidents, in her everlasting redistribution of matter in motion; like the rise and fall of the wave I lament, or like a single musical note that a screeching, rumbling railway train might happen to emit." This is a one-sided view; but suppose it were all so, what is the moral? Surely, to change our standpoint, our angle of vision; to stop looking for results among conditions that we know will not yield them; to turn our gaze to the goods, the values that exist actually and indubitably in experience; and consider by what natural conditions these particular values may be strengthened and widened. Insist if you please that Nature as a whole does not stand for good as a whole. Then, in heaven's name, just because good is both so plural (so "numerous") and so partial, bend your energies of intelligence and of effort to selecting the specific plural and partial natural conditions which will at least render values that we do have more secure and more extensive. Any other course is the way of madness; it is the way of the spoilt child who cries at the seashore because the waves do not stand still, and who cries even more frantically in the mountains because the hills do not melt and flow.

But no. Moore and his school will not have it so: we must "go back of the returns." All this science, after all, is a mode of knowledge. Examine knowledge itself and find it implies a complete all-inclusive intelligence; and then find (by taking another tack) that intelligence involves sentiency, feeling, and also will. Hence your very physical science, if you will only criticize it, examine it, shows that its object, mechanical nature, is itself an included and superseded element in an all-embracing spiritual and ideal whole. And there you are.

Well, I do not now insist that all this is mere dialectic prestidigitation. No; accept it; let it go at its face value. But what of it? Is any value more concretely and securely in life than it was before? Does this perfect intelligence enable us to correct one single mis-step, one paltry error, here and now? Does this perfect all-inclusive goodness serve to heal one disease? Does it rectify one transgression? Does it even give the slightest inkling of how to go to work at any of these things? No; it just tells you: Never mind, for they are al-

ready eternally corrected, eternally healed in the eternal consciousness which alone is really Real. Stop: there is one evil,
one pain, which the doctrine mitigates—the hysteric sentimentalism which is troubled because the universe as a whole
does not sustain good as a whole. But that is the only thing
it alters. The "pathetic fallacy" of Ruskin magnified to the nth
power is the *motif* of modern idealism.

Moore. Certainly nobody will accuse Eaton of tender-
mindedness—except in his logic, which, *as* certainly, is not
tough-minded. His excitement, however, convinces me that
he has at least an inkling that he is begging the question;
and like the true pragmatist that he is, is trying to prevent
by action (to wit, his flood of speech) his false logic from
becoming articulate to him. The question being whether the
values we seem to apprehend, the purposes we entertain, the
goods we possess, are anything more than transitory waves,
Eaton meets it by saying: "Oh, of course, they are waves;
but don't think about that—just sit down hard on the wave
or get another wave to buttress it with!" No wonder he recom-
mends action instead of thinking! Men have tried this method
before, as a counsel of desperation or as cynical pessimism.
But it remained for contemporary pragmatism to label the
drowning of sorrow in the intoxication of thoughtless action,
the highest achievement of philosophic method, and to
preach wilful restlessness as a doctrine of hope and illumination. Meantime, I prefer to be tender-minded in my attitude toward Reality, and to make that attitude more reasonable by a tough-minded logic.

Eaton. I am willing to be quiet long enough for you to
translate your metaphor into logic, and show how I have
begged the question.

Moore. It is plain enough. You bid us turn to the cultivation, the nurture, of certain values in human life. But the
question is whether these are or are not values. And that is
a question of their relation to the Universe—to Reality. If
Reality substantiates them, then indeed they are values; if
it mocks and flouts them—as it surely does if what mechanical science calls Nature be ultimate and absolute—then they
are *not* values. You and your kind are really the sentimental-
ists, because you are sheer subjectivists. You say: Accept the

dream as real; do not question about it; add a little iridescence to its fog and extend it till it obscure even more of
Reality than it naturally does, and all is well! I say: Perhaps
the dream is no dream but an intimation of the solidest and
most ultimate of all realities; and a thorough examination
of what the positivist, the materialist, accepts as solid,
namely, science, reveals as its own aim, standard, and presupposition that Reality is one all-exhaustive spiritual Being.

Eaton. This is about the way I thought my begging of
the question would turn out. You insist upon translating my
position into terms of your own; I am not then surprised to
hear that it would be a begging of the question for *you* to hold
my views. My point is precisely that it is only as long as you
take the position that some Reality beyond—some metaphysical or transcendental reality—is necessary to substantiate
empirical values that you can even discuss whether the latter
are genuine or illusions. Drop the presupposition that you
read into everything I say, the idea that the reality of things
as they are is dependent upon something beyond and behind,
and the facts of the case just stare you in the eyes: Goods
are, a multitude of them—but, unfortunately, evils also *are*;
and all grades, pretty much, of both. Not the contrast and
relation of experience *in toto* to something beyond experience drives men to religion and then to philosophy; but the
contrast *within* experience of the better and the worse, and
the consequent problem of how to substantiate the former
and reduce the latter. Until you set up the notion of a transcendental reality at large, you cannot even raise the question of whether goods and evils are or only seem to be. The
trouble and the joy, the good and the evil, is *that* they are;
the hope is that they may be regulated, guided, increased in
one direction and minimized in another. Instead of neglect-
ing thought, we (I mean the pragmatists) exalt it, because
we say that intelligent discrimination of means and ends is
the sole final resource in this problem of all problems, the
control of the factors of good and ill in life. We say, indeed,
not merely that that is what intelligence *does*, but rather
what it *is*.

Historically, it is quite possible to show how under certain social conditions this human and practical problem of

the relation of good and intelligence generated the notion
of the transcendental good and the pure reason. As Grimes
reminded us, Plato——

Moore. Yes, and Protagoras—don't forget him; for unfortunately we know both the origin and the consequences
of your doctrine that being and seeming are the same. We
know quite well that pure empiricism leads to the identification of being and seeming, and that is just why every
deeply moral and religious soul from the time of Plato and
Aristotle to the present has insisted upon a transcendent reality.

Eaton. Personally I don't need an absolute to enable me
to distinguish between, say, the good of kindness and the evil
of slander, or the good of health and the evil of valetudinarianism. In experience, things bear their own specific characters. Nor has the absolute idealist as yet answered the
question of *how* the absolute reality enables him to distinguish between being and seeming in one single concrete
case. The trouble is that for him *all* Being is on the other
side of experience, and *all* experience is seeming.

Grimes. I think I heard you mention history. I wish both
of you would drop dialectics and go to history. You would
find history to be a struggle for existence—for bread, for a
roof, for protected and nourished offspring. You would find
history a picture of the masses always going under—just
missing—in the struggle, because others have captured the
control of natural resources, which in themselves, if not as
benign as the eighteenth century imagined, are at least abun-
dantly ample for the needs of all. But because of the mo-
nopolization of Nature by a few persons, most men and
women only stick their heads above the welter just enough
to catch a glimpse of better things, then to be shoved down
and under. The only problem of the relation of Nature to
human good which is real is the economic problem of the
exploitation of natural resources in the equal interests of all,
instead of in the unequal interests of a class. The problem
you two men are discussing has no existence—and never
had any—outside of the heads of a few metaphysicians. The
latter would never have amounted to anything, would never
have had any career at all, had not shrewd monopolists or

tyrants (with the skill that characterizes them) have seen
that these speculations about reality and a transcendental
world could be distilled into opiates and distributed among
the masses to make them less rebellious. That, if you would
know, Eaton, is the real historic origin of the ideal world
beyond. When you realize that, you will perceive that the
pragmatists are only half-way over. You will see that practical questions *are* practical, and are not to be solved merely
by having a theory *about* theory, different from the traditional one—which is all your pragmatism comes to.

Moore. If you mean that your own crass Philistinism is
all that pragmatism comes to, I fancy you are about right.
Forget that the only end of action is to bring about an ap-
proximation to the complete inclusive consciousness; make,
as the pragmatists do, consciousness a means to action, and
one form of external activity is just as good as another. Art,
religion, all the generous reaches of science which do not
show up immediately in the factory—these things become
meaningless, and all that remains is that hard and dry satisfaction of economic wants which is Grimes's ideal.

Grimes. An ideal which exists, by the way, only in your
imagination. I know of no more convincing proof of the
futile irrelevancy of idealism than the damning way in
which it narrows the content of actual daily life in the minds
of those who uphold idealism. I sometimes think I am the
only true idealist. If the conditions of an equitable and ample physical existence for all were once secured, I, for one,
have no fears as to the bloom and harvest of art and science,
and all the "higher" things of leisure. Life is interesting
enough for me; give it a show for all.

Arthur. I find myself in a peculiar position in respect
to this discussion. An analysis of what is involved in this
peculiarity may throw some light on the points at issue, for
I have to believe that analysis and definition of what exists
is the essential matter both in resolution of doubts and in
steps at reform. For brevity, not from conceit, I will put the
peculiarity to which I refer in a personal form. I do not believe for a moment in some different Reality beyond and behind Nature. I do not believe that a manipulation of the logical implications of science can give results which are to be

put in the place of those which Science herself yields in her
direct application. I accept Nature as something which is,
not seems, and Science as her faithful transcript. Yet because I believe these things, not in spite of them, I believe
in the existence of purpose and of good. How Eaton can believe that fulfilment and the increasing realization of purpose can exist in human consciousness unless they first exist
in the world which is revealed in that consciousness is as
much beyond me as how Moore can believe that a manipulation of the method of knowledge can yield considerations of
a totally different order from those directly obtained by use
of the method. If purpose and fulfilment exist as natural
goods, then, and only then, can consciousness itself be a
fulfilment of Nature, and be also a natural good. Any other
view is inexplicable to sound thinking—save, historically, as
a product of modern political individualism and literary romanticism which have combined to produce that idealistic
philosophy according to which the mind in knowing the universe creates it.

The view that purpose and realization are profoundly
natural, and that consciousness—or, if you will, experience
—is itself a culmination and climax of Nature, is not a new
view. Formulated by Aristotle, it has always persisted wherever the traditions of sound thinking have not been obscured
by romanticism. The modern scientific doctrine of evolution
confirms and specifies the metaphysical insight of Aristotle.
This doctrine sets forth in detail, and in verified detail, as a
genuine characteristic of existence, the tendency toward cumulative results, the definite trend of things toward culmination and achievement. It describes the universe as possessing,
in terms of and by right of its own subject-matter (not as
an addition of subsequent reflection), differences of value
and importance—differences, moreover, that exercise selective influence upon the course of things, that is to say, genuinely determine the events that occur. It tells us that
consciousness itself is such a cumulative and culminating
natural event. Hence it is relevant to the world in which it
dwells, and its determinations of value are not arbitrary, not
obiter dicta, but descriptions of Nature herself.

Recall the words of Spencer which Moore quoted this

morning: "There is no pleasure in the consciousness of being an infinitesimal bubble on a globe that is infinitesimal compared with the totality of things. Those on whom the unpitying rush of changes inflicts sufferings which are often without remedy, find no consolation in the thought that they are at the mercy of blind forces,—which cause indifferently now the destruction of a sun and now the death of an animalcule. Contemplation of a universe which is without conceivable beginning or end and without intelligible purpose, yields no satisfaction." I am naïve enough to believe that the only question is whether the object of our "consciousness," of our "thought," of our "contemplation," is or is not as the quotation states it to be. If the statement be correct, pragmatism, like subjectivism (of which I suspect it is only a variation, putting emphasis upon will instead of idea), is an invitation to close our eyes to what is, in order to encourage the delusion that things are other than they are. But the case is not so desperate. Speaking dogmatically, the account given of the universe is just—not true. And the doctrine of evolution of which Spencer professedly made so much is the evidence. A universe describable in evolutionary terms is a universe which shows, not indeed design, but tendency and purpose; which exhibits achievement, not indeed of a single end, but of a multiplicity of natural goods at whose apex is consciousness. No account of the universe in terms *merely* of the redistribution of matter in motion is complete, no matter how true as far as it goes, for it ignores the cardinal fact that the character of matter in motion and of its redistribution is such as cumulatively to achieve ends—to effect the world of values we know. Deny this and you deny evolution; admit it and you admit purpose in the only objective— that is, the only intelligible—sense of that term. I do not say that in addition to the mechanism there are other ideal causes or factors which intervene. I only insist that the whole story be told, that the character of the mechanism be noted— namely, that it is such as to produce and sustain good in a multiplicity of forms. Mechanism is the mechanism of achieving results. To ignore this is to refuse to open our eyes to the total aspects of existence.

Among these multiple natural goods, I repeat, is consciousness itself. One of the ends in which Nature genuinely terminates is just awareness of itself—of its processes and ends. For note the implication as to why consciousness is a natural good: not because it is cut off and exists in isolation, nor yet because we may, pragmatically, cut off and cultivate certain values which have no existence beyond it; but because it *is* good that things should be known in their own characters. And this view carries with it a precious result: to know things as they are is to know them as culminating in consciousness; it is to know that the universe genuinely achieves and maintains its own self-manifestation.

A final word as to the bearing of this view upon Grimes's position. To conceive of human history as a scene of struggle of classes for domination, a struggle caused by love of power or greed for gain, is the very mythology of the emotions. What we call history is largely non-human, but so far as it is human, it is dominated by intelligence: history is the history of increasing consciousness. Not that intelligence is actually sovereign in life, but that at least it is sovereign over stupidity, error, and ignorance. The acknowledgment of things as they are—that is the causal source of every step in progress. Our present system of industry is not the product of greed or tyrannic lust of power, but of physical science giving the mastery over the mechanism of Nature's energy. If the existing system is ever displaced, it will be displaced not by good intentions and vague sentiments, but by a more extensive insight into Nature's secrets.

Modern sentimentalism is revolted at the frank naturalism of Aristotle in saying that some are slaves by nature and others free by nature. But let socialism come to-morrow and somebody—not anybody, but *some*body—will be managing its machinery and somebody else will be managed by the machinery. I do not wonder that my socialistic friends always imagine themselves active in the first capacity—perhaps by way of compensation for doing all of the imagining and none of the executive management at present. But those who are managed, who are controlled, deserve at least a moment's attention. Would you not at once agree that if there is any justice at all in these positions of relative inferiority and superiority, it is because those who are capable by insight deserve to rule, and those who are incapable on account of ignorance, deserve to be ruled? If so, how do you differ, save verbally, from Aristotle? Or do you think that all that men want in order to *be* men is to have their bellies filled, with assurance of constant plenty and without too much antecedent labor? No; believe me, Grimes, men *are* men, and hence their aspiration is for the divine—even when they know it not; their desire is for the ruling element, for intelligence. Till they achieve that they will still be discontented, rebellious, unruly—and hence ruled—shuffle your social cards as much as you may.

Grimes (after shrugging his shoulders contemptuously, finally says): There is one thing I like about Arthur: he is frank. He comes out with what you in all your hearts really believe—theory, supreme and sublime. All is to the good in this best of all possible worlds, if only someone be defining and classifying and syllogizing, according to the lines already laid down. Aristotle's God of pure intelligence (as *he* well knew) was the glorification of leisure; and Arthur's point of view, if Arthur but knew it, is as much the intellectual snobbery of a leisure class economy, as the luxury and display he condemns are its material snobbery. There is really nothing more to be said.

Moore. To get back into the game which Grimes despises. Doesn't Arthur practically say that the universe is good because it culminates in intelligence, and that intelligence is good because it perceives that the universe culminates in—itself? And, on this theory, are ignorance and error, and consequent evil, any less genuine achievements of Nature than intelligence and good? And on what basis does he call by the titles of achievement and end that which at best is an infinitesimally fragmentary and transitory episode? I said Eaton begged the question. Arthur seems to regard it as proof of a superior intelligence (one which realistically takes things as they are) to beg the question. What is this Nature, this universe in which evil is as stubborn a fact as good, in which good is constantly destroyed by the very power that produces it, in which there resides a temporary bird of passage—consciousness doomed to ultimate extinction—what is such a Nature (all that Arthur offers us) save the problem, the contradiction originally in question? A complacent optimism may gloss over its intrinsic self-contradictions, but a more serious mind is forced to go behind and beyond this scene to a permanent good which includes and transcends goods defeated and hopes suborned. Not because idealists have refused to note the facts as they are, but precisely because Nature is, on its face, such a scene as Arthur describes, idealists have always held that it is but Appearance, and have attempted to mount through it to Reality.

Stair. I had not thought to say anything. My attitude is so different from that of any one of you that it seemed unnecessary to inject another varying opinion where already disagreement reigns. But when Arthur was speaking, I felt that perhaps this disagreement exists precisely because the solvent word had not been uttered. For, at bottom, all of you agree with Arthur, and that is the cause of your disagreement with him and one another. You have agreed to make reason, intellect in some sense, the final umpire. But reason, intellect, is the principle of analysis, of division, of discord. When I appeal to feeling as the ultimate organ of unity, and hence of truth, you smile courteously; say—or think—mysticism; and the case for you is dismissed. Words like feeling, sensation, immediate appreciation, self-communication of Being, I must indeed use when I try to tell the truth I see. But I well know how inadequate the words are. And why? Because language is the chosen tool of intelligence, and hence inevitably bewrayeth the truth it would convey. But remember that words are but symbols, and that intelligence must dwell in the realm of symbols, and you realize a way out. These words, sensation, feeling, etc., as I utter them are but invitations to woo you to put yourselves into the one attitude that reveals truth—an attitude of direct vision.

The beatific vision? Yes, and No. No, if you mean something rare, extreme, almost abnormal. Yes, if you mean the commonest and most convincing, the *only* convincing self-impartation of the ultimate good in the scale of goods; the vision of blessedness in God. For this doctrine is empirical; mysticism is the heart of all positive empiricism, of all empiricism which is not more interested in denying rationalism than in asserting itself. The mystical experience marks every man's realization of the supremacy of good, and hence measures the distance that separates him from pure materialism. And since the unmitigated materialist is the rarest of creatures, and the man with faith in an unseen good the commonest, every man is a mystic—and the most so in his best moments. What an idle contradiction that Moore and Arthur should try to adduce proofs of the supremacy of ideal values in the universe! The sole possible proof is the proof that actually exists—the direct unhindered realization of those values. For each value brings with it of necessity its own depth of being. Let the pride of intellect and the pride of will cease their clamor, and in the silences Being speaks its own final word, not an argument or external ground of belief, but the self-impartation of itself to the soul. Who are the prophets and teachers of the ages? Those who have been accessible at the greatest depths to these communications.

Grimes. I suppose that poverty—and possibly disease—are specially competent ministers to the spiritual vision? The moral is obvious. Economic changes are purely irrelevant, because purely material and external. Indeed, upon the whole, efforts at reform are undesirable, for they distract attention from the fact that the final thing, the vision of good, is totally disconnected from external circumstance. I do not say, Stair, you personally believe this; but is not such a quietism the logical conclusion of all mysticism?

Stair. This is not so true as to say that in your efforts at reform you are really inspired by the divine vision of justice; and that this mystic vision and not the mere increase of quantity of eatables and drinkables is your animating motive.

Grimes. Well, to my mind this whole affair of mystical values and experiences comes down to a simple straightaway proposition. The submerged masses do not occupy themselves with such questions as those you are discussing. They haven't the time even to consider whether they want to consider them. Nor does the occasional free citizen who even now exists—a sporadic reminder and prophecy of ultimate democracy—bother himself about the relation of the

cosmos to value. Why? Not from mystic insight any more
than from metaphysical proof; but because he has so many
other interests that are worth while. His friends, his vocation
and avocations, his books, his music, his club—these things
engage him and they reward him. To multiply such men with
such interests—that is the genuine problem, I repeat; and it
is a problem to be solved only through an economic and
material redistribution.

   Eaton. Gladly, Stair, do all of us absolve ourselves from
the responsibility of having to create the goods that life—
call it God or Nature or Chance—provides. But we cannot,
if we would, absolve ourselves from responsibility for maintaining and extending these goods when they have happened.
To find it very wonderful—as Arthur does—that intelligence
perceives values as they are is trivial, for it is only an elaborate way of saying that they have happened. To invite us,
ceasing struggle and effort, to commune with Being through
the moments of insight and joy that life provides, is to bid
us to self-indulgence—to enjoyment at the expense of those
upon whom the burden of conducting life's affairs falls. For
even the mystics still need to eat and drink, be clothed and
housed, and somebody must do these unmystic things. And
to ignore others in the interest of our own perfection is not
conducive to genuine unity of Being.

   Intelligence is, indeed, as you say, discrimination, distinction. But why? Because we have to *act* in order to keep
secure, amid the moving flux of circumstance, some slight
but precious good that Nature has bestowed; and because,
in order to act successfully, we must act after conscious selection—after discrimination of means and ends. Of course,
all goods arrive, as Arthur says, as natural results, but so do
all bads, and all grades of good and bad. To label the results
that occur culminations, achievements, and then argue to a
quasi-moral constitution of Nature because she effects such
results, is to employ a logic which applies to the life-cycle of
the germ that, in achieving itself, kills man with malaria,
as well as to the process of human life that in reaching its
fulness cuts short the germ-fulfilment. It is putting the cart
before the horse to say that because Nature is so constituted as to produce results of all types of value, therefore

Nature is actuated by regard for differences of value. Nature, till it produces a being who strives and who thinks in order that he may strive more effectively, does not know whether it cares more for justice or for cruelty, more for the ravenous wolf-like competition of the struggle for existence, or for the improvements incidentally introduced through that struggle. Literally it has no mind of its own. Nor would the mere introduction of a consciousness that pictured indifferently the scene out of which consciousness developed, add one iota of reason for attributing eulogistically to Nature regard for value. But when the sentient organism, having experienced natural values, good and bad, begins to select, to prefer, and to make battle for its preference; and in order that it may make the most gallant fight possible picks out and gathers together in perception and thought what is favorable to its aims and what hostile, then and there Nature has at last achieved significant regard for good. And this is the same thing as the birth of intelligence. For the holding an end in view and the selecting and organizing out of the natural flux, on the basis of this end, conditions that are means, *is* intelligence. Not, then, when Nature produces health or efficiency or complexity does Nature exhibit regard for value, but only when it produces a living organism that has settled preferences and endeavors. The mere happening of complexity, health, adjustment, is all that Nature effects, as rightly called accident as purpose. But when Nature produces an intelligence—ah, then, indeed Nature has achieved something. Not, however, because this intelligence impartially pictures the nature which has produced it, but because in human consciousness Nature becomes genuinely partial. Because in consciousness an end is preferred, is selected for maintenance, and because intelligence pictures not a world, just as it is *in toto*, but images forth the conditions and obstacles of the continued maintenance of the selected good. For in an experience where values are demonstrably precarious, an intelligence that is not a principle of emphasis and valuation (an intelligence which defines, describes, and classifies merely for the sake of knowledge,) is a principle of stupidity and catastrophe.

As for Grimes, it is indeed true that problems are solved

only where they arise—namely, in action, in the adjustments
of behavior. But, for good or for evil, they can be solved
there only with method; and ultimately method is intelligence, and intelligence is method. The larger, the more human, the less technical the problem of practice, the more
open-eyed and wide-viewing must be the corresponding
method. I do not say that all things that have been called
philosophy participate in this method; I do say, however,
that a catholic and farsighted theory of the adjustment of
the conflicting factors of life *is*—whatever it be called—philosophy. And unless technical philosophy is to go the way
of dogmatic theology, it must loyally identify itself with such
a view of its own aim and destiny.

INTELLIGENCE AND MORALS[1]

"Except the blind forces of Nature," said Sir Henry Maine, "nothing moves in this world which is not Greek in its origin." And if we ask why this is so, the response comes that the Greek discovered the business of man to be pursuit of good, and intelligence to be central in this quest. The utmost to be said in praise of Plato and Aristotle is not that they invented excellent moral theories, but that they rose to the opportunity which the spectacle of Greek life afforded. For Athens presented an all but complete microcosm for the study of the interaction of social organization and individual character. A public life of rich diversity in concentrated and intense splendor trained the civic sense. Strife of faction and the rapid oscillations of types of polity provided the occasion for intellectual inquiry and analysis. The careers of dramatic personalities, habits of discussion, ease of legislative change, facilities for personal ambitions, distraction by personal rivalries, fixed attention upon the elements of character, and upon consideration of the effect of individual character on social vitality and stability. Happy exemption from ecclesiastic preoccupations, susceptibility to natural harmony, and natural piety conspired with frank and open observation to acknowledgment of the rôle played by natural conditions. Social instability and shock made equally pertinent and obvious the remark that only intelligence can confirm the values that natural conditions generate, and that intelligence is itself nurtured and matured only in a free and stable society. In Plato the resultant analysis of the mutual implica-

1. A public lecture delivered at Columbia University in March, 1908, under the title of "Ethics," in a series of lectures on "Science, Philosophy, and Art."

[First published as *Ethics* (New York: Columbia University Press, 1908), 26 pp. Revised and reprinted in *The Influence of Darwin on Philosophy* (New York: Henry Holt and Co., 1910), pp. 46–76, with the title "Intelligence and Morals."]

tions of the individual, the social and the natural, converged
in the ideas that morals and philosophy are one: namely, a
love of that wisdom which is the source of secure and social
good; that mathematics and the natural sciences focused
upon the problem of the perception of the good furnish the
materials of moral science; that logic is the method of the
pregnant organization of social conditions with respect to
good; that politics and psychology are sciences of one and
the same human nature, taken first in the large and then in
the little. So far that large and expansive vision of Plato.

But projection of a better life must be based upon reflection of the life already lived. The inevitable limitations of
the Greek city-state were inevitably wrought into the texture
of moral theory.

The business of thought was to furnish a substitute for
customs which were then relaxing from the pressure of
contact and intercourse without and the friction of strife
within. Reason was to take the place of custom as a guide
of life; but it was to furnish rules as final, as unalterable
as those of custom. In short, the thinkers were fascinated by
the afterglow of custom. They took for their own ideal the
distillation from custom of its essence—ends and laws which
should be rigid and invariable. Thus Morals was set upon
the track which it dared not leave for nigh twenty-five
hundred years: search for *the* final good, and for *the* single
moral force.

Aristotle's assertions that the state exists by nature, and
that in the state alone does the individual achieve independence and completeness of life, are indeed pregnant say-
ings. But as uttered by Aristotle they meant that, in an
isolated state, the Greek city-state, set a garlanded island in
the waste sea of *barbaroi*, a community indifferent when not
hostile to all other social groupings, individuals attain their
full end. In a social unity which signified social contraction,
contempt and antagonism, in a social order which despised
intercourse and glorified war, is realized the life of excellence!

There is likewise a profound saying of Aristotle's that the
individual who otherwise than by accident is not a member
of a state is either a brute or a god. But it is generally for-

gotten that elsewhere Aristotle identified the highest excellence, the chief virtue, with pure thought, and identifying
this with the divine, isolated it in lonely grandeur from the
life of society. That man, so far as in him lay, should be
godlike, meant that he should be non-social, because supra-
civic. Plato the idealist had shared the belief that reason is
the divine; but he was also a reformer and a radical and he
would have those who attained rational insight descend again
into the civic cave, and in its obscurity labor patiently for
the enlightenment of its blear-eyed inhabitants. Aristotle, the
conservative and the definer of what is, gloried in the exaltation of intelligence in man above civic excellence and social
need; and thereby isolated the life of truest knowledge from
contact with social experience and from responsibility for
discrimination of values in the course of life.

Moral theory, however, accepted from social custom
more than its cataleptic rigidity, its exclusive area of common good and its unfructified and irresponsible reason. The
city-state was a superficial layer of cultured citizens, cultured through a participation in affairs made possible by relief from economic pursuits, superimposed upon the dense
mass of serfs, artisans and laborers. For this division, moral
philosophy made itself spiritual sponsor, and thus took it up
into its own being. Plato wrestled valiantly with the class
problem; but his outcome was the necessity of decisive
demarcation, after education, of the masses in whom reason
was asleep and appetite much awake, from the few who
were fit to rule because alertly wise. The most generously
imaginative soul of all philosophy could not far outrun the
institutional practices of his people and his times. This might
have warned his successors of the danger of deserting the
sober path of a critical discernment of the better and the
worse within contemporary life for the more exciting adventure of a final determination of absolute good and evil.
It might have taught the probability that some brute resid-
uum or unrationalized social habit would be erected into an
apotheosis of pure reason. But the lesson was not learned.
Aristotle promptly yielded to the besetting sin of all philosophers, the idealization of the existent: he declared that the
class distinctions of superiority and inferiority as between

man and woman, master and slave, liberal-minded and base
mechanic, exist and are justified by nature—a nature which
aims at embodied reason.

What, finally, is this Nature to which the philosophy of
society and the individual so bound itself? It is the nature
which figures in Greek customs and myth; the nature re-
splendent and adorned which confronts us in Greek poetry
and art: the animism of savage man purged of grossness
and generalized by unerring aesthetic taste into beauty and
system. The myths had told of the loves and hates, the
caprices and desertions of the gods, and behind them all,
inevitable Fate. Philosophy translated these tales into formulae of the brute fluctuation of rapacious change held in
bounds by the final and supreme end: the rational good.
The animism of the popular mind died to reappear as
cosmology.

Repeatedly in this course we have heard of sciences
which began as parts of philosophy and which gradually
won their independence. Another statement of the same
history is that both science and philosophy began in subjection to mythological animism. Both began with acceptance
of a nature whose irregularities displayed the meaningless
variability of foolish wants held within the limits of order
and uniformity by an underlying movement toward a final
and stable purpose. And when the sciences gradually assumed the task of reducing irregular caprice to regular conjunction, philosophy bravely took upon itself the task of
substantiating, under the caption of a spiritual view of the
universe, the animistic survival. Doubtless Socrates brought
philosophy to earth; but his injunction to man to know
himself was incredibly compromised in its execution by the
fact that later philosophers submerged man in the world to
which philosophy was brought: a world which was the
heavy and sunken centre of hierarchic heavens located in
their purity and refinement as remotely as possible from the
gross and muddy vesture of earth.

The various limitations of Greek custom, its hostile indifference to all outside the narrow city-state, its assumption
of fixed divisions of wise and blind among men, its inability
socially to utilize science, its subordination of human inten-

tion to cosmic aim—all of these things were worked into moral theory. Philosophy had no active hand in producing the condition of barbarism in Europe from the fifth to the fifteenth centuries. By an unwitting irony which would have shocked none so much as the lucid moralists of Athens, their philosophic idealization, under captions of Nature and Reason, of the inherent limitations of Athenian society and Greek science, furnished the intellectual tools for defining, standardizing and justifying all the fundamental clefts and antagonisms of feudalism. When practical conditions are not frozen in men's imagination into crystalline truths, they are naturally fluid. They come and go. But when intelligence fixes fluctuating circumstances into final ideals, petrifaction is likely to occur; and philosophy gratuitously took upon itself the responsibility for justifying the worst defects of barbarian Europe by showing their necessary connection with divine reason.

The division of mankind into the two camps of the redeemed and the condemned had not needed philosophy to produce it. But the Greek cleavage of men into separate kinds on the basis of their position within or without the city-state was used to rationalize this harsh intolerance. The hierarchic organization of feudalism, within church and state, of those possessed of sacred rule and those whose sole excellence was obedience, did not require moral theory to generate or explain it. But it took philosophy to furnish the intellectual tools by which such chance episodes were emblazoned upon the cosmic heavens as a grandiose spiritual achievement. No; it is all too easy to explain bitter intolerance and desire for domination. Stubborn as they are, it was only when Greek moral theory had put underneath them the distinction between the irrational and the rational, between divine truth and good and corrupt and weak human appetite, that intolerance on system and earthly domination for the sake of eternal excellence were philosophically sanctioned. The health and welfare of the body and the securing for all of a sure and a prosperous livelihood were not matters for which medieval conditions fostered care in any case. But moral philosophy was prevailed upon to damn the body on principle, and to relegate to insignificance as merely mun-

dane and temporal the problem of a just industrial order.
Circumstances of the times bore with sufficient hardness
upon successful scientific investigation; but philosophy
added the conviction that in any case truth is so supernal
that it must be supernaturally revealed, and so important
that it must be authoritatively imparted and enforced. Intelligence was diverted from the critical consideration of the
natural sources and social consequences of better and worse
into the channel of metaphysical subtleties and systems,
acceptance of which was made essential to participation in
the social order and in rational excellence. Philosophy bound
the once erect form of human endeavor and progress to the
chariot wheels of cosmology and theology.

Since the Renaissance, moral philosophy has repeatedly
reverted to the Greek ideal of natural excellence realized in
social life, under the fostering care of intelligence in action.
The return, however, has taken place under the influence of
democratic polity, commercial expansion and scientific reorganization. It has been a liberation more than a reversion.
This combined return and emancipation, having transformed
our practice of life in the last four centuries, will not be
content till it has written itself clear in our theory of that
practice. Whether the consequent revolution in moral philosophy be termed pragmatism or be given the happier title
of the applied and experimental habit of mind is of little account. What is of moment is that intelligence has descended
from its lonely isolation at the remote edge of things, whence
it operated as unmoved mover and ultimate good, to take its
seat in the moving affairs of men. Theory may therefore
become responsible to the practices that have generated it;
the good be connected with nature, but with nature naturally,
not metaphysically, conceived, and social life be cherished
in behalf of its own immediate possibilities, not on the
ground of its remote connections with a cosmic reason and
an absolute end.

There is a notion, more familiar than correct, that
Greek thought sacrificed the individual to the state. None
has ever known better than the Greek that the individual
comes to himself and to his own only in association with
others. But Greek thought subjected, as we have seen, both

state and individual to an external cosmic order; and thereby it inevitably restricted the free use in doubt, inquiry and experimentation, of the human intelligence. The *anima libera*, the free mind of the sixteenth century, of Galileo and his successors, was the counterpart of the disintegration of cosmology and its animistic teleology. The lecturer on political economy reminded us that his subject began, in the Middle Ages, as a branch of ethics, though, as he hastened to show, it soon got into better association. Well, the same company was once kept by all the sciences, mathematical and physical as well as social. According to all accounts it was the integrity of the number one and the rectitude of the square that attracted the attention of Pythagoras to arithmetic and geometry as promising fields of study. Astronomy was the projected picture book of a cosmic object lesson in morals, Dante's transcript of which is none the less literal because poetic. If physics alone remained outside the moral fold, while noble essences redeemed chemistry, occult forces blessed physiology, and the immaterial soul exalted psychology, physics is the exception that proves the rule: matter was so inherently immoral that no high-minded science would demean itself by contact with it.

If we do not join with many in lamenting the stripping from nature of those idealistic properties in which animism survived, if we do not mourn the secession of the sciences from ethics, it is because the abandonment by intelligence of a fixed and static moral end was the necessary precondition of a free and progressive science of both things and morals; because the emancipation of the sciences from ready-made, remote and abstract values was necessary to make the sciences available for creating and maintaining more and specific values here and now. The divine comedy of modern medicine and hygiene is one of the human epics yet to be written; but when composed it may prove no unworthy companion of the medieval epic of other-worldly beatific visions. The great ideas of the eighteenth century, that expansive epoch of moral perception which ranks in illumination and fervor along with classic Greek thought, the great ideas of the indefinitely continuous progress of humanity and of the power and significance of freed intelligence, were borne by a single mother—experimental inquiry.

The growth of industry and commerce is at once cause and effect of the growth in science. Democritus and other ancients conceived the mechanical theory of the universe. The notion was not only blank and repellent, because it ignored the rich social material which Plato and Aristotle had organized into their rival idealistic views; but it was scientifically sterile, a piece of dialectics. Contempt for machines as the accoutrements of despised mechanics kept the mechanical conception aloof from these specific and controllable experiences which alone could fructify it. This conception, then, like the idealistic, was translated into a speculative cosmology and thrown like a vast net around the universe at large, as if to keep it from coming to pieces. It is from respect for the lever, the pulley and the screw that modern experimental and mathematical mechanics derives itself. Motion, traced through the workings of a machine, was followed out into natural events and studied just as motion, not as a poor yet necessary device for realizing final causes. So studied, it was found to be available for new machines and new applications, which in creating new ends also promoted new wants, and thereby stimulated new activities, new discoveries and new inventions. The recognition that natural energy can be systematically applied, through experimental observation, to the satisfaction and multiplication of concrete wants is doubtless the greatest single discovery ever imported into the life of man—save perhaps the discovery of language. Science, borrowing from industry, repaid the debt with interest, and has made the control of natural forces for the aims of life so inevitable that for the first time man is relieved from overhanging fear, with its wolflike scramble to possess and accumulate, and is freed to consider the more gracious question of securing to all an ample and liberal life. The industrial life had been condemned by Greek exaltation of abstract thought and by Greek contempt for labor as representing the brute struggle of carnal appetite for its own satiety. The industrial movement, offspring of science, restored it to its central position in morals. When Adam Smith made economic activity the

moving spring of man's unremitting effort, from the cradle
to the grave, to better his own lot, he recorded this change.
And when he made sympathy the central spring in man's
conscious moral endeavor, he reported the effect which the
increasing intercourse of men, due primarily to commerce,
had in breaking down suspicion and jealousy and in liberat-
ing man's kindlier impulses.

Democracy, the crucial expression of modern life, is
not so much an addition to the scientific and industrial
tendencies as it is the perception of their social or spiritual
meaning. Democracy is an absurdity where faith in the individual as individual is impossible; and this faith is impossible when intelligence is regarded as a cosmic power, not
an adjustment and application of individual tendencies. It
is also impossible when appetites and desires are conceived
to be the dominant factor in the constitution of most men's
characters, and when appetite and desire are conceived to be
manifestations of the disorderly and unruly principle of
nature. To put the intellectual centre of gravity in the
objective cosmos, outside of men's own experiments and
tests, and then to invite the application of individual intelligence to the determination of society is to invite chaos. To
hold that want is mere negative flux and hence requires external fixation by reason, and then to invite the wants to
give free play to themselves in social construction and intercourse is to call down anarchy. Democracy is estimable only
through the changed conception of intelligence, that forms
modern science, and of want, that forms modern industry.
It is essentially a changed psychology. The substitution, for
a priori truth and deduction, of fluent doubt and inquiry
meant trust in human nature in the concrete; in individual
honesty, curiosity and sympathy. The substitution of moving
commerce for fixed custom meant a view of wants as the
dynamics of social progress, not as the pathology of private
greed. The nineteenth century indeed turned sour on that
somewhat complacent optimism in which the eighteenth
century rested: the ideas that the intelligent self-love of
individuals would conduce to social cohesion, and competition among individuals usher in the kingdom of social
welfare. But the conception of a social harmony of interests

in which the achievement by each individual of his own freedom should contribute to a like perfecting of the powers of all, through a fraternally organized society, is the permanent contribution of the industrial movement to morals— even though so far it be but the contribution of a problem.

Intellectually speaking, the centuries since the fourteenth are the true middle ages. They mark the transitional period of mental habit, as the so-called medieval period represents the petrifaction, under changed outward conditions, of Greek ideas. The conscious articulation of genuinely modern tendencies has yet to come, and till it comes the ethic of our own life must remain undescribed. But the system of morals which has come nearest to the reflection of the movements of science, democracy and commerce, is doubtless the utilitarian. Scientific, after the modern mode, it certainly would be. Newton's influence dyes deep the moral thought of the eighteenth century. The arrangements of the solar system had been described in terms of a homogeneous matter and motion, worked by two opposed and compensating forces: all because a method of analysis, of generalization by analogy, and of mathematical deduction back to new empirical details had been followed. The imagination of the eighteenth century was a Newtonian imagination; and this no less in social than in physical matters. Hume proclaims that morals is about to become an experimental science. Just as, almost in our own day, Mill's interest in a method for social science led him to reformulate the logic of experimental inquiry, so all the great men of the Enlightenment were in search for the organon of morals which should repeat the physical triumphs of Newton. Bentham notes that physics has had its Bacon and Newton; that morals has had its Bacon in Helvétius, but still awaits its Newton; and he leaves us in no doubt that at the moment of writing he was ready, modestly but firmly, to fill the waiting niche with its missing figure.

The industrial movement furnished the concrete imagery for this ethical renovation. The utilitarians borrowed from Adam Smith the notion that through industrial exchange in a free society the individual pursuing his own good is led, under the guidance of the "invisible hand," to promote the general good more effectually than if he had set out to do it. This idea was dressed out in the atomistic psychology which Hartley built out from Locke—and was returned at usurious rates to later economists. From the great French writers who had sought to justify and promote democratic individualism, came the conception that, since it is perverted political institutions which deprave individuals and bring them into hostility, nation against nation, class against class, individual against individual, the great political problem is such a reform of law and legislation, civil and criminal, of administration, and of education as will force the individual to find his own interests in pursuits conducing to the welfare of others.

Tremendously effective as a tool of criticism, operative in abolition and elimination, utilitarianism failed to measure up to the constructive needs of the time. Its theoretical equalization of the good of each with that of every other was practically perverted by its excessive interest in the middle and manufacturing classes. Its speculative defect of an atomistic psychology combined with this narrowness of vision to make light of the constructive work that needs to be done by the state, before all can have, otherwise than in name, an equal chance to count in the common good. Thus the age-long subordination of economics to politics was revenged in the submerging of both politics and ethics in a narrow theory of economic profit; and utilitarianism, in its orthodox descendants, proffered the disjointed pieces of a mechanism, with a monotonous reiteration that looked at aright they form a beautifully harmonious organism.

Prevision, and to some extent experience, of this failure, conjoined with differing social traditions and ambitions, evoked German idealism, the transcendental morals of Kant and his successors. German thought strove to preserve the traditions which bound culture to the past, while revising these traditions to render them capable of meeting novel conditions. It found weapons at hand in the conceptions borrowed by Roman law from Stoic philosophy, and in the conceptions by which protestant humanism had re-edited scholastic catholicism. Grotius had made the idea of natural law, natural right and obligation, the central idea of German

morals, as thoroughly as Locke had made the individual
desire for liberty and happiness the focus of English and
then of French speculation. Materialized idealism is the
happy monstrosity in which the popular demand for vivid
imagery is most easily reconciled with the equally strong
demand for supremacy of moral values; and the complete
idealistic materialism of Stoicism has always given its ideas
a practical influence out of all proportion to their theoretical
vogue as a system. To the Protestant, that is the German,
humanist, Natural Law, the bond of harmonious reason in
nature, the spring of social intercourse among men, the inward light of individual conscience, united Cicero, St. Paul
and Luther in blessed union; gave a rational, not super-
rational basis for morals, and provided room for social legislation which at the same time could easily be held back
from too ruthless application to dominant class interests.

Kant saw the mass of empirical and hence irrelevant
detail that had found refuge within this liberal and diffusive
reason. He saw that the idea of reason could be made self-
consistent only by stripping it naked of these empirical accretions. He then provided, in his critiques, a somewhat
cumbrous moving van for transferring the resultant pure
or naked reason out of nature and the objective world, and
for locating it in new quarters, with a new stock of goods
and new customers. The new quarters were particular subjects, individuals; the stock of goods were the forms of
perception and the functions of thought by which empirical
flux is woven into durable fabrics; the new customers were
a society of individuals in which all are ends in themselves.
There ought to be an injunction issued that Kant's saying
about Hume's awakening of him should not be quoted save
in connection with his other saying that Rousseau brought
him to himself, in teaching him that the philosopher is of
less account than the laborer in the fields unless he contributes to human freedom. But none the less, the new
tenant, the universal reason, and the old homestead, the
empirical tumultuous individual, could not get on together.
Reason became a mere voice which, having nothing in particular to say, said Law, Duty, in general, leaving to the
existing social order of the Prussia of Frederick the Great

the congenial task of declaring just what was obligatory in the concrete. The marriage of freedom and authority was thus celebrated with the understanding that sentimental primacy went to the former and practical control to the latter.

The effort to force a universal reason that had been used to the broad domains of the cosmos into the cramped confines of individuality conceived as merely "empirical," a highly particularized creature of sense, could have but one result: an explosion. The products of that explosion constitute the Post-Kantian philosophies. It was the work of Hegel to attempt to fill in the empty reason of Kant with the concrete contents of history. The voice sounded like the voice of Aristotle, Thomas of Aquino and Spinoza translated into Swabian German; but the hands were as the hands of Montesquieu, Herder, Condorcet and the rising historical school. The outcome was the assertion that history is reason, and reason is history: the actual is rational, the rational is the actual. It gave the pleasant appearance (which Hegel did not strenuously discourage) of being specifically an idealization of the Prussian nation, and incidentally a systematized apologetic for the universe at large. But in intellectual and practical effect, it lifted the idea of process above that of fixed origins and fixed ends, and presented the social and moral order, as well as the intellectual, as a scene of becoming, and it located reason somewhere within the struggles of life.

Unstable equilibrium, rapid fermentation and a succession of explosive reports are thus the chief notes of modern ethics. Scepticism and traditionalism, empiricism and rationalism, crude naturalisms and all-embracing idealisms, flourish side by side—all the more flourish, one suspects, because side by side. Spencer exults because natural science reveals that a rapid transit system of evolution is carrying us automatically to the goal of perfect man in perfect society; and his English idealistic contemporary, Green, is so disturbed by the removal from nature of its moral qualities, that he tries to show that this makes no difference, since nature in any case is constituted and known through a spiritual principle which is as permanent as nature is changing. An Amiel genteelly laments the decadence of the inner life, while his neighbor Nietzsche brandishes in rude ecstasy the banner of brute survival as a happy omen of the final victory of nobility of mind. The reasonable conclusion from such a scene is that there is taking place a transformation of attitude towards moral theory rather than mere propagation of varieties among theories. The classic theories all agreed in one regard. They all alike assumed the existence of *the* end, the *summum bonum*, the final goal; and of *the* separate moral force that moves to that goal. Moralists have disputed as to whether the end is an aggregate of pleasurable state of consciousness, enjoyment of the divine essence, acknowledgment of the law of duty, or conformity to environment. So they have disputed as to the path by which the final goal is to be reached: fear or benevolence? reverence for pure law or pity for others? self-love or altruism? But these very controversies implied that there was but the one end and the one means.

The transformation in attitude, to which I referred, is the growing belief that the proper business of intelligence is discrimination of multiple and present goods and of the varied immediate means of their realization; not search for the one remote aim. The progress of biology has accustomed our minds to the notion that intelligence is not an outside power presiding supremely but statically over the desires and efforts of man, but is a method of adjustment of capacities and conditions within specific situations. History, as the lecturer on that subject told us, has discovered itself in the idea of process. The genetic standpoint makes us aware that the systems of the past are neither fraudulent impostures nor absolute revelations; but are the products of political, economic and scientific conditions whose change carries with it change of theoretical formulations. The recognition that intelligence is properly an organ of adjustment in difficult situations makes us aware that past theories were of value so far as they helped carry to an issue the social perplexities from which they emerged. But the chief impact of the evolutionary method is upon the present. Theory having learned what it cannot do, is made responsible for the better performance of what needs to be done, and what only a broadly equipped intelligence can undertake: study of the conditions out of which come the obstacles and the resources of adequate life, and developing and testing the ideas that, as working hypotheses, may be used to diminish the causes of evil and to buttress and expand the sources of good. This program is indeed vague, but only unfamiliarity with it could lead one to the conclusion that it is less vague than the idea that there is a single moral ideal and a single moral motive force.

From this point of view there is no separate body of moral rules; no separate system of motive powers; no separate subject-matter of moral knowledge, and hence no such thing as an isolated ethical science. If the business of morals is not to speculate upon man's final end, and upon an ultimate standard of right, it is to utilize physiology, anthropology and psychology to discover all that can be discovered of man, his organic powers and propensities. If its business is not to search for the one separate moral motive, it is to converge all the instrumentalities of the social arts, of law, education, economics and political science upon the construction of intelligent methods of improving the common lot.

If we still wish to make our peace with the past, and to sum up the plural and changing goods of life in a single word, doubtless the term happiness is the one most apt. But we should again exchange free morals for sterile metaphysics, if we imagine that "happiness" is any less unique than the individuals who experience it; any less complex than the constitution of their capacities, or any less variable than the objects upon which their capacities are directed.

To many timid, albeit sincere, souls of an earlier century, the decay of the doctrine that all true and worthful science is knowledge of final causes seemed fraught with danger to science and to morals. The rival conception of a wide open universe, a universe without bounds in time or space, without final limits of origin or destiny, a universe with the lid off, was a menace. We now face in moral science a similar crisis and like opportunity, as well as share in a like dreadful suspense. The abolition of a fixed and final goal and causal force in nature did not, as matter of fact, render rational conviction less important or less attainable. It was accompanied by the provision of a technique of persistent and detailed inquiry in all special fields of fact, a technique which led to the detection of unsuspected forces and the revelation of undreamed of uses. In like fashion we may anticipate that the abolition of *the* final goal and *the* single motive power and *the* separate and infallible faculty in morals, will quicken inquiry into the diversity of specific goods of experience, fix attention upon their conditions and bring to light values now dim and obscure. The change may relieve men from responsibility for what they cannot do, but it will promote thoughtful consideration of what they may do and the definition of responsibility for what they do amiss because of failure to think straight and carefully. Absolute goods will fall into the background, but the question of making more sure and extensive the share of all men in natural and social goods will be urgent, a problem not to be escaped nor evaded.

Morals, philosophy, returns to its first love; love of the wisdom that is nurse, as nature is mother, of good. But it returns to the Socratic principle equipped with a multitude of special methods of inquiry and testing; with an organized mass of knowledge, and with control of the arrangements by which industry, law and education may concentrate upon the problem of the participation by all men and women, up to their capacity of absorption, in all attained values. Morals may then well leave to poetry and to art, the task (so unartistically performed by philosophy since Plato) of gathering together and rounding out, into one abiding picture, the separate and special goods of life. It may leave this task with the assurance that the resultant synthesis will not depict any final and all-inclusive good, but will add just one more specific good to the enjoyable excellencies of life.

Humorous irony shines through most of the harsh glances turned towards the idea of an experimental basis and career for morals. Some shiver in the fear that morals will be plunged into anarchic confusion—a view well expressed by a recent writer in the saying that if the *a priori* and transcendental basis of morals be abandoned "we shall have merely the same certainty that now exists in physics and chemistry"! Elsewhere lurks the apprehension that the progress of scientific method will deliver the purposive freedom of man bound hand and foot to the fatal decrees of iron necessity, called natural law. The notion that laws govern and forces rule is an animistic survival. It is a product of reading nature in terms of politics in order to turn around and then read politics in the light of supposed sanctions of nature. This idea passed from medieval theology into the science of Newton, to whom the universe was the dominion of a sovereign whose laws were the laws of nature. From Newton it passed into the deism of the eighteenth century, whence it migrated into the philosophy of the Enlightenment, to make its last stand in Spencer's philosophy of the fixed environment and the static goal.

No, nature is not an unchangeable order, unwinding itself majestically from the reel of law under the control of deified forces. It is an indefinite congeries of changes. Laws are not governmental regulations which limit change, but are convenient formulations of selected portions of change followed through a longer or shorter period of time, and then registered in statistical forms that are amenable to mathematical manipulation. That this device of shorthand symbolization presages the subjection of man's intelligent effort to fixity of law and environment is interesting as a culture survival, but is not important for moral theory. Savage and child delight in creating bogeys from which, their origin and structure being conveniently concealed, interesting thrills and shudders may be had. Civilized man in the nineteenth century outdid these bugaboos in his image of a fixed universe hung on a cast-iron framework of fixed, necessary and universal laws. Knowledge of nature does not mean subjection to predestination, but insight into courses of change; an insight which is formulated in "laws," that is, methods of subsequent procedure.

Knowledge of the process and conditions of physical and social change through experimental science and genetic history has one result with a double name: increase of control and increase of responsibility; increase of power to direct natural change, and increase of responsibility for its equitable direction toward fuller good. Theory located within progressive practice instead of reigning statically supreme over it, means practice itself made responsible to intelligence; to intelligence which relentlessly scrutinizes the consequences of every practice, and which exacts liability by an equally relentless publicity. As long as morals occupies itself with mere ideals, forces and conditions as they are will be good enough for "practical" men, since they are then left free to their own devices in turning these to their own account. As long as moralists plume themselves upon possession of the domain of the categorical imperative with its bare precepts, men of executive habits will always be at their elbows to regulate the concrete social conditions through which the form of law gets its actual filling of specific injunctions. When freedom is conceived to be transcendental, the coercive restraint of immediate necessity will lay its harsh hand upon the mass of men.

In the end, men do what they can do. They refrain from doing what they cannot do. They do what their own specific powers in conjunction with the limitations and resources of the environment permit. The effective control of their powers is not through precepts, but through the regulation of their conditions. If this regulation is to be not merely physical or coercive, but moral, it must consist of the intelligent selection and determination of the environments in which we act; and in an intelligent exaction of responsibility for the use of men's powers. Theorists inquire after the "motive" to morality, to virtue and the good, under such circumstances. What then, one wonders, is their conception of the make-up of human nature and of its relation to virtue and to goodness? The pessimism that dictates such a question, if it be justified, precludes any consideration of morals.

The diversion of intelligence from discrimination of plural and concrete goods, from noting their conditions and obstacles, and from devising methods for holding men responsible for their concrete use of powers and conditions, has done more than brute love of power to establish inequality and injustice among men. It has done more, because it has confirmed with social sanctions the principle of feudal domination. All men require moral sanctions in their conduct: the consent of their kind. Not getting it otherwise, they go insane to feign it. No man ever lived with the exclusive approval of his own conscience. Hence the vacuum left in practical matters by the remote irrelevancy of transcendental morals has to be filled in somehow. It is filled in. It is filled in with class-codes, class-standards, class-approvals —with codes which recommend the practices and habits already current in a given circle, set, calling, profession, trade, industry, club or gang. These class-codes always lean back upon and support themselves by the professed ideal code. This latter meets them more than half-way. Being in its pretense a theory for regulating practice, it must demonstrate its practicability. It is uneasy in isolation, and travels hastily to meet with compromise and accommodation the actual situation in all its brute unrationality. Where the pressure is greatest—in the habitual practice of the political and economic chieftains—there it accommodates the most.

Class-codes of morals are sanctions, under the caption of ideals, of uncriticized customs; they are recommendations, under the head of duties, of what the members of the class are already most given to doing. If there are to obtain more equable and comprehensive principles of action, exacting a more impartial exercise of natural power and resource in the interests of a common good, members of a class must no longer rest content in responsibility to a class whose traditions constitute its conscience, but be made responsible to a society whose conscience is its free and effectively organized intelligence.

In such a conscience alone will the Socratic injunction to man to know himself be fulfilled.

THE INTELLECTUALIST CRITERION
FOR TRUTH[1]

I

Among the influences that have worked in contemporary philosophy towards disintegration of intellectualism of the epistemological type, and towards the substitution of a philosophy of experience, the work of Mr. Bradley must be seriously counted. One has, for example, only to compare his metaphysics with the two fundamental contentions of T. H. Green, namely, that reality is a single, eternal and all-inclusive system of relations, and that this system of relations is one in kind with that process of relating which constitutes our thinking, to be instantly aware of a changed atmosphere. Much of Bradley's writings is a sustained and deliberate polemic against intellectualism of the Neo-Kantian type. When, however, we find conjoined to this criticism an equally sustained contention that the philosophic conception of reality must be based on an exclusively intellectual criterion, a criterion belonging to and confined to theory, we have a situation that is thought-provoking. The situation grows in interest when it is remembered that there is a general and growing tendency among those who appeal in philosophy to a strictly intellectualistic *method* of defining "reality," to insist that the reality reached by this method

1. Reprinted, with many changes, from an article in *Mind*, Vol. XVI, n.s., July, 1907. Although the changes have been made to render the article less technical, it still remains, I fear, too technical to be intelligible to those not familiar with recent discussions of logical theory.

[First published in *Mind*, n.s. 16 (1907): 317–42, with the title "Reality and the Criterion for the Truth of Ideas." Revised and reprinted in *The Influence of Darwin on Philosophy* (New York: Henry Holt and Co., 1910), pp. 112–53, with the title "The Intellectualist Criterion for Truth."]

has a super-intellectual *content*: that intellectual, affectional,
and volitional features are all joined and fused in "ultimate"
reality. The curious character of the situation is that Reality
is an "absolute experience" of which the intellectual is simply
one partial and transmuted moment. Yet this reality is attained unto, in philosophic method, by exclusive emphasis
upon the intellectual aspect of present experience and by
systematic exclusion of exactly the emotional, volitional features which with respect to content are insisted upon! Under such circumstances the cynically-minded are moved to
wonder whether this tremendous insistence upon one factor
in present experience at the expense of others, is not because
this is the only way to maintain the notion of "Absolute Experience," and to prevent it from collapsing into ordinary
every-day experience. This paradox is not peculiar to Mr.
Bradley. Looking at the Neo-Kantian movement in the broad
in its modern form, one might almost say that its prominent
feature is its insistence upon reaching a "Reality" that includes extra-intellectual factors and phases, traits that are
ideal in a moral and emotional sense, by an exclusive
recognition of the function of knowledge in its isolation.

Such being the case, an examination of Mr. Bradley's
method and criterion may have far-reaching implications.
First, let us set before ourselves the general points of Mr.
Bradley's indictment of intellectualism.[2] Knowledge or judgment works by means of thought; it is predication of idea
(meaning) of existence as its subject. Its final aim is to
effect a complete union or harmony of existence and meaning. But it is fore-doomed to failure, for in realizing its end
it must employ means which contradict its own purpose.
This inherent incapacity lurks in judgment with respect to
subject, predicate and copula. The predicate or meaning
necessary to complete the reality presented in the subject
can be referred to the latter and united with it only by being
itself alienated from existence. It heals the wounds or
deficiencies of its own subject (and in the end all deficiencies
are to the modern idealist discrepancies) only on condition
of inflicting another wound,—only by sundering meaning

2. I follow chiefly Ch. 15 of *Appearance and Reality*—the chapter
on "Thought and Reality."

from a prior union with existence in some other phase. This latter existence, therefore, is always left out in the cold. It is as if we wanted to get all the cloth in the world into one garment and our only way of accomplishing this were to tear off a portion from one piece of goods in order to patch it on to another.

The subject of the judgment, moreover, as well as the predicate, stands in the way of judgment fulfilling its own task. It has "sensuous infinitude" and it has "immediacy," but these two traits contradict each other. The details of the subject always go beyond itself, being indefinitely related to something beyond. "In its given content it has relations which do not terminate within that content" (*Appearance and Reality*, p. 176), while in its immediacy it presents an undivided union of existence and meaning. No subject can be mere existence any more than it can be mere meaning. It is always existent or embodied meaning. As such it claims individuality or the character of a single subsistent whole. But this indispensable claim is inconsistent with its ragged-edged character, its indefinite external reference, which is indispensable to it as subject that it may require and receive further meaning from predication.

With respect to the copula the following quotation from the *Principles of Logic* (p. 10) may serve: "Judgment proper is the *act* which refers the ideal content (recognized as such) to the reality beyond the act." In other words, judgment as act (and it is the act which is expressed in the copula) must always fall outside of the content of knowledge as such; yet since this act certainly falls within reality, it would have to be recognized and stated by any knowledge pretending to competency with respect to reality as a whole. These considerations, stated in this way, are highly technical and presuppose a knowledge not merely of Mr. Bradley's own logic, but also of the logical analysis of knowledge initiated by Kant and carried on by Herbart, Lotze, and others. Their main import may, however, be stated in comparatively non-technical form. Human experience is full of discrepancies. Were experience purely a matter of brute existence (such as we sometimes imagine the animals' experience to be) it would be totally lacking in meaning and there would be no problems, no thinking, no occasion for thinking, and hence no philosophy. On the other hand, if experience were a complete, tight-jointed union of existence and meaning, there would be no dissatisfaction, no problems, no cause for efforts to patch up defects and contradictions. Existences, things, would embody all the meanings that they suggest; while abstract meanings, values that are *merely* ideal, that are projected or thought of but not fulfilled, would be totally unheard of. But our experience stands in marked contrast to both these types of experience. It is neither an affair of meaningless existence nor of existence self-luminous with fulfilled meaning. All things that we experience have *some* meaning, but that meaning is always so partially embodied in things that we cannot rest in them. They point beyond themselves; they indicate meanings which they do not fulfil; they suggest values which they fail to embody, and when we go to other things for the fruition of what is denied, we either find the same situation of division over again, or we find even more positive disappointment and frustration—we find contrary meanings set up. Now all thinking grows out of this discrepancy between existence and the meaning which it partially embodies and partially refuses, which it suggests but declines to express. Yet thinking, the mode of bringing existence and meaning into harmony with each other, always works by selection, by abstraction; it sets up and projects meanings which are ideal only, footless, in the air, matters of thought only, not of sentiency or immediate existence. It emphasizes the ideal of a completed union of existence and meaning, but is helpless to effect it. And this helplessness (according to Mr. Bradley) is not due to external pressure but to the very structure of thought itself.

From every point of view knowledge operates under conditions, (and these not externally imposed but inherent in its own nature as judgment,) that render it incapable of realizing its aim of complete union of existence and meaning. Granted the argument, and it is difficult to imagine a more serious indictment against the pretensions of philosophy to reach "Reality" *via* the exclusive path of knowledge.

The presence of contradiction is Mr. Bradley's criterion

for "appearance," just as its absence is his criterion for
"reality." It thus goes without saying that knowledge and
truth which we can attain are matters of appearance. Contradiction between existence and meaning is its last word.
This is not merely a logical deduction from Mr. Bradley's
position, but is expressly stated by him. "Thus the truth belongs to existence, but it does not as such exist. . . . Truth
shows a dissection but never an actual life" (*Appearance
and Reality*, p. 167). Again, "every truth is appearance since
in it we have divorce of quality from being" (*Appearance
and Reality*, p. 187). "Even absolute truth seems in the end
to turn out erroneous. . . . Internal discrepancy belongs irremovably to truth's proper character. . . . Truth is one
aspect of experience and is therefore made imperfect and
limited by what it fails to include" (*Appearance and Reality*,
pp. 544–45). Nothing could be more explicit as to the inherently contradictory character of truth, both as an ideal
and as an accomplished fact; nothing more positive as to
the unreality or appearance-character of truth. We cannot,
on Mr. Bradley's method, stop here. Not only is knowledge
—working as it does through thought which is always partial,
selective, abstractive—doomed to failure in accomplishing its
task, but the existence of the contradiction between the
suggestion of meanings by existence and this realization in
existence is itself due to thought.

Speaking of thought he says: "The relational form is a
compromise on which thought stands and which it develops."
And all the particular antinomies which he discusses are
interpreted as having their basis in the category of relation
(*Appearance and Reality*, p. 180). In his section on Appearance he goes through various aspects and distinctions
of the world, such as primary and secondary qualities, substance and its properties, relation and qualitative elements,
space and time, motion and change, causation, etc., pointing
out irreconcilable discrepancies in them. He does not, in a
generalized way, expressly refer them to any common source
or root. But it seems a fair inference that the relational
character of thought is at the bottom of the whole trouble:
so that we have in the cases mentioned precisely the same
situation *in concreto* which is set forth *in abstracto* in the
discussion of thought. The contradictions brought up are in

every case resolved into the fundamental discrepancy supposed to exist between relations and elements related. In each case there is the ideal of a final unity in which relations and elements as such disappear, while in every case the nature of relation is such as to prevent the desired consummation. In at least one place, it is expressly declared that it is the knowledge function which is responsible for the degradation of reality to appearance. "We do not suggest that the thing always itself is an appearance. We mean its character is such *that it becomes one as soon as we judge it.* And this character we have seen throughout our work, is ideality. Appearance consists in the looseness of content from existence. . . . And we have found that everywhere throughout the world such ideality prevails" (*Appearance and Reality*, pp. 485–86, italics not in the original). It is not then strictly true that the divorce of meaning and existence instigates thought; rather thought is the unruly member that creates the divorce and then engages in the task (in which it is self-condemned to failure) of trying to establish the unity which it has gratuitously destroyed. Thinking, self-consciousness, is disease of the naïve unity of thoughtless experience.

On the one hand there is a systematic discrediting of the ultimate claims of the knowledge function, and this not from external physiological or psychological reasons such as are sometimes alleged against its capacity, but on the basis of its own interior logic. But on the other hand, a strictly logical criterion is deliberately adopted and employed as the fundamental and final criterion for the philosophic conception of reality. Long familiarity has not dulled my astonishment at finding exactly the same set of considerations which in the earlier portion of the book are employed to condemn things as experienced by us to the region of Appearance, employed in the latter portion of the book to afford a triumphant demonstration of the existence and character of Absolute Reality. The argument I take up first on its formal side, and then with reference to material considerations.[3]

The positive conception of Reality is reached by the

3. The crux of the argument is contained in Chs. 13 and 14, on the "General Nature of Reality."

conception that "ultimate reality must be such that it does
not contradict itself; here is an absolute criterion. And it is
proved absolute by the fact that either in endeavouring to
deny it or even in attempting to doubt it, we tacitly assume
its validity" (*Appearance and Reality*, pp. 136–37). That is
to say, when one sets out to think one must avoid self-
contradiction; this avoidance, or, put positively, the attain-
ment of consistency, harmony, is the basic law of all thinking.
Since in thinking we set out to attain reality, it follows that
reality itself must be self-consistent, and that its self-consistency determines the law of thought. Or, as Mr. Bradley
again puts the matter, "In order to think at all you must
subject yourself to the standard, a standard which implies
an absolute knowledge of reality; and while you doubt this,
you accept it, and obey, while you rebel" (*Appearance and
Reality*, p. 153). The absolute knowledge referred to is, of
course, the knowledge of the thoroughly self-consistent, non-
contradictory character of reality. Every reader of Mr. Bradley's book knows how he goes on from this point to supply
positive content to reality; to give an outline sketch of the
characters it must possess and the way in which it must
possess them in order to maintain its thoroughly self-consistent character. It is, however, only the strictly formal
aspect of the matter that I am here concerned with.

On this side we reach, I think, the heart of the matter
by asking, in reference to the first quotation: Absolute *for
what*? Surely absolute for the process under consideration,
that is absolute for thought. But the significance of this absolute for thought is, one may say, "absolutely" (since we
are here confessedly in the realm just of thought) determined
by the nature of thought itself. Now this nature has been
already referred by considerations "belonging irremovably to
truth's proper character," to the world of appearance and of
internal discrepancy. Yes, one may say (speaking formally),
the criterion of thought is absolute—that is to say absolute
or final for thought; but how can one imagine that this in
any way alters the essential nature and value of thought? If
knowledge works by thought, and thought institutes appearance over against reality, any further fact about thought
—such as a statement of its criterion—falls wholly within

the limits of this situation. It is comical to suppose that a
special trait of thought can be employed to alter the fundamental and essential nature of thought. The criterion of
thought must be infected by the nature of thought, instead
of being a redeeming angel which at a critical juncture
transforms the fragile creature, thought, into an ambassador
with power plenipotentiary to the court of the Absolute.

There really seems to be ground for supposing that the
whole argument turns on an ambiguity in the use of the
word "absolute." Keeping strictly within the limits of the
argument, it means nothing more than that thinking has a
certain principle, a law of its own; that it has an appropriate
mode of procedure which must not be violated. It means, in
short, whatever is finally controlling for the thought-function.
But Mr. Bradley immediately takes the word to mean absolute
in the sense of describing a reality which by its very nature
is totally contradistinguished from appearance—that is to
say, from the realm of thought. Upon the ambiguity of a
word, the systematic indictment of intellectualism becomes
the corner-stone of a systematically intellectualistic method
of conceiving reality!

Mr. Bradley has himself recognized the seeming contradiction between his indictment of thought and his use of the
criterion of thought as the exclusive path to a philosophic
notion of the real. In dealing with it, he (to my mind) comes
within an ace of stating a truer doctrine, and also exhibits
even more clearly the weakness of his own position. He goes
so far as to put the following words into the mouth of an
objector, and to accept their general import: "All axioms, as
a matter of fact, are practical . . . for none of them in the
end can amount to more than the impulse to behave in a
certain way. And they cannot express more than this impulse, together with the impossibility of satisfaction unless
it is complied with" (p. 151). After accepting this (p. 152)
he goes on to say: "Take for example the law of avoiding
contradiction. When two elements will not remain quietly
together, but collide and struggle, we cannot rest satisfied
with that state. Our impulse is to alter it and, on the theoretical side, to bring the content to such shape that the variety
remains peaceably in one. And this inability to rest otherwise

and this tendency to alter in a certain way and direction is, *when reflected upon and made explicit*, our axiom and our intellectual standard" (p. 152; italics mine).

The retort is obvious: if *the* intellectual criterion, the principle of non-contradiction on which his whole Absolute Reality rests, is itself a practical principle, then surely the ultimate criterion for regulating intellectual undertakings is practical. To this obvious answer Mr. Bradley makes reply as follows: "You may call the intellect, if you like, a mere tendency to a movement, but you must remember that it is a movement of a *very special kind*. . . . Thinking is the attempt to satisfy a *special* impulse, and the attempt implies an assumption about reality. . . . But why, it may be objected, is this assumption better than what holds for practice? Why is the theoretical to be superior to the practical end? I have never said that this is so, only *here*, that is in *metaphysics*, I must be allowed to reply, we are acting theoretically. . . . The *theoretical standard within theory must surely be absolute*" (pp. 152–53. The italics again are mine; compare with the quotation this, from p. 485: "Our attitude, however, in metaphysics must be theoretical." So, also, p. 154, "Since metaphysics is mere theory and since theory from its nature must be made by the intellect, it is here the intellect alone which is to be satisfied").

Grant that intellect is a special movement or mode of practice; grant that we are not merely acting (are we ever *merely* acting?) but are "specially occupied and therefore subject to special conditions," and the problem remains *what* special kind of activity is thinking? what is its experienced differentia from other kinds? what is its commerce with them? When the problem is *what* special kind of an activity is thinking and of *what* nature is the consistency which is its criterion, somehow we do not get forward by being told that thinking *is* a special mode of practice and that its criterion *is* consistency. The unquestioned presupposition of Mr. Bradley is that thinking is such a wholly separate activity (the "intellect *alone*" which has to be satisfied), that to give it autonomy is to say that it, and its criterion, have nothing to do with other activities; that it is "independent" as to criterion, in a way which excludes interdependence in function and outcome. Unless the term "special" be interpreted to mean *isolated*, to say that thinking is a *special* mode of activity no more nullifies the proposition that it arises in a practical context and operates for practical ends, than to say that blacksmithing is a *special* activity, negates its being one connected mode of industrial activity.

His underlying presupposition of the separate character of thought comes out in the passage last quoted. "Our impulse," he says, "is to alter the conflicting situation and, *on the theoretical side*, to bring its contents into peaceable unity." If one substitutes for the word "on" the word "through," one gets a conception of theory and of thinking that does justice to the autonomy of the operation and yet so connects it with other activities as to give it a serious business, real purpose and concrete responsibility and hence testability. From this point of view the theoretical activity is simply the form that certain practical activities take after colliding, as the most effective and fruitful way of securing their own harmonization. The collision is not theoretical; the issue in "peaceable unity" is not theoretical. But theory names the type of activity by which the transformation from war to peace is most amply and securely effected.[4]

Admit, however, the force of Mr. Bradley's contention on its own terms and see how futile is the result. It is quite true, as Mr. Bradley says (p. 153), that if a man sits down to play the metaphysical game, he must abide by the rules of thinking; but if thinking be already, with respect to reality, an idle and futile game, simply abiding by the rules does not give additional value to its stakes. Grant the premises as to the character of thought, and the assertion of the final char-

---

4. The same point comes out in Mr. Bradley's treatment of the way in which the practical demand for the good or satisfaction is to be taken account of in a philosophical conception of the nature of reality. He admits that it comes in; but holds that it enters not directly, but because if left outside it indirectly introduces a feature of "discontent" on the intellectual side (see p. 155). This, as an argument for the supremacy of the isolated theoretical standard, loses all its force if we cease to conceive of intellect as from the start an independent function, and realize that intellectual discontent *is* the practical conflict becoming deliberately aware of itself as the most effective means of its own rectification.

acter of the theoretical standard within metaphysics—since
metaphysics is a form of theory—is a warning against metaphysics. If the intellect involves self-contradiction, it is either
impossible that it should be satisfied, or else self-contradiction
is its satisfaction.

II

Let us, however, turn from Mr. Bradley's formal proof
that the criterion of philosophic truth must be exclusively a
canon of formal thought. Let us ignore the contradiction involved in first making the work of thought to be the producing of appearance and then making the law of this thought
the law of an Absolute Reality. What about the intellectualist
criterion? The intellectualism of Mr. Bradley's philosophy is
represented in the statement that it is "the theoretical standard which guarantees that Reality is a self-consistent system"
(p. 148). But how can the fact that the criterion of thinking
is consistency be employed to determine the nature of the
consistency of its object? Consistency in one sense, consistency of reasoning with itself, we know; but what is the
nature of the consistency of reality which this consistency
necessitates? Thinking without doubt must be logical; but
does it follow from this that the reality about which one
thinks, and about which one must think consistently if one
is to think to any purpose, must itself be already logical? The
pivot of the argument is, of course, the old ontological argument, stripped of all theological irrelevancies and reduced to
its fighting weight as a metaphysical proposition. Those who
question this basic principle of intellectualism will, of course,
question it here. They will urge that, instead of the consistency of "reality" resting on the basis of consistency in the
reasoning process the latter derives its meaning from the material consistency at which it aims. They will say that the definition of the nature of the consistency which is the end of
thinking and which prescribes its technique is to be reached
from inquiry into such questions as these: What sort of an
activity in the concrete is thinking? what are the specific conditions which it has to fulfil? what is its use; its relevancy; its

purport in present concrete experiences? The more it is insisted that the theoretical standard—consistency—is final within theory, the more germane and the more urgent is the question: What then in the concrete *is* theory? and of what nature *is* the material consistency which is the test of its formal consistency?[5]

Take the instance of a man who wishes to deny the criterion of self-consistency in thinking. Is he refuted by pointing to the "fact" that eternal reality is eternally self-consistent? Would not his obvious answer to such a mode of refutation be: "What of it? What is the relevancy of that proposition to my procedure in thinking here and now? Doubtless absolute reality may be a great number of things, possibly very sublime and precious things; but what I am concerned with is a particular job of thinking, and until you show me the intermediate terms which link that job to the asserted self-consistent character of absolute reality, I fail to see what difference this doubtless wholly amiable trait of reality has to make in what I am here and now concerned with. You might as well quote any other irrelevant fact, such as the height of the Empress of China." We take another tack in dealing with the man in question. We call his attention to his specific aim in the situation with reference to which he is thinking, and point out the conditions that have to be observed if that aim is to fulfil itself. We show that if he does not observe the conditions imposed by his aim his thinking will go on so wildly as to defeat itself. It is to consistency of means with the end of the concrete activity that we appeal. "Try thinking," we tell such a man, "experiment with it, taking pains sometimes to have your reasonings consistent with one another, and at other times deliberately introducing in-

5. This suggests that many of the stock arguments against pragmatism fail to take its contention seriously enough. They proceed from the assumption that it is an account of truth which leaves untouched current notions of the nature of intelligence. But the essential point of pragmatism is that it bases its changed account of truth on a changed conception of the nature of intelligence, both as to its objective and its method. Now this different account of intelligence may be wrong, but controversy which leaves standing the conventionally current theories about thought and merely discusses "truth" will not go far. Since truth is the adequate fulfilment of the function of intelligence, the question turns on the nature of the latter.

consistencies; then see what you get in the two cases and how
the result reached is related to your purpose in thinking." We
point out that since that purpose is to reach a settled conclusion, that purpose will be defeated unless the steps of reasoning are kept consistent with one another. We do not appeal
from the mere consistency of the reasoning process—the intellectual aspect of the matter—to an absolute self-consistent
reality; but we appeal from the material character of the end
to be reached to the type of the formal procedure necessary
to accomplish it.

With all our heart, then, the standard of thinking is absolute (that is final) within thinking. But what is thinking?
The standard of black-smithing must be absolute within
black-smithing, but what is black-smithing? No prejudice prevents acknowledging that black-smithing is one practical activity existing as a distinct and relevant member of a like
system of activities: that it is because men use horses to
transport persons and goods that horses need to be shod. The
ultimate criterion of black-smithing is producing a good shoe,
but the nature of a good shoe is fixed, not by black-smithing,
but by the activities in which horses are used. The end is
ultimate (absolute) for the operation, but this very finality is
evidence that the operation is not absolute and self-enclosed,
but is related and responsible. Why must the fact that the end
of thinking is ultimate for thought stand on any different
footing?

Let us then, by way of experiment, follow this suggestion. Let us assume that among real objects in their values
and significances, real oppositions and incompatibilities exist; that these conflicts are both troublesome in themselves,
and the source of all manner of further difficulties—so much
so that they may be suspected of being the source of all man's
woe, of all encroachment upon and destruction of value, of
good. Suppose that thinking is, not accidentally but essentially, a way, and the only way that proves adequate, of dealing with these predicaments—that being "in a hole," in difficulty, is the fundamental "predicament" of intelligence.
Suppose when effort is made in a brute way to remove these
oppositions and to secure an arrangement of things which
means satisfaction, fulfilment, happiness, that the method of

brute attack, of trying directly to force warrings into peace fails; suppose then an effort to effect the transformation by an indirect method—by inquiry into the disordered state of affairs and by framing views, conceptions, of what the situation would be like were it reduced to harmonious order. Finally, suppose that upon this basis a plan of action is worked out, and that this plan, when carried into overt effect, succeeds infinitely better than the brute method of attack in bringing about the desired consummation. Suppose again this indirection of activity is precisely what we mean by thinking. Would it not hold that harmony is the end and the test of thinking? that observations are pertinent and ideas correct just in so far as, overtly acted upon, they succeed in removing the undesirable, the inconsistent.

But, it is said, the very process of thinking makes a certain assumption regarding the nature of reality, *viz.*, that reality is self-consistent. This statement puts the end for the beginning. The assumption is not that "reality" *is* self-consistent, but that by thinking it may, for some special purpose, or as respects some concrete problem, attain greater consistency. Why should the assumption regarding "reality" be other than that specific realities with which thought is concerned are *capable of receiving* harmonization? To say that thought must assume, in order to go on, that reality already possesses harmony is to say that thought must begin by contradicting its own direct data, and by assuming that its concrete aim is vain and illusory. Why put upon thought the onus of introducing discrepancies into reality in order just to give itself exercise in the gymnastic of removing them? The assumption that concrete thinking makes about "reality" is that things just as they exist may acquire *through activity, guided by thinking,* a certain character which it is excellent for them to possess; and may acquire it more liberally and effectively than by other methods. One might as well say that the blacksmith could not think to any effect concerning iron, without a Platonic archetypal horseshoe, laid up in the heavens. His thinking also makes an assumption about present, given reality, *viz.*, that this piece of iron, through the exercise of intelligently directed activity, may be shaped into a satisfactory horseshoe. The assumption is practical: the assumption that a specific thing may take on in a specific way a specific needed value. The test, moreover, of this assumption is practical; it consists in acting upon it to see if it will do what it pretends it can do, namely, guide activities to the required result. The assumption about reality is not something in addition to the idea, which an idea already in existence makes; some assumption about the possibility of a change in the state of things as experienced *is* the idea—and its test or criterion is whether this possible change can be effected when the idea is acted upon in good faith.

In any case, how much simpler the case becomes when we stick by the empirical facts. According to them there is no wholesale discrepancy of existence and meaning; there is simply a "loosening" of the two when objects do not fulfil our plans and meet our desires; or when we project inventions and cannot find immediately the means for their realization. The "collisions" are neither physical, metaphysical, nor logical; they are moral and practical. They exist between an aim and the means of its execution. Consequently the object of thinking is not to effect some wholesale and "Absolute" reconciliation of meaning and existence, but to make a specific adjustment of things to our purposes and of our purposes to things at just the crucial point of the crisis. Making the utmost concessions to Mr. Bradley's account of the discrepancy of meaning and existence in our experience, to his statement of the relation of this to the function of judgment (as involving namely an explicit *statement* at once of the actual sundering and the ideal union) and to his account of consistency as the goal and standard, there is still not a detail of the account that is not met amply and with infinitely more empirical warrant by the conception that the "collision" in which thinking starts and the "consistency" in which it terminates are practical and human.

III

This brings us explicitly to the question of truth, "truth" being confessedly the end and standard of thinking. I confess to being much at a loss to realize just what the intellectualists

conceive to be the relation of truth to ideas on one side and
to "reality" on the other. My difficulty occurs, I think, because
they describe so little in analytical detail; in writing of truth
they seem rather to be under a strong emotional influence —
as if they were victims of an uncritical pragmatism — which
leaves much of their thought to be guessed at. The implication of their discussions assigns three distinct values to the
term "truth." On the one hand, truth is something which
characterizes ideas, theories, hypotheses, beliefs, judgments,
propositions, assertions, etc., — anything whatsoever involving
intellectual statement. From this standpoint a criterion of
truth means the test of the worth of the intellectual intent,
import or claim of any intellectual statement as intellectual.
This is an intelligible sense of the term truth. In the second
place, it seems to be assumed that a certain kind of reality
is already, apart from ideas or meanings, Truth, and that
this Truth is the criterion of that lower and more unworthy
kind of truth that may be possessed or aimed at by ideas.
But we do not stop here. The conception that *all* truth must
have a criterion haunts the intellectualist, so that the reality,
which, as contrasted with ideas, is taken to be The Truth
(and the criterion of *their* truth) is treated as if it itself had
to have support and warrant from some other Reality, lying
back of it, which is *its* criterion. This, then, gives the third
type of truth, *The Absolute Truth*. (Just why this process
should not go on indefinitely is not clear, but the necessity
of infinite regress may be emotionally prevented by always
referring to this last type of truth as Absolute.) Now this
scheme may be "true," but it is not self-explanatory or even
easily apprehensible. In just what sense truth is (1) that
to which ideas as ideas lay claim and yet is (2) Reality
which as reality is the criterion of truth of ideas, and yet
again is (3) a Reality which completely annuls and transcends all reference to ideas, is not in the least clear to me:
nor, till better informed, shall I believe it to be clear to
anyone.

In his more strictly logical discussions, Mr. Bradley sets
out from the notion that truth refers to intellectual statements and positions as such. But the Truth soon becomes a
sort of transcendent essence on its own account. The identi-

fication of reality and truth on page 146 may be a mere casual phrase, but the distinction drawn between validity and absolute truth (p. 362), and the discussion of Degrees of Truth and Reality, involve assumptions of an identity of truth and reality. Truth in this sense turns out to be the criterion for the truth, the truth, that is, of ideas. But, again (p. 545), a distinction is made between "Finite Truth," that is, a view of reality which would completely satisfy intelligence as such, and "Absolute Truth," which is obtained only by *passing beyond intelligence* — only when intelligence as such is absorbed in some Absolute in which it loses its distinctive character.

It would advance the state of discussion, I am sure, if there were more explicit statements regarding the relations of "true idea," "truth," "the criterion of truth" and "reality" to one another. A more explicit exposition also of the view that is held concerning the relation of verification and truth could hardly fail to be of value. Not infrequently the intellectualist admits that the process of verification is experimental, consisting in setting on foot various activities that express the intent of the idea and confirm or refute it according to the changes effected. This seems to mean that truth is simply the tested or verified belief as such. But then a curious reservation is introduced; the experimental process *finds*, it is said, that an idea is true, while the error of the pragmatist is to take the process by which truth is *found* as one by which it is made. The claim of "making truth" is treated as blasphemy against the very notion of truth: such are the consequences of venturing to translate the Latin "verification" into the English "making true."

If we face the bogie thus called up, it will be found that the horror is largely sentimental. Suppose we stick to the notion that truth is a character which belongs to a meaning so far as tested through action that carries it to successful completion. In this case, to make an idea true is to modify and transform it until it reaches this successful outcome: until it initiates a mode of response which in its issue realizes its claim to be the method of harmonizing the discrepancies of a given situation. The meaning is remade by constantly acting upon it, and by introducing into its content such characters as are indicated by any resulting failures to secure harmony. From this point of view, verification and truth are two names for the same thing. We call it "verification" when we regard it as process; when the development of the idea is strung out and exposed to view in all that makes it true. We call it "truth" when we take it as product, as process telescoped and condensed.

Suppose the idea to be an invention, say of the telephone. In this case, is not the verification of the idea and the construction of the device which carries out its intent one and the same? In this case, does the truth of the idea mean anything else than that the issue proves the idea can be carried into effect? There are certain intellectualists who are not of the absolutist type; who do not believe that all of men's aims, designs, projects, that have to do with action, whether industrial, social or moral in scope, have been from all eternity registered as already accomplished in reality. How do such persons dispose of this problem of the truth of practical ideas?

Is not the truth of *such* ideas an affair of *making* them true by constructing, through appropriate behavior, a condition that satisfies the requirements of the case? If, in this case, truth means the effective capacity of the idea "to make good," what is there in the logic of the case to forbid the application of analogous considerations to any idea?

I hear a noise in the street. It suggests as its meaning a street-car. To test this idea I go to the window and through listening and looking intently—the listening and the looking being modes of behavior—organize into a single situation elements of existence and meaning which were previously disconnected. In this way an idea is made true; that which was a proposal or hypothesis is no longer merely a propounding or a guess. If I had not reacted in a way appropriate to the idea it would have remained a mere idea; at most a candidate for truth that, unless acted upon upon the spot, would always have remained a theory. Now in such a case—where the end to be accomplished is the discovery of a certain order of facts—would the intellectualist claim that apart from the forming and entertaining of some interpretation, the category of truth has either existence or meaning? Will he claim that without an original practical uneasiness introducing a practical aim of inquiry there must have been, whether or no, an idea? Must the world for some purely intellectual reason be intellectually reduplicated? Could not that occurrence which I now identify as a noisy street-car have retained, so far as pure intelligence is concerned, its unidentified status of being mere physical alteration in a vast unidentified complex of matter-in-motion? Was there any *intellectual* necessity that compelled the event to arouse just this judgment, that it meant a street-car? Was there any physical or metaphysical necessity? Was there any necessity save a need of characterizing it for some purpose of our own? And why should we be mealy-mouthed about calling this need practical? If the necessity which led to the formation and development of an intellectual judgment was purely objective (whether physical or metaphysical) why should not the thing have also to be characterized in countless millions of other ways; for example, as to its distance from some crater in the moon, or its effect upon the circulation of my blood, or upon my irascible neighbor's temper, or bearing upon the Monroe Doctrine? In short, do not intellectual positions and statements mean new and significant events in the treatment of things?

It is perhaps dangerous to attempt to follow the inner workings of the processes by which truth is first identified with some superior type of Reality, and then this Truth is taken as the criterion of the truth of ideas; while all the time it is held that truth is something already possessed by ideas as purely intellectual. But there seems to be some ground for believing that this identification is due to a twofold confusion, one having to do with ideas, and the other with things. As to the first point: After an idea is made true, we naturally say, in retrospect, "it *was* true all the time." Now this truism is quite innocuous as a truism, being just a restatement of the fact that the idea has, as matter of fact, worked successfully. But it may be regarded not as a truism but as furnishing some additional knowledge, as if it were, indeed, the dawning of a revelation regarding truth. Then it is said that the idea worked or was verified because it was already inherently, just as idea, the truth, the pragmatist, so it is said, making the error of supposing that it is true because it works. If one remembers that what the experimentalist means is that the effective working of an idea and its truth are one and the

same thing—this working being neither the cause nor the
evidence of truth but its nature—it is hard to see the point of
this statement. A man under peculiarly precarious circumstances has been rescued from drowning. A by-stander remarks that now he is a saved man. "Yes," replies someone,
"but he was a saved man all the time, and the process of
rescuing, while it gives evidence of that fact, does not constitute it." Now even such a statement, as pure tautology,
as characterizing the entire process in terms of its issue, is
objectionable only in the fact that, like all tautology, it seems
to say something but does not. But if it be regarded as revealing the earlier condition of affairs, apart from the active
process by which it was carried to a happy conclusion, such
a statement would be monstrously false; and would declare
its falsity in the fact that, if acted upon, the man would have
been left to drown. In like fashion, to say, *after the event*,
that a given idea was true all the time, is to lose sight of what
makes an idea an idea, its hypothetical character; and
thereby deliberately to transform it into brute dogma—something to which no canon of verification can ever be applied.
The intellectualist almost always treats the pragmatic account as if it were, from the standpoint of the pragmatist as
well as from his own, a denial of the existence of truth, while
it is nothing but a statement of its nature. When the intellectualist realizes this, he will, I hope, ask himself: What
then on the pragmatic basis is meant by the proposition that
an idea is true all the time? If the statement that an idea was
true all the time has no meaning except that the idea was
one which as matter of fact succeeded through action in
achieving its intent, mere reiteration that the idea was true
all the time or it could not have succeeded, does not take
us far.[6]

6. Such a statement as, for example, Mr. Bradley's (*Mind*, Vol.
XIII, No. 51, n.s., p. 311, article on "Truth and Practice") "The
idea works . . . but is able to work because I have chosen the
right idea" surely loses any argumentative force it may seem
to have, when it is recalled that, upon the theory argued against,
ability to work and rightness are one and the same thing. If the
wording is changed to read "The idea is able to work because I
have chosen an idea which is able to work" the question-begging
character of the implied criticism is evident. The change of
phraseology also may suggest the crucial and pregnant question:
How does anyone know that an idea is able to work excepting
by setting it at work?

On the side of things, *reality* is identified with truth; then on the principle that two things that are equal to the same thing are equal to each other, truth as idea and truth as reality are taken to be one and the same thing. Wherever there is an improved or tested idea, an idea which has made good, there is a concrete existence in the way of a completed or harmonized situation. The same activity which proves the idea constructs an inherently satisfied situation out of an inherently dissentient one,—for it is precisely the capacity of the idea as an aim and method of action to determine such transformation that is the criterion of its truth. Now unless all the elements in the situation are held steadily in view, the specific way in which the harmonized reality affords the criterion of truth (namely, through its function of being the last term of a process of active determination) is lost from sight; and the achieved existence in its merely existent character, apart from its practical or fulfilment character, is treated as The Truth. But when the reality is thus separated from the process by which it is achieved, when it is taken just as given, it is neither truth nor a criterion of truth. It is a state of facts like any other. The achieved telephone is a criterion of the validity of a certain prior idea in so far as it is the fulfilment of activities that embody the nature of that idea, but just as telephone, as a machine actually in existence, it is no more truth nor criterion of truth than is a crack in the wall or a cobble-stone on the street.

The intervening term that mediates and completes the confusion of truth with ideas on one hand and "reality" on the other, is, I think, the fact that ideas after they have been tested in action are employed in the development and grounding of further beliefs. There are cases in which an idea ceases to exist as idea as soon as it is made true; this is so as matter of fact and it is impossible to conceive any reason why it should not be so in point of theory. Such is the case, I take it, with a large part—possibly the major portion—of the ideas that mediate the smaller and transient crises of daily practice. I cannot imagine the situation in which the truth to which I have referred above—the verification of a certain idea about a certain noise—would ever function again as truth—save as I have given it a function in this paper by using it as a corroboration of a certain theory. Such ideas mostly cease, giving way to a matter-of-fact status: say, the perception of the noisy street-car. One at the time may say "My idea regarding that noise was a true idea"; or one may not even go so far as that, he may just stop with the eventual perception. But the tested idea need not ever recur as a factor of proof in any other problem. Such, however, is conspicuously not the case with our scientific ideas. In its first value, the idea or hypothesis of gravitation entertained by Newton, stood, when verified, on exactly the same level as the hypothesis regarding the noise in the street. Theoretically, that truth might have been so isolated that its truth character would disappear from thought as soon as a certain factual condition was ascertained. But practically quite the opposite has happened. The idea operates in many other inquiries, and operates no longer as mere idea, but as *proved* idea. Such truths get an "eternal" status—one irrespective of application just now and here, because there are so many nows and heres in which they are useful. Just as to say an idea was true all the time is a way of saying *in retrospect* that it has come out in a certain fashion, so to say that an idea is "eternally true" is to indicate *prospective* modes of application which are indefinitely anticipated. Its meaning, therefore, is strictly pragmatic. It does not indicate a property inherent in the idea as intellectualized existence, but denotes a property of use and employment. Always at hand when needed is a good enough eternal for reasonably minded persons.

IV

I have gone from the very general considerations which occupied us in the earlier portions of this article to matters which relatively at least are specific. I conclude with a summary in the hope that it may bind together the earlier and the later parts of this paper.

1. The condition which antecedes and provokes any particular exercise of reflective knowing is always one of discrepancy, struggle, "collision." This condition is practical, for it involves the habits and interests of the organism, an

agent. This does not mean that the struggle is merely personal, or subjective, or psychological. The agent or individual
is one factor in the situation—not the situation something
subsisting in the individual. The individual has to be identified in the situation, before any situation can be referred—
as in psychology—to the individual. But the discrepancy calls
out and controls reflective knowing only as the fortunes of
an agent are implicated in the crisis. Certain elements stand
out as obstacles, as interferences, as deficiencies—in short as
unsatisfactory and as requiring something for their completion. Other elements stand out as wanted—as required, as a
satisfaction which does not exist. This clash (an accompaniment of all desire) between the given and the wanted, between the present and the absent, is at once the root and the
type of that peculiar paradoxical relation between existence
and meaning which Bradley insists upon as the essence of
judgment. It is not irrational in the sense that we are dealing
with appearance wholesale, but it is non-rational—an evidence that we are dealing with a practical affair.

2. The intellectual or reflective and logical is a *statement* of this conflict: an attempt to describe and define it.
It is, as it were, the practical clash held off at arm's length
for inspection and investigation. In this way brute blind reaction against the unsatisfactoriness of the situation is suspended. Action is turned into the channel of observing, of
inferring, of reasoning, or defining means and end. It is this
change in the quality of activity, from directly overt, to indirect, or inquiring with view to stating, that constitutes the
specific nature of reflective practice to which Mr. Bradley
calls attention. The discovery of the nature of the conflict
supplies materials for the fact or existence side of the judgment. The conception or projection of the object in which the
conflict would be terminated furnishes material for the meaning side of the judgment. It is ideal because anticipatory, just
as the fact side is existential, because reminiscent or record-
ing. Hence the two are necessarily both distinguished from
and yet referred to each other: only through location of a
problem can a solution be conceived; only in reference to the
intent of finding a solution can the elements of a problem be
selected and interpreted. In origin and in destiny, this cor-

relative determination of existence and meaning is tentative and experimental. The aim of the subject of the judgment is not to include all possible reality, but to select those elements of a reality that are useful in locating the source and nature of the difficulty in hand. The aim of the predicate is not to bunch all possible meaning and refer it in one final act indiscriminately to all existence, but to state the standpoint and method through which the difficulty of the particular situation may most effectively be dealt with. The selection of what is relevant to the characterization of the problem and the projection of the method of dealing with it are theoretic, hypothetic, intellectual: —that is, they are tentative ways of viewing the matter for the sake of guiding, economizing and freeing the activities through which it may *really* be dealt with.

3. The criterion of the worth of the idea is thus the capacity of the idea (as a definition of the end or outcome in terms of what is likely to be serviceable as a method) to operate in fulfilling the object for the sake of which it was projected. Capacity of operation in this fashion is the test, measure, or criterion of truth. Hence the criterion is practical in the most overt sense of that term. We may, if we choose, regard the object in which the idea terminates through its use in guiding action, as the criterion; but if we so choose, it is at our peril that we forget that this object serves as criterion in its capacity of fulfilment and not as sheer objective existence.

4. Difficulties overlap; problems recur which resemble each other in the kind of treatment they demand for solution. Various modes of activity with their respective ends, going on at some time more or less independently, get organized into single comprehensive systems of behavior. The solution of one problem is found to create difficulties elsewhere; or the truth that is made in the solution of one problem is found to afford an effective method of dealing with questions arising apparently from unallied sources. Thus certain tested ideas in performing a constant or recurrent function secure a certain permanent status. The prospective use of such truths, the satisfaction that we anticipate in their employ, the assurance of control that we feel in their posses-

sion, becomes relatively much more important than the
circumstances under which they were first made true. In
becoming permanent resources, such tested ideas get a generalized energy of position. They are truths in general, truths
"in themselves" or in the abstract, truths to which positive
value is assigned on their own account. Such truths are the
"eternal truths" of current discussion. They naturally and
properly add to their intellectual and to their practical worth
a certain aesthetic quality. They are interesting to contemplate, and their contemplation arouses emotions of admiration and reverence. To make these emotions the basis of assigning peculiar inherent sanctity to them, apart from their
warrant in use, is simply to give way to that mood which in
primitive man is the cause of attributing magical efficacy to
physical things. Aesthetically such truths are more than instrumentalities. But to ignore both the instrumental and the
aesthetic aspect, and to ascribe values due to an instrumental
and aesthetic character to some interior and *a priori* constitution of truth is to make fetishes of them.

We may not exaggerate the permanence and stability of
such truths with respect to their recurring and prospective
use. It is only relatively that they are unchanging. When applied to new cases, used as resources for coping with new
difficulties, the oldest of truths are to some extent remade.
Indeed it is only through such application and such remak-
ing that truths retain their freshness and vitality. Otherwise
they are relegated to faint reminiscences of an antique tradition. Even the truth that two and two make four has gained
a new meaning, has had its truth in some degree remade, in
the development of the modern theory of number. If we put
ourselves in the attitude of a scientific inquirer in asking
what is the meaning of truth *per se*, there spring up before
us those ideas which are actively employed in the mastery of
new fields, in the organization of new materials. This is the
essential difference between truth and dogma; between the
living and the dead and decaying. Above all, it is in the region
of moral truth that this perception stands out. Moral truths
that are not recreated in application to the urgencies of the
passing hour, no matter how true in the place and time of
their origin, are pernicious and misleading, *i.e.*, false. And it

is perhaps through emphasizing this fact, embodied in one form or another in every system of morals and in every religion of moral import, that one most readily realizes the character of truth.

THE DILEMMA OF THE INTELLECTUALIST THEORY OF TRUTH

Is the intellectualist in his theory of truth an anarchistic subjectivist? Considerably to my own surprise, reflection has convinced me that he usually is. He insists that truth is a property of ideas (the term is used to include judgments, beliefs, all mental functions having cognitional value) *antecedent* to any process of verification; he insists that this antecedent self-possessed, self-contained property determines the working of an idea, or its verification. It follows that truths come into existence (arise or first subsist) when certain ideas are entertained. Until Columbus (or somebody else) entertained the idea that the world was round, the truth (being a self-contained property of the idea) that the world was round was non-existent. When the idea that the value of π is 3.1415926 arose in someone's mind, *this* truth was then and there created, and so on.[1] Such is the logical implication of this "antecedent property" theory. Note, further, the accidental and arbitrary way in which ideas arise, if truth is an independent property of them. They just happen. For the intellectualist can not deny that a large share of the ideas of men possess an antecedent property of falsity rather than of truth. If these properties of truth and falsity are ultimate, self-contained, and unique properties; if an idea is as likely to have one kind of property as the other; and if there is nothing in an idea which reveals upon bare inspection which of the two kinds of property is possessed, surely the intellectualist is committed to a belief in the thoroughly atomistic nature of truths.

A reply which the intellectualist might presumably make to these statements will be found only to enforce them. The

---

1. I do not raise the question whether truths cease to exist when their ideas vanish, though this would seem also to follow.

[First published in *Journal of Philosophy, Psychology and Scientific Methods* 6 (1909): 433–34.]

reply is that the intellectualist holds that the self-contained truth-property of ideas consists in their relation of agreement or correspondence to things. Precisely: he makes the relation of agreement with things which constitutes truth a self-contained property of ideas. It is this very fact which commits him to the baldest kind of psychical idea-ism—not to dignify it with the title of idealism. If there were anything in the so-called cognitive self-transcendency of ideas which concretely lighted upon their intended objects so that their truth or falsity was self-luminous, the appeal of the intellectualist to "agreement with reality" would have some bearing; but since such phosphorescence is notoriously lacking, this so-called "self-transcendency" is obviously, after all, only an internal property of an idea *qua* idea.

I shall, however, be properly reminded that not all intellectualists make truth a property of ideas. Some make it a property of things, events, objects. That Columbus discovered America, that water is H_2O, are truths independent of *any* ideas. Well then, is not *this* type of intellectualism committed to absolutistic rationalism? If things, events, are properly called truths, then the universe must be conceived as a truth-system, *i.e.*, a system of relations of reason, or as "objective thought." The frantic disclaimers of many contemporary anti-pragmatists of sympathy with the Hegelian theory of truth (or that of Bradley or Royce) seem rather amusing. What escape from sophistic subjectivism have they except this theory? The other day I ran across the following quotation from Bossuet in Janet's *Final Causes*: "If I now ask where and in what subject these truths subsist, eternal and immutable as they are, I am obliged to own a being wherein truth eternally subsists and is always understood; and this being must be the truth itself, and must be all truth; and from it is derived the truth in all that is."[2] Why not, if truths exist *per se* in the order of nature?

The non-pragmatist, if logical, thus appears as either a pure subjectivist or as an objective absolutist. Usually he is not logical, but oscillates at will between the two positions, using one at need to cover up the weakness of the other.

2. English translation, page 395.

THE CONTROL OF IDEAS BY FACTS

I

There is something a little baffling in much of the current discussion regarding the reference of ideas to facts. The not uncommon assumption is that there was a satisfactory and consistent theory of their relation in existence prior to the somewhat impertinent intrusion of a functional and practical interpretation of them. The way the instrumental logician has been turned upon by both idealist and realist is suggestive of the way in which the outsider who intervenes in a family jar is proverbially treated by both husband and wife, who manifest their unity by berating the third party.

I feel that the situation is due partly to various misapprehensions, inevitable perhaps in the first presentation of a new point of view[1] and multiplied in this instance by the coincidence of the presentation of this logical point of view with that of the larger philosophical movements, humanism and pragmatism. I wish here to undertake a summary statement of the logical view on its own account, hoping it may receive clearer understanding on its own merits.

In the first place it was (apart from the frightful confusion of logical theories) precisely the lack of an adequate and generally accepted theory of the nature of fact and idea, and of the kind of agreement or correspondence between them which constitutes the truth of the idea, that led to the development of a functional theory of logic. A brief statement of the difficulties in the traditional views may therefore be pertinent. That fruitful thinking—thought that terminates

1. *Studies in Logical Theory*, University of Chicago Press, 1903.

[First published in *Journal of Philosophy, Psychology and Scientific Methods* 4 (1907): 197–203, 253–59, 309–19. Revised and reprinted in *Essays in Experimental Logic* (Chicago: University of Chicago Press, 1916), pp. 230–49.]

in valid knowledge—goes on in terms of the distinction of facts and judgment, and that valid knowledge is precisely genuine correspondence or agreement, *of some sort*, of fact and judgment, is the common and undeniable assumption. But the discussions are largely carried on in terms of an epistemological dualism, rendering the solution of the problem impossible in virtue of the very terms in which it is stated. The distinction is at once identified with that between mind and matter, consciousness and objects, the psychical and the physical, where each of these terms is supposed to refer to some fixed order of existence, a world in itself. Then, of course, there comes up the question of the nature of the agreement, and of the recognition of it. What is the experience in which the survey of both idea and existence is made and their agreement recognized? Is it an idea? Is the agreement ultimately a matter of self-consistency of ideas? Then what has become of the postulate that truth is agreement of idea with existence beyond idea? Is it an absolute which transcends and absorbs the difference? Then, once more, what is the test of any specific judgment? What has become of the correspondence of fact and thought? Or, more urgently, since the pressing problem of life, of practice and of science is the discrimination of the *relative*, or *superior*, validity of this or that theory, plan or interpretation, what is the criterion of truth within present non-absolutistic experience, where the distinction between factual conditions and thoughts and the necessity of some working adjustment persist?

Putting the problem in yet another way, either both fact and idea are present all the time or else only one of them is present. But if the former, why should there be an idea at all and why should it have to be tested by the fact? When we already have what we want, namely, existence, reality, why should we take up the wholly supernumerary task of forming more or less imperfect ideas of those facts and then engage in the idle performance of testing them by what we already know to be? But if only ideas are present, it is idle to speak of comparing an idea with facts and testing its validity by its agreement. The elaboration and refinement of ideas to the uttermost still leaves us with an idea, and while a self-

consistent idea stands a show of being true in a way in which
an incoherent one does not, a self-consistent idea is still but
a hypothesis, a candidate for truth. Ideas are not made true
by getting bigger. But if only "facts" are present, the whole
conception of agreement is once more given up—not to mention that such a situation is one in which there is by definition no thinking or reflective factor at all.

This suggests that a strictly monistic epistemology,
whether idealistic or realistic, does not get rid of the problem.
Suppose, for example, we take a sensationalistic idealism. It
does away with the ontological gulf between ideas and facts,
and by reducing both terms to a common denominator seems
to facilitate fruitful discussion of the problem. But the problem of the distinction and reference (agreement, correspondence) of two types or sorts of sensations still persists. If I
say the box there is square, and call "box" one of a group of
ideas or sensations and "square" another sensation or "idea,"
the old question comes up: Is "square" already a part of the
"facts" of the box, or is it not? If it is, it is a supernumerary,
an idle thing, both as an idea and as an assertion of fact; if
it is not, how can we compare the two ideas, and what on
earth or in heaven does their agreement or correspondence
mean? If it means simply that we experience the two "sensations" in juxtaposition, then the same is true, of course, of
any casual association or hallucination. On the sensational
basis, accordingly, there is still a distinction of something
"given," "there," brutally factual, the box, and something
else which stands on a different level, ideal, absent, intended,
demanded, the "square," which is asserted to hold good or
be true of the thing "box." The fact that both are sensations
throws no light on the logical validity of any proposition or
belief, because by theory a like statement holds of every possible proposition.[2]

2. Mill's doctrine of the ambiguity of the copula (*Logic*, Bk. I, Ch.
4, Sec. 1) is an instance of one typical way of evading the problem. After insisting with proper force and clearness upon the
objective character of our intellectual beliefs and propositions,
viz., that when we say fire causes heat we mean actual phenomena, not our ideas of fire and heat (Bk. I, Ch. 2 and Ch. 11,
Sec. 1, and Ch. 5, Sec. 1), he thinks to dispose of the whole problem of the "is" in judgment by saying that it is only a sign of

The same problem recurs on a realistic basis. For example, there has recently been propounded[3] the doctrine of the distinction between relations of space and time and relations of meaning or significance, as a key to the problem of knowledge. Things exist in their own characters, in their temporal and spatial relations. When knowledge intervenes, there is nothing new of a subjective or psychical sort, but simply a new relation of the things—the suggesting or signifying of one thing by another. Now this seems to be an excellent way of stating the logical problem, but, I take it, it states and does not solve. For the characteristic of such situations, claiming to terminate in knowledge, is precisely that the meaning-relation is predicated *of* the other relations; it is referred to them; it is not simply a supervention existing side by side with them, like casual suggestions or the play of phantasy. It is something which the facts, the qualitative space and time things, must bear the burden of, must accept and take unto themselves as part of themselves. Until this happens, we have only "thinking," not accomplished knowledge. Hence, logically, the existential relations play the rôle of fact, and the relation of signification that of idea,[4] distinguished from fact and yet, if valid, to hold *of* fact.

This appears quite clearly in the following quotation: "It is the ice which means that it will cool the water, just as much as it is the ice which does cool the water when put into it." There is, however, a possible ambiguity in the statement, to which we shall return later. That the "ice" (the thing regarded as ice) *suggests* cooling is as real as is a case of actual cooling. But, of course, not every suggestion is valid. The "ice" may be a crystal, and it will not cool water at all. So far

affirmation (Ch. 1, Sec. 2, and Ch. 4, Sec. 1). Of course it is. But unless the affirmation (the sign of thought) "agrees" or "corresponds with" the relations of the phenomena, what becomes of the doctrine of the objective import of propositions? How otherwise shall we maintain with Mill (and with common sense and science) the difference between asserting "a fact of external nature" and "a fact in my mental history"?
3. *Studies in Philosophy and Psychology*, article by Woodbridge on "The Problem of Consciousness," especially pp. 159–60.
4. In other words, "ideas" is a term capable of assuming any definition which is logically appropriate—say, meaning. It need not have anything to do with the conception of little subjective entities or psychical stuffs.

as it is already certain that this *is* ice, and also certain that ice, under all circumstances, cools water, the meaning-relation stands on the same level as the physical, being not merely suggested, but part of the facts ascertained. It is not a meaning-relation as such at all. We already have truth; the entire work of knowing as logical is done; we have no longer the relation characteristic of reflective situations. Here again, the implication of the thinking situation is of some "correspondence" or "agreement" between two sets of distinguished relations; the problem of valid determination remains the central question of any theory of knowing in its relation to facts and truth.[5]

II

I hope this statement of the difficulty, however inadequate, will serve at least to indicate that a functional logic inherits the problem in question and does not create it; that it has never for a moment denied the *prima facie* working distinction between "ideas," "thoughts," "meanings" and "facts," "existences," "the environment," nor the necessity of a control of meaning by facts. It is concerned not with denying, but with understanding. What is denied is not the genuineness of the problem of the terms in which it is stated, but the reality and value of the orthodox interpretation. What is insisted upon is the relative, instrumental or working character of the distinction—that it *is* a *logical* distinction, instituted and maintained in the interests of intelligence with all that intelligence imports in the exercise of the life functions. To this positive side I now turn.

In the analysis it may prove convenient to take an illustration of a man lost in the woods, taking this case as typical of any reflective situation in so far as it involves perplexity—a problem to be solved. The problem is to find a correct idea of the way home—a practical idea or plan of action which will lead to success, or the realization of the pur-

5. Of course, the monistic epistemologies have an advantage in the statement of the problem over the dualistic—they do not state it in terms which presuppose the impossibility of the solution.

pose to get home. Now the critics of the experimental theory of logic make the point that this practical idea, the truth of which is evidenced in the successful meeting of a need, is dependent for its success upon a purely presentative idea, that of the existent environment, whose validity has nothing to do with success but depends on agreement with the given state of affairs. It is said that what makes a man's idea of his environment true is its agreement with the actual environment, and "generally a true idea in any situation consists in its agreement with reality." I have already indicated my acceptance of this formula. But it was long my misfortune not to be possessed offhand of those perfectly clear notions of just what is meant in this formula by the terms "idea," "existence" and "agreement" which are possessed by other writers on epistemology; and when I analyzed these notions I found the distinction between the practical idea and the theoretical not fixed nor final, and I found a somewhat startling similarity between the notions of "success" and "agreement."

Just what is the environment of which an idea is to be formed: *i.e.*, what is the intellectual content or objective detail to be assigned to the term "environment"? It can hardly mean the actual visible environment—the trees, rocks, etc., which a man is actually looking at. These things are there and it seems superfluous to form an idea of them; moreover, the wayfaring man, though lost, would have to be an unusually perverse fool if under such circumstances he were unable to form an idea (supposing he chose to engage in this luxury) in agreement with these facts. The environment must be a larger environment than the visible facts; it must include things not within the direct ken of the lost man; it must, for instance, extend from where he is now to his home, or to the point from which he started. It must include unperceived elements in their contrast with the perceived. Otherwise the man would not be lost. Now we are at once struck with the facts that the lost man has no alternative except either to wander aimlessly or else to *conceive* this inclusive environment, and that this conception is just what is meant by idea. It is not some little psychical entity or piece of consciousness-stuff, but is *the interpretation of the locally pres-*

ent environment in reference to its absent portion, that part
to which it is referred as another part so as to give a view of
a whole. Just how such an idea would differ from one's plan
of action in finding one's way, I do not know. For one's plan
(if it be really a plan, a method) is a conception of what is
given in its hypothetical relations to what is not given, employed as a guide to that act which results in the absent being also given. It is a map constructed with one's self lost
and one's self found, whether at starting or at home again,
as its two limits. If this map in its specific character is not
also the only guide to the way home, one's only plan of action, then I hope I may never be lost. It is the *practical* facts
of being lost and desiring to be found which constitute the
limits and the content of the "environment."

Then comes the test of *agreement* of the idea and the
environment. Supposing the individual stands still and attempts to compare his idea with the reality, with what reality is he to compare it? Not with the presented reality, for
that reality is the reality of himself lost; not with the complete reality, for at this stage of proceedings he has only the
idea to stand for the complete theory. What kind of comparison is possible or desirable then, save to treat the mental
layout of the whole situation as a working hypothesis, as a
plan of action, and proceed to *act* upon it, to use it as a director and controller of one's divagations instead of stumbling
blindly around until one is either exhausted or accidentally
gets out? Now suppose one uses the idea—that is to say, the
present facts projected into a whole in the light of absent
facts—as a guide of action. Suppose, by means of its specifications, one works one's way along until one comes upon
familiar ground—finds one's self. *Now*, one may say, my idea
was right, it was in accord with facts; it agrees with reality.
That is, acted upon sincerely, it has led to the desired conclusion; it has, *through action*, worked out the state of things
which it contemplated or intended. The agreement, correspondence, is between purpose, plan, and its own execution,
fulfillment; between a map of a course constructed for the
sake of guiding behavior and the result attained in acting
upon the indications of the map. Just how does such agreement differ from success?

III

If we exclude acting upon the idea, no conceivable amount or kind of intellectualistic procedure can confirm or refute an idea, or throw any light upon its validity. How does the non-pragmatic view consider that verification takes place? Does it suppose that we first look a long while at the facts and then a long time at the idea until by some magical process the degree and kind of their agreement become visible? Unless there is some such conception as this, what conception of agreement is possible except the experimental or practical one? And if it be admitted that verification involves action, how can that action be relevant to the truth of an idea, unless the idea is itself already relevant to action? If by acting in accordance with the experimental definition of facts, *viz.*, as obstacles and conditions, and the experimental definition of the end or intent, *viz.*, as plan and method of action, a harmonized situation effectually presents itself, we have the adequate and the only conceivable verification of the intellectual factors. If the action indicated be carried out and the disordered or disturbed situation persists, then we have not merely confuted the tentative positions of intelligence, but we have in the very process of acting introduced new data and eliminated some of the old ones, and thus afforded an opportunity for the resurvey of the facts and the revision of the plan of action. By acting faithfully upon an inadequate reflective presentation, we have at least secured the elements for its improvement. This, of course, gives no absolute guarantee that the reflection will at any time be so performed as to prove its validity in fact. But the self-rectification of intellectual content through acting upon it in good faith is the "absolute" of knowledge, loyalty to which is the religion of intellect.

The intellectual definition or delimitation assigned to the "given" is thus as tentative and experimental as that ascribed to the idea. In form both are categorical, and in content both are hypothetical. Facts really exist just as facts, and meanings exist as meanings. One is no more superfluous, more subjective, or less necessitated than the other. In and of themselves as existences both are equally realistic and compulsive. But on the basis of existence, there is no element in either which may be strictly described as intellectual or cognitional. There is only a practical situation in its brute and unrationalized form. What is uncertain about the facts as given at any moment is whether the right exclusions and selections have been made. Since that is a question which can be decided finally only by the experimental issue, this ascription of character is itself tentative and experimental. If it works, the characterization and delineation are found to be proper ones; but every admission prior to inquiry, of unquestioned, categorical, rigid objectivity, compromises the probability that it will work. The character assigned to the datum must be taken as hypothetically as possible in order to preserve the elasticity needed for easy and prompt reconsideration. Any other procedure virtually insists that all facts and details anywhere happening to exist and happening to present themselves (all being equally real) must all be given equal status and equal weight, and that their outer ramifications and internal complexities must be indefinitely followed up. The worthlessness of this sheer accumulation of realities, its total irrelevancy, the lack of any way of judging the significance of the accumulations, are good proofs of the fallacy of any theory which ascribes objective logical content to facts wholly apart from the needs and possibilities of a situation.

The more stubbornly one maintains the *full* reality of either his facts or his ideas, just as they stand, the more accidental is the discovery of relevantly significant facts and of valid ideas—the more accidental, the less rational, is the issue of the knowledge situation. Due progress is reasonably probable in just the degree in which the meaning, categorical in its existing imperativeness, and the fact, equally categorical in its brute coerciveness, are assigned only a provisional and tentative nature with reference to control of the situation. That this surrender of a rigid and final character for the content of knowledge on the sides both of fact and of meaning, in favor of experimental and functioning estimations, is precisely the change which has marked the development of modern from medieval and Greek science, seems undoubted. To learn the lesson one has only to contrast the rigidity of phenomena and conceptions in Greek

thought (Platonic ideas, Aristotelian forms) with the modern experimental selection and determining of facts and experimental employment of hypotheses. The former have
ceased to be ultimate realities of a nondescript sort and have
become provisional data; the latter have ceased to be eternal
meanings and have become working theories. The fruitful
application of mathematics and the evolution of a technique
of experimental inquiry have coincided with this change.
That realities exist independently of their use as intellectual
data, and that meanings exist apart from their utilization as
hypotheses, are the permanent truths of Greek realism as
against the exaggerated subjectivism of modern philosophy;
but the conception that this existence is to be defined in the
same way as are contents of knowledge, so that perfect being
is object of perfect knowledge and imperfect being object of
imperfect knowledge, is the fallacy which Greek thought projected into modern. Science has advanced in its methods in
just the degree in which it has ceased to assume that prior
realities and prior meanings retain fixedly and finally, when
entering into reflective situations, the characters they had
prior to this entrance, and in which it has realized that their
very presence within the knowledge situation signifies that
they have to be redefined and revalued from the standpoint
of the new situation.

IV

This conception does not, however, commit us to the
view that there is any conscious situation which is totally
non-reflective. It may be true that any experience which can
properly be termed such comprises something which is *meant*
over and against what is given or there. But there are many
situations into which the rational factor—the mutual distinction and mutual reference of fact and meaning—enters
only incidentally and is slurred, not accentuated. Many disturbances are relatively trivial and induce only a slight and
superficial redefinition of contents. This passing tension of
facts against meaning may suffice to call up and carry a
wide range of meaningful facts which are quite irrelevant to

the intellectual problem. Such is the case where the individual is finding his way through any field which is upon the whole familiar, and which, accordingly, requires only an occasional resurvey and revaluation at moments of slight perplexity. We may call these situations, if we will, knowledge situations (for the reflective function characteristic of knowledge is present), but so denominating them does not do away with their sharp difference from those situations in which the critical qualification of facts and definition of meanings constitute the main business. To speak of the passing attention which a traveler has occasionally to give to the indications of his proper path in a fairly familiar and beaten highway as knowledge, in just the same sense in which the deliberate inquiry of a mathematician or a chemist or a logician is knowledge, is as confusing to the real issue involved as would be the denial to it of *any* reflective factor. If, then, one bears in mind these two considerations—(1) the unique problem and purpose of every reflective situation, and (2) the difference as to range and thoroughness of logical function in different types of reflective situations—one need have no difficulty with the doctrine that the great obstacle in the development of scientific knowing is that facts and meanings enter such situations with stubborn and alien characteristics imported from other situations.

This affords an opportunity to speak again of the logical problem to which reference and promise of return were made earlier in this paper. Facts may be regarded as existing qualitatively and in certain spatial and temporal relations; when there is knowledge another relation is added, that of one thing meaning or signifying another. Water exists, for example, as water, in a certain place, in a certain temporal sequence. But it may signify the quenching of thirst; and this signification-relation constitutes knowledge.[6] This state-

6. This view was originally advanced in the discussion of quite another problem than the one here discussed, *viz.*, the problem of consciousness; and it may not be quite just to dissever it from that context. But as a formula for knowledge it has enough similarity with the one brought out in this paper to suggest further treatment; it is not intended that the results reached here shall apply to the problem of consciousness as such.

ment may be taken in a way congruous with the account developed in this paper. But it may also be taken in another sense, consideration of which will serve to enforce the point regarding the tentative nature of the characterization of the given, as distinct from the intended and absent. Water means quenching thirst; it is drunk, and death follows. It was not water, but a poison which "looked like" water. Or it is drunk and is water, but does not quench thirst, for the drinker is in an abnormal condition and drinking water only intensifies the thirst. Or it is drunk and quenches thirst; but it also brings on typhoid fever, being not merely water, but water plus germs. Now all these events demonstrate that error may appertain quite as much to the characterization of existing things, suggesting or suggested, as to the suggestion qua suggestion. There is no ground for giving the "things" any superior reality. In these cases, indeed, it may fairly be said that the mistake is made because qualitative thing and suggested or meaning-relation were *not* discriminated. The "signifying" force was regarded as a part of the direct quality of the given fact, quite as much as its color, liquidity, etc.; it is only in another situation that it is discriminated as a relation instead of being regarded as an element.

It is quite as true to say that a thing is called water because it suggests thirst-quenching as to say that it suggests thirst-quenching because it is characterized as water. *The knowledge function becomes prominent or dominant in the degree in which there is a conscious discrimination between the fact-relations and the meaning-relations.* And this inevitably means that the "water" ceases to be *surely* water, just as it becomes doubtful or hypothetical whether this thing, whatever it is, really means thirst-quenching. If it really means thirst-quenching, it is water; so far as it may not mean it, it perhaps is not water. It is now just as much a question *what* this *is* as what it means. Whatever will resolve one question will resolve the other. In just the degree, then, in which an existence or thing gets intellectualized force or function, it becomes a fragmentary and dubious thing, to be circumscribed and described for the sake of operating as *sign* or clue of a *future* reality to be realized through action. Only as "reality" is reduced to a sign, and questions of its nature as sign are considered, does it get intellectual or cognitional status. The bearing of this upon the question of practical character of the distinctions of fact and idea is obvious. No one, I take it, would deny that action of some sort *does* follow upon judgment; no one would deny that this action *does* somehow serve to test the value of the intellectual operations upon which it follows. But if this subsequent action is *merely* subsequent, if the intellectual categories, operations and distinctions are complete in themselves, without inherent reference to it, what guarantee is there that they pass into relevant action, and by what miracle does the action manage to test the worth of the idea? But if the intellectual identification and description of the thing are as tentative and instrumental as is the ascription of significance, then the exigencies of the active situation are operative in all the categories of the knowledge situation. Action is not a more or less accidental appendage or after-thought, but is undergoing development and giving direction in the entire knowledge function.

In conclusion, I remark that the ease with which the practical character of these fundamental logical categories, fact, meaning and agreement, may be overlooked or denied is due to the organic way in which practical import is incarnate in them. It can be overlooked because it is so involved in the terms themselves that it is assumed at every turn. The pragmatist is in the position of one who is charged with denying the existence of something because, in pointing out a certain fundamental feature of it, he puts it in a strange light. Such confusion always occurs when the familiar is brought to definition. The difficulties are more psychological—difficulties of orientation and mental adjustment—than logical, and in the long run will be done away with by our getting used to the different viewpoint, rather than by argument.

THE LOGICAL CHARACTER OF IDEAS

Said John Stuart Mill: "To draw inferences has been said to be the great business of life. . . . It is the only occupation in which the mind never ceases to be engaged." If this be so, it seems a pity that Mill did not recognize that this business identifies what we mean when we say "mind." If he had recognized this, he would have cast the weight of his immense influence not only against the conception that mind is a substance, but also against the conception that it is a collection of existential states or attributes without any substance in which to inhere; and he would thereby have done much to free logic from epistemological metaphysics. In any case, an account of intellectual operations and conditions from the standpoint of the role played and position occupied by them in the business of drawing inferences is a different sort of thing from an account of them as having an existence *per se*, from treating them as making up some sort of existential material distinct from the *things* which figure in inference-drawing. This latter type of treatment is that which underlies the psychology which itself has adopted uncritically the remnants of the metaphysics of soul substance: the idea of accidents without the substance.[1] This assumption from metaphysical psychology—the assumption of consciousness as an existent stuff or existent process—is then carried over into an examination of knowledge, so as

1. This conception of "consciousness" as a sort of reduplicate world of things comes to us, I think, chiefly from Hume's conception that the "*mind* is nothing but a heap, a collection of different perceptions, united together by certain relations."—*Treatise of Human Nature*, Bk. I, Part Four, Sec. 2. For the evolution of this sort of notion out of the immaterial substance notion, see Bush, "A Factor in the Genesis of Idealism," in the James *Festschrift*.

[First published in *Journal of Philosophy, Psychology and Scientific Methods* 5 (1908): 375–81. Revised and reprinted in *Essays in Experimental Logic* (Chicago: University of Chicago Press, 1916), pp. 220–29.]

to make the theory of knowledge not logic (an account of the ways in which valid inferences or conclusions from things to other things are made), but epistemology.

We have, therefore, the result (so unfortunate for logic) that logic is not free to go its own way, but is compromised by the assumption that knowledge goes on not in terms of things (I use "things" in the broadest sense, as equaling *res*, and covering affairs, concerns, acts, as well as "things" in the narrower sense), but in terms of a relation *between* things and a peculiar existence made up of consciousness, or else between things and functional operations of this existence. If it could be shown that psychology is essentially not a science of states of consciousness, but of behavior, conceived as a process of continuous readjustment, then the undoubted facts which go by the name of sensation, perception, image, emotion, concept, would be interpreted to mean peculiar (*i.e.*, specifically qualitative) epochs, phases, and crises in the scheme of behavior. The supposedly scientific basis for the belief that states of consciousness inherently define a separate type of existence would be done away with. Inferential knowledge, knowledge involving reflection, *psychologically* viewed, would be assimilated to a certain mode of readaptation of functions, involving shock and the need of control; "knowledge" in the sense of direct non-reflective presence of things would be identified (psychologically) with relatively stable or completed adjustments. I can not profess to speak for psychologists, but it is an obvious characteristic of the contemporary status of psychology that one school (the so-called functional or dynamic) operates with nothing more than a conventional and perfunctory reference to "states of consciousness"; while the orthodox school makes constant concessions to ideas of the behavior type. It introduces the conceptions of fatigue, practice, and habituation. It makes its fundamental classifications on the basis of physiological distinctions (*e.g.*, the centrally initiated and the peripherally initiated), which, from a biological standpoint, are certainly distinctions of structures involved in the performance of acts.

One of the aims of the *Studies in Logical Theory* was to show, on the negative or critical side, that the type of

logical theory which professedly starts its account of knowledge from mere states of consciousness is compelled at every
crucial juncture to assume *things*, and to define its so-called
mental states in terms of things;[2] and on the positive side, to
show that, logically considered, such distinctions as sensation, image, etc., mark instruments and crises in the development of controlled judgment, *i.e.*, of inferential conclusions. It was perhaps not surprising that this effort should
have been criticized, not on its own merits, but on the assumption that this correspondence of the (functional) psychological and the logical points of view was intended in
terms of the psychology which obtained in the *critic's* mind—
to wit, the psychology based on the assumption of consciousness as a separate existence or process.

These considerations suggest that before we can intelligently raise the question of the truth of ideas, we must consider their status in judgment, judgment being regarded as
the typical expression of the inferential operation. (1) Do
ideas present themselves except in situations which are
doubtful and inquired into? Do they exist side by side with
the facts when the facts are themselves known? Do they
exist except when judgment is in suspense? (2) Are "ideas"
anything else except the suggestions, conjectures, hypotheses,
theories (I use an ascending scale of terms) tentatively entertained during a suspended conclusion? (3) Do they have
any part to play in the conduct of inquiry? Do they serve to
direct observation, colligate data, and guide experimentation,
or are they otiose?[3] (4) If the ideas have a function in directing the reflective process (expressed in judgment), does
success in performing the function (that is, in directing to
a conclusion which is stable) have anything to do with the

2. See, for example, p. 31 [*Middle Works of John Dewey* 2:322].
"Thus that which is 'nothing but a state of our consciousness'
turns out straightway to be a specifically determined objective
fact in a system of facts," and, p. 58, [*Middle Works of John
Dewey* 2:344] "actual sensation is determined as an event in a
world of events."
3. When it is said that an idea is a "plan of action," it must be
remembered that the term "plan of action" is a formal term. It
throws no light upon *what* the action is with respect to which
an idea is the plan. It may be chopping down a tree, finding a
trail, or conducting a scientific research in mathematics, history
or chemistry.

logical worth or validity of the ideas? (5) And finally, does validity have anything to do with truth? Does "truth" mean something inherently different from the fact that the conclusion of one judgment (the known fact, previously unknown, in which judging terminates) is itself applicable in further situations of doubt and inquiry? And is judgment properly more than tentative save as it terminates in a known fact, *i.e.*, a fact present without the intermediary of reflection?

When these questions—I mean, of course, questions which are exemplified in these queries—are answered, we shall, perhaps, have gone as far as it is possible to go with reference to the *logical* character of ideas. The question may then recur as to whether the "ideas" of the epistemologist (that is, existences in a purely "private stream of consciousness") remain as something over and above, not yet accounted for; or whether they are perversions and misrepresentations of logical characters. I propose to give a brief dogmatic reply in the latter sense. Where, and in so far as, there are unquestioned objects, there is no "consciousness." There are just things. When there is uncertainty, there are dubious, suspected objects—things hinted at, guessed at. Such objects have a distinct status, and it is the part of good sense to give them, as occupying that status, a distinct caption. "Consciousness" is a term often used for this purpose; and I see no objection to that term, *provided* it is recognized to mean such objects as are problematic, plus the fact that in their problematic character they may be used, as effectively as accredited objects, to direct observations and experiments which finally relieve the doubtful features of the situation. Such "objects" may turn out to be valid, or they may not. But, in any case, they may be used. They may be internally manipulated and developed through ratiocination into explicit statement of their implications; they may be employed as standpoints for selecting and arranging data, and as methods for conducting experiments. In short, they are not merely hypothetical; they are *working* hypotheses. Meanwhile their aloofness from accredited objectivity may lead us to characterize them as merely ideas, or even as "mental states," provided once more we mean by mental state just this logical status.

We have examples of such ideas in symbols. A symbol, I take it, is always itself, existentially, a particular object. A word, an algebraic sign, is just as much a concrete existence as is a horse, a fire-engine or a fly-speck. But its value resides in its representative character: in its suggestive and directive force for operations that when performed lead us to non-symbolic objects, which without symbolic operations would not be apprehended, or at least would not be so easily apprehended. It is, I think, worth noting that the capacity (*a*) for regarding objects as mere symbols and (*b*) for employing symbols instrumentally furnishes the only safeguard against dogmatism, *i.e.*, uncritical acceptance of any suggestion that comes to us vividly; and also that it furnishes the only basis for intelligently controlled experiments.

I do not think, however, that we should have the tendency to regard ideas as *private*, as personal, if we stopped short at this point. If we had only words or other symbols uttered by others, or written or printed, we might call them, when in objective suspense, mere ideas. But we should hardly think of these ideas as our own. Such extra-organic stimuli, however, are not adequate logical devices. They are too rigid, too "objective" in their own existential status. Their meaning and character are too definitely fixed. For effective discovery we need things which are more easily manipulated, which are more transitive, more easily dropped and changed. Intra-organic events, adjustments *within* the organism, that is, adjustments of the organism considered not with reference to the environment but with reference to one another, are much better suited to stand as representatives of genuinely dubious objects. An object which is *really* doubted is by its nature precarious and inchoate, vague. What *is* a thing when it is not yet discovered and yet is tentatively entertained and tested?

Ancient logic never got beyond the conception of an object whose logical *place*, whose subsumptive position as a particular with reference to some universal, was doubtful. It never got to the point where it could search for particulars which in themselves as particulars are doubtful. Hence it was a logic of proof, of deduction, not of inquiry, of discovery, and of induction. It was hard up against its own dilemma: How can a man inquire? For either he knows that

for which he seeks, and hence does not seek: or he does not
know, in which case he can not seek nor could he tell if he
found. The individualistic movement of modern life detached, as it were, the individual, and allowed personal (*i.e.*,
intra-organic) events to have, transitively and temporarily,
a worth of their own. These events are continuous with extra-
organic events (in origin and eventual outcome); but they
may be considered in temporary displacement as uniquely
existential. In this capacity they serve as means for the
elaboration of a delayed but more adequate response in a
radically different direction. So treated, they are tentative,
dubious but experimental, anticipations of an object. They
are "subjective" (*i.e.*, individualistic) surrogates of public,
cosmic things, which may be so manipulated and elaborated
as to terminate in public things which without them would
not exist as empirical objects.[4]

The recognition then of intra-organic events, which are
not merely effects or distorted refractions of cosmic objects,
but inchoate *future* cosmic objects in process of experimental
construction, resolves, to my mind, the paradox of so-called
subjective and private things that have objective and universal reference, and that operate so as to lead to objective
consequences which test their own value. When a man can
say: This color is not necessarily the color of the glass nor
the picture nor even of an object reflected, but is at least an
event in my nervous system, an event which I may refer to
my organism till I get *surety of other reference*—he is for
the first time emancipated from the dogmatism of unquestioned reference, and is set upon a path of experimental inquiry.

I am not here concerned with trying to demonstrate
that this is the correct mode of interpretation. I am only
concerned with pointing out its radical difference from the
view of a critic who, holding to the two-world theory of existences which from the start are divided into the fixedly objective and the fixedly psychical, interprets in terms of his
own theory the view that the distinction between the objec-

4. I owe this idea, both in its historical and in its logical aspects,
to my former colleague, Professor Mead, of the University of
Chicago.

tive and the subjective is a logical-practical distinction. Whether the logical, as against the ontological, theory be true or false, it can hardly be fruitfully discussed without a preliminary apprehension of it as a logical conception.

WHAT PRAGMATISM MEANS BY PRACTICAL

Pragmatism, according to Mr. James, is a temper of mind, an attitude; it is also a theory of the nature of ideas and truth; and, finally, it is a theory about reality. It is pragmatism as method which is emphasized, I take it, in the subtitle, "a new name for some old ways of thinking."[1] It is this aspect which I suppose to be uppermost in Mr. James's own mind; one frequently gets the impression that he conceives the discussion of the other two points to be illustrative material, more or less hypothetical, of the method. The briefest and at the same time the most comprehensive formula for the method is: "The attitude of looking away from first things, principles, 'categories,' supposed necessities; and of looking towards last things, fruits, consequences, facts" (pp. 54–55). And as the attitude looked "away from" is the rationalistic, perhaps the chief aim of the lectures is to exemplify some typical differences resulting from taking one outlook or the other.

But pragmatism is "used in a still wider sense, as meaning also a certain theory of truth" (p. 55); it is "a genetic theory of what is meant by truth" (pp. 65–66). Truth means, as a matter of course, agreement, correspondence, of idea and fact (p. 198), but what do agreement, correspondence, mean? With rationalism they mean "a static, inert relation," which is so ultimate that of it nothing more can be said. With pragmatism they signify the guiding or leading power

---

1. William James, *Pragmatism. A New Name for Some Old Ways of Thinking*. Popular Lectures on Philosophy. New York: Longmans, Green, & Co., 1907. Pp. xiii+309.

[First published in *Journal of Philosophy, Psychology and Scientific Methods* 5 (1908): 85–99, with the title "What Does Pragmatism Mean by Practical?" Revised and reprinted in *Essays in Experimental Logic* (Chicago: University of Chicago Press, 1916), pp. 303–29, with the title "What Pragmatism Means by Practical."]

of ideas by which we "dip into the particulars of experience again," and if by its aid we set up the arrangements and connections among experienced objects which the idea intends, the idea is verified; it corresponds with the things it means to square with (pp. 205–6). The idea is true which works in leading us to what it purports (p. 80).[2] Or, "any idea that will carry us prosperously from any one part of experience to any other part, linking things satisfactorily, working securely, simplifying, saving labor, is true for just so much, true in so far forth" (p. 58). This notion presupposes that ideas are essentially intentions (plans and methods), and that what they, as ideas, ultimately intend is *prospective*—certain changes in prior existing things. This contrasts again with rationalism, with its copy theory, where ideas, *as* ideas, are ineffective and impotent since they mean only to mirror a reality (p. 69) complete without them. Thus we are led to the third aspect of pragmatism. The alternative between rationalism and pragmatism "concerns the structure of the universe itself" (p. 258). "The essential contrast is that reality . . . for pragmatism is still in the making" (p. 257). And in a recent number of the *Journal of Philosophy, Psychology and Scientific Methods*,[3] he says: "I was primarily concerned in my lectures with contrasting the belief that the world is still in the process of making with the belief that there is an eternal edition of it ready-made and complete."

I

It will be following Mr. James's example, I think, if we here regard pragmatism as primarily a method, and treat the account of ideas and their truth and of reality somewhat incidentally so far as the discussion of them serves to exemplify or enforce the method. Regarding the attitude of orientation which looks to outcomes and consequences, one readily sees that it has, as Mr. James points out, points of

2. Certain aspects of the doctrine are here purposely omitted, and will meet us later.
3. Vol. IV, p. 547.

contact with historic empiricism, nominalism, and utilitarianism. It insists that general notions shall "cash in" as particular objects and qualities in experience; that "principles" are ultimately subsumed under facts, rather than the reverse; that the empirical consequence rather than the *a priori* basis is the sanctioning and warranting factor. But all of these ideas are colored and transformed by the dominant influence of experimental science: the method of treating conceptions, theories, etc., as working hypotheses, as directors for certain experiments and experimental observations. Pragmatism as attitude represents what Mr. Peirce has happily termed the "laboratory habit of mind" extended into every area where inquiry may fruitfully be carried on. A scientist would, I think, wonder not so much at the method as at the lateness of philosophy's conversion to what has made science what it is. Nevertheless it is impossible to forecast the intellectual change that would proceed from carrying the method sincerely and unreservedly into all fields of inquiry. Leaving philosophy out of account, what a change would be wrought in the historical and social sciences—in the conceptions of politics and law and political economy! Mr. James does not claim too much when he says: "The centre of gravity of philosophy must alter its place. The earth of things, long thrown into shadow by the glories of the upper ether, must resume its rights. . . . It will be an alteration in the 'seat of authority' that reminds one almost of the protestant reformation" (pp. 122–23).

I can imagine that many would not accept this method in philosophy for very diverse reasons, perhaps among the most potent of which is lack of faith in the power of the elements and processes of experience and life to guarantee their own security and prosperity; because, that is, of the feeling that the world of experience is so unstable, mistaken, and fragmentary that it must have an absolutely permanent, true, and complete ground. I can not imagine, however, that so much uncertainty and controversy as actually exists should arise about the content and import of the doctrine on the basis of the general formula. It is when the method is applied to special points that questions arise. Mr. James reminds us in his preface that the pragmatic movement has found expression "from so many points of view, that much unconcerted statement has resulted." And speaking of his lectures, he goes on to say: "I have sought to unify the picture as it presents itself to my own eyes, dealing in broad strokes." The "different points of view" here spoken of have concerned themselves with viewing pragmatically a number of different things. And it is, I think, Mr. James's effort to combine them, as they stand, which occasions misunderstanding among Mr. James's readers. Mr. James himself applied it, for example, in 1898 to philosophic controversies to indicate what they mean in terms of practical issues at stake. Before that, Mr. Peirce himself (in 1878) had applied the method to the proper way of *conceiving* and defining objects. Then it has been applied to *ideas* in order to find out what they mean in terms of what they intend, and what and how they must intend in order to be true. Again, it has been applied to *beliefs*, to what men actually accept, hold to, and affirm. Indeed, it lies in the nature of pragmatism that it should be applied as widely as possible; and to things as diverse as controversies, beliefs, truths, ideas, and objects. But yet the situations and problems *are* diverse; so much so that, while the meaning of each may be told on the basis of "last things," "fruits," "consequences," "facts," *it is quite certain that the specific last things and facts will be very different in the diverse cases, and that very different types of meaning will stand out.* "Meaning" will itself *mean* something quite different in the case of "objects" from what it will mean in the case of "ideas," and for "ideas" something different from "truths." Now the explanation to which I have been led of the unsatisfactory condition of contemporary pragmatic discussion is that in composing these "different points of view" into a single pictorial whole, the distinct type of consequence and hence of meaning of "practical" appropriate to each has not been sufficiently emphasized.

1. When we consider separately the subjects to which the pragmatic method has been applied, we find that Mr. James has provided the necessary formula for each—with his never-failing instinct for the concrete. We take first the question of the significance of an object: the meaning which should properly be contained in its conception or definition.

"To attain perfect clearness in our thoughts of an object, then, we need only consider what conceivable effects of a practical kind the object may involve—what sensations we are to expect from it and what reactions we must prepare" (pp. 46–47). Or, more shortly, as it is quoted from Ostwald, "All realities influence our practice, and that influence is their meaning for us" (p. 48). Here it will be noted that the start is from objects already empirically given or presented, existentially vouched for, and the question is as to their proper conception—What is the proper meaning, or idea, of an object? And the meaning is the effects *these given objects produce*. One might doubt the correctness of this theory, but I do not see how one could doubt its import, or could accuse it of subjectivism or idealism, since the object with its power to produce effects is assumed. Meaning is expressly distinguished from objects, not confused with them (as in idealism), and is said to consist in the practical reactions objects exact of us or impose upon us. When, then, it is a question of an object, "meaning" signifies its *conceptual content or connotation, and "practical" means the future responses which an object requires of us or commits us to.*

2. But we may also start from a given idea, and ask what the *idea* means. Pragmatism will, of course, look to future consequences, but they will clearly be of a different sort when we start from an idea as idea, than when we start from an object. For what an idea as idea means, is precisely that an object is *not* given. The pragmatic procedure here is to set the idea "at work within the stream of experience. It appears less as a solution than as a program for more work, and particularly as an indication of the ways in which existing realities may be changed. Theories, thus, become instruments. . . . We don't lie back on them, we move forward, and, on occasion, make nature over again by their aid" (p. 53). In other words, an idea is a draft drawn upon existing things, an intention to act so as to arrange them in a certain way. From which it follows that if the draft is honored, if existences, following upon the actions, rearrange or readjust themselves in the way the idea intends, the idea is true. When, then, it is a question of an idea, it is the idea itself which is practical (being an intent) and its *meaning*

resides in the existences which, as changed, it intends. While the meaning of an object is the changes it requires in our attitude,[4] the meaning of an idea is the changes it, as our attitude, effects in objects.

3. Then we have another formula, applicable not to objects or ideas as objects and ideas, but to *truths* — to things, that is, where the meaning of the object and of the idea is assumed to be already ascertained. It reads: "What difference would it practically make to anyone if this notion rather than that notion were true? If no practical difference whatever can be traced, then the alternatives mean practically the same thing, and all dispute is idle" (p. 45). There can be "no difference in abstract truth that does n't express itself in a difference in concrete fact, and in conduct consequent upon that fact, imposed on somebody" (p. 50).[5] Now when we start with something which is already a truth (or taken to be truth), and ask for its meaning in terms of its consequences, it is implied that the conception, or conceptual significance, is already clear, and that the existences it refers to are already in hand. Meaning here, then, can be neither the connotative nor denotative reference of a term; they are covered by the two prior formulae. Meaning here means *value*, importance. The practical factor is, then, the worth character of these consequences: they are good or bad; desirable or undesirable; or merely *nil*, indifferent, in which latter case belief is idle, the controversy a vain and conventional, or verbal, one.

The term "meaning" and the term "practical" taken in isolation, and without explicit definition from their specific context and problem, are triply ambiguous. The meaning may be the conception or definition of an *object*; it may be the denotative existential reference of an *idea*; it may be actual value or *importance*. So practical in the corresponding cases may mean the attitudes and conduct exacted of us by

4. Only those who are already lost in the idealistic confusion of existence and meaning will take this to mean that the object *is* those changes in our reactions.

5. I assume that the reader is sufficiently familiar with Mr. James's book not to be misled by the text into thinking that Mr. James himself discriminates as I have done these three types of problems from one another. He does not; but, none the less, the three formulae for the three situations are there.

objects; or the capacity and tendency of an idea to effect changes in prior existences; or the desirable and undesirable quality of certain ends. The general pragmatic attitude, none the less, is applied in all cases.

If the differing problems and the correlative diverse significations of the terms "meaning" and "practical" are borne in mind, not all will be converted to pragmatism, but the present uncertainty as to what pragmatism is, anyway, and the present constant complaints on both sides of misunderstanding will, I think, be minimized. At all events, I have reached the conclusion that what the pragmatic movement just now wants is a clear and consistent bearing in mind of these different problems and of what is meant by practical in each. Accordingly the rest of this paper is an endeavor to elucidate from the standpoint of pragmatic method the importance of enforcing these distinctions.

II

First, as to the problems of philosophy when pragmatically approached, Mr. James says: "The whole function of philosophy ought to be to find out what definite difference it will make to you and me, at definite instants of our life, if this world-formula or that world-formula be true" (p. 50). Here the world-formula is assumed as already given; it is there, defined and constituted, and the question is as to its import if believed. But from the second standpoint, that of idea as working hypothesis, the chief function of philosophy is not to find out what difference ready-made formulae make, *if true*, but to arrive at and to clarify their *meaning as programs of behavior for modifying the existent world*. From this standpoint, the meaning of a world-formula is practical and moral, not merely in the consequences which flow from accepting a certain conceptual content as true, but as regards that content itself. And thus at the very outset we are compelled to face this question: Does Mr. James employ the pragmatic method to discover the value in terms of consequences in life of some formula which has its logical content already fixed; or does he employ it to criticize and re-

vise and, ultimately, to constitute the meaning of that formula? If it is the first, there is danger that the pragmatic
method will be employed only to vivify, if not validate, doctrines which in themselves are pieces of rationalistic metaphysics, not inherently pragmatic. If the last, there is danger
that some readers will think old notions are being confirmed
when in truth they are being translated into new and inconsistent notions.

Consider the case of design. Mr. James begins with accepting a ready-made notion, to which he then applies the
pragmatic criterion. The traditional notion is that of a "seeing force that runs things." This is rationalistically and retro-
spectively empty: its being there makes no difference. (This
seems to overlook the fact that the past world may be just
what it is in virtue of the difference which a blind force or
a seeing force has already made in it. A pragmatist as well
as a rationalist may reply that it makes no difference retro-
spectively only because we leave out the most important
retrospective difference.) But "returning with it into experience, we gain a more confiding outlook on the future. If not
a blind force, but a seeing force, runs things, we may reasonably expect better issues. *This vague confidence in the
future is the sole pragmatic meaning at present discernible
in the terms design and designer*" (p. 115, italics mine).
Now is this meaning intended to *replace* the meaning of a
"seeing force which runs things"? Or is it intended to superadd a pragmatic value and validation to that concept of a
seeing force? Or, does it mean that, irrespective of the existence of any such object, a belief in it has that value? Strict
pragmatism would seem to require the first interpretation.

The same difficulties arise in the discussion of spiritual-
istic theism *versus* materialism. Compare the two following
statements: "The notion of God . . . guarantees an ideal order that shall be permanently preserved" (p. 106). "Here,
then, in these different emotional and practical appeals, in
these adjustments of our attitudes of hope and expectation,
and all the delicate consequences which their differences en-
tail, *lie the real meanings of materialism and spiritualism*"
(p. 107, italics mine). Does the latter method of determining the meaning of, say, a spiritual God afford the substitute

for the conception of him as a "superhuman power" effecting the eternal preservation of something; does it, that is, define God, supply the content for our notion of God? Or, does it merely superadd a value to a meaning already fixed? And, if the latter, does the object, God as defined, or the notion, or the belief (the acceptance of the notion) effect these consequent values? In either of the latter alternatives, the good or valuable consequences can not clarify the meaning or conception of God; for, by the argument, they proceed from a prior definition of God. They can not prove, or render more probable, the existence of such a being, for, by the argument, these desirable consequences depend upon accepting such an existence; and not even pragmatism can prove an existence from desirable consequences which themselves exist only when and if that other existence is there. On the other hand, if the pragmatic method is not applied simply to tell the value of a belief or controversy, but to fix the meaning of the terms involved in the belief, resulting consequences would serve to constitute the entire meaning, intellectual as well as practical, of the terms; and hence the pragmatic method would simply abolish the meaning of an antecedent power which will perpetuate eternally some existence. For that consequence flows not from the belief or idea, but from the existence, the power. It is not pragmatic at all.

Accordingly, when Mr. James says: "Other than this *practical* significance, the words God, free will, design, *have none*. Yet dark though they be in themselves, or intellectualistically taken, when we bear them on to life's thicket with us, the darkness then grows light about us" (p. 121, italics mine), what is meant? Is it meant that when we take the intellectualistic notion and employ it, it gets value in the way of results, and hence then has some value of its own; or is it meant that the intellectual content itself must be determined in terms of the changes effected in the ordering of life's thicket? An explicit declaration on this point would settle, I think, not merely a point interesting in itself, but one essential to the determination of what is pragmatic method. For myself, I have no hesitation in saying that it seems unpragmatic for pragmatism to content itself with finding out the value of a conception whose own inherent significance pragmatism has not first determined; a fact which entails that it be taken not as a truth but simply as a working hypothesis. In the particular case in question, moreover, it is difficult to see how the pragmatic method could possibly be applied to a notion of "eternal perpetuation," which, by its nature, can never be empirically verified, or cashed in any particular case.

This brings us to the question of truth. The problem here is also ambiguous in advance of definition. Does the problem of what is truth refer to discovering the "true meaning" of something; or to discovering what an idea has to effect, and how, in order to be true; or to discovering what the value of truth is when it is an existent and accomplished fact? (1) We may, of course, find the "true meaning" of a thing, as distinct from its incorrect interpretation, without thereby establishing the truth of the "true meaning"—as we may dispute about the "true meaning" of a passage in the classics concerning Centaurs, without the determination of its true sense establishing the truth of the notion that there are Centaurs. Occasionally this "true meaning" seems to be what Mr. James has in mind, as when, after the passage upon design already quoted, he goes on: "But if cosmic confidence is right, not wrong, better, not worse, that [vague confidence in the future] is a most important meaning. That much at least of possible 'truth' the terms will then have in them" (p. 115). "Truth" here seems to mean that design has a genuine, not merely conventional or verbal, meaning: that something is at stake. And there are frequently points where "truth" seems to mean just meaning that is genuine as distinct from empty or verbal. (2) But the problem of the meaning of truth may also refer to the meaning or value of truths that already exist as truths. We have them; they exist: now what do they mean? The answer is: "True ideas lead us into useful verbal and conceptual quarters as well as directly up to useful sensible termini. They lead to consistency, stability, and flowing human intercourse" (p. 215). This, referring to things already true, I do not suppose the most case-hardened rationalist would question; and even if he questions the pragmatic contention that these consequences define the meaning of truth, he should see that here is not given an account of what it means for an idea to *become true*, but only of what it means *after* it has become true, truth as *fait accompli*. It is the meaning of truth as *fait accompli* which is here defined.

Bearing this in mind, I do not know why a mild tempered rationalist should object to the doctrine that truth is valuable not *per se*, but because, when given, it leads to desirable consequences. "The true thought is useful here because the home which is its object is useful. The practical value of true ideas is thus primarily derived from the practical importance of their objects to us" (p. 203). And many besides confirmed pragmatists, any utilitarian, for example, would be willing to say that our duty to pursue "truth" is conditioned upon its leading to objects which upon the whole are valuable. "The concrete benefits we gain are what we mean by calling the pursuit a duty" (p. 231, compare p. 76). (3) Difficulties have arisen chiefly because Mr. James is charged with converting simply the foregoing proposition, and arguing that since true ideas are good, any idea if good in any way is true. Certainly transition from one of these conceptions to the other is facilitated by the fact that ideas are tested as to their validity by a certain goodness, viz., whether they are good for accomplishing what they intend, for what they claim to be good for, that is, certain modifications in prior given existences. In this case, it is the idea which is practical, since it is essentially an intent and plan of altering prior existences in a specific situation, which is indicated to be unsatisfactory by the very fact that it needs or suggests a specific modification. Then arises the theory that ideas as ideas are always working hypotheses concerning the attaining of particular empirical results, and are tentative programs (or sketches of method) for attaining them. If we stick consistently to this notion of ideas, only *consequences which are actually produced by the working of the idea in cooperation with, or application to, prior existences are good consequences in the specific sense of good which is relevant to establishing the truth of an idea*. This is, at times, unequivocally recognized by Mr. James. (See, for example, the reference to veri-*fication*, on p. 201; the acceptance of the idea that verification means the advent of the object intended, on p. 205.)

But at other times any good which flows from acceptance of a belief is treated as if it were an evidence, *in so far*, of the truth of the idea. This holds particularly when theological notions are under consideration. Light would be thrown upon how Mr. James conceives this matter by statements on such points as these: If ideas terminate in good consequences, but yet the goodness of the consequences was no part of the intention of an idea, does the goodness have any verifying force? If the goodness of consequences arises from the context of the idea in belief rather than from the idea itself, does it have any verifying force?[6] If an idea leads to consequences which are good in the *one* respect only of fulfilling the intent of the idea (as when one drinks a liquid to test the idea that it is a poison), does the badness of the consequences in every other respect detract from the verifying force of consequences?

Since Mr. James has referred to me as saying "truth is what gives satisfaction" (p. 234), I may remark (apart from the fact that I do not think I ever said that truth is what *gives* satisfaction) that I have never identified any satisfaction with the truth of an idea, save *that* satisfaction which arises when the idea as working hypothesis or tentative method is applied to prior existences in such a way as to fulfill what it intends.

My final impression (which I can not adequately prove) is that upon the whole Mr. James is most concerned to enforce, as against rationalism, two conclusions about the character of truths as *faits accomplis*: namely, that they are made, not *a priori*, or eternally in existence,[7] and that their value or importance is not static, but dynamic and practical.

6. The idea of immortality or the traditional theistic idea of God, for example, may produce its good consequences, not in virtue of the idea as idea, but from the character of the person who entertains the belief; or it may be the idea of the supreme value of ideal considerations, rather than that of their temporal duration, which works.

7. "Eternal truth" is one of the most ambiguous phrases that philosophers trip over. It may mean eternally in existence; or that a statement which is ever true is always true (if it is true a fly is buzzing, it is eternally true that just now a fly buzzed); or it may mean that some truths, *in so far as wholly conceptual*, are irrelevant to any particular time determination, since they are non-existential in import—*e.g.*, the truth of geometry dialectically taken—that is, without asking whether any particular existence exemplifies them.

The special question of *how* truths are made is not particularly relevant to this anti-rationalistic crusade, while it is the chief question of interest to many. Because of this conflict of problems, what Mr. James says about the value of truth when accomplished is likely to be interpreted by some as a criterion of the truth of ideas; while, on the other hand, Mr. James himself is likely to pass lightly from the consequences that determine the worth of a belief to those which decide the worth of an idea. When Mr. James says the function of giving "satisfaction in marrying previous parts of experience with newer parts" is necessary in order to establish truth, the doctrine is unambiguous. The satisfactory character of consequences is itself measured and defined by the conditions which led up to it; the inherently satisfactory quality of results is not taken as validating the antecedent intellectual operations. But when he says (not of his own position, but of an opponent's[8]) of the idea of an absolute, "so far as it affords such comfort it surely is not sterile, it has that amount of value; it performs a concrete function. As a good pragmatist I myself ought to call the Absolute true *in so far forth* then; and I unhesitatingly now do so" (p. 73), the doctrine seems to be as unambiguous in the other direction: that any good, consequent upon acceptance of a belief, is, in so far forth,[9] a warrant of truth. In such passages as

8. Such statements, it ought in fairness to be said, generally come when Mr. James is speaking of a doctrine which he does not himself believe, and arise, I think, in that fairness and frankness of Mr. James, so unusual in philosophers, which cause him to lean over backward—unpragmatically, it seems to me. As to the claim of his own doctrine, he consistently sticks to his statement: "Pent in, as the pragmatist, more than any one, sees himself to be, between the whole body of funded truths squeezed from the past and the coercions of the world of sense about him, who, so well as he, feels the immense pressure of objective control under which our minds perform their operations? If any one imagines that this law is lax, let him keep its commandments one day, says Emerson" (p. 233).
9. Of course, Mr. James holds that this "in so far" goes a very small way. See pp. 77–79. But even the slightest concession is, I think, non-pragmatic unless the satisfaction is relevant to the idea as intent. Now the satisfaction in question comes not from the idea as *idea*, but from its acceptance as *true*. Can a satisfaction dependent on an assumption that an idea is already true be relevant to testing the truth of an idea? And can an idea, like that of the absolute, which, if true, "absolutely" precludes any appeal to consequences as test of truth, be confirmed by use of

the following (which are of the common type) the two notions seem blended together: "Ideas become true just in so
far as they help us to get into satisfactory relations with
other parts of our experience" (p. 58); and, again, on the
same page: "Any idea that will carry us *prosperously* from
any one part of our experience to any other part, linking
things *satisfactorily*, working securely, simplifying, saving
labor, is true for just so much" (italics mine). An explicit
statement as to whether the carrying function, the linking
of things, is satisfactory and prosperous and hence true in
so far as it executes the intent of an idea; or whether the
satisfaction and prosperity reside in the material consequences on their own account and in that aspect make the
idea true, would, I am sure, locate the point at issue and
economize and fructify future discussion. At present pragmatism is accepted by those whose own notions are thoroughly rationalistic in make-up as a means of refurbishing,
galvanizing, and justifying those very notions. It is rejected
by non-rationalists (empiricists and naturalistic idealists)
because it seems to them identified with the notion that
pragmatism holds that the desirability of certain beliefs
overrides the question of the meaning of the ideas involved
in them and the existence of objects denoted by them. Others
(like myself), who believe thoroughly in pragmatism as a
method of orientation as defined by Mr. James, and who
would apply the method to the determination of the meaning of objects, the intent and worth of ideas as ideas, and
to the human and moral value of beliefs, when these various
problems are carefully distinguished from one another, do
not know whether they are pragmatists in some other sense,
because they are not sure whether the practical, in the sense
of desirable facts which define the worth of a belief, is confused with the practical as an attitude imposed by objects,
and with the practical as a power and function of ideas to
effect changes in prior existences. Hence the importance of

---

the pragmatic test without sheer self-contradiction? In other
words, we have a confusion of the test of an idea as idea, with
that of the value of a belief as belief. On the other hand, it is
quite possible that all Mr. James intends by truth here is true
(*i.e.*, genuine) meaning at stake in the issue—true not as distinct
from false, but from meaningless or verbal.

knowing which one of the three senses of practical is conveyed in any given passage.

It would do Mr. James an injustice, however, to stop
here. His real doctrine is that a belief is true when it satisfies both personal needs and the requirements of objective
things. Speaking of pragmatism, he says, "Her only test of
probable truth is what works best in the way of *leading us*,
what fits every part of life best and *combines with the collec-
tivity of experience's demands*, nothing being omitted" (p.
80, italics mine). And again, "That new idea is truest which
performs most felicitously its function of satisfying *our double urgency*" (pp. 63–64). It does not appear certain from
the context that this "double urgency" is that of the personal
and the objective demands, respectively, but it is probable
(see, also, p. 217, where "consistency with previous truth
and novel fact" is said to be "always the most imperious
claimant"). On this basis, the "in so far forth" of the truth
of the absolute because of the comfort it supplies, means
that one of the two conditions which need to be satisfied has
been met, so that if the idea of the absolute met the other
one also, it would be quite true. I have no doubt this is Mr.
James's meaning, and it sufficiently safeguards him from
the charge that pragmatism means that anything which is
agreeable is true. At the same time, I do not think, in logical
strictness, that satisfying one of two tests, when satisfaction of both is required, can be said to constitute a belief true
even "in so far forth."

III

At all events this raises a question not touched so far:
the place of the personal in the determination of truth. Mr.
James, for example, emphasizes the doctrine suggested in
the following words: "We say this theory solves it [the prob-
lem] more satisfactorily than that theory; but that means
more satisfactorily *to ourselves*, and individuals will emphasize their points of satisfaction differently" (p. 61, italics
mine). This opens out into a question which, in its larger
aspects—the place of the personal factor in the constitution

of knowledge systems and of reality—I can not here enter upon, save to say that a synthetic pragmatism such as Mr. James has ventured upon will take a very different form according as the point of view of what he calls the "Chicago School" or that of humanism is taken as a basis for interpreting the nature of the personal. According to the latter view, the personal appears to be ultimate and unanalyzable, the metaphysically real. Associations with idealism, moreover, give it an idealistic turn, a translation, in effect, of monistic intellectualistic idealism into pluralistic, voluntaristic idealism. But, according to the former, the personal is not ultimate, but is to be analyzed and defined biologically on its genetic side, ethically on its prospective and functioning side.

There is, however, one phase of the teaching illustrated by the quotation which is directly relevant here. Because Mr. James recognizes that the personal element enters into judgments passed upon whether a problem has or has not been satisfactorily solved, he is charged with extreme subjectivism, with encouraging the element of personal preference to run rough-shod over all objective controls. Now the question raised in the quotation is primarily one of fact, not of doctrine. Is or is not a personal factor found in truth evaluations? If it is, pragmatism is not responsible for introducing it. If it is not, it ought to be possible to refute pragmatism by appeal to empirical fact, rather than by reviling it for subjectivism. Now it is an old story that philosophers, in common with theologians and social theorists, are as sure that personal habits and interests shape their opponents' doctrines as they are that their own beliefs are "absolutely" universal and objective in quality. Hence arises that dishonesty, that insincerity characteristic of philosophic discussion. As Mr. James says (p. 8), "The potentest of all our premises is never mentioned." Now the moment the complicity of the personal factor in our philosophic valuations is recognized, is recognized fully, frankly and generally, that moment a new era in philosophy will begin. We shall have to discover the personal factors that now influence us unconsciously, and begin to accept a new and moral responsibility for them, a responsibility for judging and testing them by their consequences. So long as we ignore this factor, its deeds will be largely evil, not because *it* is evil, but because, flourishing in the dark, it is without responsibility and without check. The only way to control it is by recognizing it. And while I would not prophesy of pragmatism's future, I would say that this element which is now so generally condemned as intellectual dishonesty (perhaps because of an uneasy, instinctive recognition of the searching of hearts its acceptance would involve) will in the future be accounted unto philosophy for righteousness' sake.

So much in general. In particular cases, it is possible that Mr. James's language occasionally leaves the impression that the fact of the inevitable involution of the personal factor in every belief gives some special sanction to some special belief. Mr. James says that his essay on the *right* to believe was unluckily entitled the *"Will* to Believe" (p. 258). Well, even the term "right" is unfortunate, if the personal or belief factor is inevitable—unfortunate because it seems to indicate a privilege which might be exercised in special cases, in religion, for example, though not in science; or, because it suggests to some minds that the fact of the personal complicity involved in belief is a warrant for this or that special personal attitude, instead of being a warning to locate and define it so as to accept responsibility for it. If we mean by "will" not something deliberate and consciously intentional (much less, something insincere), but an active personal participation, then belief *as* will rather than either the right or the will to believe seems to phrase the matter correctly.

I have attempted to review not so much Mr. James's book as the present status of the pragmatic movement which is expressed in the book; and I have selected only those points which seem to bear directly upon matters of contemporary controversy. Even as an account of this limited field, the foregoing pages do an injustice to Mr. James, save as it is recognized that his lectures were "popular lectures," as the title-page advises us. We can not expect in such lectures the kind of explicitness which would satisfy the professional and technical interests that have inspired this review. Moreover, it is inevitable that the attempt to compose different points of view, hitherto uncoordinated, into a single whole should give rise to problems foreign to any one factor of the synthesis, left to itself. The need and possibility of the discrimination of various elements in the pragmatic meaning of "practical," attempted in this review, would hardly have been recognized by me were it not for by-products of perplexity and confusion which Mr. James's combination has effected. Mr. James has given so many evidences of the sincerity of his intellectual aims, that I trust to his pardon for the injustice which the character of my review may have done *him*, in view of whatever service it may render in clarifying the problem to which he is devoted.

As for the book itself, it is in any case beyond a critic's praise or blame. It is more likely to take place as a philosophical classic than any other writing of our day. A critic who should attempt to appraise it would probably give one more illustration of the sterility of criticism compared with the productiveness of creative genius. Even those who dislike pragmatism can hardly fail to find much of profit in the exhibition of Mr. James's instinct for concrete facts, the breadth of his sympathies, and his illuminating insights. Unreserved frankness, lucid imagination, varied contacts with life digested into summary and trenchant conclusions, keen perceptions of human nature in the concrete, a constant sense of the subordination of philosophy to life, capacity to put things into an English which projects ideas as if bodily into space till they are solid things to walk around and survey from different sides—these things are not so common in philosophy that they may not smell sweet even by the name of pragmatism.

DISCUSSION ON REALISM AND IDEALISM

Josiah Royce. (No abstract has been furnished.)

John Dewey.

The conclusion of the paper was that realism and idealism arise from differences in logical attitude and mode of attack, realism standing for the function and rôle of observation, description, definition and classification, while idealism sets store by the function of reflection, interpretation, reorganization of facts through the projection of ideas and hypotheses. Since, however, these functions are mutually cooperative and limiting in the pursuit of knowledge, the real problem of the realistic-idealistic controversy turns out to be why and how each of these *motifs* is isolated from the other, and thereby exaggerated into the basis of an independently complete system.

The answer is to be sought in historic considerations. The background of ancient thought was custom and habit; a world of fixed characters, the world of natural and social acknowledgments, or observations, corresponds to custom and habit. Thus the logic of observation was entangled with a cosmology which was both false and irrelevant, and the result of classic thought was an ontology which even when idealistic *as a theory of existence* (as in the case of Plato and Aristotle) was realistic as a theory of knowledge.

Under the conditions of the origin of modern thought, the emphasis fell upon progress, and hence upon protest and rebellion against acceptance of the given and customary order, whether that of the senses or of institutions. The individual was magnified, and in the individual the power of

[First published in *Philosophical Review* 18 (1909): 182–83.]

projecting ideas, of discovery, of inferring the new and the different. The logical stress was thus transferred to "ideas" and interpretation at the expense of "data" and observation, which were transformed from finalities into fragmentary raw material for thought. Individual consciousness thus took the place of the perceptible cosmos as the clue to the metaphysical characterization of Reality, and epistemological idealism was born.

Present indications are towards giving up the attempt at wholesale characterizations of "Reality" as such. In this case, the cooperation and mutual limitations of observation and interpretation, of custom and progress, in the pursuit of knowledge will be recognized, and the absolutistic opposition of realism and idealism will become an historic episode.

[Discussion on the "Concept of a Sensation"]

A discussion on the "Concept of a Sensation" was opened by Professor John Dewey, who distinguished the following meanings of the term:

1. The anatomical—for so it must be called—according to which the sense organ and its central connections are thought of as if dissected out, isolated from the rest of the system, and acting alone. The isolation is unreal; the activity of any part is interlinked with simultaneous activities in other parts, and preceding and following activities in the same and other parts. There is never a state of rest, which might serve to isolate the subsequent activity, but everything is really a process of readjustment throughout the system.

2. The physiological or biological conception of a sensori-motor reaction, as frequently stated, is subject to the same criticism: the reaction is not isolated, nor is the stimulus exclusively peripheral, for the existing condition of the central organs is part cause of the reaction, and this reaction helps determine the stimulus finally operative.

3. A sensation is often conceived in psychology as a "sensory quality," and these qualities are assumed to be primitive and to correspond with elementary processes in the sense organs. This is a good deal of an assumption, since the qualities are known to us only as the apex of a whole system of physiological functioning. We see the color of an object rather than the color itself; we do not start with the sensory qualities and build up the object by putting them together, but we begin with the object, and only reach the sensory quality by an elaborate process of differentiation. The sensory quality is a late achievement, not a primary datum. The "elements" of structural psychology are the last terms of intellectual discrimination.

[First published in *Journal of Philosophy, Psychology and Scientific Methods* 6 (1909): 211–12.]

4. The sensory qualities—as equivalent to Locke's simple ideas—are thought of as the units of knowledge, as the irreducible minimum which can not be torn off by any amount of criticism of the percept. Locke, however, does not mean, nor would it be true, that all apparent knowledge is made up of single ideas. He was interested not in tracing the genetic psychology of knowledge, but in providing a logical device for testing knowledge and for appealing against prejudice, dogma, and authority. His sensations were not elements of composition, but ultimate, and hence elementary, criteria and tests of assurance.

5. The every-day use of the term sensation is illustrated by the phrase "sensational newspaper." Here the sensation is not an element, but a total concrete experience, the essential fact about which is that it is a shock, an interruption of an adjustment which had been running smoothly. While the "sensory qualities" are thoroughly objective, these shock experiences have the true subjective quality, since they have, for the instant, no meaning or objective reference. Their character as sensations is exhausted by this absence of reference; there is but one true sensory quality—the quality of shock. From the point of view of logic, the shock experience is valuable, since a state of suspended reference is the basis of the inductive method. Dogmatism, on the contrary, consists in the prompt interpretation of every new shock into terms of some well-established habit. In its true sense, the mental state, or the subjective, is the conscious starting-point of a qualitatively new habit.

PURE EXPERIENCE AND REALITY:
A DISCLAIMER

It is hard to judge how far it is advisable to enter into controversial discussion in reply to criticism. Observation of its usual course tends to the conclusion that the time devoted to it might ordinarily better be spent upon independent analysis or construction. And if one's original writings, put forth without controversial entanglements, are so awkwardly phrased as to provoke serious misunderstanding, why give the philosophic brethren additional cause for offense? But "Silence gives assent," and may propagate misunderstanding in minds hitherto innocent. Moreover, Professor McGilvary's misconception of my position, as he sets it forth in the May number of the *Philosophical Review*, under the caption of "Pure Experience and Reality" (Vol. XVI, pp. 266–84), is so extreme that, to some extent, it may be categorically dealt with.

1. He refers to me as among those who hold that the "reality of anything is the reality it has as experienced and *only when experienced*" (p. 266, italics mine); and again "No *contemporaneous* experience, *no* reality" (p. 274). I do not hold, never have held, and, to the best of my knowledge and belief, have never intimated nor implied any such views. That experience means experienced things; that all philosophic conclusions are to be drawn from the things as experienced (not from the concept of experience, which I have held to be purely empty excepting as indicating a *method* of procedure and recourse); that things are what they are experienced *as*, or experienced *to be*, I have asserted. The "only when" in the quotation has no standing in anything I have written. And books, chairs, geological ages, etc., are experienced, so far as I am aware, *as* existent at other times than the moments *when* they are experienced. Does not Pro-

[First published in *Philosophical Review* 16 (1907): 419–22. For McGilvary's article, see this volume, pp. 295–313.]

fessor McGilvary *experience* them *as* that sort of thing, *to be* that sort of thing?

2. The question raised in the paper upon which Professor McGilvary bases his criticism is (granting the existence of things prior to experiencing organisms), "What is the better index, for philosophy, of reality: its earlier or its later form?" (These words are in the original text and are quoted by Professor McGilvary himself.) That is to say, shall philosophy build its interpretation of reality upon reality as existent prior to its experience, or upon the reality of *that as now experienced?* The answer given is in the latter sense that the earlier (say Eozoic geological age) is experienced as the condition of a present experience which expresses reality more adequately (for philosophy, not for science) than the conception of it as merely pre-existent. This may be a false conception, but it is a totally different idea from that to which Professor McGilvary devotes much poetry, eloquence, and humor. How could it be a *condition* of the present experience unless it existed prior in time? But Professor McGilvary is so well aware that the prior existence of one thing to another thing in time leaves entirely untouched the question of the nature of the reality of time, and hence of the reality, for philosophy, of the temporal sequence, that I do not understand the satisfaction he gets from writing as if I were totally ignorant of this rudimentary distinction. Moreover, if the doctrine be false, it is still one that Professor McGilvary himself holds. He writes: "No experience somewhere and somewhen, no meaningful reality anywhere and anytime. *This is the truth which is contained in Professor Dewey's contention*" (p. 274, italics mine). I should say it was; the only truth for which I contended. My enjoyment, accordingly, of the ludicrous position in which Professor McGilvary places the "pure empiricist," with me as *corpus vile*, is heightened by the fact, that in view of his expressed agreement, I can stand the joke—if he can.

3. Professor McGilvary quotes from me: "The present experience of the veriest unenlightened ditch-digger does philosophic justice to the earlier reality [whose existence he charges me with denying!] in a way which the scientific statement does not and cannot; *cannot*, that is, *as formu-*

lated knowledge" (p. 273, italics mine). Unfortunately for his logic (though doubtless fortunately for his humor and poetic metaphor), he fails to quote, or take into account, the next sentence, which runs as follows: "As itself vital or direct experience . . . the latter is more valuable and is truer in the sense of worth more for other interpretations." The point at issue is not in the least whether the experience *creates* the things known, but whether the scientific formula as such or the direct, vital experience as such is, for the philosopher, a better index of the nature of reality, it being expressly declared that a direct experience which *includes* the scientific formulation is better than one which does not. When Professor McGilvary himself comes out strongly for the *representative* character of knowledge, he seems to be again in favor of my contention that a direct experience is a better index for philosophy than the knowledge phase as such of an experience. But perhaps only the erring empiricist holds that direct is better than merely representative experience. If so, I am still content to err; and shall abide by my conviction that an experience in which a symbol is experienced in its fulfillment or embodiment, is better than one in which the symbol alone is experienced, just as it is also better than one which remains as yet unrepresentative. And there are certain echoes from one Hegel, who held that the mediation finds its fruition in a new immediacy which I hope still also reaches the ears of Professor McGilvary.

4. Professor McGilvary refers to *Studies in Logical Theory* as follows: "In that work he [*i.e.*, the present writer] insisted that the *object of thought*, when it has emerged from the experience of stress and strain and appears in a subsequent tranquil experience as the result of pragmatic adjustment, must not be read back anachronistically into the time preceding the adjustment. The reader was therefore left to infer that no *truth* made out by intellectual labor is *to be held valid* of anything real that may have existed before that labor was ended" (p. 267, italics mine).

The reader was not only left to "infer" this, but the reader who did infer it was "left." The point of the contention to which Professor McGilvary refers is the anachronism of referring back the "object of *thought*" (as characteristically a *thought* object) to reality prior to the thinking. The old-fashioned empiricist held that thinking has no forms or modes of its own at all, being merely a complex of sensations or a disintegration of a prior complex; the epistemological idealist held that such forms or categories not only exist but are characteristic of reality as such, which therefore is to be conceived, philosophically, as a system of thought-relations; that thought as such is constitutive of reality as such. Now one object of the *Studies* was to insist, as against the sensationalist, that thinking does determine a characteristic objective situation, and, *against the idealist*, that it determines an object in process, through doubt and inquiry, of *redetermination*. Its purport, in short, is that all thinking is reflective, and that it is constitutive not of reality *per se* or at large, but only of such reality as has been reorganized through specific thinking, the reorganization finally taking place through *an action* in which the thinking terminates and by which it is tested. Thought is thus conceived of as a control-phenomenon biological in origin, humane, practical, or moral in import, involving in its issue real transformation of real reality. Hence the text abounds in assertions of reality existing prior to thinking, prior to coming to know, which, through the organic issue of thinking in experimental action, is reconstructed.

That it should be possible for a thinker of Professor McGilvary's equipment—to say nothing of his command of wit and of the poetry of picturesque and catastrophic metaphor—completely to invert the sense of my writing, even after its obscure and awkward character is taken into account, would be finally discouraging, were it not that I am buoyed up by three considerations. In the first place, he holds that knowledge is by subjective images which acquire a "transsubjective reference" to the realities to which they subjectively mean to refer,—the connection of the intention with the image, unfortunately, not being elucidated. Hence it would not be surprising if an image of my logical beliefs should spring up in Professor McGilvary's subjective resort for such creatures which should be totally unlike its object. If such an "image" were of great aesthetic brilliancy and of an unusually vivacious quality, it might easily impose upon him.

Or the image might get switched off during its "transsubjective" travels and finally light upon my devoted head, though originally intended, say, for some sensationalistic idealist. It would be obviously unjust to hold Professor McGilvary responsible for such a *faux pas* on the part of his image after it left him.

Again, thinkers who have got habituated to a mode of psychological analysis, which, in the interests of psychology, resolves experience into certain transient acts and states of a person, into sensations and images of a psycho-physical organism, may forget that others employ the term experience in a more vital, concrete, and pregnant sense. Hence, when others talk about experience, it is assumed that this means the psychological abstract which it means to the critic. Finally, modern philosophy has been built up on the foundations of epistemology; that is, it has held that reality is to be reached by the philosopher on the basis of an analysis of the procedure of knowledge. Hence, when a writer endeavors to take naïvely a frankly naturalistic, biological, and moral attitude, and to account for knowledge on the basis of the place it occupies in such a reality, he is treated as if his philosophy were only, after all, just another kind of epistemology.

DOES REALITY POSSESS
PRACTICAL CHARACTER?

I

Recently I have had an experience which, insignificant in itself, seems to mean something as an index-figure of the present philosophic situation. In a criticism of the neo-Kantian conception that *a priori* functions of thought are necessary to constitute knowledge, it became relevant to deny its underlying postulate: viz., the existence of anything properly called mental states or subjective impressions precedent to all objective recognitions, and requiring accordingly some transcendental function to order them into a world of stable and consistent reference. It was argued that such so-called original mental data are in truth turning points of the readjustment, or making over, through a state of incompatibility and shock, of objective affairs. This doctrine was met by the cry of "subjectivism"! It had seemed to its author to be a criticism, on grounds at once naturalistic and ethical, of the ground proposition of subjectivism. Why this diversity of interpretations? So far as the writer can judge, it is due to the fact that certain things characteristic of practical life, such things as lack and need, conflict and clash, desire and effort, loss and satisfaction, had been frankly referred to reality; and to the further fact that the function and structure of knowing were systematically connected with these practical features. These conceptions are doubtless radical enough; the latter was perhaps more or less revolutionary. The probability, the antecedent probability, was that hostile critics

[First published in *Essays, Philosophical and Psychological*, in Honor of William James, Professor in Harvard University, by his Colleagues at Columbia University (New York: Longmans, Green, and Co., 1908), pp. 53–80. Reprinted in *Philosophy and Civilization* (New York: Minton, Balch and Co., 1931), pp. 36–55, with the title "The Practical Character of Reality." For McGilvary's reply, see this volume, pp. 314–16.]

would have easy work in pointing out specific errors of fact
and interpretation. But no: the simpler, the more effective
method, was to dismiss the whole thing as anarchic subjectivism.

This was and remains food for thought. I have been
able to find but one explanation: In current philosophy, everything of a practical nature is regarded as "merely" personal, and the "merely" has the force of denying legitimate
standing in the court of cosmic jurisdiction. This conception
seems to me the great and the ignored assumption in contemporary philosophy: many who might shrink from the
doctrine if expressly formulated hang desperately to its implications. Yet surely as an underlying assumption, it is
sheer prejudice, a culture-survival. If we suppose the traditions of philosophic discussion wiped out and philosophy
starting afresh from the most active tendencies of to-day,—
those striving in social life, in science, in literature, and art,
—one can hardly imagine any philosophic view springing
up and gaining credence, which did not give large place, in
its scheme of things, to the practical and personal, and to
them without employing disparaging terms, such as phenomenal, merely subjective, and so on. Why, putting it
mildly, should what gives tragedy, comedy, and poignancy
to life, be excluded from things? Doubtless, what we call
life, what we take to be genuinely vital, is not all of things,
but it is a part of things; and is that part which counts most
with the philosopher—unless he has quite parted with his
ancient dignity of lover of wisdom. What becomes of philosophy so far as humane and liberal interests are concerned,
if, in an age when the person and the personal loom large
in politics, industry, religion, art, and science, it contents
itself with this parrot cry of phenomenalism, whenever the
personal comes into view? When science is carried by the
idea of evolution into introducing into the world the principles of initiative, variation, struggle, and selection; and
when social forces have driven into bankruptcy absolutistic
and static dogmas as authorities for the conduct of life, it
is trifling for philosophy to decline to look the situation in
the face. The relegation, as matter of course, of need, of
stress and strain, strife and satisfaction, to the merely per-

sonal and the merely personal to the limbo of something
which is neither flesh, fowl, nor good red herring, seems the
thoughtless rehearsal of ancestral prejudice.

When we get beyond the echoing of tradition, the sticking point seems to be the relation of knowledge to the practical function of things. Let reality be in itself as "practical"
as you please, but let not this practical character lay profane
hands on the ark of truth. Every new mode of interpreting
life—every new gospel—is met with the charge of antinomi-
anism. An imagination bound by custom apprehends the re-
strictions that are relaxed and the checks that are removed,
but not the inevitable responsibilities and tests that the new
idea brings in. And so the conception that knowledge makes
a difference in and to things looks licentious to those who
fail to see that the necessity of doing well this business, of
making the right difference puts intelligence under bonds
it never yet has known: most of all in philosophy, the most
gayly irresponsible of the procedures, and the most irrespon-
sively sullen, of the historic fruits of intelligence.

Why should the idea that knowledge makes a difference
to and in things be antecedently objectionable? If one is already committed to a belief that Reality is neatly and finally
tied up in a packet without loose ends, unfinished issues or
new departures, one would object to knowledge making a
difference just as one would object to any other impertinent
obtruder. But if one believes that the world itself is in transformation, why should the notion that knowledge is the most
important mode of its modification and the only organ of
its guidance be *a priori* obnoxious?

There is, I think, no answer save that the theory of
knowledge has been systematically built up on the notion
of a static universe, so that even those who are perfectly free
in accepting the lessons of physics and biology concerning
moving energy and evolution, and of history concerning the
constant transformation of man's affairs (science included),
retain an unquestioning belief in a theory of knowledge
which is out of any possible harmony with their own theory
of the matters to be known. Modern epistemology, having
created the idea that the way to frame right conceptions is
to analyze knowledge, has strengthened this view. For it at

once leads to the view that realities must themselves have
a theoretic and intellectual complexion—not a practical one.
This view is naturally congenial to idealists; but that realists
should so readily play into the hands of idealists by asserting
what, on the basis of a formal theory of knowledge, realities
must be, instead of accepting the guidance of things in
divining what knowledge *is*, is an anomaly so striking as to
support the view that the notion of static reality has taken
its last stand in ideas about knowledge. Take, for example,
the most striking, because the extreme case—knowledge of a
past event. It is absurd to suppose that knowledge makes a
difference to the final or appropriate content of knowledge:
to the subject-matter which fulfils the requirements of
knowing. In this case, it would get in its own way and trip
itself up in endless regress. But it seems the very superstition
of intellectualism to suppose that this fact about knowledge
can decide what is the nature of that reference to the past
which when rightly made is final. No doctrine about knowledge can hinder the belief—if there be sufficient specific evidence for it—that what we know as past may be something
which has *irretrievably* undergone just the difference which
knowledge makes.

Now arguments against pragmatism—by which I mean
the doctrine that reality possesses practical character and
that this character is most efficaciously expressed in the
function of intelligence[1]—seem to fall blandly into this fallacy. They assume that to hold that knowledge makes a difference in existences is equivalent to holding that it makes
a difference in the object *to be* known, thus defeating its own
purpose; witless that the reality which is the appropriate object of knowledge in a given case may be precisely a reality
in which knowing has succeeded in making the needed difference. This question is not one to be settled by manipula-

1. This definition, in the present state of discussion, is an arbitrary
or personal one. The text does not mean that "pragmatism" is
currently used exclusively in this sense; obviously there are
other senses. It does not mean it is the sense in which it *ought*
to be used. I have no wish to legislate either for language or for
philosophy. But it marks the sense in which it *is* used in this
paper; and the pragmatic movement is still so loose and variable
that I judge one has a right to fix his own meaning, provided
he serves notice and adheres to it.

tion of the concept of knowledge, nor by dialectic discussion
of its essence or nature. It is a question of facts, a question
of what knowing exists as in the scheme of existence. If
things undergo change without thereby ceasing to be real,
there can be no *formal* bar to knowing being one specific
kind of change in things, nor to its test being found in the
successful carrying into effect of the kind of change intended. If knowing be a change in a reality, then the more
knowing reveals this change, the more transparent, the more
adequate, it is. And if all existences are in transition, then
the knowledge which treats them as if they were something
of which knowledge is a kodak fixation is just the kind of
knowledge which refracts and perverts them. And by the
same token a knowing which actively participates in a
change in the way to effect it in the needed fashion would
be the type of knowing which is valid. If reality be itself in
transition—and this doctrine originated not with the objectionable pragmatist but with the physicist and naturalist and
moral historian—then the doctrine that knowledge *is* reality
making a particular and specified sort of change in itself
seems to have the best chance at maintaining a theory of
knowing which itself is in wholesome touch with the genuine and valid.

II

If the ground be cleared of *a priori* objections, and if it
be evident that pragmatism cannot be disposed of by any
formal or dialectic manipulations of "knowledge" or "truth,"
but only by showing that some specific things are not of the
sort claimed, we may consider some common-sense affilia-
tions of pragmatism. Common sense regards intelligence as
having a purpose and knowledge as amounting to something. I once heard a physicist, quite innocent of the pragmatic controversy, remark that the knowledge of a mechanic
or farmer was what the Yankee calls gumption—acknowledgment of things in their belongings and uses, and that to his
mind natural science was only gumption on a larger scale:
the convenient cataloguing and arranging of a whole lot of

things with reference to their most efficacious services. Popularly, good judgment is judgment as to the relative values of things: good sense is horse sense, ability to take hold of things right end up, to fit an instrument to an obstacle, to select resources apt for a task. To be reasonable is to recognize things in their offices as obstacles and as resources. Intelligence, in its ordinary use, is a practical term; ability to size up matters with respect to the needs and possibilities of the various situations in which one is called to do something; capacity to envisage things in terms of the adjustments and adaptations they make possible or hinder. Our objective test of the presence or absence of intelligence is influence upon behavior. No capacity to make adjustments means no intelligence; conduct evincing management of complex and novel conditions means a high degree of reason. Such conditions at least suggest that a reality-to-be-known, a reality which is the appropriate subject-matter of knowledge is reality-of-use-and-in-use, direct or indirect, and that a reality which is not in any sort of use, or bearing upon use, may go hang, *so far as knowledge is concerned.*

No one, I suppose, would deny that all knowledge issues in some action which changes things to some extent—be the action only a more deliberate maintenance of a course of conduct already instinctively entered upon. When I see a sign on the street corner I can turn or go on, knowing what I am about. The perceptions of the scientist need have no such overt or "utilitarian" uses, but surely after them he behaves differently, as an inquirer if in no other way; and the cumulative effect of such changes finally modifies the overt action of the ordinary man. That knowing, *after the event*, makes a difference of this sort, few I suppose would deny: if that were all pragmatism means, it would perhaps be accepted as a harmless truism. But there is a further question of fact: just how is the "consequent" action related to the "precedent" knowledge? When *is* "after the event"? What degree of continuity exists? Is the difference between knowing and acting intelligently one of kind or simply one of dominant quality? How does a thing, if it is not already in change in the knowing, manage to issue at its term in action? Moreover, do not the changes actively effected constitute the whole *import* of the knowledge, and hence its final measure and test of validity? If it merely *happens* that knowing when it is done with passes into some action, by what miracle is the subsequent action so pat to the situation? Is it not rather true that the "knowledge" is instituted and framed in anticipation of the consequent issue, and, in the degree in which it is wise and prudent, is held open to revision during it? Certainly the moralist (one might quote, for example, Goethe, Carlyle, and Mazzini) and the common man often agree that full knowledge, adequate assurance, of reality is found only in the issue which fulfils ideas; that we have to do a doctrine to *know* its truth; otherwise it is only dogma or doctrinaire program. Experimental science is a recognition that no idea is entitled to be termed knowledge till it has passed into such overt manipulation of physical conditions as constructs the object to which the idea refers. If one could get rid of his traditional logical theories and set to work afresh to frame a theory of knowledge on the basis of the procedure of the common man, the moralist and the experimentalist, would it be the forced or the natural procedure to say that the realities which we *know*, which we are sure of, are precisely those realities that have taken shape in and through the procedures of knowing?

I turn to another type of consideration. Certainly one of the most genuine problems of modern life is the reconciliation of the scientific view of the universe with the claims of the moral life. Are judgments in terms of the redistribution of matter in motion (or some other closed formula) alone valid? Or are accounts of the universe in terms of possibility and desirability, of initiative and responsibility, also valid? There is no occasion to expatiate on the importance of the moral life, nor upon the supreme importance of intelligence within the moral life. But there does seem to be occasion for asking how moral judgments—judgments of the would and should—relate themselves to the world of scientific knowledge. To frame a theory of knowledge which makes it necessary to deny the validity of moral ideas, or else to refer them to some other and separate kind of universe from that of common sense and science, is both provincial and arbitrary. The pragmatist has at least tried to face, and not to dodge, the question of how it is that moral and scientific "knowledge" can both hold of one and the same world. And whatever the difficulties in his proffered solution, the conception that scientific judgments are to be assimilated to moral is closer to common sense than is the theory that validity is to be denied of moral judgments because they do not square with a preconceived theory of the nature of the world to which scientific judgments must refer. And all moral judgments are about changes to be made.

III

I turn to one affiliation of the pragmatic theory with the results of recent science. The necessity for the occurrence of an event in the way of knowledge, of an organism which reacts or behaves in a specific way, would seem to be as well established as any scientific proposition. It is a peculiar fact, a fact fit to stir curiosity, that the rational function seems to be intercalated in a scheme of practical adjustments. The parts and members of the organism are certainly not there primarily for pure intellection or for theoretic contemplation. The brain, the last physical organ of thought, is a part of the same practical machinery for bringing about adaptation of the environment to the life requirements of the organism, to which belong legs and hand and eye. That the brain frees organic behavior from complete servitude to immediate physical conditions, that it makes possible the liberation of energy for remote and ever expanding ends is, indeed, a precious fact, but not one which removes the brain from the category of organic devices of behavior.[2] That the organ of thinking, of knowledge, was at least originally an organ of conduct, few, I imagine, will deny. And even if we try to believe that the cognitive function has supervened as a different operation, it is difficult to

2. It is interesting to note how the metaphysical puzzles regarding "parallelism," "interaction," "automatism," the relation of "consciousness" to "body," evaporate when one ceases isolating the brain into a peculiar physical substrate of mind at large, and treats it simply as one portion of the body as the instrumentality of adaptive behavior.

believe that the transfiguration has been so radical that knowing has lost all traces of its connection with vital impulse. But unless we so assume, have we any alternatives except to hold that this continual presence of vital impulse is a disturbing and refracting factor which forever prevents knowledge from reaching its own aim; or else that a certain promoting, a certain carrying forward of the vital impulse, importing certain differences in things, *is* the aim of knowledge?

The problem cannot be evaded—save ostrich-wise—by saying that such considerations are "merely genetic," or "psychological," having to do only with the origin and natural history of knowing. For the point is that the organic reaction, the behavior of the organism, affects the *content* of awareness. The subject-matter of all awareness is thing-related-to-organism—related as stimulus direct or indirect or as material of response, present or remote, ulterior or achieved. No one—so far as I know—denies this with respect to the perceptual field of awareness. Pains, pleasures, hunger, and thirst, all "secondary" qualities, involve inextricably the "interaction" of organism and environment. The perceptual field is distributed and arranged as the possible field of selective reactions of the organism at its centre. Up and down, far and near, before and behind, right and left, hard and soft (as well as white and black, bass and alto), involve reference to a centre of behavior.

This material has so long been the stock in trade of both idealistic arguments and proclamations of the agnostic "relativity" of knowledge that philosophers have grown aweary of listening. But even this lethargy might be quickened by a moderate hospitality to the pragmatic interpretation. That red, or far and near, or hard and soft, or big and little, involve a relation between organism and environment, is no more an argument for idealism than is the fact that water involves a relation between hydrogen and oxygen.[3] It is, however, an argument for the ultimately practical value of these distinctions—that they are *differences* made in what things would have been without organic behavior—differences made

3. I owe this illustration to my colleague, Dr. Montague.

not by "consciousness" or "mind," but by the organism as
the active centre of a system of activities. Moreover, the
whole agnostic sting of the doctrine of "relativity" lies in the
assumption that the ideal or aim of knowledge is to repeat
or copy a prior existence—in which case, of course, the making of contemporaneous differences by the organism in the
very fact of awareness would get in the way and forever
hinder the knowledge function from the fulfilment of its
proper end. Knowledge, awareness, in this case suffers from
an impediment which no surgery can better. But if the aim
of knowing be precisely to make *certain* differences in an
environment, to carry on to *favorable issue*, by the readjustment of the organism, certain changes going on indifferently
in the environment, then the fact that the changes of the
organism enter pervasively into the subject-matter of awareness is no restriction or perversion of knowledge, but part
of the fulfilment of its end.

The only question would then be whether the *proper*
reactions take place. The whole agnostic, positivistic controversy is flanked by a single move. The issue is no longer an
ideally necessary but actually impossible copying, *versus* an
improper but unavoidable modification of reality through organic inhibitions and stimulations: but it is the right, the
economical, the effective, and, if one may venture, the useful and satisfactory reaction *versus* the wasteful, the enslaving, the misleading, and the confusing reaction. The presence of organic responses, influencing and modifying every
content, every subject-matter of awareness, is the undoubted
fact. But the significant thing is the *way* organic behavior
enters in—the *way* it influences and modifies. We assign very
different values to different types of "knowledge,"—or subject-
matters involving organic attitudes and operations. Some
are only guesses, opinions, suspicious characters; others are
"knowledge" in the honorific and eulogistic sense—science;
some turn out mistakes, blunders, errors. Whence and how
this discrimination of character in what is taken at its own
time to be good knowledge? Why and how is the matter
of some "knowledge" genuine-knowing and of other mis-
knowing? Awareness is itself a blanket term, covering, in the
same bed, delusion, doubt, confusion, ambiguity, and defini-

tion, organization, logical conclusiveness assured by evidence
and reason. Any naturalistic or realistic theory is committed
to the idea that all of these terms bear impartially the same
relation to things considered as sheer existences. What we
must have in any case is the same existences—the same in
kind—only differently arranged or linked up. But why then
the tremendous difference in value? And if the unnaturalist,
the non-realist, says the difference is one of existential kind,
made by the working here malign, there benign, of "consciousness," "psychical" operations and states, upon the
existences which are the direct subject-matter of knowledge,
there is still the problem of discriminating the conditions and
nature of the respective beneficent and malicious interven-
tions of the peculiar "existence" labelled consciousness.[4] The
realness of error, ambiguity, doubt and guess poses a problem. It is a problem which has perplexed philosophy so long
and has led to so many speculative adventures, that it would
seem worth while, were it only for the sake of variety, to
listen to the pragmatic solution. It is the business of that organic adaptation involved in all knowing to make a *certain*
difference in reality, but *not* to make any old difference, any
casual difference. The right, the true and good, difference is
that which carries out satisfactorily the specific purpose for
the sake of which knowing occurs. All manufactures are the
product of an activity, but it does not follow that all manufactures are equally good. And so all "knowledges" are differences made in things by knowing, but some differences
are not calculated or wanted in the knowing, and hence are
disturbers and interlopers when they come—while others
fulfil the intent of the knowing, being in such harmony with
the consistent behavior of the organism as to reinforce and
enlarge its functioning. A mistake is literally a mishandling;
a doubt is a temporary suspense and vacillation of reactions;
an ambiguity is the tension of alternative but incompatible
mode of responsive treatment; an inquiry is a tentative and
retrievable (because intra-organic) mode of activity entered

4. Of course on the theory I am interested in expounding, the so-
called action of "consciousness" means simply the organic releases in the way of behavior which are the conditions of
awareness, and which also modify its content.

upon prior to launching upon a knowledge which is public, ineluctable—without anchors to windward—*because* it has taken physical effect through overt action.

It is practically all one to say that the norm of honorable knowing is to make no difference in *its* object, and that its aim is to attain and buttress a specific kind of difference in reality. Knowing fails in its business if it makes a change in its *own* object—that is a mistake; but its own object is none the less a prior existence changed in a certain way. Nor is this a play upon the two senses—end and subject-matter— of "object." The organism has its appropriate functions. To maintain, to expand adequate functioning is its business. This functioning does not occur *in vacuo*. It involves cooperative and readjusted changes in the cosmic medium. Hence the appropriate subject-matter of awareness is not reality at large, a metaphysical heaven to be mimeographed at many removes upon a badly constructed mental carbon paper which yields at best only fragmentary, blurred, and erroneous copies. Its proper and legitimate object is that relationship of organism and environment in which functioning is most amply and effectively attained; or by which, in case of obstruction and consequent needed experimentation, its later eventual free course is most facilitated. As for the other reality, metaphysical reality at large, it may, so far as awareness is concerned, go to its own place.

For ordinary purposes, that is for practical purposes, the truth and the realness of things are synonymous. We are all children who say "really and truly." A reality which is so taken in organic response as to lead to subsequent reactions that are off the track and aside from the mark, while it is, existentially speaking, perfectly real, is not *good* reality. It lacks the hall-mark of value. Since it is a certain *kind* of object which we want, that which will be as favorable as possible to a consistent and liberal or growing functioning, it is this kind, the *true* kind, which for us monopolizes the title of reality. Pragmatically, teleologically, this identification of truth and "reality" is sound and reasonable: rationalistically, it leads to the notion of the duplicate versions of reality, one absolute and static because exhausted; the other phenomenal and kept continually on the jump because otherwise its own inherent nothingness would lead to its total annihilation. Since it is only genuine or sincere things, things which are good for what they pretend to in the way of consequences, that we want or are after, *morally* they alone are "real."

IV

So far we have been dealing with awareness as a fact—a fact there like any fact—and have been concerned to show that the subject-matter of awareness is, in any case, things in process of change; and in such change that the knowing function takes a hand in trying to guide it or steer it, so that *some* (and *not* other) differences accrue. But what about the awareness itself? What happens when it is made the subject-matter of awareness? What sort of a thing is it? It is, I submit, mere sophistication (futile at that), to argue either that we cannot become aware of awareness without involving ourselves in an endless regress, or that whenever we are aware of anything we are thereby necessarily aware of awareness once for all, so that it has no character save this purely formal and empty one. Taken concretely, awareness is an event with certain specifiable conditions. We may indeed be aware of it formally, as a bare fact, just as we may be cognizant of an explosion without knowing anything of its nature. But we may also be aware of it in a curious and analytic spirit, undertaking to study it in detail. This inquiry, like any other inquiry, proceeds by determining conditions and consequences. Here awareness is a characteristic fact, presenting to inquiry its own characteristic ear-marks; and a valid knowledge of awareness is the same sort of thing as valid knowledge of the spectrum or of a trotting horse; it proceeds generically in the same way and must satisfy the same generic tests.

What, then, is awareness found to be? The following answer, dogmatically summary in form, involves positive difficulties, and glides over many points where our ignorance is still too great. But it represents a general trend of scientific inquiry, carried on, I hardly need say, on its own merits

without respect to the pragmatic controversy. Awareness
means *attention*, and attention means a crisis of some sort
in an existent situation; a forking of the roads of some material, a tendency to go this way and that. It represents
something the matter, something out of gear, or in some
way menaced, insecure, problematical and strained. This
state of tension, of ambiguous indications, projects and tendencies, is not merely in the "mind," it is nothing merely
emotional. It is in the facts of the situation as transitive
facts; the emotional or "subjective" disturbance is just a part
of the larger disturbance. And if, employing the *language*
of psychology, we say that attention is a phenomenon of conflicting habits, being the process of resolving this conflict
by finding an act which functions all the factors concerned,
this language does not make the facts "merely psychological"
—whatever that means.[5] The habits are as biologic as they
are "personal," and as cosmic as they are biologic. They are
the total order of things expressed in one way; just as a
physical or chemical phenomenon is the same order expressed in another way. The statement in terms of conflict
and readjustment of habits is at most one way of locating
the disturbance in *things*; it furnishes no substitute for, or
rival of, reality, and no "psychical" duplication.

If this be true, then awareness, even in its most perplexed and confused state, a state of maximum doubt and
precariousness of subject-matter, means things entering, *via*
the particular thing known as organism, into a peculiar condition of differential—or additive—change. How can we refuse to raise and consider the question of how things in this
condition are related to the prior state which emerges into
it, and to the subsequent state of things into which it issues?[6]

5. What does it mean? Does the objectivity of fact disappear when
   the biologist gives it a biological statement? Why not object to
   his conclusions on the ground that they are "merely" biological?
6. It is this question *of the relation to one another of different successive states of things* which the pragmatic method substitutes
   for the epistemological inquiry of how one sort of existence,
   purely mental, temporal but not spatial, immaterial, made up of
   sublimated gaseous consciousness, can get beyond itself and
   have valid reference to a totally different kind of existence—
   spatial and extended; and how it can receive impressions from
   the latter, etc.,—all the questions which constitute that species
   of confirmed intellectual lock-jaw called epistemology.

Suppose the case to be awareness of a chair. Suppose
that this awareness comes only when there is some problematic affair with which the chair is in some way—in whatever degree of remoteness—concerned. It may be a wonder
whether that is a chair at all; or whether it is strong enough
to stand on; or where I shall put it; or whether it is worth
what I paid for it; or, as not infrequently happens, the situation involved in uncertainty may be some philosophic matter in which the perception of the chair is cited as evidence
or illustration. (Humorously enough, the awareness of it may
even be cited in the course of a philosophic argument intended to show that awareness has nothing to do with situations of incompleteness and ambiguity.) Now what of the
change the chair undergoes in entering this way into a situation of perplexed inquiry? Is this any part of the genuineness of that chair with which we are concerned? If not,
where is the change found? In something totally different
called "consciousness"? In that case how can the operations
of inquiry, of observation and memory and reflection, ever
have any assurance of getting referred back to the *right* object? Positively the presumption is that the *chair-of-which-
we-are-speaking*, *is* the chair *of-which-we-are-speaking*; it is
the *same* thing that is out there which is involved also in
the doubtful situation. Moreover, the reference to "consciousness" as the exclusive locus of the doubt only repeats the
problem, for "consciousness," by the theory under consideration, means, after all, only the chair *as* concerned in the
problematical situation. The *physical* chair remains un-
changed, you say. Surely, if as is altogether likely, what is
meant by physical is precisely *that part* of the chair as object
of total awareness which remains unaffected, for certain possible purposes, by entering for certain other actual purposes
into the situation of awareness. But how can we segregate,
antecedently to experimental inquiry, the "physical" chair
from the chair which is now the object to be known; into
what contradictions do we fall when we attempt to define
the object of one awareness not in its own terms, but in
terms of a selected type of object which is the appropriate
subject-matter of some other cognizance!

But awareness means inquiry as well as doubt—these

are the negative and positive, the retrospective and the prospective relationships of the thing. This means a genuinely *additive* quale—one of readjustment in prior things.[7] I know the dialectic argument that nothing can assume a new relation, because in order to do so it must already be completely related—when it comes from an absolutist I can understand why he holds it, even if I cannot understand the idea itself. But apart from this conceptual reasoning we must follow the lead of our subject-matter; and when we find a thing assuming new relations in the process of inquiry, must accept the fact and frame our theory of things and of knowing to include it, not assert that it is impossible because we already have a theory of knowledge which precludes it. In inquiry, the existence which has become doubtful always undergoes experimental reconstruction. This may be largely imaginative or "speculative." We may view certain things *as if* placed under varying conditions, and consider what then happens to them. But such differences are really transformative so far as they go,—and besides, such inquiries never reach conclusions finally justifiable. In important and persistent inquiry, we insist upon something in the way of actual physical making—be it only a diagram. In other words, *science*, or knowing in its honorific sense, is experimental, involving physical construction. We insist upon something being *done about* it, that we may see how the idea when carried into effect comports with the other things through which our activities are hedged in and released. To avoid this conclusion by saying that knowing makes no difference in the "truth," but merely is the preliminary exercise which discovers it, is that old friend whose acquaintance we have repeatedly made in this discussion: the fallacy of confusing an existence anteceding knowing with the object which terminates and fulfils it. For knowing to make a difference in its own final term is gross self-stultification; it is none the less so when the aim of knowing is precisely to guide things straight up to this term. When "truth" means the accomplished introduction of certain new differences into condi-

---

7. We have arrived here, upon a more analytic platform, at the point made earlier concerning the fact that knowing *issues* in action which changes things.

tions, why be foolish enough to make other and more differences, which are not wanted since they are irrelevant and misleading?

Were it not for the teachings of sad experience, it would not be necessary to add that the change in environment made by knowing is not a total or miraculous change. Transformation, readjustment, reconstruction all imply prior existences: existences which have characters and behaviors of their own which must be accepted, consulted, humored, manipulated or made light of, in all kinds of differing ways in the different contexts of different problems. Making a difference in reality does not mean making any more difference than we find by experimentation can be made under the given conditions—even though we may still hope for different fortune another time under other circumstances. Still less does it mean making a thing into an unreality, though the pragmatist is sometimes criticised as if any change in reality must be a change into non-reality. There are difficulties indeed, both dialectic, and real or practical, in the fact of change—in the fact that only a permanent can change and that change is alteration of a permanent. But till we enjoin botanists and chemists from referring to changes and transformations in their subject-matter on the ground that for anything to change means for it to part with its reality, we may as well permit the logician to make similar references.

V

Sub specie aeternitatis? or *sub specie generationis?* I am susceptible to the aesthetic charm of the former ideal— who is not? There are moments of relaxation: there are moments when the demand for peace, to be let alone and relieved from the continual claim of the world in which we live that we be up and doing something about it, seems irresistible; when the responsibilities imposed by living in a moving universe seem intolerable. We contemplate with equal mind the thought of the eternal sleep. But, after all, this is a matter in which reality and not the philosopher is

the court of final jurisdiction. Outside of philosophy, the
question seems fairly settled; in science, in poetry, in social
organization, in religion—wherever religion is not hopelessly
at the mercy of a Frankenstein philosophy which it originally
called into being as its own slave. Under such circumstances
there is danger that the philosophy which tries to escape the
form of generation by taking refuge under the form of eternity will only come under the form of a by-gone generation.
To try to escape from the snares and pitfalls of time by
recourse to traditional problems and interests—rather than
that let the dead bury their own dead. Better it is for philosophy to err in active participation in the living struggles
and issues of its own age and times than to maintain an immune monastic impeccability, without relevancy and bearing
in the generating ideas of its contemporary present. In the
one case, it will be respected, as we respect all virtue that
attests its sincerity by sharing in the perplexities and failures, as well as in the joys and triumphs, of endeavor. In the
other case, it bids fair to share the fate of whatever preserves
its gentility, but not its activity, in descent from better days;
namely, to be snugly ensconced in the consciousness of its
own respectability.

A REPLY TO PROFESSOR McGILVARY'S QUESTIONS

Circumstances connected with the time of the appearance of Professor McGilvary's courteous questions to me (see *Journal of Philosophy, Psychology and Scientific Methods* for August 17, 1911) prevented my attention to them in proper season. I hope the long lapse of time has not outlawed my reply—such as it is.

His questions were based primarily upon the following quotation from my article in the "James Memorial Volume": "The so-called action of 'consciousness' means simply the organic releases in the way of behavior which are the conditions of awareness and which also modify its content." If I am not able to answer Professor McGilvary's questions directly, or with respect to the form in which he has put them, it is because these questions, as he formulates them, seem to me to depend upon ignoring the force of the *so-called* prefixed to *action* and the quotation marks surrounding the word *consciousness*. I meant by these precautions to warn the reader that I was referring to a view for which I disowned responsibility, especially as regards "consciousness." In fact I supposed it would be evident that the *consciousness* of the quotation marks designated precisely a conception which I was engaged in criticizing, and for which I was proffering a substitute. But the form of the questions put to me seems to me (I may misapprehend their import) to depend upon supposing that I accept just what I meant to reject. Naturally, then, the questions imply that I have involved myself in serious inconsistencies.

I quote two passages which afford some overt evidence that my impression is correct. "Although elsewhere in this paper Professor Dewey defined awareness as attention, I pre-

[First published in *Journal of Philosophy, Psychology and Scientific Methods* 9 (1912): 19–21. For McGilvary's reply, to which this article is a rejoinder, see this volume, pp. 314–16.]

sume that in this sentence [the one quoted above] he would mean to include consciousness in its inattentive forms also." And in connection with his next question he says, "Knowledge is one kind of consciousness, presumably." Both of these presumptions are natural on the basis of the notion of consciousness referred to in quotation marks, but I have difficulty in placing them in connection with my own view. Now if I am right in supposing that Professor McGilvary means one thing by consciousness and I mean another, I am somewhat embarrassed in replying to his questions. If I reply in his sense, I shall misrepresent myself; if I reply in mine, I shall probably give additional cause for misunderstanding, as the answers will be read in terms of his sense. Accordingly, I shall try to indicate what my view is, and then state the form his questions would take upon its basis.

My contention was that "consciousness" is an adjective of behavior, a quality attaching to it under certain conditions. When we make a noun of "conscious" and forget that we are dealing (as in the case of other nouns in -ness) with an abstract noun, we are guilty of the same fallacy as if we abstracted red from things and then discussed the relation of redness to things, instead of the relation of red things to other things. Hence (to come to question 1) there *is* certainly a question as to the relation of conscious behavior, attentive behavior, to other kinds of behavior. But this is *not* a question that can be discussed profitably after it has been misput. If the actual question is as to the rôle of the brain in certain kinds of behavior, the parallelist, automatist, etc., are making answer after they have translated the question into another and artificial form.

So with the second question. My reply (after I have translated the question) is that the aim of knowledge (to which reference was made) is the enrichment and guidance of subsequent behaviors—of all kinds. That conscious behavior grows out of instinctive and habitual (routine) behavior and is the prerequisite of moral, technological, esthetic, etc., behaviors, and that looking at it in this way is the proper way of understanding thinking ("consciousness") and all that goes with it, may be false positions as matters of fact, but I do not see that such positions involve questions of internal consistency.

The third question reads: "If it is the organic releases that change the environment in the act of knowing, does knowing as distinct from these organic releases make any changes in the environment on its own account?" The question involves the repudiated conception of consciousness, in the distinction it propounds between knowing and behavior. If consciousness be a characteristic quality of one kind of behavior, as distinct from other kinds, Professor McGilvary's question can not be asked. The only question is as to *what* changes conscious behavior makes as contrasting with other kinds. And my answer is that just given: the changes that conduce to direction of subsequent action and to enrichment of their meanings.

The fourth question reads in one of its forms: "Once distinguish between consciousness and organic releases, what justification have we for asserting that knowledge can be only of the *effects* of the conditions of knowledge?" Here again, the distinguishing holds with the meaning that Professor McGilvary obviously attributes to "consciousness," but not upon my meaning. Translated into my own terms, the question would read: "What reasons have we for thinking that knowing (attentive) behavior comes after certain other kinds?" And I quite agree with my questioner that this question is to be studied "just as we study anything else." And considering the number of times that an "instrumental" theory of knowing has been attacked on the ground that it narrows its consideration to the functions of knowledge, it is an interesting variation to find it intimated that it declines to extend its view to take them in.[1] To me—though probably not to those who criticize it—this suggests that the instrumental theory is trying to date knowing, to place it with respect both to its generating conditions and its consequences —or functions.

---

1. "If knowledge be distinct from its conditions, should we not study it as we study anything else, not confining ourselves entirely to the functions of its conditions, but extending our view to take in any possible functions it may itself have?"

OBJECTS, DATA, AND EXISTENCES: A REPLY TO PROFESSOR McGILVARY

I can not be otherwise than grateful to Professor McGilvary for the pains he has taken in acquainting himself with my logical analysis and in setting forth his results so clearly and succinctly.[1] Gratitude, if nothing else, would lead me to respond to his friendly challenge.

I

I begin by quoting almost *in toto* one section of his criticism, having inserted letters for convenience of subsequent reference to portions involved in the discussion.

"There is one further difficulty that I wish to lay before Professor Dewey in connection with his new distinction between fact and idea. (*a*) I suppose that most of us accept the other side of the moon as a fact, on a par *as fact* with this side of it. . . . (*b*) This fact, while as accepted fact it is on a parity with this side of the moon, yet as experienced fact seems to differ considerably from it. I can see the one; I can not see the other. . . . There is, after the conclusion is reached that the moon has two hemispheres, a considerable difference in our experience between the two hemispheres, and this difference does not seem to budge however we may pry upon it with changed meanings of terms. The realist, following the ordinary usage, says that while there are two lunar hemispheres, only one can be immediately experienced, and the other is accessible to us only by means

1. In his article entitled "The Chicago 'Idea' and Idealism," in *Journal of Philosophy, Psychology and Scientific Methods*, Vol. V, p. 589.

[First published in *Journal of Philosophy, Psychology and Scientific Methods* 6 (1909): 13–21. For McGilvary's article, see this volume, pp. 317–27.]

of idea. . . . What is pragmatism going to do with this difference? If it ignores it, can it keep peace with science? . . .
(c) Science makes a thoroughgoing distinction between observation and inference, between empirical facts and scientific constructions upon the basis of facts. . . . What we
take to be a satellite, 240,000 miles distant from the planetary earth, may after all not prove to be what we think it is.
But suppose that such a change in scientific construction
should ever take place? (d) All is not lost from present scientific fact; there remains the fact that there is a bright
something occasionally in experience, growing from slender
crescent to full orb. . . . This fact may come to be interpreted as anything you please, and get accepted as that thing;
but it will be there to be accepted somehow whenever any
one constituted like us opens his eyes and turns them in the
right direction at an opportune time. This kind of fact, and
there are many of them, forms the inexpugnable datum of
thought. It is the givenest of givens, *datissimum datorum*.
. . . These data of the first order are in the game, but not
of it. They give to one lunar hemisphere a primacy which no
terrestrial thought-reorganization can give to the other. Now
a philosophy which keeps close to experience can not well ignore this distinction between the two kinds of data."

Contradictions confront one in the subject-matter of
this passage—the natural inference is that they have their
source in my position. Is this the case, or do they inhere in
the ground taken by my critic? Let me first state the grava-
men of the charge brought against me, as briefly and as impartially as may be. I have held that objects accepted at the
conclusion of a judgment (the lunar sphere, for instance)
issue from a *process* of judging in which data (brute observational facts) and hypothetical meanings (conceptual *ideata*)
are at once discriminated from and referred to each other;
and that they issue in such fashion that the finally accepted
object presents both a reorganization of the data through the
"idea" and a verification of the "idea" through the experimental processes by which a meaning is taken up into the
data. Mr. McGilvary holds that this lands me in subjective
idealism—for it admits no "facts" or "objects" except those
into whose constitution "ideas" have entered. It also puts me

in conflict with scientific method for it ignores "data of the first order" which remain the same yesterday, to-day, and forever, so far as any "thought reconstruction" is concerned.[2]

II

My reply, in substance, is (1) that I have *not* ignored the existence of *datissima datorum*; that the assertion of their existence antecedent to ideas as such is essential to my theory of the reconstructive nature and work of the reflective process; (2) that my critic confuses such data, wholly non-cognitional, non-logical in character, with data which are in and of judgment, and hence distinctively logical in quality; (3) that he puts himself in conflict with science in ascribing to data (of the second kind) a higher knowledge value than belongs to the objects which are accepted as the conclusions of judgment.

The following discussion, while involving the above propositions, will follow, however, a different order. I shall try to show that in the portions of the citation marked off by the letters (b), (c), and (d), he has repeatedly transferred what holds good in one sort of situation to another sort of situation, and that the difficulties he notes flow not from my position, but from this interchange of propositions, each sound in itself, but so distinctive in meaning and reference as to negate the possibility of such transfer.

1. The lunar sphere (it is suggestive, as we shall see below, that my critic sticks closely to "two hemispheres" rather than to one sphere) is related—as stated in (b)—to the individual's act of recognizing it in a twofold way. Just *because* the assertion in (a) is true, *viz.*, that the two hemispheres stand as accepted facts on a parity, the individual in apprehending the single total fact *can not* be related to the far and to the near sides in the same way. The statement about the *difference in the modes of experiencing* the two

---

2. Mr. Nunn in his suggestive "Aims and Achievements of the Scientific Method" has also criticized the view of hypothesis and its function set forth in the *Studies in Logical Theory* on substantially the same ground. See sections 67 and 68.

sides is thus congruous with the acceptance of the object in which a judgment is concluded—and it is congruous *only* with its acceptance. *An analysis of the way a fact is apprehended can not, by the nature of the case, be made to yield a statement of the nature of that fact which is incompatible with the nature whose method of apprehension is under analysis.* I come in the sequel to the question of why I deny I am an idealist; but the gist of the matter lies right here. All idealist epistemologies with which I am acquainted perform exactly the self-contradictory act indicated in the last sentence.

There are two alternative ways of interpreting the statement of my critic that "as an *experienced* fact" the other side of the moon differs from this side, even though it be on a *parity* "as an *accepted* fact." In one way of interpretation, the fact that "only one side can be immediately experienced, and the other is accessible to us only by means of idea," refers precisely to the ways in which the different related elements in one complex fact are *accessible* to us. The proposition has as its universe of discourse not the relative cognitional status, or respective knowledge-values, of this side and the other side of the moon, but the mode *of our access* to elements possessed of the same cognitional value. The other mode of interpretation concludes that because our mode of access is different, therefore the elements to which we have access *stand on a different footing.*[3]

2. Let us consider both of these alternatives in relation to Mr. McGilvary's argument. If we take the first (which seems to me perfectly sound) we may discriminate, with respect to the lunar sphere, different relations of the two sides to our manner of apprehension; and from the standpoint of the *relation of the moon to our cognizing organism* distinguish the *sensory* quale of this side from the *ideal* or *suggested* quale of the other side. We may even, if we wish to (but I wish nobody wished to), speak of the former qualities as, *in this relation*, sensations; the latter as *ideas*—but,

3. The implication in the quoted passage that the fact as *immediately experienced* occupies a position cognitionally superior to the fact *accepted* after judgment is somewhat startling in view of Mr. McGilvary's previous criticisms of me, on the basis of attributing this notion to me. But of this "more anon."

of course, *if* we so name them the facts control the meaning
of the names, not the names the character of the facts. "Sensations" mean what Professor McGilvary in an earlier article[4]
well termed *sensa, i.e., qualities* of an object in relation to
our mode of apprehension. It is a disappointment that Mr.
McGilvary has not borne in mind in this article what he so
clearly pointed out before—*viz.*, "that the term sensation is
an *omnibus* term" (p. 458). If he had done so, he would
have realized that in pointing out a fifth passenger in an
obscure corner of the coach in which Mr. McGilvary had already discovered four fellow-travelers, I was neither altering
the "ordinary acceptation" of the term (*which* of the four is
the "ordinary," I wonder?) nor yet denying the existence of
the facts to which any one of the other four refers. But in
any case, if Mr. McGilvary intended or accepts *this* alternative interpretation, no inconsistency lies at my door. It is true
as an accepted fact of astronomy that the two sides of the
moon are on a parity; and it is true as an accepted fact of
psychology (or whatever the universe of reference may be)
that, *given this astronomical fact*, the experience of apprehending it is related to its two sides in different fashions.

If the other interpretation is accepted, then and then
only, does *this* side have a certain priority and supremacy
over the other side; and only then can Professor McGilvary
charge me with ignoring the plain procedure of science. But
if he intends and accepts this second alternative, then he
uses his analysis of our *recognizing-experience to discredit
scientific knowledge*—the conclusion that the two sides stand
as hemispheres on a parity. In this case, it turns out to be
he, not I, who should be worried about "keeping peace with
science"—for I do not think he will persuade the astronomer
to accept a moon which is fact on this side and idea on the
other: green cheese possibly, but "idea" never.

3. In the portion designated (*c*) a further confusion
comes to view. The difference between the two modes of
cognitive access to one fact appears now to be confused with
*a distinction lying within the process of judging or coming
to know, viz.*, that between "observation and inference," "em-

4. *Journal of Philosophy, Psychology and Scientific Methods*, Vol.
IV, p. 457.

pirical facts" and scientific constructions upon them. Again
two alternatives are possible. Either it is meant that this distinction (with superiority resting on the side of "observation"
and "empirical facts") holds during the process of judging
the real form of the moon, while, that is, we are still in
search of an "acceptable" fact; or it is meant that this quality
of values persists after the conclusion is reached—even after
the problem of its form is solved! If he means the former,
he has no quarrel with me, for it is precisely this antithetical
relation of datum and ideatum which I have made the peculiar differentia of judgment-in-process, as distinct from
inconclusion. But if he means the latter, how shall he keep
peace with science? For the characteristic of *scientific* knowledge is that it finds its genuinely acceptable object in the conclusions of a systematic process of inferential inquiry rather
than in "observations" *isolated* from all inferential matter,
or in "empirical facts" set over against *rationally* organized
and explained facts. When doubt as to the objective character occurs or recurs, then, of course, the antithesis recurs;
and then the *datum* becomes the factual element and the
ideatum, the hypothetical element. But as long as the conclusion remains unchallenged, so long the object *is* as the
conclusion describes it. Moreover, when there is doubt (and
hence when judgment is going on, not concluded) the factual
superiority is only of the datum in *that* judgment over *its* hypothetically suggested interpretation, not over the accepted
facts of scientific conclusions as such. For the entire process
of re-coordinating the raw data *rests upon the acceptance
of a whole system of other facts, not questioned simultaneously, which are conclusions of other judgments in which
thought has intervened.*

4. In the passage marked (*d*) the issue shifts to what
seems to me a more tenable position. Up to this point, my
critic has assumed the hemispherical quality of *this* side of
the moon to be a given "empirical fact" from which the hemi-
sphericity of the *other* side is an inference! If we had any
direct knowledge that this side of the moon is a hemisphere,
the "conclusion" that the other side is a hemisphere might
adorn an exposition of Kant's analytic judgments, or enliven
a treatise on "immediate inference," but it would not illumi-

nate the history of astronomy. Of course, the inference is that the *moon is a sphere*, the hemi-sphere character of *both* sides being involved in this conclusion. This obvious fact is indicated in Mr. McGilvary's reference to the "bright something occasionally in experience growing from slender crescent to full orb" as the primary datum.

The substitution of this statement for the hemispherical character of this side only strengthens, however (it may be truly replied) Mr. McGilvary's argument, for here at last are indeed *datissima datorum*. But how does this bear down on me? I have insisted (much to my discredit among "objective idealists") that there are non-logical antecedents for every specific reflective situation (and that *all* reflective situations are specific) so that knowledge involving thought is occasioned by non-reflective or alogical ("practical") factors in an antecedent experience.[5] I ask for no better proof of the hold of *intellectualistic*[6] epistemology upon current thought than is afforded by the fact that the position that thought operates in all judging processes (and hence is embodied in all judgment-conclusions) has seemed to so many critics to involve an idealistic theory of the nature of existence. It would, if to *exist* and to be subject-matter or result of cognition were equivalent terms. But the very denial of intellectualism claims that to exist—to exist even as matter of "experience"—is *not* to be identified with the status of a cognized something, whether during judgment or as its conclusion. And this mode of existence furnishes me as well as Professor McGilvary an impregnable fortress, a "givenest of

5. I may remark in passing that some of the criticisms made against this position from the side of the objective idealists would not have been made if it had been seen that my position does not demand that the prior situation as prior should be non-reflective *per se*, but only *as calling out thought*—that it does this in virtue of a clash or conflict which itself is wholly non-reflective, no matter how reflective the situation in which it is found.

6. Professor McGilvary incidentally questions the use of the term "rationalism" in my "later writings." I do not recall how extensive that use is, but I plead guilty. Rationalism is too closely associated with "free thought," or free criticism, on one hand, and with the antithesis to empiricism on the other, to be conveniently used as a term to designate intellectualism as against pragmatism:—for pragmatism may be "rationalistic" in the first sense, while empiricism may be—sensational empiricism *has* been—as intellectualistic as any rationalistic theory.

givens." If to believe in it makes him a realist, then it also makes me one.

If there be a difference between us, it must be in the character assigned the prior factor. What *is* the nature of what happens "whenever one constituted like us *opens his eyes and turns them* in the right direction" (italics mine), so that a crescent or an orb is seen? I say that what happens has the nature of an *act*; that it *exists* as an act. I have said that while the act may be cogni-*tive* (that is, exercise an influence upon further knowledge) it is not itself properly called cognition.[7] What does Professor McGilvary say?

If he says that it is a mode or content or object of knowledge, *qua* knowledge, what relation does its content bear to the datum in judgment? Is it identical with the former? Are the heavens and the furniture of the earth which we see when we *open our eyes and turn our heads* the same thing as those isolated, selected data of observation which the astronomer accepts as given, and works upon in figuring out the shape of the moon? Then is the rational or objective idealist lying in wait to swallow up Professor McGilvary by his simple method of pointing out the merely particular, *merely* observational (*i.e.*, sensible), merely fragmentary, chaotic, lawless character of such data, and the necessity of conceptual (or thought) relations to organize such brute trivialities into our significant world of related objects. Or, on the other hand, does Professor McGilvary mean that looking and seeing things *is* knowledge *par excellence*? that it represents the cognitional function at its best? Then how does

7. Aside from the question of fact, a dialectical difficulty should perhaps, to avoid misapprehension, be referred to. It may be said that I am assuming that primary "data" are here known—or may be known—as acts, and hence I have myself reduced them either to "data" undergoing interpretation or else to accepted objects of judgment. This objection, so frequently made, shows again the domination of the intellectualistic assumption. My position is that the term "experience" denotes primarily a mode of *existence*; experience may *exist* as an act-of-a-certain-specific quality, and that does not have to be reduplicated as knowledge in order to possess the character which it has. As for the other objection frequently made, that this reference to an act is pure individualism, I only want here to point out that it is the critic's assumption, not mine, that an act such as seeing is something attached to or possessed by an individual. As I see it, the individual is within, not without, the act, and within it as only one of its factors.

he keep peace with science? How does he avoid the conclusion that scientific knowledge is a hoax, an intentional arbitrary perversion of or declension from what we already know in a better, truer way? But, on the other hand, if it be admitted that what occurs when "one constituted as we are" uses his organs in accordance with their own structure is not knowledge at all—in any intellectual or scientific sense of that term—we are free to admit the primary existence of something with respect to any and all thinking, and at the same time free to admit that when the standpoint of knowledge as knowledge is once taken, the conclusions of systematized inference have a status superior to any other determinations.

This, I hope, at least answers the question of Professor McGilvary as to what I mean when I say that I do not conceive my position to be idealistic. I do not think it requires "thought" to see and to hear any more than it does to digest; though I also think that after thought has intervened such an action may be performed better, more economically and effectively—and also more chaotically and wastefully—to say nothing of its results having an infinitely more precious value.

III

Professor McGilvary inquires whether I am not, in any case, an idealist in the current sense of idealism—a sense which he states as follows: "the theory which regards all reality as embraced within experiences or within Experience." He adds, "A clear unambiguous answer by Professor Dewey to the question whether he is an idealist in the current sense as defined above would, I am sure, make his view much more intelligible." Ah, my dear questioner, I am tempted to reply, there are certain prerequisite conditions for "a clear and unambiguous answer": namely, that the question be clear and unambiguous. What is meant by "embraced"? Is it to have an *existential* meaning?—that some *thing* called experience holds physically or metaphysically other things in its embrace? Then I do *not* accept the theory.

Or is its meaning *methodological*? that philosophy, like science, proceeds intelligibly and fruitfully to verifiable results only by taking experienced, not transcendental, things, and by discussing them in the characters they empirically possess, not in the characters which, according to some *a priori* method, they *ought* to possess? In that case my answer might be affirmative, coupled with the admission that I know shamefully little about "all reality," since my empiricism is precisely that the only realities I do know anything about or ever shall know anything about are just experienced realities—for I do not suppose the phrase "all reality" was a trap laid for me.

Again, would not a "clear and unambiguous" definition of experience be both a boon in general and a prerequisite to a clear and unambiguous answer to the question asked? In neither of the two senses of experience which Mr. McGilvary expressly sets forth (on page 324) can I answer his question affirmatively. In the sense in which he *uses* the term on his next page (in the passages quoted) but without defining it, my answer would probably be affirmative. But in that case I am confused, for Professor McGilvary says *that* view is realism. And a reply that made me out both realist and idealist at the same time might not strike anybody as "clear and unambiguous." But perhaps if Mr. McGilvary should make explicit the sense in which he uses the word "experienced" when he talks, for example, about our experience of the moon as changing from crescent to full orb, and should contrast that with his use of "experience" in the instance of the perceived stone, he would discover a vital and pregnant meaning of experience which would reveal that he and I as human beings are much alike in what we mean by experience. And in that case I am quite willing to leave it to my critic by what names he and I are to be labeled.

ADDRESS TO NATIONAL NEGRO CONFERENCE

The ground has already been so well covered in the matter of this scientific discussion, that I shall detain you but a moment or two; in fact I should not have appeared at all, were it not that it gave me the opportunity to express my sympathy with the purpose of this gathering and to give myself that privilege, I venture to detain you for these very few moments. One point that has been made on the scientific side, might perhaps be emphasized, namely with reference to the doctrine of heredity.

It was for a long time the assumption—an assumption because there was no evidence or consideration of evidence —that acquired characteristics of heredity, in other words capacities which the individual acquired through his home life and training, modified the stock that was handed down. Now the whole tendency of biological science at the present time is to make it reasonably certain that the characteristics which the individual acquired are not transmissible, or if they are transmissible, then in such a small degree as to be comparatively and relatively negligible. At first sight this taken by itself may seem to be a disappointing and discouraging doctrine, that what one individual attains by his own effort and training, does not modify the level from which the next generation then starts. But we have put over against that this other point that has been made with reference to social heredity, and the fact that there is a great difference between mental culture from the standpoint of the individual and mental culture from the standpoint of society.

This doctrine that acquired characteristics are not transmitted becomes a very encouraging doctrine because it

[First published in *Proceedings of the National Negro Conference* 1909 (New York: National Negro Conference Headquarters, n.d.), pp. 71–73. Reprinted in facsimile "from a copy in the collection of Harvard College Library" by Arno Press and the *New York Times* (New York: Arno Press, 1969).]

means, so far as individuals are concerned, that they have a full, fair and free social opportunity. Each generation biologically commences over again very much on the level of the individuals of the past generation, or a few generations gone by. In other words, there is no "inferior race," and the members of a race so-called should each have the same opportunities of social environment and personality as those of a more favored race. Those individuals start practically to-day, where the members of the more favored race start again as individuals, and if they have more drawbacks to advance, they lie upon the side of their surrounding opportunities, the opportunities in education, not merely of school education but of that education which comes from vocation, from work responsibilities, from industrial and social responsibilities, and so on. It is therefore the responsibility of society as a whole, conceived from a strictly scientific standpoint leaving out all sentimental and all moral considerations—it is the business of society as a whole to-day, to see to it that the environment is provided which will utilize all of the individual capital that is being born into it.

For if these race differences are, as has been pointed out, comparatively slight, individual differences are very great. All points of skill are represented in every race, from the inferior individual to the superior individual, and a society that does not furnish the environment and education and the opportunity of all kinds which will bring out and make effective the superior ability wherever it is born, is not merely doing an injustice to that particular race and to those particular individuals, but it is doing an injustice to itself for it is depriving itself of just that much of social capital.

EDUCATION AS A UNIVERSITY STUDY

Using the number of years by which generations are conventionally reckoned, it is for only a little over one of them that education has had any standing as a university subject. When all the work of a university is in education, how absurd, the argument used to run, to attempt to make education a separate topic of study! And if further attention was given to the matter, beyond that summary method of disposal, it was enough to call up an image of "pedagogy" as the pretended art of teaching teachers how to teach by means of trivial devices and patent panaceas, all of which tended to make "method" a substitute for knowledge of subject-matter. Adding a few remarks about the inborn personality of the teacher, the need of experience and tact, made the case quite complete. This is not the place to record the statistics of the invasion of universities by first stray teachers of the subject of education, then by departments, and latterly by completely organized schools and colleges paralleling those of law and medicine. It is enough, perhaps, to recall that in the past year the university whose president was once credited, whether rightly or wrongly, with the remark that any intelligent person could learn in a few hours all that can be learned, theoretically, about pedagogy, has erected that subject into an independent department.

Doubtless, however, the notion still persists in the minds of some Bourbons of culture, that the main purpose of educational theory is to peddle handy and cheap ways of teaching a subject without much scholarship in it—much as if scientific medicine were thought to be exhausted in setting forth ways of making cod-liver oil and other nauseating drugs more palatable. And many of those who take a more serious view of its possibilities, rarely pause to consider the

[First published in *Columbia University Quarterly* 9 (1907): 284–90.]

impressive scope of the topic as matter of a strictly university discipline. It may be asserted, without danger of successful challenge, that no subject touches life on so many sides, and brings with itself such a wealth of materials combined with such stimulating outlook upon the past and the present of humanity. It goes without saying, that the school is a social institution. But in spite of the practical devotion of American publicists and tax-payers to the cause of the schools and of the oratorical flourishes to which the topic has lent itself ever since at least the days of Edward Everett, neither political science, nor its younger sister, sociology, has, till very recently, taken seriously all that is involved in the fact that the school is an institution like the family, like the church, like business, like government, and that it would reward as careful a study.

Consider first the institution in its more external aspects, in its mechanism. There are the economic problems of the construction, maintenance and equipment of buildings and of the fixing and grading of salaries. That these problems are political, as well as economic, is testified to by the discussions going on in practically every large American city today; questions of the inadequate supply of sittings, of half-time pupils, and inadequate rented buildings, of agitations for increase of salary, for better methods of classifying teachers with respect to rate of pay, etc., etc. Is it complimentary to the social leadership of our universities that they should ignore such investigation and discussion as will fit their graduates to speak with some authority, from the intellectual standpoint, upon the economic and political aspects of such questions, to say nothing of the ultimate human interests involved? Unless such matters somewhere are made the objects of systematic study, they will continue to be settled in the future as in the past, by clamor, rule-of-thumb and the interests of ward politicians. And still upon the external side, there are indefinitely numerous and complicated hygienic and aesthetic questions; problems of sanitation, of heat and light and ventilation, of seats and blackboards and play-ground space, etc., questions that of course in their most technical aspects must be dealt with by architects, but also questions with reference to which it is impor-

tant that the professed leaders of public education should
be competent to direct and to form public opinion.

Then there is the mechanism of administration; the
position and operation of the school as part of the whole
scheme of civic and state administration. It is not long since
the entire American literature on this subject was summed
up in compendia of "School-laws." Now we have discussions
of the relations of the federal government to education; of
various types of state, county, township and district organization; of school consolidation and transportation of pupils;
of the phases of school administration to be included in the
city charter and those to be left to school-boards; of the right
organization of such boards, and of the division of functions between it, superintendent and business-manager; of
the definition of duties and rights of all the constituent portions of the school system, superintendent, associate or district superintendents, supervisors, principals, teachers, etc.;
the formation of school budgets; the making of school reports with such degree of system and uniformity that those
from different cities may profitably be compared by students
of statistics, economics and civil government, as well as by
educators, etc. And each of these subjects ramifies in countless directions.

Passing from the outside to more vital matters, there
are the countless problems of concern to the sociologist and
the moralist, as well as to the man who claims the title of
statesman. The question of child labor is but one phase, the
reverse phase, of the question of child education; compulsory
education; parental schools, truant schools, reform schools;
the training of the defective classes, cripples, feeble-minded,
of the unfortunates, the deaf and the blind; the organization
of special schools for special classes, evening schools, industrial schools, clubs, play-grounds, recreation centres, are all
questions of the proper direction of social forces. It is only
a question of time when, whether under the head of education or under some other rubric, the sociology of the child
will gather into itself and organize a large number of topics
now scattered at large through fields of philanthropy, penol-
ogy, economics, law, and medicine. The one thing still most
certain is that every member of society is born and dies; in

other words, that society has continually to maintain its life by renewing it through the immature. Yet it is this most certain and most salient of all sociological facts which is most commonly ignored; a fact which can never receive its proper attention until education is recognized not merely as a fitting topic for serious and prolonged study, but the most important of subjects for such study.

The inventory of the capacities of education as a university study must include at least passing reference to the historical side. If it be true that an adequate knowledge of one organ enables the scientist to reconstruct the entire organism, it is surely true that an adequate knowledge of the educational machinery, subject-matter, ideals and methods of Greece, Rome, mediaeval Europe, or of the Germany, England and France of yesterday, initiates us into the inmost secrets of those people. To know their education is to know their family life, their religion, their science and their philosophy. This history covers both the history of institutions and of ideas. The history of education is the history of the social mechanisms by which the immature have been bred true to social type; of the speculations by which men have sought both to justify and to reform their social types; of the progress of mankind in the arts of war and of industry, and of the development of the various sciences. None of these things, not the most abstract of the sciences, lives in the vacuum, not even if we label this vacuum "mind"; they live only in processes of social transmission and communication —that is, in last resort, of education. The history of education is the history of intelligence, applied and "pure."

I have not touched upon that aspect of education which, since it was the first to receive recognition, through the formation of normal schools, by the teaching profession itself, still bulks most largely in the public eye—methods of dealing with children in instruction and discipline. However great errors may have been committed in the name of "method," these are none the less topics for profound and multiform scientific study here. Psychology, whether physiological, experimental or social, is still in its scientific infancy. We do not discredit medicine and surgery because they waited so long upon the necessary advances of chemistry and bacteriology and physiology to emerge from the empiric and quasi-magic stage to that of intelligent arts. And there is no subject, reading, writing, arithmetic, drawing, music, manual training, history, foreign language, or whatever, of which it can not be said that certain methods of teaching are physiologically and intellectually (and hence morally) better than others. The respective values of these methods are capable of scientific determination, and, until this determination has taken place, we are working blindly with the most important of all forces. No sensible person will hold that we have as yet got very far in these regions; but it needs no argument to show that the modern university does not exist simply to rehearse the knowledge of the past; that it exists precisely because there are so many fields in which, relatively, we have not got very far, but in which it is most important that we shall get farther; and in which the type of inquiry and discussion that the university exists to foster is the sole means of advance.

I should like to say a word about another phase of the study of education which, not of great interest to large numbers, makes up, perhaps, for this lack by the intensity of the fascination it has for a few: the philosophic side of education—its abstract theory. Philosophy is always tending to run to seed; and, as happens in such cases, the seeds both deteriorate in quality and are spread by chance to grow weeds —that is, plants which use up the soil to little avail. Philosophy, like any specialty, tends to develop its own technique to a point where the ends for the sake of which the technique was created are forgotten; problems of technique take the place of problems of life, and, by a strange irony, are regarded as the questions for which the questions of life exist. There is no more certain way of recalling to the student these basic and ultimate questions than to have philosophy presented in the concrete—in the form of its bearing upon the conduct of education. Take the group of problems centering in the theory of knowledge. When they have been worn threadbare by much discussion, when they have been reduced to questions which exist only for the philosopher and for him only in the moments in which he philosophizes, they get a pregnant vitality when they are presented as the formulation of the practical educational questions of, say, the relation between intellectual training and the better control of conduct; of the relation between science and art, of the naturalistic and the humanistic studies; of the proper division and correlation of the sciences. Then one sees that the isolated technical problems of the philosophic class-room neither begin nor end in philosophy itself, that philosophy is only a language, a way of phrasing conflicts upon which men actually divide in their more unconscious and habitual procedures. Rationalism versus empiricism, the proper reconciliation of the claims of sensation and thought, get a new meaning when one views them as questions of the right use of observation and thinking in the economy of instruction. The problem of the relation of mind and matter becomes a more humanly significant topic when one has envisaged it in terms of the adjustment of the respective claims of liberal culture and serviceable industry within the school—and so one might go through the list of all the time-honored philosophical questions.

I hope I have not said anything that is not only obvious but so obvious as to raise the question why it is worth while setting down such commonplaces. But it is commonplaces that are of chief importance and yet they are the last things to receive scientific education. Science begins with the stars and with mathematical points—with things remote and abstract—and only slowly comes to man—to the intimate and the concrete. The most common of all things is the growth of helpless infancy into trained maturity; it is so common that it is left to go its own way subject only to custom, to caprice and to the display of superior power. Yet upon the course it takes depends the direction that the course of society takes. Either there is no possibility of any deliberate, conscious direction, or else scientific study, the type of study that is at home in the university, must supply it.

There is an additional reason for attaching importance to education as a university discipline under American conditions. Our political and social traditions are against any systematic and centralized control of education from governmental centres and bureaus. Extreme local self-government is the rule in education even more, if possible, than in other parts of our administrative processes. Some regret this; others see in it a recognition of the change in the spirit and ideals of education that must come with democracy. When the aim is a suppression of many features of individuality, especially those which make for variation and initiation, by running all into a common mold, an authoritative system proceeding by hierarchical gradations, from superior to inferior, till at last it reaches the *infimus gradus*, the child, is natural. But if development of self-initiative and self-responsible personalities is the aim, there must be greater opportunity for flexibility, experimentation and local diversity. But whether one regret or approve, our educational systems are in need of some sort of direction from expert sources. If it does not come with coercion, it must come voluntarily. If it is not undertaken with the authority of a bureaucracy, it must be with the authority of science and philosophy and history. The universities are the natural centres of such free and sympathetic organization. It is for them to gather and focus the best that emerges in the practices of the present; it is for them to experiment in the development of more adequate conceptions of subject-matter, and to issue the results to the school with the *imprimatur* not of officialdom but of intelligence. Through education of leaders, through the avenues of persuasion and conviction, they must perform the task of selection and of organization, which ministers of education effect under more autocratically centralized schemes. In fine, the scientific study of education should represent the finest self-consciousness of the university of its own work and destiny—of its mission for itself and for the society of which it is both minister and organ.

RELIGION AND OUR SCHOOLS

I

A learned and self-conscious generation has fittingly discovered religion to be a universal tendency of human nature. Through its learning, anthropology, psychology, and comparative religion have been summoned to give this testimony. But because of its self-consciousness the generation is uneasy. As it surveys itself it is fearful lest, solitary among the ages, it should not be religious. The self-same learning which has made it aware that other times have had their life permeated with religious faith is part of the conditions which have rendered the religions of those periods impossible. The dilemma is striking and perplexing. Shall the very circumstances which convince us that religion is necessary also make it impossible? Shall the evidence that it is a universal tendency make those who are aware of this tendency the flagrant exception to its universality? We have learned so much about religious "instincts": shall we therefore lose them?

It indeed seems hard that a generation which has accumulated not only material wealth, but intellectual riches, to the extent that it is compelled to pull down its barns—its systems of philosophy and doctrine—and build greater, should be lacking in just that grace and sanction of life which ignorant and poor people have possessed as matter of course. But our learnedly self-conscious generation is also mechanical. It has a tool for everything, and almost every-

[First published in *Hibbert Journal* 6 (1908): 796–809. Reprinted in *Characters and Events* (New York: Henry Holt and Co., 1929), 2: 504–16; in *Intelligence in the Modern World* (New York: Modern Library, 1939), pp. 702–15, with the title "The Schools and Religions"; and in *Education Today* (New York: G. P. Putnam's Sons, 1940), pp. 74–86, all edited by Joseph Ratner.]

thing has become for it a tool. Why, then, should we longer suffer from deficiency of religion? We have discovered our lack: let us set the machinery in motion which will supply it. We have mastered the elements of physical well-being; we can make light and heat to order, and can command the means of transportation. Let us now put a similar energy, goodwill, and thoughtfulness into the control of the things of the spiritual life. Having got so far as to search for proper machinery, the next step is easy. Education is the modern universal purveyor, and upon the schools shall rest the responsibility for seeing to it that we recover our threatened religious heritage.

I cannot expect that those who are now especially concerned with the maintenance and the spread of conscious and explicit religious instruction (for the time being one must use this question-begging epithet) will recognize their attitude or intention in what I have just said. And it has no application to those who are already committed to special dogmas of religion which are the monopoly of special ecclesiastic institutions. With respect to them, the fight for special agencies and peculiar materials and methods of education in religion is a natural part of their business: just as, however, it is the business of those who do not believe that religion is a monopoly or a protected industry to contend, in the interest both of education and of religion, for keeping the schools free from what they must regard as a false bias. Those who believe that human nature without special divine assistance is lost, who believe that they have in their charge the special channels through which the needed assistance is conveyed, must, naturally, be strenuous in keeping open these channels to the minds of men. But when the arguments for special religious education at special times and places by special means proceed from philosophic sources—from those whose primary premiss is denial of any breach between man and the world and God, then a sense of unreality comes over me. The arguments perforce translate themselves ironically. They seem to say that, since religion is a universal function of life, we must particularly safeguard it lest it disappear; that since religion is the consciousness of the spiritual import of experience, we must find mechanical appliances for developing it.

Those who approach religion and education from the side of unconstrained reflection, not from the side of tradition, are of necessity aware of the tremendous transformation of intellectual attitude effected by the systematic denial of the supernatural; they are aware of the changes it imports not merely in special dogma and rites, but in the interpretation of the world, and in the projection of social, and, hence, moral life. It testifies to the current unreality of philosophy (itself probably a product of that forced idealism in which modern thought has taken refuge) that philosophers should seem to think that great intellectual generalizations may be, as it were, plastered over life to label its contents, and not imply profound practical alterations within life itself. In no other way is it easy to account for the attitude of those who are convinced of the final departure of the supernatural interpretation of the world and of man, and who yet think that agencies like the church and the school must not be thoroughly reconstructed before they can be fit organs for nurturing types of religious feeling and thought which are consistent with modern democracy and modern science.

That science has the same spiritual import as supernaturalism; that democracy translates into the same religious attitude as did feudalism; that it is only a matter of slight changes of phraseology, a development of old symbolisms into new shades of meaning—such beliefs testify to that torpor of imagination which is the uniform effect of dogmatic belief. The reconstruction of the Church is a matter which concerns, indeed, the whole community so far as its outcome is concerned; while the responsibility for its initiation belongs primarily to those within the churches. The burden of conducting the development, the reconstruction, of other educational agencies belongs, however, primarily to the community as a whole. With respect to its intellectual aspect, its philosophy, it belongs especially to those who, having become conscious in some degree of the modern ideas of nature, of man and society, are best able to forecast the direction which social changes are taking. It is lucidity, sincerity, and the sense of reality which demand that, until the non-supernatural view is more completely elaborated in all its implications and is more completely in possession of

the machinery of education, the schools shall keep hands off
and shall do as little as possible. This is indeed a *laissez-faire*
policy. It is frankly, avowedly so. And, doubtless, *laissez-
faire* policies are not in favor in self-conscious and mechanical days. One of the further ironies of our time is that,
having discovered the part played by unconscious, organic,
collective forces in the processes of human development, we
are possessed by a great eagerness, a great uneasiness, consciously to foster and to guide these forces. We need, however, to accept the responsibilities of living in an age marked
by the greatest intellectual readjustment history records.
There is undoubted loss of joy, of consolation, of some types
of strength, and of some sources of inspiration in the change.
There is a manifest increase of uncertainty; there is some
paralysis of energy, and much excessive application of energy in materialistic directions. Yet nothing is gained by
deliberate effort to return to ideas which have become incredible, and to symbols which have been emptied of their
content of obvious meaning. Nothing can be gained by moves
which will increase confusion and obscurity, which tend to
an emotional hypocrisy and to a phrasemongering of formulae which seem to mean one thing and really import the
opposite. Bearing the losses and inconveniences of our time
as best we may, it is the part of men to labor persistently
and patiently for the clarification and development of the
positive creed of life implicit in democracy and in science,
and to work for the transformation of all practical instrumentalities of education till they are in harmony with these
ideas. Till these ends are further along than we can honestly
claim them to be at present, it is better that our schools
should do nothing than that they should do wrong things.
It is better for them to confine themselves to their obviously
urgent tasks than that they should, under the name of
spiritual culture, form habits of mind which are at war with
the habits of mind congruous with democracy and with science. It is not laziness nor cynicism which calls for the
laissez-faire policy; it is honesty, courage, sobriety, and faith.

　　If one inquires why the American tradition is so strong
against any connection of state and church, why it dreads
even the rudiments of religious teaching in state-maintained

schools, the immediate and superficial answer is not far to
seek. The cause was not, mainly, religious indifference, much
less hostility to Christianity, although the eighteenth-century
deism played an important rôle. The cause lay largely in
the diversity and vitality of the various denominations, each
fairly sure that, with a fair field and no favor, it could make
its own way; and each animated by a jealous fear that, if
any connection of state and church were permitted, some
rival denomination would get an unfair advantage. But there
was a deeper and by no means wholly unconscious influence
at work. The United States became a nation late enough in
the history of the world to profit by the growth of that modern (although Greek) thing—the state consciousness. This
nation was born under conditions which enabled it to share
in and to appropriate the idea that the state life, the vitality
of the social whole, is of more importance than the flourishing of any segment or class. So far as church institutions
were concerned, the doctrine of popular sovereignty was a
reality, not a literary or legal fiction. Upon the economic side,
the nation was born too soon to learn the full force of the
state idea as against the class idea. Our fathers naïvely
dreamed of the continuation of pioneer conditions and the
free opportunity of every individual, and took none of the
precautions to maintain the supremacy of the state over that
of the class which newer commonwealths are taking. For
that lack of foresight we are paying dearly, and are like to
pay more dearly. But the lesson of the two and a half centuries lying between the Protestant revolt and the formation
of the nation was well learned as respected the necessity of
maintaining the integrity of the state as against all divisive
ecclesiastical divisions. Doubtless many of our ancestors
would have been somewhat shocked to realize the full logic
of their own attitude with respect to the subordination of
churches to the state (falsely termed the *separation* of church
and state); but the state idea was inherently of such vitality
and constructive force as to carry the practical result, with
or without conscious perception of its philosophy. And any
general agitation in the United States of the question of religious instruction in the schools could have but one explanation. It would mean that, from economic segregation and

unassimilated immigration, the state-consciousness of the country had been sapped by the growth of social factions. I write, then, from the standpoint of that country with whose traditions and tendencies I am directly acquainted. But so far as it is true that circumstances have permitted the United States merely to travel a certain course more rapidly than other contemporary nations (save France), what is based upon American conditions must apply, in its measure, to the conditions of education in other countries.

II

As I recall, some of the Platonic dialogues discuss the question whether virtue can be taught, and all of them contain overtones or reminiscences of the topic. For the discussion led a long way. What is virtue? That is not an altogether easy question; and since to answer it we must know virtue and not merely have opinions about it, it will be well to find out what knowledge is. Moreover, teaching implies learning, and learning is coming to know, or knowledge in process of learning. What then is the connection of the becoming of knowledge with the being of knowledge? And since the teaching of virtue means, not getting knowledge "about" virtue, but the conversion of character to the good, what, after all, is the relation between becoming good and that becoming wise which is the result of learning?

Somehow, I am more aware that Plato discusses all these questions than I am certain of any final answer to the question whether virtue may be taught. Yet I seem to recall some hypothetical suggestions for an answer. If, as we have reason to believe, the soul of man is naturally akin to good— if, indeed, it truly *is* only through participation in the good —then may various objects, also in their measure expressions of good, serve to remind the soul of its own or original nature. If these various reminders may be organized into a comprehensive scheme, continuous and continual in operation—if, in other words, there may be found a state organized in righteousness—then may the soul be finally brought to the apprehension of its own being or good; and this com-

ing to know and to be we may term learning. But, if I remember rightly, Plato always classed endeavors to teach
virtue apart from an accompanying thorough reorganization
of social life and of science as a piece of confused and self-
contradictory thinking—as a case, that is, of sophistic.

Have we any reason for taking the present problem of
teaching religion to be simpler in conception or easier in execution? The contemporary problem appears, indeed, to be
more intricate and difficult. Varied and conflicting as were
the views of Plato's Greek contemporaries as to what things
should be included and taught under the head of virtues, the
question of just what concretely comes under the caption
of religion to-day is as much harder to decide as our social
life is more heterogeneous in origin and composition than
was the Athenian. We certainly cannot teach religion as an
abstract essence. We have got to teach *something* as religion, and that means practically *some* religion. Which? In
America, at least, the answer cannot be summarily given
even as Christianity in general. Our Jewish fellow-citizens
not only have the same "hands, organs, dimensions, senses,
affections, passions" as the Christians, but, like them, they
pay taxes, vote, and serve on school boards. But we should
not be very much better off even if it were a question of
Christianity alone. *Which* Christianity? Oriental in its origin, it has been since Latinized and Germanized, and there
are even those who have dreamed of humanizing it.

The problem of to-day is more complex as respects also
the process of learning, of coming to know. In the day of
Plato, art and science, skilled practice and theory, were only
beginning to be separated. Just as a man learned shoemaking
in process of becoming a shoemaker, so might a man learn
virtue in becoming a member of a good state—if such a thing
could be found. To-day knowledge is something specialized,
and learning does not consist in intelligent mastery of an activity, but in acquiring a diversity of information about
things, and control over technical methods for instituting
symbolic references to things. Knowledge to Plato was the
sort of thing that the forefathers of some of us called "getting religion." It was a personal experiencing and a vital
realization. But what shall knowledge of religion as an out-

come of instruction mean to-day? Shall it mean the conversion of character into spirituality? Shall it mean the accumulation of information *about* religion? Or are there those who
still believe in some magic power resident in memorized
words, phrases, and facts of transmuting themselves into
personal insight, the development of fundamental mood and
the formation of permanent attitudes towards experience?

When we consider knowledge from the side of its
method and from the standpoint of what it takes to get something really worthy to be called knowledge, the problem increases in difficulty. As yet, the standpoint of science, its
spirit, has not of course leavened very adequately our methods of teaching. From the standpoint of those methods of
inquiry and testing which we call science, much, perhaps
most, of what passes for knowledge is in reality what Plato
called opinion. Our science is still an outward garb more
or less awkwardly worn rather than a habit of mind. But
none the less the scientific norm of mental activity presses
daily more close upon life and upon the schools. We are getting daily further away from the conditions in which one
subject more or less taught by dogmatic, catechetical and
memoriter methods was of slight consequence. We are becoming aware of the absurdity implied in calling things
which happen to be studied and learned in school "knowledge," when they have been acquired by methods frequently
at odds with those necessary to give science. Can those who
take the philosophic and historic view of religion as a flower
and fruition of the human spirit in a congenial atmosphere
tolerate the incongruity involved in "teaching" such an intimate and originally vital matter by external and formal
methods? And can those who hold that true religion is something externally imported tolerate any other methods? Is it
not confusion to seek a reconciliation of two such disparate
ideas?

Already the spirit of our schooling is permeated with
the feeling that every subject, every topic, every fact, every
professed truth must submit to a certain publicity and im-
partiality. All proffered samples of learning must go to the
same assay-room and be subjected to common tests. It is the
essence of all dogmatic faiths to hold that any such "show-

down" is sacrilegious and perverse. The characteristic of religion, from their point of view, is that it is—intellectually—secret, not public; peculiarly revealed, not generally known; authoritatively declared, not communicated and tested in ordinary ways. What is to be done about this increasing antinomy between the standard for coming to know in other subjects of the school, and coming to know in religious matters? I am far from saying that the antinomy is an inherent one, or that the day may not come when religion will be so thoroughly naturalized in the hearts and minds of men that it can be considered publicly, openly, and by common tests, even among religious people. But it is pertinent to point out that, as long as religion is conceived as it now is conceived by the great majority of professed religionists, there is something self-contradictory in speaking of education in religion in the same sense in which we speak of education in topics where the method of free inquiry has made its way. The "religious" would be the last to be willing that either the history or the content of religion should be taught in this spirit; while those to whom the scientific standpoint is not a merely technical device, but is the embodiment of integrity of mind, must protest against its being taught in any other spirit.

As Plato brought out with reference to the teaching of virtue, there is one other factor in coming to know—the teachers. Plato was quite sure that, whether or no virtue might be taught, it might not be taught by its professed teachers—the sophists. I express my appreciation of Plato rather than my lack of appreciation of the professional teachers of our own day, when I say that if Plato were to return to take part in the current discussion, he would raise questions about those who were to teach religion analogous to those he brought up about the teachers of his own time. It is not that those into whose hands the giving of instruction would fall are so irreligious or so non-religious as to be unfitted for the task. The sophists were doubtless superior rather than inferior in personal virtues to their average neighbor. It is one thing to be fairly or even exceptionally virtuous; it is another thing to command the conditions and the qualifications for successful importation of virtue to others. Where are the experts in religion? and where are the authoritative teachers? There are theologians: do we want theology taught? There are historians, but I fear the day has not come when the history of religion can be taught as history. Here precisely is one of those fields of clarification and criticism where much labor needs to be done, and where the professional religionist is one of the most serious obstacles to reckon with, since a wider and deeper historic knowledge would overthrow his traditional basis.

There are preachers and catechists, but, unless we are committed to some peculiar faith or institution, it is not exhortation or discipline of this sort that constitutes religious instruction. There are psychologists: but is introspection our aim? There remains, indeed, the corps of faithful, more or less well-prepared, hard-working and hard-worked teachers. This brings us to the crux of the whole matter. Is religion a thing so specialized, so technical, so "informational" that, like geography or history or grammar, it may be taught at special hours, times, and places by those who have properly "got it up," and been approved as persons of fit character and adequate professional training?

This question of the mode, time, and stuff of specific instruction trenches indeed upon a question in which national temper and tradition count for much. I am quite aware that upon this subject it is almost impossible for an Englishman and an American whose actual intellectual attitude in general is very much the same to understand each other. Nothing, I think, struck the American who followed the debates on the last English Educational Bill with more emphasis than the fact that even the more radical upon the Liberal side disclaimed, almost with horror, any intention of bringing about the state of things which we, upon this side, precisely take for granted as normal—all of us except Lutherans and Roman Catholics. I have no right to suppose that these protests and disclaimers were discreet concessions to political expediency. We must assume a profound difference of attitude and conviction. Consequently what I have now to say is conceived so definitely from the American point of view that it may not be intelligible in a different situation. But we do not find it feasible or desirable to put upon the regular teachers the burden of teaching a subject which has the nature of religion. The alternative plan of parcelling out pupils among religious teachers drawn from their respective churches and denominations brings us up against exactly the matter which has done most to discredit the churches, and to discredit the cause, not perhaps of religion, but of organized and institutional religion: the multiplication of rival and competing religious bodies, each with its private inspiration and outlook. Our schools, in bringing together those of different nationalities, languages, traditions, and creeds, in assimilating them together upon the basis of what is common and public in endeavor and achievement, are performing an infinitely significant religious work. They are promoting the social unity out of which in the end genuine religious unity must grow. Shall we interfere with this work? shall we run the risk of undoing it by introducing into education a subject which can be taught only by segregating pupils and turning them over at special hours to separate representatives of rival faiths? This would be deliberately to adopt a scheme which is predicated upon the maintenance of social divisions in just the matter, religion, which is empty and futile save as it expresses the basic unities of life. An acute English critic has recently called us, with much truth, a "nation of villagers." But in this matter of education at least we have no intention or desire of letting go our hard-won state-consciousness in order to relapse into divisive provinciality. We are far, indeed, from having attained an explicit and articulated consciousness of the religious significance of democracy in education, and of education in democracy. But some underlying convictions get ingrained in unconscious habit and find expression in obscure intimation and intense labor, long before they receive consistent theoretic formulation. In such dim, blind, but effective way the American people is conscious that its schools serve best the cause of religion in serving the cause of social unification; and that under certain conditions schools are more religious in substance and in promise without any of the conventional badges and machinery of religious instruction than they could be in cultivating these forms at the expense of a state-consciousness.

We may indeed question whether it is true that in any

relative sense this is a peculiarly irreligious age. Absolutely
speaking, it doubtless is so; but have superficiality, flippancy,
and externality of life been such uniformly absent traits of
past ages? Our historic imagination is at best slightly developed. We generalize and idealize the past egregiously. We
set up little toys to stand as symbols for long centuries and
the complicated lives of countless individuals. And we are
still, even those who have nominally surrendered supernatural dogma, largely under the dominion of the ideas of
those who have succeeded in identifying religion with the
rites, symbols, and emotions associated with these dogmatic
beliefs. As we see the latter disappearing, we think we are
growing irreligious. For all we know, the integrity of mind
which is loosening the hold of these things is potentially
much more religious than all that it is displacing. It is increased knowledge of nature which has made supra-nature
incredible, or at least difficult of belief. We measure the
change from the standpoint of the supranatural and we call
it irreligious. Possibly if we measured it from the standpoint
of the natural piety it is fostering, the sense of the permanent and inevitable implication of nature and man in a common career and destiny, it would appear as the growth of
religion. We take note of the decay of cohesion and influence among the religiously organized bodies of the familiar
historic type, and again we conventionally judge religion to
be on the decrease. But it may be that their decadence is the
fruit of a broader and more catholic principle of human intercourse and association which is too religious to tolerate
these pretensions to monopolize truth and to make private
possessions of spiritual insight and aspiration.

It may be so; it may be that the symptoms of religious
ebb as conventionally interpreted are symptoms of the coming of a fuller and deeper religion. I do not claim to know.
But of one thing I am quite sure: our ordinary opinions
about the rise and falling off of religion are highly conventional, based mostly upon the acceptance of a standard of
religion which is the product of just those things in historic
religions which are ceasing to be credible. So far as education is concerned, those who believe in religion as a natural
expression of human experience must devote themselves to

the development of the ideas of life which lie implicit in our still new science and our still newer democracy. They must interest themselves in the transformation of those institutions which still bear the dogmatic and the feudal stamp (and which do not?) till they are in accord with these ideas. In performing this service, it is their business to do what they can to prevent all public educational agencies from being employed in ways which inevitably impede the recognition of the spiritual import of science and of democracy, and hence of that type of religion which will be the fine flower of the modern spirit's achievement.

THE BEARINGS OF PRAGMATISM
UPON EDUCATION

First Paper

According to pragmatism, intelligence or the power of thought is developed out of the struggles of organic beings to secure a successful exercise of their functions. The doctrine may be compared to the theory of "economic interpretation of history," taken in its broad sense. According to this theory, the main features of the structure of any particular society are best understood by looking first into how that society went at the problem of maintaining itself in existence —how it undertook the primary business of "making its living." Similarly, the transformation and evolution of successive social states depend upon the introduction of new factors and forces into industrial production and exchange, so that men's points of view—judgment of values—and the location of power—of control of nature and hence of others— are changed. Now, in a somewhat analogous way, pragmatism holds that all the higher achievements of individual organic life result from the stress and strain of the problem of maintaining the functions of life. For life can be kept going only as the organism *"makes* its living," by proper manipulation of the environment and adjustment of the latter to its own vital ends. Reduced to their simplest terms, the biological problem of the individual and the economic problem of society are exactly the same. In each case the aim is to subordinate the materials and forces of the natural environment so that they shall be rendered tributary to life-functions.

Now, while this requires direct contact with things in seizing, digesting, etc., the limitations of the direct method of subjugation of materials to function are very great. The

[First published in *Progressive Journal of Education* 1 (Dec. 1908): 1–3; 1 (Jan. 1909): 5–8; 1 (Feb. 1909): 6–7.]

evolution of the nervous system represents the discovery of the advantages of indirect control by manipulation of the present environment on the basis of the past and future, of the felt and seen on the basis of the remote and foreseen.

On this basis, it is not the business of thought to mirror with theoretical or speculative exactness an outside world. It is its business to select whatever is relevant to the most effective carrying on of life functions, and to arrange what is selected, not on the basis of some outside pattern, but with reference to facilitating the complete practical performance of all the activities possible to an organic being. Knowledge, accordingly, is not an attempt to copy, after the fashion of an encyclopaedia, all the facts of the universe. It is the expression of man's past most successful achievements in effecting adjustments and adaptations, put in a form so as best to help sustain and promote the future still greater control of the environment.

This theory of the nature of intelligence and knowledge is contrasted with the two other theories which have practically divided the field between them in the past. One, which may be called the transcendental theory of pure rationalism, is that the mind is an immaterial entity, temporarily housed in a material organism, having thought or reason as its own independent or *a priori* power, and creating knowledge by the exercise of its faculties, just because it is the very nature of thought to produce knowledge. Knowledge, on this view, is an end complete in itself. It simply represents the deposit that results from the exercise of a purely theoretic faculty. It may possibly have some useful application in activity, but that is purely accidental—it is an afterthought. Knowledge is complete in itself just as soon as the purely theoretic capacity of reason has expressed itself.

The other contrasting view is that mind is a blank piece of paper, or a passive waxlike something on which objects impress themselves, and the accumulation of the records left behind constitutes knowledge. This view underlies, for example, Spencer's theory of evolution, according to which mental forms and powers have been developed by the constant impact of environmental forces, the more transient features obliterating one another's effects, while the more permanent have molded intelligence into their own likeness. Knowledge, on this view, is a replica or duplicate edition within consciousness of what already exists ready-made without.

Now the pragmatic view of mind and knowledge agrees with this latter account in that it regards mind as a development and lays a great stress upon the relation between organism and the environment. But it regards the evolution of mind as a growth out of the constant tendency of life to sustain and fulfill its own functions through subordinating environment to itself rather than by passively accommodating itself to a coercion working from without. It does not regard intelligence, therefore, as merely a result of evolution, but as also a factor in guiding the evolutionary process; for it regards intelligence as an evolution of the functions of life to the point at which they can be performed most effectively. Similarly, knowledge, on this view, is not a copy whose truth is to be judged by its fidelity to an original; *it is an instrument or organ of successful action.*

We do not judge the value of the hand or eye on the basis of their being copies of something previously existing in the environment, but on the basis of their worth as instrumentalities of adjustments. On the pragmatic view, the case is the same with knowledge. What measures its value, its correctness and truth, is the degree of its availability for conducting to a successful issue the activities of living beings.

What we call "theory" and pure science are not then academic exercises of an isolated or transcendental reason, working according to its own *a priori* laws. They are simply the product of an unbiased, *unprejudiced* view of the conditions and consequences of the most efficient and fruitful action. For the success of an activity may be judged from either a narrow or a wide standpoint. When the individual views everything with reference to his ends and needs in isolation from the society of which he is a member, we do not get scientific knowledge, but knowledge in the form of opinion and dogma. When the individual considers the conditions and results of his activities from the standpoint of their bearing on the successful issue, or welfare, of the activities of the community, he gets the broadest, most general (or objective) point of view possible for human beings from which to know. The result of taking this social, instead of the purely personal, point of view is knowledge in its best sense—namely, science. And history shows that the advance of science represents the gradual victory of the more generic, or social point of view over purely individual points of view, opinions, and merely class points of view—dogmas. *Pure* knowledge, in short, is knowledge on the basis of the widest and most effective application or service in social progress instead of that of individual advantage secured at the expense of others. It is therefore not properly opposed to applied or useful knowledge.

Since one of the main offices of education is the training of mind—since, indeed, this is the only office of education when we consider mind in its organic connections with character—a changed view of the nature and purpose of mind carries with it a very great change in educational ideas and practices. Education in the past has been dominated almost entirely by a combination of the two older views of mind which I have noted—that of a pure reason or of a purely passive and receptive vessel. In general, the education of the "leisure class," the prevalent idea of "culture," is based on the notion of a mind separate, so far as possible, from material conditions and soiled by contact with them, a mind whose highest end is production of knowledge for its own sake. On the other hand, education for the "masses" has been considered a process by which certain features of their environment were ground in upon them, till their minds were molded into passive and obedient conformity to the existing type about them. The distinctive and contrasted bearings of the pragmatic view of mind upon education must be for a further paper.

Second Paper

In the December number of this journal I showed that in the past educational theory and practice have been associated with two different theories of the nature of mind. One theory is that the highest faculty of mind is reason or pure thought, whose exercise results in knowledge. This view goes along with the notion that knowledge is an end in itself, apart from social uses and applications; it results in a theoretic type of education, one which its opponents condemn as scholastic and academic, while its upholders always defend it on the ground of "culture" and a "liberal," "humanistic" education. This type of education has prevailed almost entirely in the schools aiming to produce "gentlemen" in the English conventional sense—that is, members of the ruling and leisure class.

Another philosophy of mind has regarded mind as something purely passive, to be impressed from without by sensations and images which are then arranged to produce knowledge and beliefs. This notion has had its practical vogue mainly in education of the masses or "lower classes," with the effect, more or less consciously designed, of making them the passive and willing upholders of the existing order. For the things that were impressed upon the children of the lower schools were not, for the most part, natural objects and events; but the *symbols* of knowledge and of the art of calculation—the written and printed forms of language and the rudiments of arithmetic. The effect was two-fold. On the one hand, it developed mental dependency and submissiveness. *Docility*, or *obedient* absorption of material presented by school teacher and text-book, has been the traditional and conventional virtue of the schools. On the other hand, the social and economic conditions of elementary education have been such as to invite and to compel the great bulk of elementary school children to leave school at the point where they had enough reading, 'riting and 'rithmetic to make them more useful in subordinate economic positions, but not enough to encourage or enable them (save in rare instances) to rise to the point where they were masters of the direction of their own physical and mental powers.

Now, as was suggested in my prior article, the pragmatic theory of mind and of knowledge is adapted both to a different scheme of educational practice and to a different social aim for it. The pragmatic view of mind is that intelligence has developed primarily as an organ of readaptation and readjustment amid the needs of active functions that are continually increasing their complexity. The amoeba has little need of mind and knowledge. Its functions are simple, largely undifferentiated, and exercised in a medium which is simple, mainly all of one kind. Man lives in a highly differentiated environment, a natural and social world in which there is an endless diversity of factors to be taken account of; and where the maintenance of life and the successful achievement of ends depends upon delicate and far-reaching combinations of various factors. Every advance in civilization, every progressive social change, increases the number of factors at work and also the difficulty of keeping them balanced up (or coordinated, as we say, technically) with one another. The meal of the savage, his clothes, his shelter, bring into relation to one another only a scanty number of elements, existing at most over a short period of time, covering only a few square miles of space, and involving the cooperation of but a few score of people at most. The corresponding satisfactions of a modern denizen of a city, even of the poorest, are syntheses or coordinations of factors that operate almost over the entire world, cover a period of some years of successive activities and require the coadjustments of thousands of people.

Now this is only one illustration of a general law of development. The modern astronomer or chemist not only has thousands of facts to deal with where his ancestor had one, but he also has the problem of classifying, grouping each new fact; of fitting in with other facts, a process which perhaps requires the correction and reclassification of old facts as well as the interpretation of new ones. In this way, for example, the new facts discovered by Darwin were not merely added to old ones, but their discovery compelled a thorough re-examination and restatement of every previously known detail of botany and zoology. Wherever we look we find organic evolution both multiplying the number of details or elements that enter in, and also increasing the problem and the task of keeping these all properly balanced up with regard to one another. Otherwise, the mere increase in number and the unlikeness of parts would lead to utter confusion and a breakdown from dead weight. Because the human organism has so many more specialized parts or organs than the

amoeba or the oyster, it is exposed to the danger of thousands of maladjustments and failures of cooperative activities which do not confront the other animals. And the same
is true in comparing modern societies with savage groups.

The pragmatic theory points out that mind or intelligence is an accompaniment of just this process of organic
growth in nature and in society. Mind is, so to speak, a device for keeping track of the increased differentiation and
multiplication of conditions, and planning for, arranging for
in advance, ends and means of activity which will keep these
various factors in proper adjustment to one another. This explains the fact that all intelligence involves a peculiar combination of the sensory and receptive factor (emphasized by
the passive theory of education) with the active, intellectual
factor—emphasized by the theory of pure rational activity.
The function of sensation is to afford stimuli to properly directed behavior—i.e., to behavior which will keep the life
functions properly adjusted. With respect to knowledge, sensations indicate the condition of things with respect to which
the organism has to act. The object of sensations is not to
mirror or even register the whole external world, but simply
to make the individual agent aware of those things in the
environment which threaten its welfare or which afford the
resources needed at the given time in the life adjustments of
the individual. If we regard sensations as intended to give
knowledge of the external world in its entirety they are
ludicrously incompetent to the end. If we regard them as
devices for warning an agent of threatening dangers and for
calling out responses which will enable the agent to protect
himself and to avoid or destroy the obstacles, they are admirably fit for the purpose.

When, however, situations are complicated, the reports
that come to an organism of the state of things that require
attention if the organism is to hold its own are very diverse
and incompatible. It would be impossible for the organism
to react to them all at once; but it might be fatal for it arbitrarily to select one or a few, and ignore the others. A mistake in the selection must destroy the organism. Thinking
develops accordingly as a method of *valuing the importance*
of the various stimuli that demand attention. Judgment, in

the popular usage, is precisely power to estimate the *relative value* of things as claimants for notice and responsive behavior. A faint sound may be of more importance in the long run than a loud one; a dim light more fraught with consequence upon the welfare of the organism than a bright one. Thought is required to discount their immediate strength, and to interpret them on the basis of their *indirect* and remote *consequences*. The power of imagination weighs the various stimuli that are struggling to control action up against one another; devises a method for discounting those which may be only momentarily more violent, and works up seemingly insignificant reports. Thus imagination and thought are processes of estimating observed objects in the light of their possible future consequences. They are forecasts, tentative predictions or conjectures as to what present conditions indicate or prophesy regarding future developments. All ideas are of the nature of what the scientist calls "working hypotheses"; forecasts of what will happen under future conditions; forecasts employed moreover to guide and direct activities so that if possible the desirable conditions will be realized. Those ideas that really "work"; the forecasts that future events verify when they arrive; the plans and methods of behavior which successfully modify conditions in the direction desired, are *true*; and the term truth as applied to judgments and ideas has no other meaning than this.

I now touch briefly upon the bearings of this conception of mind upon the question of educational *method*, reserving for a later paper its bearings upon the *subject-matter* of study, and upon the social or moral basis and aim of schools:

1. Every educative process should begin with *doing something*; and the necessary training of sense perception, memory, imagination and judgment should grow out of the conditions and needs of what is being done. The something done should not be of the nature of an arbitrary task imposed by a taskmaster; but something inherently significant, and of such a nature that the pupil appreciates for himself its importance enough to take a vital interest in it. This is the way the child gets all the first training of his powers and all his first knowledge of the world. In carrying out his instinctive tendency to reach, handle, throw, a baby learns to

know his own limbs and their capacities, and becomes acquainted with the properties of things—their hardness, colors, form, size and a thousand and one properties. He did not start to know these things, nor did any teacher set him the lesson of finding out about them. He started to *do* something, and these results came necessarily.

For a few years of his life, the first few, a child's instinctive eagerness and the natural environment are so well adjusted that this educative training goes on at a very rapid rate and, relatively speaking, almost without oversight or guidance. There comes a time when a richer, fuller and more carefully selected and arranged environment is required to afford the stimuli and conditions of the most educative activity—an environment more varied than that of the ordinary home, and yet one not so varied, disorderly, overpowering and overspecialized as that of social life in general.

Conscious education begins at this point. If it were what it ought to be and what it may become, it would consist in the selection and arrangement of an environment of materials and tools, with models of the best artistic achievement of such a nature as to call out and exercise the child's life functions—to suggest to him, in other words, things worth doing and to keep him engaged in doing them. Teachers would be present, more competent, more experienced members of a society; but they would be present as fellow-workers and fellow-players—comrades in carrying on the scheme of play and work activities, and in building up, along with the children, a miniature world as the obvious result and reward of their joint activities.

2. Sense training would inevitably result from engaging in these various activities. The boy who plays marbles and ball, the girl who dresses and undresses her doll and makes clothes for her, gets a training of the senses which is all the more effective because it is incidental to the carrying on of some line of action, and is not set up as a special task or end in itself. Clay modeling, gardening, shop-work in wood or metal, cooking, weaving, etc.—these are the normal methods for cultivating power of observation and accurate interpretation of sensations. The race did not acquire its original store of information for the sake of knowledge, nor yet by

having natural objects impress themselves on the mind. It
learned about plants, animals, stones, metals, weather, etc.,
because a knowledge of these things was required to solve
problems of food, shelter, clothing, social cooperation and
defense and so on.

3. The more intellectual side of education, the store of
general ideas and principles, the requisition of habits of reflection and deliberation, should be placed on the same basis.
All thinking at its outset is planning, forecasting, forming
purposes, selecting and arranging means for their most economical and successful realization. Comparatively little opportunity is afforded in our present school systems for the
practical activities which are necessary to develop this type
of thought. Opportunities for independent manipulation of
materials, initiative and responsibility for getting results, for
detecting and correcting errors, are few and far between. As
a result, the power of thinking remains comparatively unde-
veloped except in the few who are naturally adapted to more
specialized and purely theoretic interests—children and youth
whose thinking clusters about the symbols for things, rather
than things themselves. Such persons get specialized naturally into an academic class of investigators and speculators.
The world doubtless owes a great deal to its pure "research-
ers" and scholars; but it would owe a great deal more still to
them if they had been educated into habits of thinking out
the bearings of their abstract ideas upon social matters. As
it is, they have been largely shunted off into an isolated and
remote class—isolated and remote socially, that is—where
the results of their thinking are quite "safe," because not
translated from symbols into the facts of action.

In an educational scheme which should embody practically the pragmatic conception of thought, intellectual instruction would have then the following traits: (a) It would
grow—all of it—out of the needs and opportunities of activities engaged in by the students themselves. This principle
would be universal. At present it is expressed sporadically; to
some extent in the kindergarten at the lower end, in the scientific laboratories at the upper, and in the manual and occupational activities of shop-work, cooking, etc., along the
line. (b) Information would not be amassed and accumu-

lated and driven into pupils as an end in itself, but would cluster about the development of activities. Some information is immediately required in order to do anything successfully; a child cannot garden intelligently without learning about soils, seeds, measures, plants and their growth, the facts of rain, sunshine, etc. Interest in the continuous carrying on of such an activity would, however, generate curiosity and openness of mind about many things not directly related to the immediate needs. Methods of agriculture in this and other lands, the historic evolution of this occupation, the social and economic problems connected with it, have a natural interest and avenue to the mind of one who has developed personal interest in a similar activity which they cannot have for one who merely hears or reads about them second hand. One great object then in having school work organized mainly about certain continuous lines of occupation is that these afford natural axes for the collection and organization of all kinds of facts and ideas. (c) Instruction carried on upon this basis would teach the mind that all ideas, truths, theories, etc., are of the nature of *working hypotheses*. One of the chief obstacles to the progress of the race has been the *dogmatic* habit of mind, the belief that some principles and ideas have such a final value and authority that they are to be accepted without question and without revision. The *experimental* habit of mind, that which regards ideas and principles as tentative methods of solving problems and organizing data, is very recent. An education based upon the pragmatic conception would inevitably turn out persons who were alive to the necessity of continually testing their ideas and beliefs by putting them into practical application, and of revising their beliefs on the basis of the results of such application.

Concluding Paper

Having spoken of the pragmatic theory in general and of its special bearings upon educational method, I propose to speak briefly of its connection with educational subject-matter, or the material of the course of study. For the last

two or three centuries educational reformers have protested
against the conventional scheme of studies on the ground
of its artificiality and remoteness from life. At first they protested against its verbal and linguistic character, against the
fact that it was devoted so exclusively to symbols of learning. This protest has been more or less effectual and material from nature (the sciences) and from the life of man
(history) introduced into the schools. Then there was a protest against the exclusively informational character of these
studies—against the emphasis upon memorizing and the accumulation of knowledge—and a demand for what would
connect more directly and more usefully with contemporary
social requirements. Industrial drawing, manual training, the
rudiments of various arts have been introduced in response
to this demand. If we add to the list of studies finally pursued in the schools the subjects of music and the other "fine"
arts, we do not wonder that there has grown up an outcry
against an overloaded curriculum, lacking in unity and concentration, scattering and overstraining the activities of both
teachers and children. There has even been a cry for a return
to the simplicity of the meagre fare of the old-fashioned
three R's. But is there not some other way of securing organization of material and unity of purpose?

The education of the human race, upon the whole, has
been gained through the *occupations* which it has pursued
and developed. The vocations, the professions, the lines of
activity which have been socially evolved, have furnished the
social stimuli to knowledge and the centres about which it
has been organized. If occupations were made fundamental
in education, school work would conform to the natural principles of social and mental development. The beginnings of
this reform have already been introduced. Froebel got a
glimpse of this conception in his scheme of education for infancy, though his policy was too romantic and symbolic to
permit the idea to get adequate expression. Engineering and
technical schools, in which the sciences are pursued in reference to their social uses, illustrate, at the upper end of the
school ladder, another aspect of the same principle. The increasing emphasis upon gardening, horticulture, cooking,
weaving, shop-work in wood and metal in the elementary

and secondary schools is another symptom of the same movement. The ultimate value and (let us hope) destiny of the present movement toward industrial education will depend upon whether it becomes switched off into a method of class-education—in which case it would be better for it to perish immediately—or whether it recognizes the fundamental importance of training in typical and continuous lines of activity, which are of social value for everybody.

It is a serious error to think of occupational activities as if they were merely of prosaic and utilitarian, or even commercial, worth. Their primary value is educational. It consists in training the thinking of the boys and girls in connection with things that appeal to them as worth doing, instead of training thought-power by partly formal tasks and gymnastic exercises. It does not exclude, but includes a broad and liberal scheme of knowledge. All typical social occupations rest upon scientific insight and information. One of the chief values of shop-work, weaving, gardening, etc., even in elementary schools, is that they introduce the pupil to natural facts and forces and give him a motive for becoming thoroughly acquainted with the concrete facts and laws of nature. The historic development of the occupations by which men have subjugated nature by learning its secrets, and have learned how to cooperate with another for common ends, gives the key to the study of history; it indicates what is important and what is trivial in the mass of facts that has come down from the past. An adequate mastery of typical occupations brings the pupil to a study of the social conditions and aims of the present; to facts which, when classified, form sociology, political economy, civics and politics. The fine arts are naturally included; for, as Morris and others have pointed out, all embodiment of ideas in external form, when done freely and with joy in the activity, tends to gain an artistic quality. In short, there is nothing of science, history or art which the educational experience of the past has shown to be of worth which an occupational education would not include. Old values would be conserved, but would be centralized about a new principle and acquire the vitality of a new motive.

Finally, such an education would change the morale of

the school. Since the activities of the latter would be continuous with the interests and activities of men and women at large, the school would lose the special code of ethics and moral training, which must characterize it as long as it is isolated. It would take up into itself the moral aims and forces of social sympathy, cooperation and progress. Occupations bring people naturally together in groups, develop a group of consciousness and power to divide and yet cooperate harmoniously. Knowledge, scholastic attainments, aesthetic culture, pursued, as at present, with only personal ends in view, tend to egoism, social stratifications and antagonisms.

HISTORY FOR THE EDUCATOR

If history be regarded as just the record of the past, it is hard to see any grounds for claiming that it should play any large role in the curriculum of elementary education. The past is the past, and the dead may be safèly left to bury its dead. There are too many urgent demands in the present, too many calls over the threshold of the future, to permit the child to become deeply immersed in what is forever gone by. Not so when history is considered as an account of the forces and forms of social life. Social life we have always with us; the distinction of past and present is indifferent to it. Whether it was lived just here or just there is a matter of slight moment. It is life for all that; it shows the motives which draw men together and push them apart and depicts what is desirable and what is hurtful. Whatever history may be for the scientific historian, for the educator it must be an indirect sociology—a study of society which lays bare its process of becoming and its modes of organization. Existing society is both too complex and too close to the child to be studied. He finds no clues in its labyrinth of detail and can mount no eminence whence to get a perspective of arrangement.

If the aim of historical instruction is to enable the child to appreciate the values of social life, to see in imagination the forces which favor men's effective cooperation with one another, to understand the sorts of character that help and that hold back, the essential thing in its presentation is to make it moving, dynamic. History must be presented, not as an accumulation of results or effects, a mere statement of what happened, but as a forceful, acting thing. The motives —that is, the motors—must stand out. To study history is not to amass information, but to use information in constructing

[First published in *Progressive Journal of Education* 1 (Mar. 1909): 1–4.]

a vivid picture of how and why men did thus and so;
achieved their successes and came to their failures.

When history is conceived as dynamic, as moving, its
economic and industrial aspects are emphasized. These are
but technical terms which express the problem with which
humanity is unceasingly engaged—how to live, how to master and use nature so as to make it tributary to enrichment
of human life. The great advances in civilization have come
through those manifestations of intelligence which have
lifted man from his precarious subjection to nature and revealed to him how he may make its forces cooperate with his
own purposes.

The social world in which the child now lives is so rich
and full that it is not easy to see how much it cost, how much
effort and thought lie back of it. Man has a tremendous
equipment ready at hand. The child may be led to translate
these ready-made resources into fluid terms; he may be led
to see man face to face with nature, without inherited capital, without tools, without manufactured materials. And,
step by step, he may follow the processes by which man recognized the needs of his situation, thought out the weapons
and instruments that enabled him to cope with them; and
may learn how these new resources opened new horizons of
growth and created new problems. The industrial history of
man is not a materialistic or merely utilitarian affair. It is
a matter of intelligence. Its record is the record of how man
learned to think, to think to some effect, to transform the
conditions of life so that life itself became a different thing.
It is an ethical record as well; the account of the conditions
which men have patiently wrought out to serve their ends.

The question of how human beings live, indeed, represents the dominant interest with which the child approaches
historic material. It is this point of view which brings those
who worked in the past close to the beings with whom he is
daily associated, and confers upon him the gift of sympathetic penetration.

The child who is interested in the way in which men
lived, the tools they had to do with, the new inventions they
made, the transformations of life that arose from the power
and leisure thus gained, is eager to repeat like processes in

his own action, to remake utensils, to reproduce processes, to rehandle materials. Since he understands their problems and their successes only by seeing what obstacles and what resources they had from nature, the child is interested in field and forest, ocean and mountain, plant and animal. By building up a conception of the natural environment in which lived the people he is studying, he gets his hold upon their lives. This reproduction he cannot make excepting as he gains acquaintance with the natural forces and forms with which he is himself surrounded. The interest in history gives a more human coloring, a wider significance, to his own study of nature. His knowledge of nature lends point and accuracy to his study of history. This is the natural "correlation" of history and science.

This same end, a deepening appreciation of social life, decides the place of the biographic element in historical instruction. That historical material appeals to the child most completely and vividly when presented in individual form, when summed up in the lives and deeds of some heroic character, there can be no doubt. Yet it is possible to use biographies so that they become a collection of mere stories, interesting possibly, to the point of sensationalism, but yet bringing the child no nearer to comprehension of social life. This happens when the individual who is the hero of the tale is isolated from his social environment; when the child is not brought to feel the social situations which evoked his acts and the social progress to which his deeds contributed. If biography is presented as a dramatic summary of social needs and achievements, if the child's imagination pictures the social defects and problems that clamored for the man and the ways in which the individual met the emergency, then the biography is an organ of social study.

A consciousness of the social aim of history prevents any tendency to swamp history in myth, fairy story, and merely literary renderings. I cannot avoid the feeling that much as the Herbartian school has done to enrich the elementary curriculum in the direction of history, it has often inverted the true relationship existing between history and literature. In a certain sense the *motif* of American colonial history and of De Foe's "Robinson Crusoe" are the same. Both represent man who has achieved civilization, who has attained a certain maturity of thought, who has developed ideals and means of action; but suddenly thrown back upon his own resources, having to cope with a raw and often hostile nature, and to regain success by sheer intelligence, energy, and persistence of character. But when "Robinson Crusoe" supplies the material for the curriculum of the third or fourth grade child are we not putting the cart before the horse? Why not give the child the reality with its much larger sweep, its intenser forces, its more vivid and lasting value for life, using the "Robinson Crusoe" as an imaginative idealization in a particular case of the same sort of problem and activities? Again, whatever may be the worth of the study of savage life in general, and of the North American Indians in particular, why should that be approached circuitously through the medium of "Hiawatha" instead of at first hand?—employing, indeed, the poem to furnish the idealized and culminating touches to a series of conditions and struggles which the child has previously realized in more specific form. Either the life of the Indian presents some permanent questions and factors in social life or it has next to no place in a scheme of instruction. If it has such a value, this should be made to stand out on its own account instead of being lost in the very refinement and beauty of a purely literary presentation.

The same end, the understanding of character and social relations in their natural dependence, enables us, I think, to decide upon the importance to be attached to chronological order in historical instruction. Considerable stress has been laid upon the supposed necessity of following the development of civilization through the successive steps in which it actually took place—beginning with the valleys of the Euphrates and the Nile, and coming on down through Greece, Rome, etc. The point urged is that the present depends upon the past, and each phase of the past upon a prior past.

We are here introduced to a conflict between the logical and psychological interpretation of history. If the aim be an appreciation of what social life is and how it goes on, then, certainly, the child must deal with what is near in spirit, not with the remote. The difficulty with the Babylonian or Egyp-

tian life is not so much its remoteness in time as its remoteness from the present interests and aims of social life. It does
not simplify enough and it does not generalize enough; or, at
least, it does not do so in the right way. It does it by omission
of what is significant now rather than by presenting these
factors arranged on a lower scale. Its salient features are hard
to get at and to understand, even by the specialist. It undoubtedly presents factors which contributed to later life and
which modified the course of events in the stream of time.
But the child has not arrived at a point where he can appreciate abstract causes and specialized contributions. What he
needs is a picture of typical relations, conditions and activities. In this respect there is much of prehistoric life which is
much closer to him than the complicated and artificial life
of Babylon or of Egypt. When a child is capable of appreciat-
ing institutions he is capable of seeing what special institutional idea each historic nation stands for and what factor
it has contributed to the present complex of institutions. But
this period arrives only when the child is beginning to be
capable of abstracting causes in other realms as well; in other
words, when he is approaching the time of secondary education.

The principle stated, together with the applications indicated to industrial history, to biography and story, and to
chronological sequence, will explain, in a general way, a
program which has been outlined. In this general scheme
three periods of phases are recognized:

First comes the generalized and simplified history—history which is hardly history at all in the local or chronological sense, but which aims at giving the child insight into,
and sympathy with, a variety of social activities. This period
includes the work of the six-year-old children in studying typical occupations of people in the country and city at present;
of the seven-year-old children in working out the evolution
of inventions and their effect upon life, and of the eight-
year-old children in dealing with the great movements of
migration, exploration and discovery which have brought the
whole round world into human ken. The work of the first two
years is evidently quite independent of any particular people or any particular person—that is, of historical data in the

ESSAYS 197

strict sense of the term. At the same time, plenty of scope is
provided through dramatization for the introduction of the
individual factor. The account of the great explorers and the
discoverers serves to make the transition to what is local and
specific, that which depends upon certain specified persons
who lived at certain specified places and times.

This introduces us to the second period where local conditions and the definite activities of particular bodies of people become prominent—corresponding to the child's growth
in power of dealing with limited and positive fact. Since Chicago, since the United States, are localities with which the
child can, by the nature of the case, most effectively deal, the
material of the next three years is derived directly and indirectly from this source. Here, again, the third year is a transitional year, taking up the connections of American life with
European.

By this time the child should be ready to deal, not with
social life in general, or even with the social life with which
he is most familiar, but with certain thoroughly differentiated, and, so to speak, peculiar types of social life; with the
special significance of each and the particular contribution it
has made to the whole world history. Accordingly, in the next
period the chronological order is followed, beginning with the
ancient world about the Mediterranean and coming down
again through European history to the peculiar and differen-
tiating factors of American history.

The program is not presented as the only one meeting
the problem, but as a contribution, the outcome not of
thought but of considerable experimenting and shifting of
subjects from year to year, to the problem of giving material
which takes vital hold upon the child; and, at the same time,
leads on, step by step, to more thorough and accurate knowledge of both the principles and facts of social life, and makes
a preparation for later specialized historic studies.

THE PURPOSE AND ORGANIZATION OF PHYSICS TEACHING IN SECONDARY SCHOOLS

One not professionally or technically acquainted with a subject of instruction can, without presumption, only state the *points of view* from which he thinks that subject should be treated to obtain its maximum efficiency. With material so comprehensive and so detailed as that of physics, selections and rejections must in any case take place and take place from some standpoint. And the material thus selected must be brought to the student in a certain atmosphere of context and motive. Concerning these principles of selection and motivation a non-physicist may, perhaps, say a few words without trespassing where he has no business.

1. The importance of the social applications of physical science in modern life should be borne constantly in mind both in selecting and in presenting subject-matter. The business of the high school is primarily a social business, not of creating a class of specialists. The public that pays taxes for the support of schools is justified in requiring that whenever it can be accomplished without doing violence to the subject taught, the subject shall be so taught as to make individuals more intelligent and hence more competent in doing their share in social life. Contemporary civilization rests so largely upon applied science that no one can really understand it who does not grasp something of the scientific methods and results that underlie it; on the other hand, a consideration of scientific resources and achievements from the standpoint of their application to the control of industry, transportation, communication, not only increases the future social efficiency of those instructed, but augments the immediate vital appeal and interest of the subject.

2. Scientific method in its largest sense is the justification on its intelligent side of science teaching, and the forma-

[First published in *School Science and Mathematics* 9 (1909): 291–92.]

tion of scientific habits of mind should be the primary aim
of the science teacher in the high school. Scientific methods
in their largest sense are more than matter of pure technique
of measurement, manipulation and experimentation. There
may come a period in the training of scientific specialists
when these things for the time being become ends in themselves. In secondary education their value and hence their
limits are fixed by the extent to which they react to create
and develop logical attitudes and habits of mind. The methods of experimental inquiry and testing which give intellectual integrity, sincerity and power in *all* fields, rather than
those which are peculiar to his specialty, are what the high-
school teacher should bear in mind. A *new type of mind* is
gradually developing under the influence of scientific methods; the physics teacher should do what in him lies to hasten
the extension and the supremacy of this type of mind.

I want to add a word about one aspect of the training
on its logical side. Almost all intellectual subjects have inherited notions of *law* from earlier thought which are essentially "metaphysical" in character—in the bad sense of metaphysical. Laws are conceived either after the analogy of jural
and legal ordinances as cast iron decrees which somehow
"govern" facts and events; or else as mere sequences and
coexistences that happen to be uniformly repeated in these
facts and events. In the popular mind there is a fusion of
these two views. Anyone who knows the history of philosophy can put his finger on the origin of these notions; they
arose outside of science and were imported into science from
outside. Conceived in either of these ways, laws lack intellectual vitality and significance. Instead of being organic aids
to thinking, they mark fixed external limits that have been
set to thinking. The very notion of law, in addition, becomes
a confusing puzzle. Logically laws are the general methods
by which we introduce continuity and order in experiences
otherwise discrepant and mixed up. They are instrumentalities of bridging over the gaps in our experience of things;
they are instrumentalities of reducing seeming conflicts to
harmony. In other words, treat laws as *logical* tools and
weapons and their wonderful value becomes self-evident.
Otherwise laws are metaphysical puzzles. Intellectual devices

of introducing continuity and system laws *certainly* are; let us begin with what is certain; if laws are also more than logical instrumentalities, this surplus over and above the logical can safely be left for discussion when the student comes to metaphysical studies.

TEACHING THAT DOES NOT EDUCATE

With the development of reflective attention come the need and the possibility of a change in the mode of the child's instruction. The direct, spontaneous attitude marks the child till into his seventh year, caused by his demand for new experiences, and his desire to complete his partial experiences by building up images and expressing them in play. This attitude is typical of what writers call spontaneous attention, or, as some say, non-voluntary attention.

The child is simply absorbed in what he is doing; the occupation in which he is engaged lays complete hold on him. He gives himself without reserve. Hence, while there is much energy spent, there is no *conscious* effort; while the child is intent, to the point of engrossment, there is no *conscious* intention.

With the development of a sense of more remote ends, and of the need of directing acts so as to make them means for these ends, we have the transition to what is termed indirect, or, as some writers prefer to say, voluntary, attention. A result is imagined, and the child attends to what is before him or what he is immediately doing, because it helps to secure the result. Taken by itself, the object or the act might be indifferent or even repulsive. But because it is felt to belong to something desirable or valuable, it borrows the latter's attracting or holding power.

This is the transition to "voluntary" attention, but only the transition. The latter comes fully into being only when the child entertains results in the form of problems or questions, the solution of which he is to seek for himself. In the intervening stage (in the child from eight to, say, eleven or twelve), while the child directs a series of intervening activities on the basis of some end he wishes to reach, this end

[First published in *Progressive Journal of Education* 1 (June 1909): 1-3.]

is something to be done or made, or some tangible result to be reached; the problem is a practical difficulty, rather than an intellectual question. But with growing power, the child can conceive of the end as something to be found out, discovered, and can control his acts and images so as to help in the inquiry and solution. This is reflective attention proper.

In history work there is change from the story and biography form, from the discussion of questions that arise to the formulation of questions. Points about which difference of opinion is possible, matters upon which experience, reflection, etc., can be brought to bear, are always coming up in history. But to use the discussion to develop this matter of doubt and difference into a definite problem, to bring the child to feel just what the difficulty is, and then throw him upon his own resources in looking up material bearing upon the point and upon his judgment in bringing it to bear, or getting a solution, is a marked intellectual advance. In Latin there is the change from hearing and reading stories, speaking and writing answers upon certain points, to problems of inflection and syntax—bringing to light the theoretical significance of matters already practically dealt with.

In general this growth is a natural psychical process. But the proper recognition and use of it is perhaps the most serious problem in instruction upon the intellectual side. A person who has gained the power of reflective attention, the power to hold problems, questions, before the mind, *is*, in so far, intellectually speaking, *educated*. He has mental discipline—the power *of* the mind and *for* the mind. Without this the mind remains at the mercy of custom and external suggestions. Some of the difficulties may be barely indicated by referring to an error that almost dominates instruction of the usual type. Too often it is assumed that attention can be given directly to any subject-matter, if only the proper will or disposition be at hand, failure being regarded as a sign of unwillingness or indocility. Lessons in arithmetic, geography and grammar are put before the child, and he is told to attend in order to learn. But excepting as there is some question, some doubt, present in the mind as a *basis* for this attention, *reflective* attention is impossible. If there is sufficient *intrinsic* interest in the material, there will be direct or spontaneous attention, which is excellent so far as it goes, but which barely of itself does not give power of thought or internal mental control. If there is not an inherent attracting power in the material, then (according to his temperament and training, and the precedents and expectations of the school) the teacher will either attempt to surround the material with foreign attractiveness, making a bid or offering a bribe for attention by "making the lesson interesting"; or else will resort to counter-irritants (low marks, threats of non-promotion, staying after school, personal disapprobation, expressed in a great variety of ways, naggings, continuous calling upon the child to "pay attention," etc.), or, probably, will use some of both means.

But (1) the attention thus gained is never more than partial, or divided, and (2) it always remains dependent upon something external—hence, when the attraction ceases or the pressure lets up, there is little or no gain in inner or intellectual control. And (3) such attention is always for the sake of "learning," *i.e., memorizing ready-made answers to possible questions to be put by another.* True attention, reflective attention, on the other hand, always involves judging, reasoning, deliberation; it means that the child has a question of his own, and is actively engaged in seeking and selecting relevant material with which to answer it, considering the bearings and relations of this material—the kind of solution it calls for. The problem is one's own, hence also the impetus, the stimulus to attention, is one's own; hence also the training secured is one's own—it is discipline, or gain in power of control; that is, a *habit* of considering problems.

It is hardly too much to say that in the traditional education so much stress has been laid upon the presentation to the child of ready-made material (books, object-lessons, teacher's talks, etc.), and the child has been so almost exclusively held to bare responsibility for reciting upon this ready-made material that there has been only accidental occasion and motive for developing reflective attention. Next to no consideration has been paid to the fundamental necessity—leading the child to realize a problem as his own, so that he is self-induced to attend in order to find out its answer. So completely have the conditions for securing this

self-putting of problems been neglected that the very idea of
voluntary attention has been radically perverted. It is regarded as measured by unwilling effort—as activity called
out by foreign, and even repulsive, material under conditions
of strain, instead of as self-initiated effort. "Voluntary" is
treated as meaning the reluctant and disagreeable instead
of the free, the self-directed, through personal interest, insight and power.

THE MORAL SIGNIFICANCE OF THE COMMON SCHOOL STUDIES

It may assist comprehension of the more specific portions of this paper if we begin with stating the standpoint from which the paper is conceived. Why should we expect the subject-matter of school studies to have any moral value? How can bodies of knowledge, of information, get transmuted into character? Have we any right to suppose that the miracle of changing facts, ideas, artistic products into the fibre of personal endeavor can be wrought? Unless we bear two principles in mind—bear them in mind by engraving them in practice—the expectation is unreasonable.

The two principles are that the subject-matter of the studies represents the results of past human social struggles and achievements, and that mind—the capacities of knowing by which the subject-matter is laid hold of and digested—is a manifestation of primary impulses in their efforts to master the environments. Because art, natural science, and mathematics have been evolved in the doings and sufferings of man, they are something more than merely intellectual; they are the outcome of human desire, passion, endeavor, success and failure. They have not been produced by some mind in the abstract, interested only in knowing, but have been worked out in the long-continued, arduous struggle of man to come into sound and effective connection with nature and with fellowman. Because of this fact they are full of moral meaning.

In like fashion, the powers with which children assimilate subject-matter are outgrowths of native instincts and reactions, tendencies much more akin to hunger, thirst, reach-

[First published in Northern Illinois Teachers' Association, *Topics for General Sessions: Moral and Religious Training in the Public Schools, November 5th and 6th, 1909, Elgin, Illinois*, pp. 21–27.]

ing, handling, moving about than to separate independent faculties of theoretical knowing.

These general statements indicate the source both of failure and of success in using subject-matter as a means of moral nurture. When studies are treated as just so many studies to be learned by pure intellectual faculties of memory, thought, etc., the moral outcome is insecure and accidental. When they are treated as human achievements, appealing to tendencies in childhood which are aiming however unconsciously and partially at similar achievements, the moral connection is positive and direct.

Art, of which literature is only one branch, though the one most readily available for school uses, is perhaps the most unmixed and the simplest record of the consummation of human endeavor. For this reason, it has been overworked in the schools as a moral force compared with other subjects. Children are easily stimulated,—their emotions are stirred,— and teachers are apt to assume that a somewhat momentary reaction of the feelings is a distinct ethical gain. In the early years, serious limitations attend the use of reading matter. The child's capacity to take in ideas through eye-symbols is so slight that "literature" is apt to be puerile intellectually, and the best of intentions to point a moral do not make up for triviality and paucity of ideas. For this reason, the ear is the natural channel, but there is danger that even oral stories and poems be made up on the basis of success in catching momentary attention and arousing signs of excitement. It is not a matter of accident that classic stories, as nearly as possible in their classic form, are more valuable than stories or poems composed for children. They *are* classics because they have passed through the medium of successive generations and have been proved true to the essentials of human experience. Their endurance is the stamp of their sterling, their genuine nature, while things written for children are mostly only paper money, even if not counterfeit. The chief protection lies in remembering that literature is a branch of *art*, so that if the literary material, whether prose or poetry, oral or printed, does not show the marks of highly selected, purified and refined experience, its effect upon children, even when striking, is likely to be sensational rather than morally educative. Physical reactions and the emotional thrills that accompany them closely simulate moral responses, and the parent or teacher who judges the worth of story and poems on the basis of the immediate excitement aroused instead of judging the latter on the basis of the intrinsic significance of the experiences condensed in the work of art is turning the scale of values upside down.

Given genuine art, genuine crystallization of what is important in life, in literature and the chief condition of its moral influence is that it be unconsciously absorbed, not consciously driven in, raked over and pulled up. Nothing is more absurd in theory or harmful in practice than first insisting upon the intrinsic ethical value of literature, and then impressing by suggestion, question, and discourse, the moral point or lesson to be derived from the piece of literature. What this really means is that the teacher has no faith in the moral force of the scene and ideas presented, but has great faith in his own conversation and personal influence. Consequently, while he talks about the moral import of a poem or story, in fact he only uses it as an occasion for his own moralizings. The result is the destruction of the piece in question as a work of art; and whatever accidental moral influence accrues being due to the teacher's personality and method, it could have been got as well from the multiplication table by the exercise of a little ingenuity.

One can hardly remind himself too often that works of art are appreciated, not consciously dissected. To say that they are appreciated means that the organ for taking them in is a sympathetic imagination. They are apprehended in terms of the analogous instincts and experience which they arouse in the spectator or auditor. The appeal is direct and hence unconscious. Somehow, nobody can tell just how, the person responds; he puts himself in tune with the theme and its mode of treatment, he takes on the color of the scene presented. The process is one of silent adjustment, of absorption, of assimilation, involving a gradual making over of personal fibre. Conscious effort to secure the desired moral result may arrest the process of assimilation; it cannot hasten it. Intellectual digestion and reconstruction are slow and organic processes. Conscious and short cuts to the end only leave superficial, perverted, and conventional results behind.

Appreciation of literature is moreover a personal, a highly individual matter. The teacher, like any skilled critic, may heighten another's appreciation of a work of art by indicating how he himself is affected, what memories and expectations are aroused in himself. But when he decides in advance that the moral truth of a given poem or literary transcript *is* just thus and so, and then enforces this upon a class as a whole, a class composed of individuals of different temperaments, experiences, and preferences, he tends to fix in the pupils' minds a conventional, superficial interpretation, and thus arbitrarily prevent the work of art accomplishing its own and perfect work. There is a certain impertinence in any case in forestalling the deeper and organic responses of other persons, whether children or adults; a certain presumptuous lack of sympathy in insisting upon one's own reaction as typical and essential. And the worst of it is when the teacher undertakes to make a piece of literary art an excuse for tagging on "morals," he rarely gets the benefit even of his own genuine response, but falls back upon nondescript stereotyped generalities.

In short, since art represents the purified consummation, the selected consummation of human experience, its ethical value, at its best, is indeed supreme. But because its work is so vital, its mode of operation is most delicate, is most easily disturbed and disarranged. "Literature" has no magical automatic efficacy simply because it is called literature. Its importance measures also the dangers of its use, and hence while it cannot be said that current pedagogical traditions exaggerate the moral value of literature, it is nevertheless true that they are highly misleading so far as they create the belief that literature is the chief *conscious* moral resource of the teacher with respect to the various branches of subject-matter.

History, rather than literature, represents doubtless the most effective conscious tool (I am not speaking of the various active occupations and exercises of the pupil, but of the stock studies of the curriculum). Here conscious analysis, the study of motives and results, comes into play. Even here it must be remembered, however, that conscious attention

ESSAYS   209

should be directed not to what the teacher regards as the
peculiar moral truth embodied in the portion of history under consideration, but to the *subject-matter itself*, to clear up
its obscurities, to render it more vivid and vital, to build up,
in short, a complete scene to which pupils may respond as a
whole. That the "kingdom of God cometh not with observation" may be taken to mean, among other things, that the
reactions which induce moral growth are too total and too
personal to be laid out in advance by even the most competent teacher. *His* work, in the case of history as well as of
literature, is to so see that full justice is done in the presentation of the objective subject-matter that the moral response
must come in the pupil's assimilative reactions.

This being premised, we naturally ask what it is in the
historical subject-matter that specially lends itself to a growth
of desirable personal attitudes. Putting the matter first in a
somewhat technical way, we may say that as literature affords the occasion for realizing the select consummation, the
achieved ideals and standards of human experience, so history affords the materials for apprehending its typical *problems*, the chief *obstructions* to development, the chief *methods* of progress. It gives *processes* rather than results—and
for this reason lends itself so rapidly to analytic discussion.[1]

It is commonly stated that history must be studied from
the standpoint of cause and effect. The truth of this statement depends upon its interpretation. Social life is so complex and the various parts of it are so organically related to
one another and to the natural environment, that it is impossible to say that this or that thing is the cause of some
other particular thing. But the study of history can reveal
the main instruments in the discoveries, inventions, new
modes of life, etc., which have initiated the great epochs of
social advance; and it can present to the child types of the
main lines of social progress, and can set before him what
have been the chief difficulties and obstructions in the way
of progress. This can be done so far as it is recognized that
social forces in themselves are always the same,—that the

1. From this point on, this paper follows the lines of my *Moral
Principles in Education*, pp. 32–43 (Houghton, Mifflin and Co.,
1909). [This volume, pp. 279–85.]

same kind of influences were at work one hundred and one thousand years ago that are now working,—and that particular historical epochs afford illustration of the way in which the fundamental forces work.

Everything depends, then, upon history being treated from a social standpoint; as manifesting the agencies which have influenced social development, and as presenting the typical institutions in which human experience naturally assumes form. The culture-epoch theory, while working in the right direction, has failed to recognize the importance of treating past periods with relation to the present,—as affording insight into the representative factors of its structure; it has treated these periods too much as if they had some meaning or value in themselves. The biographical method is often treated in such a way as to exclude from the child's consciousness (or at least not sufficiently to emphasize) the social values involved, which give the biographies their moral significance. Isolated stories about heroes, about George Washington and Abraham Lincoln, belong to literature rather than to history, and, except when told by a master, to second-rate literature. Of course, it is individuals who are important, not abstract forces and causes; but there is a fundamental difference between methods which dole out isolated anecdotes however thrilling or however calculated to impress a moral, and methods in which the leader is seen as one individual among many, summing up, by guidance, their powers and meeting needs which help in the peculiar social environment in which he lives and works. The individual disconnected from his social situation is ethically unreal, and no devices for instilling, through stories about him, lessons of truth-telling, patriotism, industry, etc., succeed in really concealing the moral unreality of the case.

In short, the ethical value of history teaching is measured by the extent to which past events are made the means of understanding the present,—affording insight into what makes up the structure and working of society today. Existing social structure is exceedingly complex. It is practically impossible for the child to attack it en masse and get any definite mental image of it. But type phases of historical development may be selected which will exhibit, as through a telescope, the essential constituents of the existing order.

The separation of geography from history on one side, and from "nature study" on the other, is quite artificial. History does not go on "in the air," and even if it did, the air would still be intimately one with the earth. Human action takes place under natural conditions; it is modified by geographical conditions, and in turn it transforms them. History would be meaningless if it were writ in water; if it did not leave behind itself permanent changes in nature which make it possible for later generations to take up their work on a higher plane of activity. Reverence for the natural, the physical, conditions of human well-being is perhaps the chief moral accomplishment of the study of science.

Hence, the beginning must be social geography, the frank recognition of the earth as the home of men acting in relations to one another. The essence of any geographical fact is the consciousness of two persons, or two groups of persons, who are at once separated and connected by their physical environment, and that the interest is in seeing how these people are at once kept apart and brought together in their actions by the instrumentality of the physical environment. The ultimate significance of lake, river, mountain, and plain is not physical but social,—the part played in modifying and directing human relationships. This evidently involves an extension of commercial geography, which has to do not simply with business in the narrow sense, but with whatever relates to human intercourse and intercommunication as affected by natural forms. Political geography represents the same social interaction in a static, instead of in a dynamic way; that is, as temporarily crystallized in certain forms.

If it be asked what this has to do with the moral bearing of geography, the answer is not far to seek. The development of character is not exhausted in learning the nature of the various virtues and in having their importance emotionally impressed. Effective character—and this is increasingly true under modern conditions of life—requires intelligence regarding the natural resources and conditions of action. Morality severed from an understanding of the conditions in which action takes effect is sentimental or else routine.

In its broad sense, the study of the earth as genuinely

the *home* of man, geography includes nature study. Plants and animals live on the earth; knowledge of them disconnected from the total scene of which they are a part, results in mere scrappy information, futile intellectually and hence morally. Electricity, heat, light, gravity, etc., may be studied by specialists as separate themes; but in general education they owe their significance to the fact that they too belong to the earth as the home of man, while their laws express the ways in which natural resources have been adapted to human ends.

A word in conclusion about mathematics. What the study of number suffers from in elementary education is lack of motivation. Back of this and that and the other particular bad method is the radical mistake of treating number as if it were an end in itself, instead of the means of accomplishing some end. Let the child get a consciousness of what is the use of number, of what it really is for, and half the battle is won. Now this consciousness of the use or reason implies some end which is implicitly social.

One of the absurd things in the more advanced study of arithmetic is the extent to which the child is introduced to numerical operations which have no distinctive mathematical principles characterizing them, but which represent certain general principles found in business relationships. To train the child in these operations, while paying no attention to the business realities in which they are of use, or to the conditions of social life which make these business activities necessary, is neither arithmetic nor common sense. The child is called upon to do examples in interest, partnership, banking, brokerage, and so on through a long string, and no pains are taken to see that, in connection with the arithmetic, he has any sense of the social realities involved. This part of arithmetic is essentially sociological in its nature. It ought either to be omitted entirely, or else be taught in connection with a study of the relevant social realities.

The training in exactness, neatness, and thoroughness which it is customary to associate with mathematics is real enough, but after all it extends beyond its own particular sphere only when mathematical relations are seen in their connection with the realities, where strictness, definiteness, accuracy and leaving nothing out of account are recognized as important.

In conclusion, we may say that in many respects, the subject-matter used in school life decides both the general atmosphere of the school and the methods of instruction and discipline which rule. A barren "course of study," that is to say, a meagre and narrow field of school activities cannot possibly lend itself to the development of a vital social spirit or to methods that appeal to sympathy and cooperation instead of to absorption, exclusiveness, and competition.

"Studies" are of moral value in the degree in which they enable the pupil sympathetically and imaginatively to appreciate the social scene in which he is a partaker; to realize his own indebtedness to the great stream of human activities which flow through and about him; the community of purpose with the large world of nature and society and his consequent obligation to be loyal to his inheritance and sincere in his devotion to the interests which have made him what he is and given him the opportunities he possesses. If such moral training seems slow and roundabout, we may yet encourage ourselves with the reflection that virtue is not a miracle but a conquest, and character not an accident but the efficacious growth of organic powers.

Reviews

Studies in Philosophy and Psychology
By Former Students of Charles Edward Garman, in
Commemoration of Twenty-five Years of Service as
Teacher of Philosophy in Amherst College. Boston and
New York, Houghton, Mifflin and Co., 1906.

This volume, edited by a committee of five of Professor
Garman's former students, is a significant fruit of the advance of serious thought and independent research in American college life, an evidence of increasing solidarity among
men of scholarship, and an indication of the growth of a desirable intellectual piety. The stimulating influence of Professor Garman as a teacher has long been a familiar fact to
those interested in philosophy, and has palliated, although
it has not removed, the regret that he has not sent forth in
print the products of his vigorous intellect. A recent investigation of the collegiate education of American teachers and
writers in philosophy and psychology showed, I believe, that,
considering the relative size of institutions, a greater proportion of these teachers came from Amherst College than from
any other one institution. It was in every way appropriate
that the rounding off of Professor Garman's twenty-five years
as a teacher of philosophy in that institution should be com-
memorated in this *Festschrift*.

An introduction to the volume is found in a ten-page
letter written by Professor Garman and published in the
American Journal of Psychology in 1898, giving an account
of his ideals and methods in teaching. The following quotation is indicative of the spirit in which he has conceived
training in philosophy; and is, perhaps, the most significant
commentary on the freshness and diversity of the philosophical positions which are, as a matter of fact, presented
in the essays which make up the bulk of the volume: "If you
can get the man so far along as to make him have confidence
in the power of weighing evidence, to realize how much
civilization owes to it, how every department of life can be
progressive only through scientific thinking, and then make

[First published in *Philosophical Review* 16 (1907): 312–21.]

it a moral question, and show that intellectual honesty and supreme choice of truth for truth's sake, and determination to follow evidence to the best of one's ability, is the great line of cleavage between the saints and the sinners,—if you can force the issue here and win, then the class are entirely different afterwards. I do not believe without this moral battle, without considering the ethical phases of the question, it would be possible to get the best intellectual results."[1]

The essays in this volume are divided into "Studies in Philosophy," of which there are eight, and "Studies in Psychology," of which there are five. Two of those in philosophy are, however, strictly speaking, sociological, and of them, accordingly, a few words may first be said.

In his essay upon "The Expansion of Europe in its Influence upon Population," Professor Willcox suggests that the centre of modern history has been the effort of Europe at expansion outside of Europe itself,—an expansion quite as much economic as political and military. The influence of this was the increase of the population of the world from, say, one billion in 1750 to one and one-half billion in 1900. This expansion, Professor Willcox thinks, has not been merely quantitative, but a development in the direction of a higher quality of living, representing a greater mastery over the powers of nature and the living of a more consciously progressive life.

Mr. Woods's essay on "Democracy a New Unfolding of Human Power," might be termed a plea for an ethical, as distinct from a purely economic and political, socialism. It identifies the democratic movement with increasing capacity of mankind for living an associated life, and considers the new impetus and widened outlook which come to the individual in consequence of the growth of his capacity to see himself in the light of an associated cooperative whole. It was, according to Mr. Woods, largely a matter of historical accident that the earlier period of democracy threw the emphasis

---

1. As Professor Garman's death has occurred since this review was penned, I venture to add another quotation which presents even more clearly, perhaps, the spirit of his teaching. "The young man who philosophizes, who really understands himself and appreciates the truth, is no longer a slave of form, but is filled with admiration that is genuine and lasting."

upon the elements of liberty and equality, minimizing the value of deliberate political and social organization, and in economics laying the emphasis upon the *laissez faire* notion. As the democratic movement works itself free from the circumstances which conditioned its early development, its inherently fraternal and cooperative nature is released. The modern industrial system, with its influences upon social and political life, is not to be referred exclusively to mechanical inventions, but more fundamentally to the growing spirit of association which made it possible to utilize these inventions. Mr. Woods argues that, as the ultimate tendency of political democracy has been to enhance individual initiative and force so that even the great productiveness of modern industry is largely to be credited to the indirect influence of political freedom, there is every reason to suppose that, whatever the difficulties of temporary adjustment, the ultimate effect of industrial democracy will be also to multiply initiation and stimulate capable leadership. The outcome of the argument is that "democratic association, instead of in any way restricting and hardening the issues of life, provides to the vital impulse an infinitely varied number of natural, invigorating, inspiring outlets."

The first essay of the volume is by Professor Tufts on "Moral Evolution." He endeavors to utilize the results of modern general and genetic psychology and of social psychology to give a sketch of the development of the moral self. Psychological ideas which are especially laid under tribute are three: namely, (1) the beginnings of mental and moral development in instinct and impulses of a biological sort; intelligent personality developing out of these as the simpler and more immediate discharge of instinct is checked, and a circuitous route of response built up on the basis of thinking and planning; (2) the recognition that the self is many as well as one, and many before it is one—the self as at first a more or less loosely connected aggregate of various instincts and impulses reacting to their own specific cues, rather than an organized system of capacities held together through the recognition of the principles of unity and generality in the situations in which they have to function; (3) the social character of the self: the fact that unconscious solidarity is the status at the outset, that only gradually are separate and individual interests split off and organized, until conscious individuality and conscious social interests are a final outcome. These general conceptions are applied to the interpretation of the development of moral character on its two sides, inner control, purpose, feeling, and external mastery of environment.

Professor Tufts's essay is very compact, many portions of it being sketched in summary, almost diagrammatic outline, so that further condensation is extremely difficult. I shall accordingly refer the interested reader to the article itself for details, and confine myself to certain general impressions which it has made upon me. In the first place, I should say that Professor Tufts has been unusually successful in avoiding the fallacy which easily besets the discussions of moral evolution, that of the fixed separation of "higher" and "lower." It is not uncommon to find the earlier stages conceived in such a way as to make the development of present ethical status inconceivable except at the expense of explaining away most of its significant features. This stimulates a reaction which insists, accordingly, either that moral evolution is inherently impossible, or else that the higher and later elements are already "latent" or "potential" in the earlier stages. Professor Tufts, however, has conceived the earlier stages in such a vitally concrete way as to realize that there are in them factors which are strictly analogous to those of more developed ethical situations, so that the evolution of the latter out of the former can be treated without denying the essential features of morality on the one hand, or falling into very dubious metaphysics, on the other.

The second impression is the concrete hold the writer has kept upon the social character of the individual as individual. "Social psychology" is used not as an annex to the normal psychology of the individual, much less as a recourse to a mystic over-soul labelled "social mind," but as a method of interpreting the actual constitution and functioning of the self. At every point of the discussion we find ourselves face to face with an individual into whose structure social factors are already built; and face to face with a social environment viewed as the medium in which the sociality of the past, consolidated into an individual, displays itself, is developed, and, through opposition and effort, reconstructed. It is this standpoint, more than anything else, I think, which is responsible for the first point I have mentioned; for it enables Professor Tufts to seize upon the genuinely moral problem, elements, and processes in every situation, at whatever plane of historic progress.

Dr. Sharp's paper on "Moral Judgment" is noteworthy among ethical discussions for the consistency with which it takes a single and simple point of view and sticks to it through various windings and turnings. His thesis is that the fact of approbation is the fundamental phenomenon of moral life. He first differentiates moral approbation from other forms by showing that, while all involve a union of an intellectual element and an emotional satisfaction, in an idea thought of as realized, moral approbation is directed at the purpose, the intended aim of an agent, which, since it is a disclosure of the agent's interests, may be treated as identical with "the system of a man's desires, considered in respect to their power to determine action." Yet this is not exhaustive. We may disapprove a purpose, as that of a lawyer opposed to us to win a case for his client, which is injurious to us, without regarding it as morally wrong. Only if we regard such a purpose as wrong for everyone, under the same circumstances, would the disapprobation be moral; or, put positively, "a purpose is morally approved when placing ourselves in a social order large or small we wish every member of it to make it his own under the given conditions."

Hence the right is not merely that which we *do* approve; all moral discussion in the concrete involves the supposition of an object which is universally approvable. There is an objectivity to rightness behind the mere fact of actual approbation. This is involved in the notion of the object of moral approbation as concerned with the purposes of *all* placed in a given situation. This involves the ideal of consistency in the various desires,—that they are really a system. On this basis, obligation can easily be explained as a concomitant of the approbation process under certain conditions, with no need of making the notion fundamental to morals. When we find a purpose morally approvable and yet disagreeable, there is a situation of constraint, and this in its emotional aspect is what we call consciousness of duty.

I hope even this inadequate sketch gives an idea of the clear and simple way in which Professor Sharp has worked out his point. I am not sure, however, that at bottom this clearness is not delusive,—not sure, that is, whether his argument does not either beg or evade the real issue. Professor Sharp denies, it will be observed, the Kantian notion of the fundamental character of the category of duty, while he adopts the allied Kantian notion of the universalization of purpose as the test and mark of rightness. Why, a Kantian might ask, do we not simply accept the fact that we find something good,—that we *do* approve,—as indicative of the right? Why do we look at the desire or the intent in which the desire expresses itself with reference to its place in a rationalized, universalized system? Surely, the Kantian would argue, only because it is a duty so to do,—*the* duty: *this* obligation is the moral law, and the essence of morality. In other words, Professor Sharp makes, without justifying it, the transition from the *fact* of approbation to the *ideal* of a certain kind of approbation, which is precisely the crux of all valuational or approbational theories of conduct. In passing, I would remark that, if Professor Sharp had concerned himself with this problem of transition and the *modus operandi* of its achievement, he would be likely to esteem (apart from details which may be eliminated or reconstructed) the machinery of Adam Smith's "Impartial Spectator" more highly than he does. As it is, in ignoring the problem of getting from a particular or *de facto* valuation to a *de jure,* or universalized one, he has no use for that, or any other social-psychology method.

The most important strictly metaphysical paper in the volume is that by Professor Woodbridge on "The Problem of Consciousness." This paper, on its critical and historic side, is a statement that a certain conception of consciousness controls the development of epistemology from Locke to Hegel, ending inevitably in idealistic constructions of the universe; and, on its suggested constructive side, the presentation of an idea of consciousness whose realistic implications are as marked as are the idealistic of the older conception, and one affording a point of departure for various logical problems of basic import. The historic criticism is worked out with force and almost dramatic clearness; considering the space taken, in detail. The constructive portion will suffer, with most readers, from its extreme compression, severe in any case, but additionally so when the conception is avowedly offered not as "a solvent for philosophic problems, but rather a creator of them."

The three underlying notions of modern philosophy, clearly formulated by Locke, that ideas are the sole objects of knowledge, that ideas are acquired, and that knowledge is their composition, all rest upon the notion of mind as an end-term, not as a relation of terms. As such, it is inherently a receptacle or capacity, endowed with constitutional powers and needing an alien factor to arouse it into activity,—this last being the other end-term, possibly an unknown substance, matter, possibly God, possibly nobody knows what. Now the value of such a notion of mind or consciousness (since this is empty in itself) "can be preserved only by assigning to it in increasing measure the character which may ultimately give to the whole of experience and the world their essential features." So mind is gradually supplied with everything that belongs to the universe; things "we can put in our pockets, or throw out of the window, or take into our stomachs, or shut our eyes and ears to," become "mental states"; while the principles of synthesis, the relations of the objective world of experience, become certain active or synthesizing functions of consciousness. Such is the dialectic which out of Locke has created Neo-Kantianism; Professor Woodbridge inserts Hegel as well, for no obvious reason to my mind save that it provides an interesting historic climax.

Professor Woodbridge then advances certain objections to idealism. Among these are the natural difficulty in believing it in spite of its logical systematic character, and the artificiality of its method in accordance with which sensations are declared to be immaterial because, on the basis of the theory, they ought to be immaterial, while at the same time physical things are treated as sensations. "One cannot

reach the mind by claiming that all objects are ideas and
then trying to establish this claim by insisting that by the
nature of mind ideas can be its only objects. It is precisely
the suspicion that this is just what idealism does that tends
again to make it appear artificial and incredible." Among
other exterior reasons working against the theory of idealism,
is the increasing consciousness "of a vast and enfolding nature which science by its steady progressive achievements
constantly deepens within us," which makes more and more
suspicious "those philosophies which seek to explain the
world primarily from the initial fact that man happens to
be conscious of a small part of it." The introduction of the
idea of evolution into natural science is peculiarly obnoxious
to idealism. It shifts the whole point of view so that the
problem becomes not, How does the mind know the world?
but, How does the world evolve to the consciousness of
itself?

In his constructive statement Professor Woodbridge insists that we should commence with the conscious situation
itself as exemplified in our familiar reflective conscious inquiry. Since the problem can appear only within this situation, it is reasonable to suppose that the solution must be
relevant to it,—must be an explanation and illustration of
it. Hence genetic theories as to the origin of consciousness
are rejected as right methods for attacking the problem, and
also the methods which would define consciousness through
the analysis of the process of perception. When we take the
situation of conscious inquiry in and for itself, we find it
resolvable into things related somehow to one another. Conspicuous among these relations are the temporal and the
spatial ones. Things also sustain in a conspicuous way another relationship to each other, the relationship of significance. Within the conscious situation things are not merely
beside each other or after each other, but one thing signifies
or means another. These relations of significance are capable
of organization and condensation by themselves without
modifying in any way the other relations of things. In this
contrast, they may fairly be called immaterial relations. It is
with their arrangement and condensation that logic deals,
just as the physical sciences deal with things in their other

relations. The gist of the hypothesis which Professor Woodbridge advances is, then, that consciousness means precisely the possibility of this significance of relationship among things. Take away consciousness and the things still exist in all their other relations; add consciousness and you add just the possibility of one thing signifying, symbolizing, or intending another. Philosophically, then, the theory involves a background of natural realism, a world of facts in space and of events in time of precisely the sort that physical science supposes itself to deal with. On the other hand, it assigns to consciousness a unique and important relation, that of significance, so that the theory is demarcated from those views which regard consciousness as merely an epiphenomenon.

Professor Woodbridge concludes with the sketching of certain problems which his conception inevitably suggests. The fact that things are grouped in different relations in the conscious situation raises the question whether those relations are coordinate or subordinate with respect to one another, or whether they all may be derived from a general unifying relation. This question at least suggests a relational formula as "expressing the simplest and most general type of existence." In any case what we seem to have is a relation between two variables, the fact of variation being independent of the relation, while the relation expresses the way in which the independents vary with respect to one another. Even if the relations could be deduced from one or more fundamental types, the fact of variation in the terms related would still remain underived and ultimate. Only by assuming their original independent variation would there, indeed, be any significance in the deduction of the relations. This remains true, even if we conceive consciousness to be the fundamental relation in question. "Things" would still have to be taken as the "independents" whose modes of variation with respect to one another were stated in the various relations in which consciousness (or significance) is expressed. That it should, however, be of this central type, seems to be forbidden by its intermittent character.

Another problem is suggested in the fact that consciousness belongs to the centered type of relations; that is, to that type in which one of the related things varies in such a way as to determine the scope of the relations. Here, again, it is suggested that, just as a highly general study of types of relation would throw light upon that particular relation which is exemplified in consciousness, so a study of centered types of relations in particular would throw light upon the individual aspect of consciousness. Finally, a study of the different types of relations belonging to the significance relationship affords a natural basis for a study of different systems or classes of knowledge, with their characteristic categories.

It is difficult to introduce within the casual paragraph of a review any relevant criticism of a theory which is at once so condensed in form of presentation and so far-reaching in its possible applications. I shall confine myself, accordingly, to a few summary remarks. The sketch of the evolution of idealism out of the notion of consciousness as an end-term, seems to me most illuminating. To one who grasps it and sympathizes with it, it is so conclusive as almost to render any other refutation of Kantian idealism unnecessary. Masterly and significant, however, as is the analysis with reference to one of the motifs of modern philosophy, it seems to me to leave untouched two others equally significant. The analysis from Locke to Kant succeeded in doing away with most of the fixed dualisms which Mediaevalism had extracted from Greek philosophy and handed on to modern times. The dualisms of substance and attribute, soul and matter, Absolute and finite, primary cause and derivative effects, noumenon and phenomenon, etc., etc., all went the same road. They disappeared in the distinctions and relations of plain, ordinary, everyday experience. It is this democratic community of experience which is the permanent truth of Berkeley and Hume, after one has given up the idea that there is any magic in the terms "consciousness," "sensations," "ideas," etc. The other motif is the logical analysis of judgment, which grew up through these philosophies, nominally connected with the theory of mind, but in effect independent of it. That knowledge is judgment, and that judgment involves a distinction and yet a relation of a direct given manifold and indirect or conceptual unifications, is a formula which sums up this development, and a formula which lies much nearer to Professor Woodbridge's own formula than he seems to recognize.[2] Just because the problem involved in this formula is the net outcome of this philosophic movement, Professor Woodbridge's own formula of the reflective situation as that in which physical relations and significance relations are found (and presumably distinguished from and yet referred to one another) seems to me to give a digest of that movement, freed from more or less accidental accretions regarding ideas and sensations (inherited from Greek thought through Scholastic psychology rather than genuine products of modern psychology). It exposes the problem of judgment, *i.e.*, knowledge involving reflection, as a problem. The crucial point of Professor Woodbridge's own argument is, of course, the assumption that the relational formula expresses the general type of existence. It is to be hoped that he will recur to this assumption independent of the idealistic-realistic argument, and will attempt to justify the formula as applicable to reality against the very damaging criticisms which have long been brought against it. Meantime, it is to be noted that it is precisely upon this formula that such writers as T. H. Green base their idealism; and that its outcome would seem to be an identification of reality with reason; a thought system minus consciousness except *per accidens*, like Aristotle's νόησις νοήσεως, which Aristotle seems to have regarded as conscious only in flagrant defiance of his own basic principles in psychology and logic.

Professor Norton's article upon "The Intellectual Element in Music" is an interesting and fruitful attempt to determine the logical aspects in the way of concepts and judgments in music. If the general tendency to identify the intellectual factor with judgment be valid, then the treatment of musical forms as modes of judgment ought not only to throw light upon music, but to give a fresh and unconventional way of approaching various problems regarding judgment. Professor Raub attempts to find pragmatism in

2. This impression, however, may be due to the brevity of the treatment, for in one passage Woodbridge writes: "The description which I have given of the conscious situation accords, I suppose, with an idealistic description of experience when experience is taken in its immediate and evident character."

Kantianism and Kantianism in pragmatism. His account of pragmatism is largely made up in the usual way, viz., by combining selections from Schiller's humanism, James's pragmatism and radical empiricism, and the Chicago school's instrumental logic, and is perhaps as fair a picture of an indefinite tendency as any such miscellany can possibly be. As regards Kant, his chief stumbling-block is, of course, the *a priori* categories. He deals with these not by suggesting that they might be interpreted as an effort to classify the most important working hypotheses employed in the selective determination of objects, *a priori* only with reference to *future* efforts, but by indicating that some pragmatists accept the Spencerian theory that what is *a posteriori* for the race is *a priori* for the individual. Professor Lyman attempts to mediate between theology and the modern mind by use of pragmatic methods, indicating the need of interpreting the supernatural not as the trans-experiential, but as the ethical in experience, and suggesting the possibility, by transforming dogmatic into historic theology, of conserving to man's use the great values worked out in the religious experience of the race. The essay is thoughtful, and free from both the sentimentalism and the arbitrary "fideism" which sometimes accompany a professedly pragmatic view of religion.

Of the psychological essays, I have left myself no space to speak, and some are so technical that only an experimental psychologist is equipped to speak of them. One essay by Professor Pierce, on the Subconscious, and another by Professor Woodworth, on the conditions of a voluntary act, are, however, so clear and comprehensive that they can hardly fail to afford the points of departure for further discussion in their fields.

The Life of Reason, or the Phases of Human Progress
By George Santayana. New York: Charles Scribner's
Sons, 1905–06.

That which makes it difficult for me to give, even from
my own standpoint, a just account of the criticism of life
recorded in Professor Santayana's *The Life of Reason*, is that
which seems to me, after all, a most characteristic feature
of the book. It is an interfusion of a lively, sympathetic, delicate, and direct sense for the realities of human experience,
with an equally acute, equally subtle, but correspondingly
indirect and antagonistic, sense of what almost all philosophers have thought and said about them. I know of no writing in modern philosophy which evidences more just and
kindly appreciation of the forces of human life, taken simply, frankly, and naturally,—with less refraction through the
medium of artificial philosophic lenses. But I must add that
I also know no book more indirect, more permeated with
allusions—mostly unlabelled—more colored by recollections
of other—but mostly disliked—philosophic interpretations.
The series of five volumes is (in comparison with most philosophic literature) at once ultra-direct and personal, and ultra-
academic, "learned," and reminiscent.

And it is an interfusion! We get both things not only
in the same chapter, but on the same page, in the same sentence. Rarely does Mr. Santayana let himself go for even a
paragraph. He starts to tell the truth about something as he
himself feels it and sees it, and he diverts himself (to the
diversion or the annoyance of the reader, according to the
tastes of the latter) with side-hits at three or four other
views of the same matter which, decidedly, do not commend
themselves to him. The book—it is one, though printed in
five volumes—will accordingly affect different readers in the
most extraordinarily different ways. So many philosophers
gathered together, so many opinions about not only the mer-

[First published in *Educational Review* 34 (Sept. 1907): 116–29.]

its, but the purpose and character of *The Life of Reason*. One
(and I may notify the reader that I take my own stand here)
is most stirred by those portions which give Mr. Santayana's
own evaluation of the facts and motifs of human life; another is moved—to admiration or to hostility—by his treatment of other philosophic 'isms; a third feels himself torn
asunder in the rapid panoramic transformation scenes at
which he is invited to assist and is quite sure the book is
only "literature" (though admirably written literature), quite
lacking in philosophic standpoint or method.

Truth to tell, while Mr. Santayana generally takes life
at its best, he as regularly takes philosophers and theologians, and scientists so far as they generalize, at their worst.
Views which are dangerously like Mr. Santayana's own are
vigorously criticized when proceeding from suspected quarters, and the reader, who is not willing to make as fine
distinctions as Mr. Santayana himself, accuses him of inconsistency and lack of any single standpoint. The style helps
out the impression—classic, academic, quasi-mathematical
in outward form, it is in truth clinging and yielding, almost
chameleon in its elusive adaptation to the particular matter
in hand. In it, all things flow; nothing projects. It is vibrat-
ing, but not resonant. The secret of it all, I suspect, is an
intelligence of easy sympathy conjoined with a sympathy
not always broad enough to be intelligent. Mr. Santayana's
method sometimes reminds one of what Mazzini said about
Carlyle's attitude towards social reform—he was a thorough
believer in it provided no reformers had a hand in bringing
it to pass. Mr. Santayana is thoroughly appreciative of the
various elements in experience—save when some philosopher
has formulated them.

But this is enough, and more than enough, of general
impression. The subject-matter is distributed through five
volumes devoted respectively to The Life of Reason in Common Sense, in Society, in Religion, in Art, in Science. Of
these five, the first and the last go most closely together and
hardly can be understood, in their bearing upon Mr. Santayana's own philosophy, apart from each other. The standpoint and method are, loosely, historical. The book purports
to give not a finished philosophy of reality, but an account

of the various ways in which humanity has expressed its
tentative efforts to rationalize itself, with a critical estimate
of the respective worth of these attempts, this estimate being
a further work of that clarifying, purging, and selective Life
of Reason whose tale is told. He criticizes so-called philosophies of history for virtually assuming "that events have
directed themselves prophetically upon the interests which
they arouse"—in spite of the fact that these interests are
many and contradictory; he criticizes the pompous appeal
to a "historical force which breaks up on inspection into a
cataract of miscellaneous natural processes and minute particular causes." But he suggests a purification of this method.
If the philosopher, in reviewing events, confesses that he is
scrutinizing them in order to abstract from them whatever
tends to illustrate his own ideals, as he might look over a
crowd to find his friends, the operation becomes a perfectly
legitimate one. "A sort of retrospective politics, an estimate
of events in reference to the moral ideal which they embodied
or betrayed, might supervene upon positive history. . . .
The present work is an essay in that direction." The enlightened historian will, however, recognize that the ideal
which he uses as a touchstone must not be an arbitrary personal dogma, but itself an outcome of the historical events
which he is testing and sifting by their relation to it. He
must be sensitive to all the goods which life in its various
manifestations has evolved and sustained; his standard will
be a "variegated omnipresent happiness." The philosophic
historian "needs to make himself the spokesman for all past
aspirations"—barring those of mystics, transcendentalists,
and militant liberals, it may be remarked parenthetically.

The method, as I said, is loosely historical. It is also, in
the loose sense, psychological. And since Mr. Santayana
speaks too rarely in precise terms, of his own intentions, I
quote again: "It constantly happens in philosophic writings
that what is supposed to go on in the human mind is described and appealed to in order to support some observation
or illustrate some argument—as continually, for instance, in
the older English critics of human nature, or in these very
pages. What is offered in such cases is merely an invitation
to think after a certain fashion. A way of grasping or inter-

preting some fact is suggested, with a more or less civil challenge to the reader to resist the suasion of his own experience so evoked and represented. Such a method of appeal may be called psychological, in the sense that it relies for success on the total movement of the reader's life and mind, without forcing a detailed assent through ocular demonstration or pure dialectic." In short, the appeal is to the developing experience of mankind so far as that can be imaginatively reproduced by the individual in terms of his own experience.

I make no apology for these extended quotations, because I think the reader who fails to grasp the aim and method of the book as set forth in them will not grasp the continuity of its ideas, however much of incidental delight —or irritation—they may severally furnish him.

Whether Mr. Santayana conceives that any philosophy or metaphysic, aside from critical valuation of human experience in its historic development as verified in reflection upon the individual's own experience, is or is not possible, I am not sure. At times, such critical valuation would appear to exhaust to Mr. Santayana the whole realm of profitable "metaphysics." At other times, he seems to regard such an account as *merely* genetic or "subjective"; and as presenting, if viewed as positive metaphysics, an attempt to erect an account of the processes of human discovery into an account of the reality discovered. That philosophy can be anything but a historic phenomenon, a part of man's efforts to read and criticize the story of his own life in the universe in which he is set, seems to the present writer the initial fallacy of vicious metaphysics; and he would fain believe that Mr. Santayana has renounced the heresy of supposing that, whether for himself or for someone else, history is going to stop long enough for one to step outside of its processes, and kodak reality "*sub specie aeternatatis.*" In other words, the present writer desires to take Mr. Santayana's *The Life of Reason* as representing the only type of philosophy with which it is worth while to engage one's self; a return to the ancient identification of philosophy with morals, with love of wisdom. A survey by intelligence of the past struggles, failures, and successes of intelligence with a view to directing its own further endeavors, emphasizing and safeguarding its achievements, avoiding repetitions of its futile and wasteful excesses, stimulating it to greater patience and courage—this, indeed, is a conception of philosophy fit to rescue it from the slough of disrespect and despondency into which it has fallen in evil days. It is this, I take it, in Mr. Santayana's writing which will permanently count, spite of its signs of hankering after the flesh-pots of "metaphysics."

What, then, is reason, and what is its life? The answer is implicit in the quotations already made. *"The Life of Reason* will then be a name for that part of experience which perceives and pursues ideals—all conduct so controlled and all sense so interpreted as to perfect natural happiness." As soon as man ceased to be immersed in the flux of sense, he looked to the future and the past; in this way experiences were gathered and graded in their value; they were apprehended in their relative worth. The past is judged in the light of the present it evokes and the present is judged in the light of the future it makes possible. The foresight of the consequence which the present imports is consciousness of end, of purpose. All reflection is thus ideal; reason always involves emergence from the present, the immediate, the merely existent; it is the estimate, the survey and criticism of this from the standpoint of the eventual, the ulterior. But such foresight and discrimination introduces a new complication into the existent itself; it is a modification of it which thereby modifies the future. Reason is inevitably practical as well as speculative; it is an attitude of intention, of will. "Vital impulse when it is modified by reflection and veers in sympathy with judgments pronounced on the past is properly called reason. Man's rational life consists in those moments in which reflection not only occurs but proves efficacious. What is absent then works in the present." The forecast of the possible future on the basis of the best experienced in the past is itself an impulse to realize the better, to ward off the worse.

Reflection thus functions in the interest of value, of the good, of the variegated omnipresent happiness—that *is* its life. "It is the unity given to all existence by a mind in *love with the good.* In the higher reaches of human nature,

as much as in the lower, rationality depends on distinguishing the excellent. . . . When definite interests are recognized and the values of things are estimated by that standard, then reason has been born and a moral world has
arisen."

We have here the factors upon which the whole philosophy of Mr. Santayana turns. On the one hand, there is brute
existence, shifting, transitive, in flux; sheer nature, a world
innocent of spirit, of purpose, but gifted with impulse, with
experimentation. This world in its movement bears moments of value, excellence—moments which man gladly
would have stay, they are so fair. Their memory abides;
that is, the ideal supervenes. Standing upon them, man surveys and classifies, organizes the brutally existent; through
them he reacts upon the flux and brings it into more permanent order. These values, these meanings, are, when arrested in reflection, what the ancients called the form of
things; and "we exist through form, and the love of form is
our whole real inspiration." With Mr. Santayana as with the
ancients—the Greeks, of course—"order is what is meant by
intelligence and order productive of excellence what is meant
by reason." But this order, which is intelligence, is not creative; is not original; is not absolute. It is divinely human.
Everywhere there is the fluctuating process of nature which
first bears and then sustains meanings. It is the office and
the reward of those in whom they are born to cherish and
to extend them. Thereby is the relatively unmeaning flux
further subdued and rendered more efficaciously, stably, and
pervasively the source and stay of reason.

The five volumes are variations on this theme. They
trace the directions in which, the experiments by which, that
excellence and harmony which are our happiness are secured
and spread by increased acknowledgment of that natural
basis from which they were generated. They trace also fruitless sidesteps, the inconsequential deviations which have
been the efflorescence of an exaggerated and maniacal consciousness which nature indeed generates but refuses to accept further responsibility for. They record also the relapses,
the blind surrenders, the abnegations of reason, which, in
one form or another, Mr. Santayana finds to be characteris-

tic of positivist, sceptic, mystic, and transcendentalist alike.
For as success is attained but in one way, by following nature in the conscious, deliberate, persistent, and artful love
of those values which she generates casually, occasionally,
and accidentally, so the source of all error, practical and
theoretical, is in forgetting or denying natural basis or ideal
end. On the one hand, the rooting of the spiritual in the
natural is ignored: that "it must be a resultant or synthesis
of impulses already afoot. An ideal out of relation to the actual demands of living beings is so far from being an ideal
that it is not even a good." Other philosophies, recognizing
that the good of existence *is* the good which it generates,
change this moral truth into a false physics, and hold that
therefore the good, the spiritual, and the ideal are the cause
or productive source of the physical. The Greeks first "made
a mock physics in moral terms, out of which theology was
afterwards developed." The result was the non-natural spiritual world of orthodox tradition. "A mechanism composed
of values and definitions was placed behind phenomena to
constitute a substantial world." The moral and logical sense
in which values and meanings make things what they are
was transformed into a quasi-physical, and therefore wholly
magical and mythological, mode of causation and substantia-
tion. This way lies the fallacy of false idealisms and spir-
itualities.

Another type of fallacy consists in sticking brutally by
the brute natural situation. Here are the positivists, the ma-
terialists, the over-naturalists who "look at life from the outside"; the "processes of Nature make them forget her uses."
Such, priding themselves upon their enlightenment, "have
discarded the machinery in which their ancestors embodied
the ideal; they have not perceived that those symbols stood
for the Life of Reason and gave fantastic and embarrassed
expression to what, in itself, is pure humanity; and they have
thus remained entangled in the colossal error that ideals are
something adventitious and unmeaning, not having a soil in
mortal life, nor a possible fulfilment there."

It is to this idea of nature generative of value that the
argument in every volume returns; from it the argument proceeds. The basic idea of the interpretation of society is that

"love has an animal basis; but an ideal object." But since these propositions usually seem contradictory "no writer ventures to present more than half the truth and that half out of its true relations." Popular sentiment makes the affections which are the bond of union among men divine in origin and natural in object: "which is the exact opposite of the truth." The end of the family as of other social arrangements, industry, war, government, is "to turn the friction of material forces into the light of ideal good." Relatively speaking, however, the entire function of the family and of states based on the family, is natural: it is to *produce* the individual and equip him with the *prerequisites* of moral freedoms. Then ensues free society, where physical association is elevated, through participation in some ideal interest, into friendship and sympathy. But "ideal society transcends accidental conjunctions altogether; its companions are the symbols it breeds and possesses for excellence, beauty, and truth. Religion, art, and science are the chief spheres in which ideal companionship is found."

Reason is interested in value, in meaning, in perpetuating and extending it. Religion may be said to be the emotion, imaginatively expressed, of this supremacy of the ideal as the end and standard of life. The consciousness of meaning, of worth, is always, as we have said, ideal—it is of the absent, the ulterior. And so religion is naturally born in devotion to this ulterior. "The vistas it opens and the mysteries it propounds are another world to live in; and another world to live in—whether we expect ever to pass wholly into it or no—is what we mean by having a religion." But religion, so close to rationality in its purpose, has fallen far short of it in its texture and results. Instead of using the ideal as an ethical inspiration and fulcrum, it tends to materialize it, to make it an explanation, a cause, a quasi-physical force and substance. It forgets that it is poetry and arrogates to itself "literal truth and moral authority, neither of which it possesses." To make the ideal effective in life it must be imagined, given sensuous embodiment. And these poetical conceits come to pass for reports of another objective world, somehow enveloping the natural world.

Religion fails to recognize that it is concerned with

experience as it should be, and supposes that its idealized symbols of a better reality "are information about reality elsewhere." Hence mythology; which has the genuinely poetic character of "revealing some function of nature in human life," but which is regarded as literally true of something which exists beyond nature. Hence magic, and sacrifice, and various other devices for entering into favorable relations with this other kind of existence.

None the less, under favorable circumstances religion comes to subserve the life of reason. The imagination at least maintains "an ideal standard for action and a perfect object for contemplation." In this, its proper function, it is piety and spirituality. Piety is attachment to whatever in the sources of man's being also serves as the natural and historic fount of the values which make this being worth having. It is a cherishing consciousness that the human spirit is derived and responsible, having its roots in nature and in the past endeavor of society. Spirituality is freer; it is attachment to the values themselves as ends; it is prospective as piety is retrospective. "Piety drinks at the deep, elemental sources of power and order: it studies nature, honours the past, appropriates and continues its mission. Spirituality uses the strength thus acquired, remodelling all it receives, and looking to the future and the ideal. True religion is entirely human and political. . . . Supernatural machinery is either symbolic of natural conditions and moral aims or else it is worthless."

Art is an even more potent expression of living reason —that is, of nature exercising function and use, and achieving order and stable harmony. In origin again, it is wholly natural; the spontaneous overflow of instinct and impulse. In process, it is instinct become aware of its use and shaping nature to better manifestation of that use. In effect, it is nature idealized, harmonized: the union of practical achievement, reasonable insight, and disciplined happiness. In art, happy instinct both perpetuates its own function and reproduces and extends itself, for art, being an intelligent, a deliberate process, is teachable. Art is thus doubly rational.

Beauty, the distinctively esthetic element, is thus an incident. In reshaping nature by making it a more apt embodiment of value, nature is rendered a more congenial stimulus to the soul, and the immediate apprehension of this congeniality is the beauty of the object. "The esthetic good is hatched in the same nest with the others [utility, etc.] and is incapable of flying far in a different air." Purely industrial art, on the other hand, is instrumental only. It is the liberal life, which the subjection of nature to economic use makes possible, which justifies industry. To fail to recognize this instrumental function is genuine materialism. This forgets that the worth of the end realized is the sole warrant for the labor of realization. Its moral philosophy "dwells by preference on the possibility that a violent and continual subjection in the present might issue in a glorious future dominion." Industrial art merely "gives nature that form which, if more thoroughly humane, she might have originally possessed for our benefit; liberal arts bring to spiritual fruition the matter which either nature or industry has prepared and rendered propitious."

The fine arts are a union, as already said, of original animal spontaneity or automatism, and of success in achieving the realization of value. Their goal is the complete superimposition of these two characters. Meantime, the two factors run their course somewhat apart. Much spontaneous activity is wasteful and irrelevant. Much achievement is laborious, painful, compulsory, illiberal, and, in a sense, unnatural. Some fine arts, like dancing, music, and the arts of speech,—poetry, the drama,—emphasize the factor of spontaneity. They leave less definite impress; less modification of their own conditions. Their delight is this spontaneity, but so is their weakness. "If pure music, even with its immense sensuous appeal, is so easily tedious, what a universal yawn must meet the verbiage which develops nothing but its own iridescence." The plastic arts, architecture, sculpture, painting, emphasize use; achievement; the accomplished transformation of nature through an action which makes it the more pertinent and pliant embodiment of the ideal.

The ultimate problem is the union of the industrial and the fine arts. "Art, in the better sense, is a condition of happiness for a practical and labouring creature, since without art he remains a slave; but it is one more source of unhappiness for him so long as it is not squared with his necessary labours and merely interrupts them. It then alienates him from his world without being able to carry him effectually into a better one." And present "fine" art is mainly vain, "a brief truancy from rational practice."

That science is an expression of the life of reason is perhaps only too obvious to the "modern" man, who is so conscious of it that he is apt to forget what Mr. Santayana so sincerely expresses: that society and art and religion are also of the life of reason. But I am not sure just how Mr. Santayana conceives the respective relations of art and science to reason: a doubt which makes me uncertain in just what perspective his whole scheme is to be interpreted. On its face, art would seem to be a more concrete and final expression of living reason than science; for art can hardly be regarded as other than the recognition in intelligence of order and harmony in so far as that acknowledgment functions through action in the service of conscious excellence or happiness. (To apprehend what Mr. Santayana means by happiness is to have apprehended the ultimate of morals.) In comparison with art, science would then be preliminary and preparatory—itself a form of art, indeed, but of art still halting from its ulterior destiny. There is much in Mr. Santayana that bears out this conception. Such a philosophy, in the philosophic nickname of the day, would be pragmatism— pragmatism of a noble and significant type. But there is much in Mr. Santayana (and the weight in the end falls upon this side) which prevents such an interpretation. The final paragraph in the book is entitled "It [*i.e.*, science] suffices for the Life of Reason." And, aside from words, while there are many assertions in the book that all science is moral, human, practical, eventual, symbolic, hypothetical, determined by vital bias, impulse, purpose; that it is "an instinctive product, a stepping forth of human courage in the dark,"—"a claim which we put forth"[1]: there are many other passages which declare action to be servile and instrumental; the end of life to be contemplation—in the Greek sense, of

1. See Vol. V, p. 177. "Intelligence is not a substance; it is a principle of order and of art; it requires a given situation and some particular natural interests brought into play."

course—and science to be the ultimate revealer and judge of reality. In other words, the reader—this reader at least—is left at a loss to know just what, in the end, Mr. Santayana conceives to be the relation of natural basis and ideal end to one another and to reality. Is reality for the philosopher the moral life itself, the life of reason, and are physics— the statement of the order or mechanism by which nature sustains its ends—and dialectic—the explication of the meanings, the intents which are suggested and sustained—integral instruments of this life? Or are the mechanism which science progressively reveals, and the eternal order of immutable truth which dialectic determines,[2] *the* reality, while the purposes, and endeavors, and achievements of human experience are only an evanescent and superficial mirror in which *the* Reality happens, for our passing delectation and confusion, to reflect itself? I do not know. The more explicit and official declarations of our author are all in the latter sense. The spirit and vital accomplishment of the book are in the former.

Mr. Santayana seems—I may misrepresent him—to have his own reconciliation of the apparent contradiction. One account, that of the noble, artistic, and moral "pragmatism" —I care much less for the word than for the life of reason— holds good historically; of the processes by which man has come to discover what really is; while the coldly scientific, physical, and dialectic view holds of the reality itself of which this history is but one transitory manifestation. Hence to regard the "life of reason" as the philosopher's reality is to fall into the idealist's usual fallacy of supposing that the instrumentalities, methods, and states of coming to know abrogate the realities which are known.[3]

But surely there is another alternative. Let Mr. Santayana extend his well-guarded aversion to the results of idealism—whether of the "malicious psychology" type or the tran-

---

2. Compare Vol. V, p. 315—Mathematics "is absolutely self-justified and necessary before it is discovered to be so. Here, then, is a conspicuous region of truth disclosed to the human intellect by its own internal exercise, which is nevertheless altogether independent, being eternal and indefeasible, while the thought that utters it is ephemeral."
3. See, for example, Vol. II, p. 200.

scendental type—to their postulate about the processes and methods of knowing, let him stick to his own postulate that knowing is an operation of reality (not of subjects, egos, or consciousnesses) through vital impulse; and it surely remains true that dialectic and physics hold of reality, but hold of it *not* apart from the courage, adventure, and achievement of vital impulse, but through and in so far as reality embodies itself through a vital impulse which chooses the excellent and strives to make it prevail. Mr. Santayana seems to me to be in the precarious position of at once throwing an immense burden upon "vital impulse" and of then damning it in the light of its own ulterior products in the way of "form."

But even in this respect Mr. Santayana remains, although unconsciously and perhaps against his intention, a true historian. For the contemporary life of reason still oscillates between the ancient principle of form and the modern principle of vital impulse, lacking any sure synthesis of intellect and action. We are grateful to Mr. Santayana for what he *has* given us: the most adequate contribution America has yet made—always excepting Emerson—to moral philosophy. And we may conclude with a quotation breathing its most Emersonian spirit: "The darkest spots are in man himself, in his fitful, irrational disposition. Could a better system prevail in our lives a better order would establish itself in our thinking. It has not been for want of keen senses, or personal genius, or a constant order in the outer world, that mankind have fallen back repeatedly into barbarism and superstition. It has been for want of good character, good example, and good government. There is a pathetic capacity in men to live nobly, if only they would give one another the chance."

Henry Sidgwick
A Memoir by A. S(idgwick) and E(leanor) M. S(idgwick). London and New York. The Macmillan Company, 1906.

To a leisurely reader who finds pleasure in weighty matter for meditative reflection, furnished in a discursive, sometimes scrappy, manner, this biography of one of the greatest of England's recent ethical teachers will make many appeals. It gives a reflected picture of the intellectual changes in British thought from 1860 to 1900 (the bibliography of Sidgwick's articles, given in an appendix, covers these forty years). The reflection is through the intellectual atmosphere of the University of Cambridge; that it comes with so little refraction is due to the peculiarly transparent medium of Sidgwick's own mind. It begins with the University still dominated by traditional theology, while the younger, more open minds were tremendously subjected to the influence of Mill upon one side, and tremendously stirred, upon the other, by the application of philosophical and historical criticism to the documents and dogmas of Christian theology. It continues through the emancipation of the University and cultured thought in general, to the reaction against liberalism in politics and economics and against agnosticism in theology and morals. To some it is this unintended record of the course of intellectual development of an important generation which will be most interesting.

Others will be interested in the more intimate and psychological portrayal of the development of individual attitudes and beliefs. There is nothing of the "introspective" in the morbid and emotional sense either in Sidgwick's own make-up or in this volume. There is nothing of that romantic egoism, that interest in the inner drama of one's own consciousness, which attracts—or repels—say in such a record as Amiel's *Journal*. But Sidgwick involved himself and his own ideas and beliefs to an extraordinary degree in his unusual power and habit of criticism. His self-criticism is as acute as his criticism of systems of philosophy and morals;

[First published in *Political Science Quarterly* 22 (1907): 133–35.]

indeed it is, to an extent to which no parallel occurs to me, a part of the same criticism. It is the record of a mind whose methods of intellectual analysis were always at war with its emotional desires. With more than usual ardor Sidgwick wished to be an optimistic, personal theist, but he never could find evidence, external or philosophical, to justify yielding to the desire, and his conscience as a philosopher forbade him to do so. The result is well expressed in his comments upon a distinctly unsympathetic criticism of his teaching career passed upon him by Professor Alfred Marshall; and the entire absence of any shade of resentment on Sidgwick's part, and his endeavor to analyze Marshall's words, to get the exact amount of truth contained in them, are eminently characteristic:

> I, however, am not unhappy; for Destiny, which bestowed on me the dubious gift of this *vue d'ensemble*, also gave me richly all external sources of happiness—friends, a wife, congenial occupation, freedom from material cares—but feeling that the deepest truth I have to tell is by no means "good tidings," I naturally shrink from exercising on others the personal influence which would make them resemble me, as much as men more optimistic and prophetic naturally aim at exercising such influence. Hence as a teacher I instinctively desire to limit my teaching to those whose bent or deliberate choice it is to search after ultimate truth . . . I would not, if I could, and I could not if I would, say anything which would make philosophy, my philosophy, popular.

A third point of view from which the volume is amply suggestive is the incidental insights it affords into various practical movements with which Sidgwick was more or less directly concerned. He was always interested in politics in the practical sense of that term, and his connection, through marriage, with Balfour naturally gave him much opportunity for comments on English politics. It is interesting to find him, in the early sixties, writing: "I seem to see, as clear as if it was in history, the long Conservative reaction that awaits us when the Whig party have vanished, and I also see the shock menaced by the Radical opposition when they have sufficiently agitated the country." Those interested in the history of university reform, both of administrative matters and of the curriculum and methods of teaching, will find rich and varied material; though it must be confessed that, as regards changes in the curriculum, Sidgwick fought generally on the losing side. In the nineties the large majority by which the proposition to abolish compulsory Greek was defeated discouraged him, and "he used to point despondingly to the Chinese Mandarins as an example of the effect of clinging to worn-out forms of literary examination"—an attitude which made him interestedly active in the reorganization of the University of London. His part in the promotion of higher education for women, and in the organization of Newnham College was large.

The book is also a mine of information as regards "psychical research," Sidgwick's own interest in ghosts, *etc.*, antedating by many years the formation of the society of which he was a founder. It is again characteristic of the candor of his intelligence that, while of the greatest disposition in the world to find empirical evidence for the reality of immortality and while frequently on the verge, apparently, of finding what he wanted, he never got beyond the point of a hopeful scepticism. His interest was not merely personal, but philosophical. In his ethical system, his fundamental postulate was the basic identity of happiness and duty. In this world, however, he found them discrepant. His inability, accordingly, to find proof, either empirical or rational, for the doctrine of immortality, gave him serious scruples about the very bases of his ethical system.

In its larger philosophical features, Sidgwick is an exponent of one of the most characteristic features of recent thought. He combined the scientific, inductive and empirical interest with great personal sensitiveness to ideal and spiritual aspirations, and he found himself to the last unable satisfactorily to reconcile the two tendencies. Practically he reflects the inability of the liberalism of the Mill type of the earlier half of the century to hold its own. Judged from results, it was in a state of unstable equilibrium. In part, it moved towards radicalism and socialism; in part—the part with which Sidgwick, though with many misgivings, sympathized—it moved towards conservatism. But above all Sidgwick remains a monument to all that is best in Mill—his simplicity, openmindedness, absolute fairness and sincerity. In the centenary year of Mill's birth, it is worth recalling that the ideas and methods of a man like Henry Sidgwick were largely formed under Mill's influence.

Anti-pragmatisme
Examen des droits respectifs de l'aristocratie intel-
lectuelle et de la democratie sociale. Par Albert Schinz.
Paris, Félix Alcan, 1909.

In addition to an appendix of two reprinted articles, this
volume of about three hundred pages consists of three parts.
The first part, entitled "Pragmatism and Intellectualism,"
begins with a chapter on "The Principles of Pragmatism,"
which sets forth the three arguments upon which pragmatism is based and then "refutes" them. The three fundamental principles are that (1) all purely intellectualistic systems
have failed to satisfy us; (2) all systems (whether we are
aware of the fact or not) are inspired by personal and practical motives and envisage practical ends; and, (3) pragmatism reconciles all philosophic speculations because it enables us to recognize as true whatever is useful in any of
them, while they are compelled to deny one another *in toto*.

That Professor Schinz is a consistent Anti-Empiricist,
a thorough-going conceptualist, is obvious enough in the
above summary, which sets forth, not the arguments upon
which any pragmatist has ever rested his case, but the type
of formal, rationalistic reasons that would appeal to an intellectualist of a somewhat unusually abstract sort.

That his "refutations" follow the lines of a highly formal logic might therefore be expected. (1) Even if all the
intellectualist philosophies were false, this would not add
one iota of proof to the truth of pragmatism; (2) if it be
admitted that all philosophies have been inspired by subjective and personal preferences, this, by pragmatism's own
argument, confers upon them exactly the same advantages
pragmatism claims for itself, thus negating its claim to
superiority; (3) the sciences when they employ the useful
as a criterion of selection and coordination of rival hypotheses always mean the useful to *intelligence*, while pragmatism means the *socially* useful,—a characteristically "Anglo-
Saxon" standard. Subjectivism is an established principle of

[First published in *Philosophical Review* 18 (1909): 446–49.]

all modern philosophy, made such by Hume and Kant, but there is all the difference in the world between a philosophy which holds that phenomena have to be adapted to certain fixed predetermined faculties of our intelligence, and that which holds that they are influenced by factors of desire and volition. The unusually abstract flavor of the intellectualism of these refutations is probably apparent without express indication. The average man, probably even among the "anti-pragmatists," is sufficiently empirical so that if the idea occurred to him that all other philosophies are on the same level with pragmatism because pragmatism insists that all alike are influenced by personal and practical considerations, it would also occur to him to ask whether the fact that pragmatism *recognizes* this influence while other philosophies deny and ignore it does not make a considerable difference. And, similarly, when Professor Schinz sets up the dilemma (the dilemma is his habitual mode of thought) that either the pragmatist accepts the principle of contradiction and so admits intellectualism, or else denies it, and so subverts itself as well as other philosophies, the ordinary intellectualist (at least if an Anglo-Saxon) would stop to consider that possibly the pragmatist would have a pragmatic interpretation of the principle of contradiction.

The second chapter being entitled "Le Cas Dewey," a becoming modesty forbids my dealing with it. I was somewhat surprised,—some Anti-pragmatists will probably share my surprise,—however, to learn that my chief interest was to base morals upon transcendental metaphysics, and that the traces of a naturalistic reliance upon psychology and sociology in my writing are evidences of "hesitation" and "self-contradiction" on my part! But as Professor Schinz says of himself in another portion of his work (p. 138), "Without doubt it is necessary for us to interpret pragmatism and *to read between the lines*,"—a passage which might well serve as its motto.

In the second part, "Pragmatism and Modernism," we have Professor Schinz in the very act, as it were, of reading between the lines: Industrial democracy, the insistence of America upon sheer activity for its own sake, upon success, upon the battle for victory,—that, and Pragmatism as a

hearty concession to the views of the populace in which
such ideas are current, are the vision. Democracies, especially those in which the spirit of industrialism is dominant,
—as in the United States,—are hostile to freedom of thought
and science, for they are interested only in results.

"*La philosophie de Wm. James reflète exactement cette
façon de voir; . . . il cherche à la justifier.*" There is, however, a second trait of our American life reflected in pragmatism. The furore of competitive energy leads to excessive
egoism,—the war of all against all. Some check, some restraint, is needed,—hence America is great on religion, not
to say religions. Accordingly when Professor James speaks
most as a pragmatist, the utilitarian aspects of religion are
the feature most emphasized.

One fears that Professor Schinz does not always get the
full force of his own humor, as for example in a passage he
uses to exemplify the doctrine of the prevalent recognition
in America of the financial value of religion. "There is in
Wall Street a broker's office at the head of which is a woman,
Mrs. Gailord. She began each day's work with prayers in
the office. Early in 1907 she wanted to do even more; she
arranged with a clergyman to come every Wednesday and
asked the great financiers who were her neighbors,—the
Rockefellers, the Pierpont Morgans, the Schiffs(!),—of whose
religious tendencies she was aware, to cooperate." In a
foot-note he adds that he does not know whether the undertaking went through or not,—"but after all, that matters little; the interesting fact is that it was proposed!" The American reader's appreciation of the humor of the entire chapter
(think what a boon to the French literary writer is this one
Wall Street passage!) is saddened at times by reflection upon
the nostalgia with which Professor Schinz must suffer from
living in a country such as he depicts.

The next chapter is entitled "Medieval Pragmatism and
Modern Scholasticism." Medieval philosophy was distinctly
pragmatic; it supported theology which sustained the church
in its social task. The rationalistic method of Descartes in
enfranchising philosophy made necessary a new pragmatism, for a complete disintegration of religious beliefs was
too dangerous for society. This the contemporary pragmatic

philosophy supplies; it is a new scholasticism. Pascal, Rousseau, and Kant are its great forerunners, utilitarian ethics
not being sufficiently religious to fill the bill.

The first chapter of Part III, "Pragmatism and Truth,"
is called the Triumph of Pragmatism. Pragmatism will triumph; democracy is invading the whole world. America to-
day is what we (Europe) will be to-morrow. In America the
members of the intellectual class do not have children; im-
migrants coming from lower classes increase more and more.
Strict scientific truths would be dangerous for such a people;
it could not use them. And as if to prove that his volume is
not mere non-pragmatism, but is genuine anti-pragmatism,
Professor Schinz adds: "What is this stupid prejudice that
truth has anything to do with the practice of life? It was
necessary for our epoch of crude democracy to arrive before
such enormities could be seriously affirmed." "Truth has
nothing to do with life,"—and for this reason, pragmatism,
an acceptance of popular life as a philosophy, is so thoroughly false that it will surely triumph.

In the next chapter, however, Professor Schinz recovers
a little from this gloom. "Salvation is possible, but not possible," for the Latin civilizations have kept intact the principle at least of intellectual inequality. If only "the social
organization conceived before the Revolution had been continued, and existed in our own day, even supposing that free
thought had arrived (as it has) at the notion of determinism
in nature, then just because this principle is dangerous for
the masses, society would not have to yield itself to the
acrobatic feats of pragmatism; it would have accepted the
consequences of determinism and would, from the point of
view of practical life, have formulated *a rule of conduct
adapted to the masses*, a rule which would have satisfied
the masses, and which would not have sacrificed the dignity
of thought." If it is still not too late to establish the organization of society on this basis of castes (the word is our author's own), pragmatism may still be defeated,—a pragmatic
suggestion to anti-pragmatists in America to get busy in
politics if they wish really to down pragmatism.

The final chapter is entitled "Is William James a Pragmatist?" Professor Schinz here concludes that Mr. James's

main object is, after all, to oppose to the stupid popular pragmatism he finds all about him an enlightened pragmatism,— one which recognizes that practice is so different from theory, life so different from philosophy and science, that the latter may and should have its own rights in its own sphere without any dictation from practical life. (*Query*: Had Professor Schinz got hold by mistake of a book by one of Professor James's colleagues?) These second thoughts regarding Professor James may be compared with the earlier chapter in which it is shown that Professor James "exactly reflects" the popular tendencies about him. It would be interesting to see Professor Schinz apply his favorite disjunctive dilemma to his own case.

If the reader wonders why so much space has been devoted to a book of which the foregoing is a synopsis as exact as limits of space permit, I may remind him that the book appears in Alcan's "Library of Contemporary Philosophy"; and, coming from a teacher in a representative American college, can hardly fail in France at least of a certain prestige and authority, as presumably diagnostic of American life and thought.

Syllabus
The Pragmatic Movement
of Contemporary Thought

Note

This syllabus is synoptic rather than analytic. Consequently the general considerations in Parts One and Two are developed relatively more freely than those of the subsequent parts. The bibliography is neither exhaustive nor typically selective, articles of quite varying values being represented.

Part One. Historical Background.

On the negative side, the pragmatic movement is developed by various deadlocks into which modern thought has run, thereby necessitating a reconsideration of fundamental premises. On its positive side, it grows out of the development of experimental methods and of genetic and evolutionary conceptions in science.

I. Beginning with the problem of finding a natural method of knowledge for the guidance of individual life and for control of social organization, modern thought ran, on one side, into positivism, agnosticism, scepticism or materialism, denying primary practical values; or else, on the other side, into absolutism and transcendental idealism, breaking (in the supposed interests of morals and religion) with science. Modern "epistemology" has been a futile attempt to transcend the results of science by an analysis of its presuppositions.

II. The positive side consists in:

1. Revision of logical concepts by thoroughgoing substitution of the experimental method for the prior one-sided inductive and deductive methods. Kant's attempted reconciliation of empiricism and rationalism: its fundamental mistake was changing working or functional distinctions into fixed, ready-made separations. The pragmatic versus the absolutist solution.

2. The development of the earlier mechanical and mathematical notions of nature into dynamic and genetic conceptions: the historic method and biological evolution—novelty, genuine interaction and transition versus the completed, and fixed subsumption.

Part Two. Pragmatic Motifs in Modern Thought.

Philosophy from the 17th through the 19th centuries shows an increasing conflict between inherited intellectual tools, which were static and intellectualistic, and an animating interest which was practical and human.

I. 1. The practical motif in Bacon, Descartes, Hobbes and Locke.

2. Hume's sceptical opposition of action and reason. Custom and reason.

3. Kant's fixed dualism of the theoretic and practical.

4. Bradley's "practical makeshifts"—Royce's "eternal and practical."

II. The individualism of modern philosophy. Descartes and the right of "private judgment." The British individualism. In origin and intention constructive, but becomes sceptical and disintegrating. The analytic method of Hume and Mill. A world of isolated particulars. Emancipation from tradition and custom, but no positive program. Survival of the simple soul substance in the conception of the individual. Rise of "organic" concepts in sociology and biology. The self as agent, conservative and projective.

Part Three. Philosophic Reconstruction.

The new scientific conceptions make possible a fruitful and consistent execution of the thwarted intentions of modern philosophy.

I. Biologically, knowledge is found to be one natural function among others. The so-called problem of the relation of knowledge to "reality" is the problem of the interrelation of these various functions. The nervous system as an organ of adaptation and control; connections with organs of conservation and action. The brain and sense organs: stimuli and redirected response—modification of stimulus. Habit—the conservative principle; attention, the progressive. Conflict of habits in complex situations; function of "sensations" and "ideas." "Consciousness" and the strain of readjustment. Importance of symbols as factors of emancipation and of construction. Neglect of language in orthodox theories of knowledge. Knowledge as instrumental. Experience increases in depth and range of meaning.

II. The change in the individual with the transition from custom to reflection as method of action. The function of "subjectivity" in knowledge. The cultivation of doubt and inquiry. Berkeley's identification of mind and self. Absurd as an ontological proposition; valid as expressive of moral or voluntary attitude. Connection with scientific discovery. Contrast of Greek (deductive and classificatory) with modern experimental methods. The resulting view of the individual.

Part Four. Application of Pragmatic Method to Some Technical Problems of Knowledge.

Modern philosophy has been chiefly concerned (consciously or unconsciously) with the problem of the relation of experience and knowledge. It has been caught in dilemmas in its efforts to unite an empirical (or natural) origin of knowledge with an objectively valid reference of knowledge.

I. The old concept of experience: Hobbes—transformation by Locke and Hume. Sceptical result. Transcendental solution. Habit will do all that the Kantian categories are supposed to effect. Natural organization and reason. The *a priori* and *a posteriori*. Experience continuous and vital. The genetic and the eventual, or teleologic.

II. Particulars and universals. Sensations and concepts. The Kantian theory of judgment. The trivial or analytic and the instructive or synthetic; matters of fact and relations of ideas. Mathematics, morals (common sense) and physical science all turned against one another. Pragmatic meaning of particular (existential) and universal (meaning). Reorganization of experience versus the Absolute Experience.

Part Five. Application of Results to Problem of Truth.

Problem of truth has to do with relation of meaning (ideas) to existence. Hence a correct theory of truth depends upon a correct theory of intelligence and its functions.

I. Contrast of pragmatic theory with theory

   1. That truth is a property of things. This runs into objective idealism. "Reality" as rational. Pragmatic value of the notion of objective truth.

   2. That truth is an independent antecedent property of some ideas. Sceptical and solipsistic outcome. Genuine meaning of consistency and correspondence. Ideas as projections and as hypotheses. All truths experimental in character. The scientific theory of verification. Error and mistake. The "standard of truth" means an effective method of detecting and rectifying error.

II. Objections to the pragmatic theory of truth with answers.

Part Six. The Problem of Individualism.

I. The antinomy in modern philosophy: the effort to eliminate personal factors; the antagonism to "passion" need and choice; and the exaltation of the self. Idealism (both subjective and objective) vibrate between making self all, and merging self in the impersonal. Hume and transcendentalism agree in this. The self, and its function in knowledge, a crux for realism. Spencer's and Huxley's double bookkeeping.

II. Voluntarism. Personal Idealism and Humanism. The Will to Believe. True and false interpretations: Is "will" a separate entity or interpreted as a natural and social category?

III. The self biologically considered. The self logically considered; the functions of doubt, guessing and experimenting. The individual factor in discovery and the growth of knowledge systems, and, thereby, of nature. Nature and Art.

Part Seven. Some General Considerations.

I. *Application to Religion.*—The part played by religious motives in philosophy. Frankness of James in dealing with this. Philosophy as apologetic. James's method, while empirical, not specially pragmatic. Question of philosophy of religion is relation of existential facts to values. Tendency to make value itself existential. Pluralistic panpsychism afflicted with this fallacy as much as monistic transcendentalism. Religion is moral and pragmatic, not physical, psychical or metapsychical. Irrelevancy of "supernormal" phenomena, even if genuine. Bearing on question of God and immortality.

II. *Application to Philosophy.*

 1. Pragmatism must take its own medicine. Cannot be a metaphysics in old sense, because, being itself a mode of knowledge, all its theories must be recognized to be only working hypotheses and experimental in quality.

 2. Philosophy as method instead of as doctrine.

  (1) Locates typical problems or conflicts in experience.

  (2) Projects plans of dealing with them.

 3. General conclusion as to theory and practice.

 4. Misinterpretation of pragmatism as arbitrary subjection of theory to practice. Pragmatic value of free or pure theorizing. No progress possible without independent intellectual undertakings. Theory must, however, be a responsible division of labor, and not usurp irresponsible sovereignty.

Bibliography

I. GENERAL

(1) *Books.*

James. *Pragmatism.*

Moore. *The Functional versus the Representational Theories of Knowledge in Locke's Essay.*

Schiller. *Humanism; Studies in Humanism.*
Dewey. *Significance of the Problem of Knowledge; Studies in
    Logical Theory* (editor).
Pratt. *What Is Pragmatism?*
Schinz. *Anti-pragmatisme.*
Hébert. *Le pragmatisme.* See review by James, *Journal of Philos-
    ophy, Psychology and Scientific Methods,* Vol. V (1908), p.
    689.

(2) *Articles expository and critical in general, mostly un-
favorable.*

Lalande. "Pragmatisme, humanisme et verité." *Revue philosophi-
    que,* Vol. LXV (1908), p. 1.
Chide. "Pragmatisme et intellectualisme." *Revue philosophique,*
    Vol. LXV (1908), p. 367.
Stein. "Der Pragmatismus." *Archiv für systematische Philosophie,*
    n.s. Vol. XIV (1908), pp. 1, 143. (Summary ["A German
    Critic of Pragmatism"] in *Monist,* Vol. XIX [1909], p. 136.)
Bawden. "The New Philosophy Called Pragmatism." *Popular
    Science Monthly,* Vol. LXXIII (1908), p. 61.
Aliotta. "Il pragmatismo anglo-americano." *La Cultura Filosofica,*
    Vol. III (1909), p. 104.
Chiappelli. "Philosophie des valeurs." *Revue philosophique,* Vol.
    LXVII (1909), p. 225.
Carus. "Pragmatism." *Monist,* Vol. XVIII (1908), p. 321; Parodi.
    "La signification du pragmatisme." *Bulletin de la société
    française de philosophie,* Vol. VIII (1908), p. 249 ff.
Woodbridge. "Pragmatism and Education." *Educational Review,*
    Vol. XXXIV (1907), p. 227.
Tausch. "William James, the Pragmatist." *Monist,* Vol. XIX
    (1909), p. 1. See also p. 156, letter from Professor James.
Colvin. "Pragmatism, Old and New." *Monist,* Vol. XVI (1906),
    p. 547.
Russell, B. "Some Difficulties with the Epistemology of Pragma-
    tism and Radical Empiricism." *Philosophical Review,* Vol.
    XV (1906), p. 406.
Mentré. "La valeur pragmatique du pragmatisme." *Revue de
    philosophie,* Vol. XI (1907), pp. 5–22. (Reply by Borrell,
    "La notion de pragmatisme," p. 587; rejoinder by Mentré,
    "Complément à la note sur la valeur pragmatique du prag-
    matisme," p. 591, same volume.)
Baldwin. "Limits of Pragmatism." *Psychological Review,* Vol. XI
    (1904), p. 30.
Leighton. "Pragmatism." *Journal of Philosophy, Psychology and
    Scientific Methods,* Vol. I (1904), p. 148.
Armstrong. "Evolution of Pragmatism." *Journal of Philosophy,
    Psychology and Scientific Methods,* Vol. V (1908), p. 645.

Dewey. "What Does Pragmatism Mean by Practical?" *Journal of Philosophy, Psychology and Scientific Methods,* Vol. V (1908), p. 85.

Lovejoy. "The Thirteen Pragmatisms." *Journal of Philosophy, Psychology and Scientific Methods,* Vol. V (1908), p. 29.

Cox. "Pragmatism." *American Catholic Quarterly,* Vol. XXXIV (1909), p. 139.

Hibben. "The Test of Pragmatism." *Philosophical Review,* Vol. XVII (1908), p. 365.

Moore. "Pragmatism and Its Critics." *Philosophical Review,* Vol. XIV (1905), p. 322.

Lorenz-Ightham. "Der Pragmatismus." *Internationale Wochenschrift,* 1908.

II. SPECIAL ARTICLES.

Peirce. "How to Make Our Ideas Clear." *Popular Science Monthly,* Vol. XII (1878), p. 286 (idea but not word).

James. "Pragmatic Method." *Journal of Philosophy, Psychology and Scientific Methods,* Vol. I (1904), p. 673. (Reprint of Berkeley address of 1899 in which word was first used.)

Baldwin. "Pragmatism." *Dictionary of Philosophy and Psychology,* Vol. I (1901), pp. 321–23.

Peirce. "What Pragmatism Is." *Monist,* Vol. XV (1905), p. 161; "Issues of Pragmatism." *Monist,* Vol. XV (1905), p. 481; "Apology for Pragmatism." *Monist,* Vol. XVI (1906), p. 492.

Rieber. "Pragmatism and the *a priori.*" *University of California Publications in Philosophy,* Vol. I, p. 72; Bakewell. "Latter-Day Flowing-Philosophy." *University of California Publications in Philosophy,* Vol. I, p. 92.

Creighton. "Purpose as Logical Category." *Philosophical Review,* Vol. XIII (1904), p. 284.

Dewey. "Does Reality Possess Practical Character?" In *Essays Philosophical and Psychological,* p. 53.

Gordon. "Pragmatism in Aesthetics." In *Essays Philosophical and Psychological,* p. 459.

Dewey. "Experience and Objective Idealism." *Philosophical Review,* Vol. XV (1906), p. 465.

Mead. "Definition of the Psychical." In *Investigations Representing the Departments,* Vol. III (1903), p. 75.

Moore. "Existence, Meaning, and Reality." In *Investigations Representing the Departments,* Vol. II (1903), p. 29.

Dewey. "Logical Conditions of a Scientific Treatment of Morality." In *Investigations Representing the Departments,* Vol. III (1903), p. 113.

Royce. "The Eternal and the Practical." *Philosophical Review,* Vol. XIII (1904), p. 113.

Schiller. "Pragmatism and Pseudo-Pragmatism." *Mind,* Vol. XV (1906), p. 375; also "Is Mr. Bradley Becoming a Pragma-

tist?" *Mind*, Vol. XVII (1908), p. 370; "Plato or Protagoras."
Mind, Vol. XVII (1908), p. 518.
Bradley. "Ambiguity of Pragmatism." *Mind*, Vol. XVII (1908),
p. 226.
Sidgwick. Reply to Bradley, "The Ambiguity of Pragmatism."
Mind, Vol. XVII (1908), p. 368.
Russell, B. "Pragmatism as the Salvation from Philosophic
Doubt." *Journal of Philosophy, Psychology and Scientific
Methods*, Vol. IV (1907), p. 57; and elsewhere.
Schiller. "The Pragmatic Cure of Doubt." *Journal of Philosophy,
Psychology and Scientific Methods*, Vol. IV (1907), p. 235;
"Pragmatism versus Skepticism." *Journal of Philosophy, Psy-
chology and Scientific Methods*, Vol. IV (1907), p. 482; "A
Pragmatic Babe in the Wood." *Journal of Philosophy, Psy-
chology and Scientific Methods*, Vol. IV (1907), p. 42.
Lorenz-Ightham. "Das Verhältnis des Pragmatismus zu Kant."
Kant Studien, Vol. XIV (1909), p. 8.

III. MORE DISTINCTIVELY LOGICAL ARTICLES.

Dewey. "Experimental Theory of Knowledge." *Mind*, Vol. XV
(1906), p. 293.
Moore. "Absolutism and Teleology." *Philosophical Review*, Vol.
XVIII (1909), p. 309.
Vailati. "Pragmatism and Mathematical Logic." *Monist*, Vol. VI
(1906), p. 481; "A Pragmatic Zoologist." *Monist*, Vol. XVIII
(1908), p. 142 (see p. 150, quotation from Giardina on the
nature of scientific inference).
Rogers. "James's Theory of Knowledge." *Philosophical Review*,
Vol. XV (1906), p. 577.
Bode. "Concept of Pure Experience." *Philosophical Review*, Vol.
XIV (1905), p. 684.
Woodbridge. "Field of Logic." In *Congress of Arts and Science*,
Vol. I (1905), p. 313 (see especially pp. 319–26).
Perry. "Pragmatism as a Theory of Knowledge." *Journal of Phi-
losophy, Psychology and Scientific Methods*, Vol. IV (1907),
p. 365; "Pragmatism as a Philosophical Generalization."
Journal of Philosophy, Psychology and Scientific Methods,
Vol. IV (1907), p. 421.
Moore. Reply to Perry, "Professor Perry on Pragmatism." *Journal
of Philosophy, Psychology and Scientific Methods*, Vol. IV
(1907), p. 567.
Dewey. "Control of Ideas by Facts." *Journal of Philosophy, Psy-
chology and Scientific Methods*, Vol. IV (1907), pp. 197, 253,
309; "Logical Character of Ideas." *Journal of Philosophy,
Psychology and Scientific Methods*, Vol. V (1908), p. 378.
McGilvary. "Chicago 'Idea' and Idealism." *Journal of Philosophy,
Psychology and Scientific Methods*, Vol. V (1908), p. 589.

Dewey. "Some Stages of Logical Thought." *Philosophical Review*, Vol. IX (1900), p. 465.
Schiller. "Axioms as Postulates." In *Personal Idealism*, p. 47.

IV. TRUTH DISCUSSION.

Stout. "Error." In *Personal Idealism*, p. 1.
Taylor. "Truth and Practice." *Philosophical Review*, Vol. XIV (1905), p. 265.
Bradley. "On Truth and Copying." *Mind*, Vol. XVI (1907), p. 165; "Truth and Practice." *Mind*, Vol. XIII (1904), p. 309.
Schiller. "Bradley's Theory of Truth." *Mind*, Vol. XVI (1907), p. 401.
Sturt. "Bradley on Truth and Copying." *Mind*, Vol. XVI (1907), p. 416.
Dewey. "Reality and the Criterion for the Truth of Ideas." *Mind*, Vol. XVI (1907), p. 317.
Russell, B. "The Nature of Truth." *Mind*, Vol. XV (1906), p. 528.
Taylor. "Truth and Consequences." *Mind*, Vol. XV (1906), p. 81.
James. "Humanism and Truth." *Mind*, Vol. XIII (1904), p. 457.
Baldwin. "On Truth." *Psychological Review*, Vol. XIV (1907), p. 264.
James. "Pragmatism's Conception of Truth." *Journal of Philosophy, Psychology and Scientific Methods*, Vol. IV (1907), p. 141; "Pratt on Truth." *Journal of Philosophy, Psychology and Scientific Methods*, Vol. IV (1907), p. 464.
Joachim. *The Nature of Truth: An Essay*; James. "A Word More About Truth." *Journal of Philosophy, Psychology and Scientific Methods*, Vol. IV (1907), p. 396.
Pratt. "Truth and Its Verification." *Journal of Philosophy, Psychology and Scientific Methods*, Vol. IV (1907), p. 320.
James and Russell, B. "Controversy about Truth." *Journal of Philosophy, Psychology and Scientific Methods*, Vol. IV (1907), p. 289.
Strong. "Pragmatism and Its Definition of Truth." *Journal of Philosophy, Psychology and Scientific Methods*, Vol. V (1908), p. 256.
Russell, J. E. "The Pragmatist's Meaning of Truth." *Journal of Philosophy, Psychology and Scientific Methods*, Vol. III (1906), p. 599.
Moore. "Truth Value." *Journal of Philosophy, Psychology and Scientific Methods*, Vol. V (1908), p. 429.
Pratt. "Truth and Ideas." *Journal of Philosophy, Psychology and Scientific Methods*, Vol. V (1908), p. 122.
Bush. "Provisional and Eternal Truth." *Journal of Philosophy, Psychology and Scientific Methods*, Vol. V (1908), p. 181.
Bakewell. "Meaning of Truth." *Philosophical Review*, Vol. XVII (1908), p. 579.

Creighton. "Nature and Criterion of Truth." *Philosophical Review*,
     Vol. XVII (1908), p. 592.
Gardiner. "Problem of Truth." *Philosophical Review*, Vol. XVII
     (1908), p. 113.
James. "The Pragmatist Account of Truth and Its Misunder-
     standers." *Philosophical Review*, Vol. XVII (1908), p. 1.
Knox. "Pragmatism; the Evolution of Truth." *Quarterly Review*,
     Vol. CCX (1909), p. 379.

V. PERSONAL AND VOLITIONAL FACTOR.

James. *The Will to Believe* (Title essay); *Pragmatism*.
Schiller. *Personal Idealism*, especially.
Dewey. "Beliefs and Realities." *Philosophical Review*, Vol. XV
     (1906), p. 113; "Psychology and Philosophic Method."
     University [of California] *Chronicle*, Vol. II (1899), p. 159.

VI. RELIGION.

James. *The Varieties of Religious Experience* (last chapters);
     Pragmatism (Ch. 8); *A Pluralistic Universe* (Chs. 7 and 8).
Santayana. *The Life of Reason: or the Phases of Human Progress*,
     (Vol. III) *Reason in Religion*.
Brown. "Pragmatic Value of the Absolute." *Journal of Philosophy,
     Psychology and Scientific Methods*, Vol. IV (1907), p. 459.

RELATED ARTICLES.

James. "Pure Experience." *Journal of Philosophy, Psychology and
     Scientific Methods*, Vol. I (1904), pp. 533, 561; "Does 'Con-
     sciousness' Exist?" *Journal of Philosophy, Psychology and
     Scientific Methods*, Vol. I (1904), p. 477; "Thing and Its
     Relations." *Journal of Philosophy, Psychology and Scientific
     Methods*, Vol. II (1905), p. 29; "Essence of Humanism."
     Journal of Philosophy, Psychology and Scientific Methods,
     Vol. II (1905), p. 113; "Place of Affectional Facts." *Journal
     of Philosophy, Psychology and Scientific Methods*, Vol. II
     (1905), p. 281.
Schiller. "Defence of Humanism." *Mind*, n.s. Vol. XIII (1904),
     p. 525.
Rey. "Vers le positivisme absolu." *Revue philosophique de la
     France et de l'etranger*, Vol. LXVIII (1909), p. 461.

Though not under the denomination of pragmatism, the
following articles concerning the nature of science are important.

Le Roy. "De la valeur objective des lois physiques." *Bulletin de la
     société française de philosophie*, Vol. I (1901), p. 5.
Poincaré. "Sur la valeur objective de la science." *Revue de meta-
     physique et de morale*, Vol. X (1902), p. 263.

Boutroux. "L'objectivité intrinsèque des mathématiques." *Revue de metaphysique et de morale*, Vol. XI (1903), p. 573.
An interesting discussion of knowledge and utility will be found (under the title of Ophelism) in Benn, *History of Rationalism*, Vol. I.

Moral Principles in Education

1. THE MORAL PURPOSE OF THE SCHOOL

An English contemporary philosopher has called attention to the difference between moral ideas and ideas about morality. "Moral ideas" are ideas of any sort whatsoever which take effect in conduct and improve it, make it better than it otherwise would be. Similarly, one may say, immoral ideas are ideas of whatever sort (whether arithmetical or geographical or physiological) which show themselves in making behavior worse than it would otherwise be; and non-moral ideas, one may say, are such ideas and pieces of information as leave conduct uninfluenced for either the better or the worse. Now "ideas about morality" may be morally indifferent or immoral or moral. There is nothing in the nature of ideas *about* morality, of information *about* honesty or purity or kindness which automatically transmutes such ideas into good character or good conduct.

This distinction between moral ideas, ideas of any sort whatsoever that have become a part of character and hence a part of the working motives of behavior, and ideas *about* moral action that may remain as inert and ineffective as if they were so much knowledge about Egyptian archaeology, is fundamental to the discussion of moral education. The business of the educator—whether parent or teacher—is to see to it that the greatest possible number of ideas acquired by children and youth are acquired in such a vital way that they become *moving* ideas, motive-forces in the guidance of conduct. This demand and this opportunity make the moral purpose universal and dominant in all instruction—whatsoever the topic. Were it not for this possibility, the familiar statement that the ultimate purpose of all education is character-forming would be hypocritical pretense; for as everyone knows, the direct and immediate attention of teachers and pupils must be, for the greater part of the time, upon intellectual matters. It is out of the question to keep direct moral considerations constantly uppermost. But it is not out of the question to aim at making the methods of learning, of acquiring intellectual power, and of assimilating subject-matter, such that they will render behavior more enlightened, more consistent, more vigorous than it otherwise would be.

The same distinction between "moral ideas" and "ideas about morality" explains for us a source of continual misunderstanding between teachers in the schools and critics of education outside of the schools. The latter look through the school programs, the school courses of study, and do not find any place set apart for instruction in ethics or for "moral teaching." Then they assert that the schools are doing nothing, or next to nothing, for character-training; they become emphatic, even vehement, about the moral deficiencies of public education. The school-teachers, on the other hand, resent these criticisms as an injustice, and hold not only that they do "teach morals," but that they teach them every moment of the day, five days in the week. In this contention the teachers *in principle* are in the right; if they are in the wrong, it is not because special periods are not set aside for what after all can only be teaching *about* morals, but because their own characters, or their school atmosphere and ideals, or their methods of teaching, or the subject-matter which they teach, are not such *in detail* as to bring intellectual results into vital union with character so that they become working forces in behavior. Without discussing, therefore, the limits or the value of so-called direct moral instruction (or, better, instruction *about* morals), it may be laid down as fundamental that the influence of direct moral instruction, even at its very best, is *comparatively* small in amount and slight in influence, when the whole field of moral growth through education is taken into account. This larger field of indirect and vital moral education, the development of character through all the agencies, instrumentalities, and materials of school life is, therefore, the subject of our present discussion.

2. THE MORAL TRAINING GIVEN BY THE SCHOOL COMMUNITY

There cannot be two sets of ethical principles, one for life in the school, and the other for life outside of the school. As conduct is one, so also the principles of conduct are one. The tendency to discuss the morals of the school as if the school were an institution by itself is highly unfortunate. The moral responsibility of the school, and of those who conduct it, is to society. The school is fundamentally an institution erected by society to do a certain specific work,—to exercise a certain specific function in maintaining the life and advancing the welfare of society. The educational system which does not recognize that this fact entails upon it an ethical responsibility is derelict and a defaulter. It is not doing what it was called into existence to do, and what it pretends to do. Hence the entire structure of the school in general and its concrete workings in particular need to be considered from time to time with reference to the social position and function of the school.

The idea that the moral work and worth of the public-school system as a whole are to be measured by its social value is, indeed, a familiar notion. However, it is frequently taken in too limited and rigid a way. The social work of the school is often limited to training for citizenship, and citizenship is then interpreted in a narrow sense as meaning capacity to vote intelligently, disposition to obey laws, etc. But it is futile to contract and cramp the ethical responsibility of the school in this way. The child is one, and he must either live his social life as an integral unified being, or suffer loss and create friction. To pick out one of the many social relations which the child bears, and to define the work of the school by that alone, is like instituting a vast and complicated system of physical exercise which would have for its object simply the development of the lungs and the power of breathing, independent of other organs and functions.

The child is an organic whole, intellectually, socially, and morally, as well as physically. We must take the child as a member of society in the broadest sense, and demand for and from the schools whatever is necessary to enable the child intelligently to recognize all his social relations and take his part in sustaining them.

To isolate the formal relationship of citizenship from the whole system of relations with which it is actually interwoven; to suppose that there is some one particular study or mode of treatment which can make the child a good citizen; to suppose, in other words, that a good citizen is anything more than a thoroughly efficient and serviceable member of society, one with all his powers of body and mind under control, is a hampering superstition which it is hoped may soon disappear from educational discussion.

The child is to be not only a voter and a subject of law; he is also to be a member of a family, himself in turn responsible, in all probability, for rearing and training of future children, thereby maintaining the continuity of society. He is to be a worker, engaged in some occupation which will be of use to society, and which will maintain his own independence and self-respect. He is to be a member of some particular neighborhood and community, and must contribute to the values of life, add to the decencies and graces of civilization wherever he is. These are bare and formal statements, but if we let our imagination translate them into their concrete details, we have a wide and varied scene. For the child properly to take his place in reference to these various functions means training in science, in art, in history; means command of the fundamental methods of inquiry and the fundamental tools of intercourse and communication; means a trained and sound body, skillful eye and hand; means habits of industry, perseverance; in short, habits of serviceableness.

Moreover, the society of which the child is to be a member is, in the United States, a democratic and progressive society. The child must be educated for leadership as well as for obedience. He must have power of self-direction and power of directing others, power of administration, ability to assume positions of responsibility. This necessity of educating for leadership is as great on the industrial as on the political side.

New inventions, new machines, new methods of transportation and intercourse are making over the whole scene of action year by year. It is an absolute impossibility to educate the child for any fixed station in life. So far as education is conducted unconsciously or consciously on this basis, it results in fitting the future citizen for no station in life, but makes him a drone, a hanger-on, or an actual retarding influence in the onward movement. Instead of caring for himself and for others, he becomes one who has himself to be cared for. Here, too, the ethical responsibility of the school on the social side must be interpreted in the broadest and freest spirit; it is equivalent to that training of the child which will give him such possession of himself that he may take charge of himself; may not only adapt himself to the changes that are going on, but have power to shape and direct them.

Apart from participation in social life, the school has no moral end nor aim. As long as we confine ourselves to the school as an isolated institution, we have no directing principles, because we have no object. For example, the end of education is said to be the harmonious development of all the powers of the individual. Here no reference to social life or membership is apparent, and yet many think we have in it an adequate and thoroughgoing definition of the goal of education. But if this definition be taken independently of social relationship we have no way of telling what is meant by any one of the terms employed. We do not know what a power is; we do not know what development is; we do not know what harmony is. A power is a power only with reference to the use to which it is put, the function it has to serve. If we leave out the uses supplied by social life we have nothing but the old "faculty psychology" to tell what is meant by power and what the specific powers are. The principle reduces itself to enumerating a lot of faculties like perception, memory, reasoning, etc., and then stating that each one of these powers needs to be developed.

Education then becomes a gymnastic exercise. Acute powers of observation and memory might be developed by studying Chinese characters; acuteness in reasoning might be got by discussing the scholastic subtleties of the Middle Ages. The simple fact is that there is no isolated faculty of observation, or memory, or reasoning any more than there is an original faculty of black-smithing, carpentering, or steam engineering. Faculties mean simply that particular impulses and habits have been coordinated or framed with reference to accomplishing certain definite kinds of work. We need to know the social situations in which the individual will have to use ability to observe, recollect, imagine, and reason, in order to have any way of telling what a training of mental powers actually means.

What holds in the illustration of this particular definition of education holds good from whatever point of view we approach the matter. Only as we interpret school activities with reference to the larger circle of social activities to which they relate do we find any standard for judging their moral significance.

The school itself must be a vital social institution to a much greater extent than obtains at present. I am told that there is a swimming school in a certain city where youth are taught to swim without going into the water, being repeatedly drilled in the various movements which are necessary for swimming. When one of the young men so trained was asked what he did when he got into the water, he laconically replied, "Sunk." The story happens to be true; were it not, it would seem to be a fable made expressly for the purpose of typifying the ethical relationship of school to society. The school cannot be a preparation for social life excepting as it reproduces, within itself, typical conditions of social life. At present it is largely engaged in the futile task of Sisyphus. It is endeavoring to form habits in children for use in a social life which, it would almost seem, is carefully and purposely kept away from vital contact with the child undergoing training. The only way to prepare for social life is to engage in social life. To form habits of social usefulness and serviceableness apart from any direct social need and motive, apart from any existing social situation, is, to the letter, teaching the child to swim by going through motions outside of the water. The most indispensable condition is left out of account, and the results are correspondingly partial.

The much lamented separation in the schools of intellectual and moral training, of acquiring information and growing in character, is simply one expression of the failure to conceive and construct the school as a social institution, having social life and value within itself. Except so far as the school is an embryonic typical community life, moral training must be partly pathological and partly formal. Training is pathological when stress is laid upon correcting wrongdoing instead of upon forming habits of positive service. Too often the teacher's concern with the moral life of pupils takes the form of alertness for failures to conform to school rules and routine. These regulations, judged from the standpoint of the development of the child at the time, are more or less conventional and arbitrary. They are rules which have to be made in order that the existing modes of school work may go on; but the lack of inherent necessity in these school modes reflects itself in a feeling, on the part of the child, that the moral discipline of the school is arbitrary. Any conditions that compel the teacher to take note of failures rather than of healthy growth give false standards and result in distortion and perversion. Attending to wrong-doing ought to be an incident rather than a principle. The child ought to have a positive consciousness of what he is about, so as to judge his acts from the standpoint of reference to the work which he has to do. Only in this way does he have a vital standard, one that enables him to turn failures to account for the future.

By saying that the moral training of the school is formal, I mean that the moral habits currently emphasized by the school are habits which are created, as it were, *ad hoc*. Even the habits of promptness, regularity, industry, non-interference with the work of others, faithfulness to tasks imposed, which are specially inculcated in the school, are habits that are necessary simply because the school system is what it is, and must be preserved intact. If we grant the inviolability of the school system as it is, these habits represent permanent and necessary moral ideas; but just in so far as the school system is itself isolated and mechanical,

insistence upon these moral habits is more or less unreal, because the ideal to which they relate is not itself necessary.
The duties, in other words, are distinctly school duties, not
life duties. If we compare this condition with that of the
well-ordered home, we find that the duties and responsibilities that the child has there to recognize do not belong to
the family as a specialized and isolated institution, but flow
from the very nature of the social life in which the family
participates and to which it contributes. The child ought to
have the same motives for right doing and to be judged by
the same standards in the school, as the adult in the wider
social life to which he belongs. Interest in community welfare, an interest that is intellectual and practical, as well as
emotional—an interest, that is to say, in perceiving whatever
makes for social order and progress, and in carrying these
principles into execution—is the moral habit to which all the
special school habits must be related if they are to be animated by the breath of life.

3. THE MORAL TRAINING FROM METHODS OF INSTRUCTION

The principle of the social character of the school as the basic factor in the moral education given may be also applied to the question of methods of instruction,—not in their details, but their general spirit. The emphasis then falls upon construction and giving out, rather than upon absorption and mere learning. We fail to recognize how essentially individualistic the latter methods are, and how unconsciously, yet certainly and effectively, they react into the child's ways of judging and of acting. Imagine forty children all engaged in reading the same books, and in preparing and reciting the same lessons day after day. Suppose this process constitutes by far the larger part of their work, and that they are continually judged from the standpoint of what they are able to take in in a study hour and reproduce in a recitation hour. There is next to no opportunity for any social division of labor. There is no opportunity for each child to work out something specifically his own, which he may contribute to the common stock, while he, in turn, participates in the productions of others. All are set to do exactly the same work and turn out the same products. The social spirit is not cultivated,—in fact, in so far as the purely individualistic method gets in its work, it atrophies for lack of use. One reason why reading aloud in school is poor is that the real motive for the use of language—the desire to communicate and to learn—is not utilized. The child knows perfectly well that the teacher and all his fellow pupils have exactly the same facts and ideas before them that he has; he is not *giving* them anything at all. And it may be questioned whether the moral lack is not as great as the intellectual. The child is born with a natural desire to give out, to do, to serve. When this tendency is not used, when conditions are such that other motives are substituted, the accumulation of an influence working against the social spirit is much larger than we have any idea of,—especially when the burden of work, week after week, and year after year, falls upon this side.

But lack of cultivation of the social spirit is not all. Positively individualistic motives and standards are inculcated. Some stimulus must be found to keep the child at his studies. At the best this will be his affection for his teacher, together with a feeling that he is not violating school rules, and thus negatively, if not positively, is contributing to the good of the school. I have nothing to say against these motives so far as they go, but they are inadequate. The relation between the piece of work to be done and affection for a third person is external, not intrinsic. It is therefore liable to break down whenever the external conditions are changed. Moreover, this attachment to a particular person, while in a way social, may become so isolated and exclusive as to be selfish in quality. In any case, the child should gradually grow out of this relatively external motive into an appreciation, for its own sake, of the social value of what he has to do, because of its larger relations to life, not pinned down to two or three persons.

But, unfortunately, the motive is not always at this relative best, but mixed with lower motives which are distinctly egoistic. Fear is a motive which is almost sure to enter in,—not necessarily physical fear, or fear of punishment, but fear of losing the approbation of others; or fear of failure, so extreme as to be morbid and paralyzing. On the other side, emulation and rivalry enter in. Just because all are doing the same work, and are judged (either in recitation or examination with reference to grading and to promotion) not from the standpoint of their personal contribution, but from that of *comparative* success, the feeling of superiority over others is unduly appealed to, while timid children are depressed. Children are judged with reference to their capacity to realize the same external standard. The weaker gradually lose their sense of power, and accept a position of continuous and persistent inferiority. The effect upon both self-respect and respect for work need not be dwelt upon. The strong learn to glory, not in their strength, but in the fact that they are stronger. The child is prematurely launched into the region of individualistic competition, and this in a direction where competition is least applicable, namely, in intellectual and artistic matters, whose law is cooperation and participation.

Next, perhaps, to the evils of passive absorption and of competition for external standing come, perhaps, those which result from the eternal emphasis upon preparation for a remote future. I do not refer here to the waste of energy and vitality that accrues when children, who live so largely in the immediate present, are appealed to in the name of a dim and uncertain future which means little or nothing to them. I have in mind rather the habitual procrastination that develops when the motive for work is future, not present; and the false standards of judgment that are created when work is estimated, not on the basis of present need and present responsibility, but by reference to an external result, like passing an examination, getting promoted, entering high school, getting into college, etc. Who can reckon up the loss of moral power that arises from the constant impression that nothing is worth doing in itself, but only as a preparation for something else, which in turn is only a getting ready for some genuinely serious end beyond? Moreover, as a rule, it will be found that remote success is an end which appeals most to those in whom egoistic desire to get ahead—to get ahead of others—is already only too strong a motive. Those in whom personal ambition is already so strong that it paints glowing pictures of future victories may be touched; others of a more generous nature do not respond.

I cannot stop to paint the other side. I can only say that the introduction of every method that appeals to the child's active powers, to his capacities in construction, production, and creation, marks an opportunity to shift the centre of ethical gravity from an absorption which is selfish to a service which is social. Manual training is more than manual; it is more than intellectual; in the hands of any good teacher it lends itself easily, and almost as a matter of course, to development of social habits. Ever since the philosophy of Kant, it has been a commonplace of aesthetic theory, that art is universal; that it is not the product of purely personal desire or appetite, or capable of merely individual appropriation, but has a value participated in by all who perceive it. Even in the schools where most conscious attention is paid to moral considerations, the methods of study and recitation may be such as to emphasize appreciation rather than power, an emotional readiness to assimilate the experiences of others, rather than enlightened and trained capacity to carry forward those values which in other conditions and past times made those experiences worth having. At all events, separation between instruction and character continues in our schools (in spite of the efforts of individual teachers) as a result of divorce between learning and doing. The attempt to attach genuine moral effectiveness to the mere processes of learning, and to the habits which go along with learning, can result only in a training infected with formality, arbitrariness, and an undue emphasis upon failure to conform. That there is as much accomplished as there is shows the possibilities involved in methods of school activity which afford opportunity for reciprocity, cooperation, and positive personal achievement.

4. THE SOCIAL NATURE OF THE COURSE OF STUDY

In many respects, it is the subject-matter used in school life which decides both the general atmosphere of the school and the methods of instruction and discipline which rule. A barren "course of study," that is to say, a meagre and narrow field of school activities, cannot possibly lend itself to the development of a vital social spirit or to methods that appeal to sympathy and cooperation instead of to absorption, exclusiveness, and competition. Hence it becomes an all-important matter to know how we shall apply our social standard of moral value to the subject-matter of school work, to what we call, traditionally, the "studies" that occupy pupils.

A study is to be considered as a means of bringing the child to realize the social scene of action. Thus considered it gives a criterion for selection of material and for judgment of values. We have at present three independent values set up: one of culture, another of information, and another of discipline. In reality, these refer only to three phases of social interpretation. Information is genuine or educative only in so far as it presents definite images and conceptions of materials placed in a context of social life. Discipline is genuinely educative only as it represents a reaction of information into the individual's own powers so that he brings them under control for social ends. Culture, if it is to be genuinely educative and not an external polish or factitious varnish, represents the vital union of information and discipline. It marks the socialization of the individual in his outlook upon life.

This point may be illustrated by brief reference to a few of the school studies. In the first place, there is no line of demarcation within facts themselves which classifies them as belonging to science, history, or geography, respectively. The pigeon-hole classification which is so prevalent at pres-

ent (fostered by introducing the pupil at the outset into a
number of different studies contained in different text-
books) gives an utterly erroneous idea of the relations of
studies to one another and to the intellectual whole to which
all belong. In fact, these subjects have to do with the same
ultimate reality, namely, the conscious experience of man.
It is only because we have different interests, or different
ends, that we sort out the material and label part of it science, part of it history, part geography, and so on. Each
"sorting" represents materials arranged with reference to
some one dominant typical aim or process of the social life.

This social criterion is necessary, not only to mark off
studies from one another, but also to grasp the reasons for
each study,—the motives in connection with which it shall
be presented. How, for example, should we define geography?
What is the unity in the different so-called divisions of geography,—mathematical geography, physical geography, political geography, commercial geography? Are they purely
empirical classifications dependent upon the brute fact that
we run across a lot of different facts? Or is there some intrinsic principle through which the material is distributed
under these various heads,—something in the interest and
attitude of the human mind towards them? I should say
that geography has to do with all those aspects of social life
which are concerned with the interaction of the life of man
and nature; or, that it has to do with the world considered
as the scene of social interaction. Any fact, then, will be
geographical in so far as it has to do with the dependence
of man upon his natural environment, or with changes introduced in this environment through the life of man.

The four forms of geography referred to above represent, then, four increasing stages of abstraction in discussing the mutual relation of human life and nature. The beginning must be social geography, the frank recognition of
the earth as the home of men acting in relations to one another. I mean by this that the essence of any geographical
fact is the consciousness of two persons, or two groups of
persons, who are at once separated and connected by their
physical environment, and that the interest is in seeing how
these people are at once kept apart and brought together in

their actions by the instrumentality of the physical environment. The ultimate significance of lake, river, mountain, and plain is not physical but social; it is the part which it plays in modifying and directing human relationships. This evidently involves an extension of the term commercial. It has to do not simply with business, in the narrow sense, but with whatever relates to human intercourse and intercommunication as affected by natural forms and properties. Political geography represents this same social interaction taken in a static instead of in a dynamic way; taken, that is, as temporarily crystallized and fixed in certain forms. Physical geography (including under this not simply physiography, but also the study of flora and fauna) represents a further analysis or abstraction. It studies the conditions which determine human action, leaving out of account, temporarily, the ways in which they concretely do this. Mathematical geography carries the analysis back to more ultimate and remote conditions, showing that the physical conditions of the earth are not ultimate, but depend upon the place which the world occupies in a larger system. Here, in other words, are traced, step by step, the links which connect the immediate social occupations and groupings of men with the whole natural system which ultimately conditions them. Step by step the scene is enlarged and the image of what enters into the make-up of social action is widened and broadened; at no time is the chain of connection to be broken.

It is out of the question to take up the studies one by one and show that their meaning is similarly controlled by social considerations. But I cannot forbear saying a word or two upon history. History is vital or dead to the child according as it is, or is not, presented from the sociological standpoint. When treated simply as a record of what has passed and gone, it must be mechanical, because the past, as the past, is remote. Simply as the past there is no motive for attending to it. The ethical value of history teaching will be measured by the extent to which past events are made the means of understanding the present,—affording insight into what makes up the structure and working of society to-day. Existing social structure is exceedingly complex. It is practically impossible for the child to attack it *en masse* and get any definite mental image of it. But type phases of historical development may be selected which will exhibit, as through a telescope, the essential constituents of the existing order. Greece, for example, represents what art and growing power of individual expression stand for; Rome exhibits the elements and forces of political life on a tremendous scale. Or, as these civilizations are themselves relatively complex, a study of still simpler forms of hunting, nomadic, and agricultural life in the beginnings of civilization, a study of the effects of the introduction of iron, and iron tools, reduces the complexity to simpler elements.

One reason historical teaching is usually not more effective is that the student is set to acquire information in such a way that no epochs or factors stand out in his mind as typical; everything is reduced to the same dead level. The way to secure the necessary perspective is to treat the past as if it were a projected present with some of its elements enlarged.

The principle of contrast is as important as that of similarity. Because the present life is so close to us, touching us at every point, we cannot get away from it to see it as it really is. Nothing stands out clearly or sharply as characteristic. In the study of past periods, attention necessarily attaches itself to striking differences. Thus the child gets a locus of imagination, through which he can remove himself from the pressure of present surrounding circumstances and define them.

History is equally available in teaching the *methods* of social progress. It is commonly stated that history must be studied from the standpoint of cause and effect. The truth of this statement depends upon its interpretation. Social life is so complex and the various parts of it are so organically related to one another and to the natural environment, that it is impossible to say that this or that thing is the cause of some other particular thing. But the study of history can reveal the main instruments in the discoveries, inventions, new modes of life, etc., which have initiated the great epochs of social advance; and it can present to the child types of the main lines of social progress, and can set before him what have been the chief difficulties and obstructions in the way of progress. Once more this can be done only in so far as it is recognized that social forces in themselves are always the same,—that the same kind of influences were at work one hundred and one thousand years ago that are now working, —and that particular historical epochs afford illustration of the way in which the fundamental forces work.

Everything depends, then, upon history being treated from a social standpoint; as manifesting the agencies which have influenced social development and as presenting the typical institutions in which social life has expressed itself. The culture-epoch theory, while working in the right direction, has failed to recognize the importance of treating past periods with relation to the present,—as affording insight into the representative factors of its structure; it has treated these periods too much as if they had some meaning or value in themselves. The way in which the biographical method is handled illustrates the same point. It is often treated in such a way as to exclude from the child's consciousness (or at least not sufficiently to emphasize) the social forces and principles involved in the association of the masses of men. It is quite true that the child is easily interested in history from the biographical standpoint; but unless "the hero" is treated in relation to the community life behind him that he sums up and directs, there is danger that history will reduce itself to a mere exciting story. Then moral instruction reduces itself to drawing certain lessons from the life of the particular personalities concerned, instead of widening and deepening the child's imagination of social relations, ideals, and means.

It will be remembered that I am not making these points for their own sake, but with reference to the general principle that when a study is taught as a mode of understanding social life it has positive ethical import. What the normal child continuously needs is not so much isolated moral lessons upon the importance of truthfulness and honesty, or the beneficent results that follow from a particular act of patriotism, as the formation of habits of social imagination and conception.

I take one more illustration, namely, mathematics. This

does, or does not, accomplish its full purpose according as it is, or is not, presented as a social tool. The prevailing divorce between information and character, between knowledge and social action, stalks upon the scene here. The moment mathematical study is severed from the place which it occupies with reference to use in social life, it becomes unduly abstract, even upon the purely intellectual side. It is presented as a matter of technical relations and formulae apart from any end or use. What the study of number suffers from in elementary education is lack of motivation. Back of this and that and the other particular bad method is the radical mistake of treating number as if it were an end in itself, instead of the means of accomplishing some end. Let the child get a consciousness of what is the use of number, of what it really is for, and half the battle is won. Now this consciousness of the use of reason implies some end which is implicitly social.

One of the absurd things in the more advanced study of arithmetic is the extent to which the child is introduced to numerical operations which have no distinctive mathematical principles characterizing them, but which represent certain general principles found in business relationships. To train the child in these operations, while paying no attention to the business realities in which they are of use, or to the conditions of social life which make these business activities necessary, is neither arithmetic nor common sense. The child is called upon to do examples in interest, partnership, banking, brokerage, and so on through a long string, and no pains are taken to see that, in connection with the arithmetic, he has any sense of the social realities involved. This part of arithmetic is essentially sociological in its nature. It ought either to be omitted entirely, or else be taught in connection with a study of the relevant social realities. As we now manage the study, it is the old case of learning to swim apart from the water over again, with correspondingly bad results on the practical side.

In concluding this portion of the discussion, we may say that our conceptions of moral education have been too narrow, too formal, and too pathological. We have associated the term ethical with certain special acts which are labeled virtues and are set off from the mass of other acts, and are still more divorced from the habitual images and motives of the children performing them. Moral instruction is thus associated with teaching about these particular virtues, or with instilling certain sentiments in regard to them. The moral has been conceived in too goody-goody a way. Ultimate moral motives and forces are nothing more or less than social intelligence—the power of observing and comprehending social situations,—and social power—trained capacities of control—at work in the service of social interest and aims. There is no fact which throws light upon the constitution of society, there is no power whose training adds to social resourcefulness that is not moral.

I sum up, then, this part of the discussion by asking your attention to the moral trinity of the school. The demand is for social intelligence, social power, and social interests. Our resources are (1) the life of the school as a social institution in itself; (2) methods of learning and of doing work; and (3) the school studies or curriculum. In so far as the school represents, in its own spirit, a genuine community life; in so far as what are called school discipline, government, order, etc., are the expressions of this inherent social spirit; in so far as the methods used are those that appeal to the active and constructive powers, permitting the child to give out and thus to serve; in so far as the curriculum is so selected and organized as to provide the material for affording the child a consciousness of the world in which he has to play a part, and the demands he has to meet; so far as these ends are met, the school is organized on an ethical basis. So far as general principles are concerned, all the basic ethical requirements are met. The rest remains between the individual teacher and the individual child.

5. THE PSYCHOLOGICAL ASPECT OF MORAL EDUCATION

So far we have been considering the make-up of purposes and results that constitute conduct—its "what." But conduct has a certain method and spirit also—its "how." Conduct may be looked upon as expressing the attitudes and dispositions of an *individual*, as well as realizing social results and maintaining the social fabric. A consideration of conduct as a mode of individual performance, personal doing, takes us from the social to the psychological side of morals. In the first place, all conduct springs ultimately and radically out of native instincts and impulses. We must know what these instincts and impulses are, and what they are at each particular stage of the child's development, in order to know what to appeal to and what to build upon. Neglect of this principle may give a mechanical imitation of moral conduct, but the imitation will be ethically dead, because it is external and has its centre without, not within, the individual. We must study the child, in other words, to get our indications, our symptoms, our suggestions. The more or less spontaneous acts of the child are not to be thought of as setting moral forms to which the efforts of the educator must conform—this would result simply in spoiling the child; but they are symptoms which require to be interpreted: stimuli which need to be responded to in directed ways; material which, in however transformed a shape, is the only ultimate constituent of future moral conduct and character.

Then, secondly, our ethical principles need to be stated in psychological terms because the child supplies us with the only means or instruments by which to realize moral ideals. The subject-matter of the curriculum, however important, however judiciously selected, is empty of conclusive moral content until it is made over into terms of the individual's own activities, habits, and desires. We must know what history, geography, and mathematics mean in psychological terms, that is, as modes of personal experiencing, before we can get out of them their moral potentialities.

The psychological side of education sums itself up, of course, in a consideration of character. It is a commonplace to say that the development of character is the end of all school work. The difficulty lies in the execution of the idea. And an underlying difficulty in this execution is the lack of a clear conception of what character means. This may seem an extreme statement. If so, the idea may be conveyed by saying that we generally conceive of character simply in terms of results; we have no clear conception of it in psychological terms—that is, as a process, as working or dynamic. We know what character means in terms of the actions which proceed from it, but we have not a definite conception of it on its inner side, as a system of working forces.

(1) Force, efficiency in execution, or overt action, is one necessary constituent of character. In our moral books and lectures we may lay the stress upon good intentions, etc. But we know practically that the kind of character we hope to build up through our education is one that not only has good intentions, but that insists upon carrying them out. Any other character is wishy-washy; it is goody, not good. The individual must have the power to stand up and count for something in the actual conflicts of life. He must have initiative, insistence, persistence, courage, and industry. He must, in a word, have all that goes under the name "*force of character.*" Undoubtedly, individuals differ greatly in their native endowment in this respect. None the less, each has a certain primary equipment of impulse, of tendency forward, of innate urgency to do. The problem of education on this side is that of discovering what this native fund of power is, and then of utilizing it in such a way (affording conditions which both stimulate and control) as to organize it into definite conserved modes of action—habits.

(2) But something more is required than sheer force. Sheer force may be brutal; it may override the interests of others. Even when aiming at right ends it may go at them in such a way as to violate the rights of others. More than

this, in sheer force there is no guarantee for the right end. Efficiency may be directed towards mistaken ends and result in positive mischief and destruction. Power, as already suggested, must be directed. It must be organized along social channels; it must be attached to valuable ends.

This involves training on both the intellectual and emotional side. On the intellectual side we must have judgment —what is ordinarily called good sense. The difference between mere knowledge, or information, and judgment is that the former is simply held, not used; judgment is knowledge directed with reference to the accomplishment of ends. Good judgment is a sense of respective or proportionate values. The one who has judgment is the one who has ability to size up a situation. He is the one who can grasp the scene or situation before him, ignoring what is irrelevant, or what for the time being is unimportant, who can seize upon the factors which demand attention, and grade them according to their respective claims. Mere knowledge of what the right is, in the abstract, mere intentions of following the right in general, however praiseworthy in themselves, are never a substitute for this power of trained judgment. Action is always in the concrete. It is definite and individualized. Except, therefore, as it is backed and controlled by a knowledge of the actual concrete factors in the situation in which it occurs, it must be relatively futile and waste.

(3) But the consciousness of ends must be more than merely intellectual. We can imagine a person with most excellent judgment, who yet does not act upon his judgment. There must not only be force to insure effort in execution against obstacles, but there must also be a delicate personal responsiveness,—there must be an emotional reaction. Indeed, good judgment is impossible without this susceptibility. Unless there is a prompt and almost instinctive sensitiveness to conditions, to the ends and interests of others, the intellectual side of judgment will not have proper material to work upon. Just as the material of knowledge is supplied through the senses, so the material of ethical knowledge is supplied by emotional responsiveness. It is difficult to put this quality into words, but we all know the difference between the character which is hard and formal,

and one which is sympathetic, flexible, and open. In the abstract the former may be as sincerely devoted to moral ideas as is the latter, but as a practical matter we prefer to live with the latter. We count upon it to accomplish more by tact, by instinctive recognition of the claims of others, by skill in adjusting, than the former can accomplish by mere attachment to rules.

Here, then, is the moral standard, by which to test the work of the school upon the side of what it does directly for individuals. (*a*) Does the school as a system, at present, attach sufficient importance to the spontaneous instincts and impulses? Does it afford sufficient opportunity for these to assert themselves and work out their own results? Can we even say that the school in principle attaches itself, at present, to the active constructive powers rather than to processes of absorption and learning? Does not our talk about self-activity largely render itself meaningless because the self-activity we have in mind is purely "intellectual," out of relation to those impulses which work through hand and eye?

Just in so far as the present school methods fail to meet the test of such questions moral results must be unsatisfactory. We cannot secure the development of positive force of character unless we are willing to pay its price. We cannot smother and repress the child's powers, or gradually abort them (from failure of opportunity for exercise), and then expect a character with initiative and consecutive industry. I am aware of the importance attaching to inhibition, but mere inhibition is valueless. The only restraint, the only holding-in, that is of any worth is that which comes through holding powers concentrated upon a positive end. An end cannot be attained excepting as instincts and impulses are kept from discharging at random and from running off on side tracks. In keeping powers at work upon their relevant ends, there is sufficient opportunity for genuine inhibition. To say that inhibition is higher than power, is like saying that death is more than life, negation more than affirmation, sacrifice more than service.

(*b*) We must also test our school work by finding whether it affords the conditions necessary for the formation of good judgment. Judgment as the sense of relative values involves ability to select, to discriminate. Acquiring information can never develop the power of judgment. Development of judgment is in spite of, not because of, methods of instruction that emphasize simple learning. The test comes only when the information acquired has to be put to use. Will it do what we expect of it? I have heard an educator of large experience say that in her judgment the greatest defect of instruction to-day, on the intellectual side, is found in the fact that children leave school without a mental perspective. Facts seem to them all of the same importance. There is no foreground or background. There is no instinctive habit of sorting out facts upon a scale of worth and of grading them.

The child cannot get power of judgment excepting as he is continually exercised in forming and testing judgments. He must have an opportunity to select for himself, and to attempt to put his selections into execution, that he may submit them to the final test, that of action. Only thus can he learn to discriminate that which promises success from that which promises failure; only thus can he form the habit of relating his purposes and notions to the conditions that determine their value. Does the school, as a system, afford at present sufficient opportunity for this sort of experimentation? Except so far as the emphasis of the school work is upon intelligent doing, upon active investigation, it does not furnish the conditions necessary for that exercise of judgment which is an integral factor in good character.

(c) I shall be brief with respect to the other point, the need of susceptibility and responsiveness. The informally social side of education, the aesthetic environment and influences, are all-important. In so far as the work is laid out in regular and formulated ways, so far as there are lacking opportunities for casual and free social intercourse between pupils and between the pupils and the teacher, this side of the child's nature is either starved, or else left to find haphazard expression along more or less secret channels. When the school system, under plea of the practical (meaning by the practical the narrowly utilitarian), confines the child to the three R's and the formal studies connected with them, shuts him out from the vital in literature and history, and deprives him of his right to contact with what is best in architecture, music, sculpture, and picture, it is hopeless to expect definite results in the training of sympathetic openness and responsiveness.

What we need in education is a genuine faith in the existence of moral principles which are capable of effective application. We believe, so far as the mass of children are concerned, that if we keep at them long enough we can teach reading and writing and figuring. We are practically, even if unconsciously, sceptical as to the possibility of anything like the same assurance in morals. We believe in moral laws and rules, to be sure, but they are in the air. They are something set off by themselves. They are so *very* "moral" that they have no working contact with the average affairs of every-day life. These moral principles need to be brought down to the ground through their statement in social and in psychological terms. We need to see that moral principles are not arbitrary, that they are not "transcendental"; that the term "moral" does not designate a special region or portion of life. We need to translate the moral into the conditions and forces of our community life, and into the impulses and habits of the individual.

All the rest is mint, anise, and cummin. The one thing needful is that we recognize that moral principles are real in the same sense in which other forces are real; that they are inherent in community life, and in the working structure of the individual. If we can secure a genuine faith in this fact, we shall have secured the condition which alone is necessary to get from our educational system all the effectiveness there is in it. The teacher who operates in this faith will find every subject, every method of instruction, every incident of school life pregnant with moral possibility.

Appendixes

Appendix 1

PURE EXPERIENCE AND REALITY
by Evander Bradley McGilvary

In this scientific age no philosopher feels comfortable, if
he finds that his doctrines bring him into conflict with scientific facts. Scientific theories at variance with his own philosophical theories he can venture to criticise and reject, but
facts made out by science he prefers not to deny. As Professor Dewey says: "One is entitled to enter a *caveat* against
any attempt to impose science, whether physical or psychological, *as* philosophy. . . . Yet most empiricists would
hardly be willing to adopt any philosophic position of which
it could be clearly shown that it depends upon ignoring, denying or perverting scientific results."[1]

Now the philosophy of pure experience which has recently been developed by Professors James and Dewey has
been suspected by many of involving just such a denial of
'scientific results.' If the reality of anything is the reality it
has as experienced and only when experienced, then it would
seem that the sciences which deal with objects purporting to
have existed before any verifiable experience do not have
to do with reality; yet these very sciences claim to prove as
scientific fact the real existence of objects prior to zoic periods. Hence the philosophers of pure experience feel it in-
cumbent on them to set themselves at rights in this matter.

Professor James has recently so defined his position
that it ceases to have any anti-realistic suggestions which
might bring him into contradiction with the sciences of geology and astronomy. In answer to a question put to him by
Mr. Pitkin, as to whether his theory precludes the possibility
of something not experienced, Professor James says: "As-
suredly not . . . how could it? Yet in my opinion we should

1. *Journal of Philosophy, Psychology and Scientific Methods*, Vol.
III, p. 253. Hereafter this journal will be referred to simply as
Journal.

[First published in *Philosophical Review* 16 (1907): 266–84.
For Dewey's reply, see this volume, pp. 120–24.]

be wise not to *consider* any thing or action of that nature,
and to restrict our universe of philosophic discourse to what
is experienced *or, at least, experienceable*."[2] What kind of
reality the experienceable has when it is not experienced,
Professor James does not tell us, at least in his recent writings. In his *Psychology* there was no attempt to abbreviate
such reality and write it down to a tentative programme,
waiting for the signature and seal of experience to put it
into execution. Likewise there is nothing in the address on
the pragmatic method, delivered before the Philosophical
Union of the University of California, which should commit
him, so far as one can see, to denying the full and genuine
reality of the things which, though not experienced, make
a tremendous difference in what we do experience and shall
continue to experience. In default, therefore, of any express
avowal by Professor James of adherence to the notion that
unexperienced but experienceable reality is incomplete reality, one may assume, provisionally at least, that there is nothing in his experientialism to which a scientist may reasonably object on the score that it deprives him of the very
objects of his investigation. Whether Professor James's
philosophy remains pure experientialism when it is interpreted in the light of the sentences just quoted, is another
question which does not concern us here.

Professor Dewey has taken another course. He has tried
to put himself at one with science by admitting *something
"non-contemporaneously experienced."*[3] But he also maintains his pure experientialism by qualifying this admission:
the pre-experiential something is not to be considered completely real. The readers of Professor Dewey's *Studies in
Logical Theory* must have been prepared for such a statement from him. In that work he insisted that the object of
thought, when it has emerged from the experience of stress
and strain and appears in a subsequent tranquil experience

2. *Journal*, Vol. IV, p. 106. The italics in the last four words are
mine.
3. *Journal*, Vol. III, p. 254; italics mine. The quotations from Professor Dewey in what follows are all from his article on "Reality
as Experience" in Volume III of the *Journal*, pp. 253–257, [*Middle Works* 3: 101–7] except where otherwise designated; and
as the article is short and the passages and phrases quoted are
easily found in it, I shall not page the references.

as the result of pragmatic adjustment, must not be read
back anachronistically into the time preceding the adjustment. The reader was therefore left to infer that no truth
made out by intellectual labor is to be held valid of anything
real that may have existed before that labor was ended. This
inference is now for the first time explicitly confirmed by
Professor Dewey in the article just referred to. This article
has therefore the importance of a definitive statement of his
attitude towards facts dealt with in some fundamental sciences. We have here a touchstone of the scientific character
of his experiential philosophy. If his philosophy cannot stand
at this point the test of comparison with the results of science, then that philosophy is anti-scientific; and the pure ex-
perientialist of Professor Dewey's type stands at the parting
of the ways. Either he must take leave of science, or he must
surrender his peculiar views and the logic which issues in
these views. We need not here decide which course anyone
would reasonably choose with these alternatives before him.
We must first see whether these are exclusive and exhaustive
alternatives. Professor Dewey himself evidently appreciates
the crisis which his system here faces. The article in question is a resolute attempt to avert the crisis. Let us see
whether it succeeds.

As we have already said, Professor Dewey admits the
existence of something prior to experience,—something "non-
contemporaneously experienced." This something, however,
though it is called an "earlier reality," is not to be set over
against the "later experience" of it, as one complete reality
against another. "It is only the earlier portion, historically
speaking, of what later is experience. So viewed, the question of reality *versus* experience turns out to be only the
question of an earlier version of reality against a later version,—or, if the term 'version' be objected to, then, of an
earlier rendering or expression or state of reality compared
with its own later condition. We can not, however, say an
earlier reality *versus* a later reality, because this denies the
salient point of *transition towards*. Continual-transformation-
in-the-direction-of-this is the fact which excludes on the basis
of science (to which we have agreed to appeal) any chopping off of the non-contemporaneously experienced earlier

reality from later experience. So viewed, the question for philosophy reduces itself to this: What is the better index, for philosophy, of reality: its earlier or its later form?"

In the earlier form "something essential to reality is still omitted," and thus the 'earlier reality' was not really and entirely real.

> "Wanting is—what?
> Summer redundant,
> Blueness abundant,
> —Where is the blot?
> Beamy the world, yet a blank all the same,
> —Framework which waits for a picture to frame:
> What of the leafage, what of the flower?
> Roses embowering with naught they embower!
> Come then, complete incompletion, O comer,
> Pant through the blueness, perfect the summer!
> Breathe but one breath
> Rose-beauty above,
> And all that was death
> Grows life, grows love,
> Grows love!"

The 'comer' fulfils the promise and potency of the past, immersing the knowledge-object, which before was only reality in the making, "in an inclusive, vital, direct experience," and lo! reality is made, perfect and entire, wanting nothing. But it does not remain made for good and all. It has a way of slipping back into its inchoate state every time it ceases to be experienced, every time it is withdrawn from the bath. Reality is invulnerable to philosophical attack only so long as the waters of experience flow over it. But this gives no serious trouble, for it can be dipped again and again. The charm, though momentarily lost, can be regained. Reality is always at hand, a portable bath for any one who needs it in his pragmatic business: a need is possible only in experience, and experience is itself the magic water. "Every experience thus holds in suspense within itself knowledge with its entire object-world, however big or little. And the experience here referred to is *any* experience in which cognition enters. It is not some ideal, or absolute, or exhaustive experience." Every pre-experiential creature is by experience delivered from the bondage of incompleteness into glorious reality. The vision beatific culminates and reifies the 'qualitative-transfor-mation-towards.'

We have in this theory a daring de-realization of the pre-experiential past. What is the justification for it? We are told that the justification is found in the fact that all the ob-jects of which astronomy and geology treat are *objects for the scientific experience*. When the scientist predicates re-ality of them apart from his experience of them, he ignores the fact that he is necessary to make this predication and therefore to *realize* them. This realization of them in his sci-entific judgment abates the perfection of the reality they had before they were ever experienced. For to realize means to make real, and when the scientist realizes the existence of long bygone things, he makes that existence real. If he *makes* that existence real, it could not have *been* real before; for what already is, why doth a man yet make? Recognize that the transformation of pre-experiential qualities towards ex-perience "is realized in present experience, and the contra-diction vanishes. Since the qualitative transformation was towards experience, where else *should* its nature be realized save in experience—and in the very experience in which O, the knowledge object, is present? . . . What is omitted from reality in the O is always restored in the experience in which O is present. The O is thus really taken as what it is—a con-dition of reality as experience."

In other words, the world of knowledge is from start to finish a performance going on before the eyes of virginal experience. Even though she cannot bar from the boards certain really objective facts, they are not objectionable, for they appear completely clad in robes she has provided. What they might have been before they were thus clothed upon she can never see. Should, perchance, visions of the dressing-room flit before her maiden fancy, she merely thinks of the occupants as undergoing continual-transformation-in-the-direction-of investiture. They could never be *real* for her, because they become real only when they appear garbed before the foot-lights.

Everything that experience touches is thereby made clean for the grace of her favor and made whole in the en-tirety of her embrace. Without such cleansing and such integration nothing can enter into her presence. The object as it existed before it was experienced, was not reality, but only a condition of reality, and the condition is not sufficient to produce reality. Only when the condition is supplemented by an experience which realizes the object does the object become real.

It is a great pity that, before writing of the realizing power of experience, Professor Dewey had not made as exhaustive a study in some dictionary of the word 'realize' as he has made of the words 'idea' and 'consciousness.' For any even fairly complete dictionary would have shown him that 'realize' means at least two things: (1) 'make real,' and (2) 'recognize or think of as real.' To argue that, because the nature of the object is 'realized' only in experience, it could not have been completely real before the experience, looks suspiciously like a play upon words. A pun can hardly be a "scientific fact on which are wrecked all strictly objectivistic realisms."

The result will not be substantially different if we regard the emphasis which Professor Dewey lays on the word 'realize' in his article as merely the employment of the convenient word to enforce a view obtained otherwise, and not as an attempt to rear a pretentious philosophic structure on such a logical study of language. The foundation of his system is laid on the fact that, before any object can be posited as real, there must be some (cognitive?) experience in which the object is thus posited. Experience as the presupposition of scientific objects, it is asserted, is ignored in the physical sciences, which deal with objects and abstract from the experience for which such objects exist as real. "The reason the scientist can suppress in his *statement* of the reality factors which the reality possesses," more specifically the factor of being experienced, "is just because (1) he is not interested in the total reality, but in such phases of it as serve as trustworthy indications of imports and projects, and because (2) the elements suppressed are not totally suppressed, but are right there in his *experience*: in its extrascientific features. In other words, the *scientist* can ignore some part of the *man's* experience just because that part is so irremediably there in experience."

There is no question that we have here a very important truth which realism may ignore to its ultimate philosophic undoing. But we have the truth stated in a way that
leads to confusion, and it is on this confusion that Professor
Dewey builds that part of his philosophy which is anti-
realistic. By avoiding the confusion and yet by recognizing
the truth which Professor Dewey expresses,—only to impress
it wrongfully into the service of a false experientialism,—the
realist can round off his realism with an idealism. He would
thus get an ontological realism and an epistemological idealism. Of course, this result would be an abomination to any
one who abhors the very word epistemology, and who has
brought himself to believe that "knowing the external world
through ideas which are merely within us is" "an inherent
self-contradiction."[4]

The confusion to which I refer is that between the intellectual cognition of a fact, as a present experience, and a
fact cognized as a reality temporally prior to the experience
which cognizes it. The former is 'pure experience,' in Professor Dewey's meaning of the term. All the mediations by
which such a cognition has been attained have also been
purely experienced as processes of tension and inner distraction, terminating in purely experienced redintegration of contents: in pure experience of rest after toil, port after stormy
seas. Nothing can enter into the kingdom of knowledge and
acquire citizenship in the scientific domain, with all the
rights and privileges appertaining thereunto, without having
taken out naturalization papers in the court of experience.
Without this preliminary process even a star cannot be domi-
ciled as a star and allowed to stake out a claim to a quarter-
section in the stellar universe—*of science!*

This necessity that something should first be experienced in some way and then be known in a scientific way,
before that thing can be treated by science, does not seem
to be overlooked by scientists to-day. Most of these worthy
gentlemen would probably be amused by the suggestion that
they could ignore the knowing part of their experience and
pay attention only to the known part, because forsooth the

4. *Studies in Logical Theory,* p. 83. [*Middle Works* 2:366.]

knowing part is irremediably there in experience. What are microscopes and telescopes and spectroscopes, from the epistemological point of view, but eloquent witnesses to the scrupulous exaction the scientist makes that every object should first be experienced before it be inventoried in the scientific catalogue? What are the method of least squares and the allowance for personal equations but the recognition that, whatever may be the final scientific statement, that statement must take as its point of departure the experience of the scientist? The scientific statement is not shot out of a pistol: it is the fruition of a developmental process whose germination and whose florescence occur in the atmosphere of 'pure experience.' Experience is the very life, the self-conscious life, of science, and of such life the scientist agonizingly exclaims:

> " 'Tis life, whereof our nerves are scant,
>   Oh life, not death, for which we pant;
>   More life, and fuller, that I want."

And then he is told by a philosopher, who desires a *rapprochement* between his philosophy and science, that "in a very real sense, the present experience of the veriest unenlightened ditch-digger does philosophic justice to the earlier reality in a way which the scientific statement does not and cannot: cannot, that is, as formulated knowledge!" I presume that the ditch-digger is dignified with laudatory mention in disparagement of the scientist because the ditch *becomes real* in the digging experience, while the fossil does not. If the geologist could only dig his fossils in while he is digging them out, then his pure digging experience would do philosophic justice to the reality. Where else should the nature of fossils be realized save in experience,—and in the very experience in which fossils as knowledge-objects are present? This kind of pure experience, however, would probably be branded by professional geologists as impure science.

It is well enough to lay emphasis on the experience of the scientist as indispensable to the scientific validity of his results. When we do, we get what I have ventured to call an epistemological idealism, or the doctrine that there would be no *scientific* reality were there no scientists, with scien-

tific ideas and ideational experiences. If there were a universe of real things which did not include somewhere or
sometime within it cognitive experience of at least some
part of it, and which were so completely self-contained that
no thinker of another universe could even guess its existence,
the reality of that universe could not be *scientific* reality,
whatever else in its meaninglessness it might be. Even the
idlest dream of such a universe would require a dream experience for which it could have a quasi-reality. The reality
we know and the reality we predicate with any intelligibility
or significance is reality for us as predicators. Even when
we think of this kind of reality as being possible in another
universe unradiated by a single gleam of intelligence or
sense-experience, we still *are thinking* of it; we cannot think
ourselves and everything else out of *such* a universe without
being in *this* universe to do this thinking away. No thinker,
no thought-object; no experience somewhere and somewhen,
no meaningful reality anywhere and anytime. This is the
truth which is contained in Professor Dewey's contention.

But it is one thing to say, No experience; no reality,
and it is another thing to say, No *contemporaneous* experience, no reality. It is this contemporaneousness that Professor Dewey surreptitiously introduces into the statement of the
truth, thereby converting it into,—well, let us say a huge assumption. "Thus, the knowledge-object *always* carries along,
contemporaneously with itself, an other, something to which
it is relevant and accountable, and whose union with it affords the condition of its testing, its correction and verification. This union is intimate and complete. The distinction
in experience between the knowledge portion, as such, and
its own experienced context, as non-cognitional, is a reflective, analytic distinction—itself real in *its* experienced content and function."[5]

By thus synchronizing the experience and the reality,
the object of knowledge, which for the scientific geologist
may be a real object belonging to the remote past, becomes
so tied down to the present by the fact that it is cognitively
experienced, that it loses the *character of past reality which*

5. All the italics are mine except the last.

it claims to have for scientific knowledge. Knowledge of the past becomes a self-contradictory thing. To use expressions of Bosanquet's,—the 'time of judgment' and the 'time in judgment' get so badly mixed that they must be reduced to the same time, the time of judging. Lotze's view that the ways of thought and the ways of things are different is ridiculed out of court to make way for the sole alternative "view which regards reality as developing in and through judgment."[6] The development of our ideas of reality and the development of reality itself are economically merged into one development, the development of objects in our cognitive experience of them.

Let us now follow the results of this merger. I think that we shall see that the stock of the holding company rises at the expense of the manipulated stock, which falls to zero. In geology the scientist deals with facts cognized as prior to his cognizing experience of them. Professor Dewey tries to acknowledge this; he goes as far as his theory will allow him. But his theory will not allow him to regard the geological fact as complete reality. It is simply reality-in-the-process-of-transformation-towards-experience. This process of transformation towards reality is a fact "as objectively real as anything else," and is "realized in present experience." Hence "what is omitted from reality" in the scientist's statement of the nature of the object "is always restored in the experience in which" that fact "is present."

In dealing with reality-in-the-process-of-transformation-towards-experience, if, dropping out the first hyphen, you try the experiment of the "chopping off of the non-contemporaneously experienced earlier reality from later experience," you do violence to "the pragmatic variety of empiricism with its interpretation of the place of reflective knowledge, or thought, in control of experience," and you must remember that this pragmatic variety of empiricism "seems to have the call" here. If you put down your axe and let the hyphen be, that hyphen will wreck every fortune that is tied up in "strictly objectivistic realisms."

The real trouble with this pragmatic variety of empiri-

6. Dr. Helen Bradford Thompson, in *Studies in Logical Theory*, p. 126.

cism is that it is so much engaged in the business of the interpretation of the place of *reflective knowledge, or thought,* in the control of experience, that it ignores the right of the *object* to the place it claims, — a place in time prior to the date of the experience. It claims that place, not as an incomplete reality, but as a genuine ready-made reality, waiting all these ages to be recognized as such. The recognition does not, in the knowing experience, pretend to *give* reality to what it recognizes as real, any more than the registration of a deed of conveyance with the registrar of deeds makes the deed real. The deed is already real, or no registrar registering to doomsday can register reality into it.

The pragmatist of Professor Dewey's type of empiricism writes as if a change in geological science involved a change in the actual past history of geological objects. But I am afraid that he would find it hard to make terms with the scientific geologist on the proposition that the discovery of geological development made that development real. The geologist would be unkind enough to say that discovery is not invention. The map of the past may be changed after the discovery, but that does not change the real past. If the map becomes more accurate in the effort of reflective knowledge to control present experience, that is because there was a real past, now fixed in its eternal state, which one map can more truthfully represent than another. It would be a queer sort of a past that should complaisantly adjust itself to conform to every change that the cartographer felt obliged to make in the effort to redintegrate his pure experience of cartographical distractions.

Or let us take the momentous day when Copernicus first hit upon his famous redintegration of astronomical experience after Ptolemaic tensions. Was the real earth at that time uprooted out of its place in the center of the universe and sent spinning in an elliptical orbit about the sun? Mighty as was the thought of Copernicus, it would be hard to suppose that it could suddenly impart a motion of many miles per second to the huge masses of the earth and the other planets, and cap the climax by performing the miracle of Joshua. The scientist is more apt to suppose that the real solar system at that moment kept on in the equable course it had been pursuing for countless millenniums, and that it did not feel a single tremor throughout its whole frame save in the little nervous system of Copernicus himself.

In all these pre-Copernican aeons, where was that "other" which the "knowledge object" of Copernicus had always carried along "contemporaneously with itself"? Had Copernicus's experience existed continuously through all pre-Copernican times? Or did the "knowledge object" of Copernicus not exist except contemporaneously with the historical Copernicus? I must confess that the attempt to think out this puzzle in terms of the "pragmatic variety of empiricism with its interpretation of the place of reflective knowledge, or thought, in control of experience" gives me a pure experience of tension and distraction, "of particular elements which are in strife." The facts I seem to get "are crude, raw, unorganized, brute. They lack relationship, that is, assured place in the universe: they are deficient as to continuity."[7] And this, I am told, is an index of pragmatic untruth.

But we are assured that we can escape all this difficulty by recognizing the objects prior to Copernicus as incompletely real. The 'real' is a sop to science, the 'incompletely' is the acknowledgment of the truth of the pragmatic variety of empiricism. This seems to be an easy way out of the difficulty, but let us look ahead a little before committing ourselves to this reconciliation of science and philosophy. "The non-contemporaneously experienced earlier reality" is not complete reality, because it is undergoing "change-in-the-direction-of, which is, to say the least, as objectively real as anything else." Does not this prove too much? The function of the solar system as an object of knowledge was not exhausted in the experience of Copernicus. It continues in the experience of every educated man to-day. If it be said that what is continuously undergoing transformation-in-the-direction-of is not complete, the solar system is incomplete yet, because it seems to be undergoing just such a hyphenated transformation every day, and it is hard to fix the term of that transformation before Byron's Last Man shall have found surcease for his unshared sorrows in the grave of all

---

7. *Studies in Logical Theory*, p. 52. [*Middle Works* 2:339.]

experience. And yet even then the solar system cannot be real, for the experience which is necessary to realize it is gone. We thus get the interesting result that nothing can be completely real till nothing is left to be possibly real. No wonder that the philosopher whose view of complete reality involves this paradox should have found that the paradox wrecks "all strictly objectivistic realisms." But why does he not see that every other ism shares the same fate?

But it may be argued that, although pure experientialism may be a floating mine which wrecks the whole philosophic navy in exploding itself, still any other philosophic doctrine negatives the value and the reality of thought. The reply is: Not in the least, unless by reality is meant the whole universe, past, present, and to come; and by value is meant inclusiveness of such total reality. Thought may be real without being *omnitudo realitatis*. It may be an integral part of the universe, with its definite place in time and its definite work to do. What its place is, is scientifically determined, as everything is properly determined in science, by appeal to the witness of harmonized and redintegrated experience. Experience assigns to itself a place in the world of reality, as posterior to much of the reality experienced in scientific ideation. Experience also recognizes its own function in the world, just as it recognizes the function of other parts of the whole of reality. When it recognizes itself as necessary for the recognition of reality, it recognizes in itself a unique value; but if it tries to emancipate itself from the duties of its sphere and to usurp the function of another sphere, it makes itself a laughing-stock, much as the would-be male females of our time do. Even though experience is bone of the bones and flesh of the flesh of reality, still she ought to realize that there were some real ribs whose prior existence was necessary to her making. She may give names to the animals brought before her, but if she arrogates to herself the power of giving reality to the very conditions that brought her into being, she is trying to become greater than Spinoza's God, who is merely *causa sui*. She wants to become *causa causae sui*. Experience may look before and after, but she may not translocate. She may embrace the real, but not reduce it to a dependency of herself.

If it be asked how the real, which may exist prior to experience, can come to be an object of subsequent experience of it, unless the obsolete doctrine of representative knowledge be true, I should answer that perhaps there is more truth in that doctrine than many would be disposed to acknowledge to-day. Let us look at experience as it actually is, and see what are the facts. At present I am experiencing my typewriter, *i.e.*, there is an awareness of it along with other things, among which is a group of contents called by Professor James 'the empirical Me.' The awareness comprehends them all, including many relations subsisting between them severally and collectively. The awareness is not *in* any one of them but *of* them together. These various things do not exist for the awareness as borrowing their reality from it. They exist for it as just being there, in various relations to each other. The awareness, as embracing the color and the shape of the typewriter, is called *seeing* it; as embracing the hardness of the keys is called *touching* them. What is thus seen and touched stands in bold relief in space before my body. Now let me close my eyes and raise my fingers. There is a change in the field of objects. Instead of the thing in clear outlines, there is now something of which I am aware as similar to what was before my body a while ago, but also as somehow different. What I formerly experienced is not now present along with this new something, and by its presence furnishing one of the 'relata' for the relation of similarity. On the contrary, I am aware only of this new something *as similar* and yet *as different*. The thing it resembles and does not entirely resemble is absent from my awareness as a definite content of my present experience, but I know that it was experienced only a moment ago. Now I move my fingers, still keeping my eyes closed; I again become aware of the kind of hardness I experienced a moment ago when I touched the keys before. The present hardness is much more similar to that previous hardness than the present color I see with closed lids is to the color viewed with open eyes. The keys I still see are ghostly white and black; the fingers I see are ghostly fingers; but the hardness I feel is not ghostly. Now this object of my vision, so 'sicklied o'er with the pale cast of thought,' is called a visual image, corresponding to and resembling the *thing* I saw once and can again see if only I open my eyes. The image is, moreover, not merely something in the field of vision; it is there as standing for something else,—for what is called the real typewriter, which I can see and do touch. I know the reality through this image. If you ask me what is the color of the typewriter frame, I answer, 'Black.' I see the black of my image and it *means* the black of the real typewriter. In this case, unquestionably, I know the reality through the image. I can do so because I am aware of the resemblance the image has to the real typewriter, which I saw a moment ago standing in its naked reality before my eyes. If I were to doubt the resemblance, I should only have to open my eyes, and lo! the real thing would stand revealed as having just the color I attributed to it, because I saw that color in the image. That is to say, when my eyes are closed I have a representative visual image of the reality I have previously seen face to face.

It is to be noted that such representative knowledge differs greatly from the representative knowledge of the school of Hamilton. Hamilton thought that the thing we saw with open eyes was not the real thing; it was merely a replica of the real thing. Hence he believed that all our knowledge is representative. According to the account given above, not all knowledge is representative. The knowledge of the real thing's visual characters which we get when our eyes are open is direct and immediate: it is intuitive. It is only when my eyes are closed that I have to depend on representative knowledge. Now as I can have both intuitive and representative knowledge of reality, and as I can be aware of the similarity or dissimilarity between them, I can, when I have intuitive knowledge, test the correctness of the representative knowledge I previously had. The arguments, therefore, which have been directed against the theory of the representative character of *all* knowledge lose their force when turned against the asserted fact of the representative character of a large part of our knowledge. If we call this representative part of our knowledge "knowing the external world through ideas which are merely within us," it is hard to see the justification which Professor Dewey has for saying that such knowing is "an inherent self-contradiction."

The question, however, may properly be asked whether the image is "merely within us." Answering from experience, I should say that it is. I have never found any reason for supposing that the image can exist apart from the awareness of it, and I presume that by "merely existing within us" Professor Dewey means "existing only when there is an awareness of what exists." On the other hand, I think that I have good reason for believing that the real thing I see continues to exist when I no longer see it, when I do not even think of it, and when so far as I know no one experiences it in any way.

The trouble with Hamilton's school is that, having convinced themselves that some of our knowledge is representative, they allowed themselves to infer that all knowledge is representative. The trouble with philosophers of Professor Dewey's way of thinking is that, having convinced themselves that some of our knowledge is not representative, and that, if all our knowledge were representative, we should never have any criterion for truth, they jump to the conclusion that none of our knowledge is representative. If people would only give up trying to reduce all knowledge to a dull uniformity of character and would describe facts as they are, we should have neither the insoluble problem of proving copies authentic when we can never get at the originals, nor the anti-scientific view that things are real only in experience, and that real things change when our purely experienced images of them change, and that the changes of these images are the changes of the things.

The theory above outlined as to the partially intuitive and partially representative character of our knowledge makes possible a meaning of *transsubjective reference*, which accords with the facts and does not involve contradictions. By transsubjective reference, according to this theory, is meant reference to what exists beyond the direct object of awareness when that object is merely subjective.

When I close my eyes and remove my fingers from the keys of my typewriter, I am aware of images (which are called merely subjective, because they are supposed to have no existence except as they appear in consciousness); but I am also aware of a 'reference' of these images to what is not now directly present in consciousness, viz., my typewriter. This transsubjective reference finds its simplest illustration in memory. The thing remembered and the image present in consciousness when we remember, are of course not the same thing. We cannot literally recall our boyhood days, but we do have images which, however, are not mere images and nothing more: we have images which reproduce with some verisimilitude those bygone days. Not only is there reproduction, there is also recognition, of the past experience. The images come to us in the character of representatives, present ambassadors bearing credentials from a court which has long been levelled in the dust of time. But we honor the credentials, and treat the embassy with all the consideration due to the power they represent. This treatment of the present image as representative of a past reality is a transsubjective reference. The image is a 'relatum' in relation to a nonexistent 'correlatum.' We might call the relation, so far as the immediate contents of experience are concerned, a one-term relation; the other term is not present in the 'pure experience' of the moment. But its absence does not mar the character of the present term as a related term, recognized as such. There is pure experience of reference to; and if the phrase is to be completed, the complement lies beyond the immediate experience. An image thus referred to what is not present in consciousness to complete the reference, is what I should call an 'idea.' All our reminiscent knowledge is by means of ideas.

Now if we may know the past, of which we are no longer immediately aware, by means of ideas, why may we not know present objects, of which we are not immediately aware, in the same way? At present, for instance, I have an image of my bed in another room. The image is not my bed, and the bed is not an object of my immediate pure experience, while I am writing. Nevertheless the image refers to the real bed, now existing, in the same way in which the memory refers to something not itself, something not now existing but having existed in the past. The fact that in the one case the object referred to is past and in the other case exists simultaneously with the image, does not make any difference in the transsubjective character of the reference.

If it be asked how I know that the bed is up in my room, a distinct reality from my image of it as my body sits here at my writing table, I should say that Hume has fairly stated the facts on which my belief in the distinction rests, although of course Hume did not think that the belief was logically valid; the belief was for him a mere fiction of the imagination. But for him, when he was consistent, the memory image had no transsubjective reference either. Whether we call the motive which prompts to the belief an instinct, or reason, or common sense, the fact is that the belief is in normal experience present; and no argument can be given for its untenableness which does not at the same time assume its tenableness and its correctness.

Now, just as I have memory images referred to realities previously experienced, and just as I have images referring to present realities not immediately experienced, so I can have images referring to past or future realities which have never been experienced. The fall of Constantinople, the martyrdom of Bruno, the next Fourth of July, and my death-bed experience are all present to me by representative images. I know them more or less accurately by means of ideas. All my knowledge of the past, all my forecast of the future, and all my knowledge of facts now existing save the few I have before me in the way of sense-perception 'inner' and 'outer,' are representative. Bosanquet, therefore, does not seem to be far from the truth when he says that we come into contact with reality in sense-perception. Everywhere else, we have images referring to reality, ideas of reality, but not reality itself.

If I read Professor James aright, this view is not far from his, yet it differs from his in one important respect. He seems to make the truth of experience where substitutional images are employed, to consist in the fact that these images do actually continue uninterruptedly into the experience where the reality becomes an object of sense-perception. I should rather say that one important *test* of my imaging experience is found in subsequent or prior sense-perceptions. The *truth* of the images, however, consists in the correspondence of the images with a transsubjective reality which now exists, or with a transsubjective reality which has existed in the past or will exist in the future, whether ever actually an object of immediate experience or not. The sense-perception confirms the truth, but is not the truth. Truth is the agreement between ideas and reality. Such agreement does not necessitate exact correspondence, point for point, between images and reality. But for truth there must be correspondence in regard to the feature which is transsubjectively referred.

Appendix 2

PROFESSOR DEWEY'S "ACTION OF CONSCIOUSNESS"
by Evander Bradley McGilvary

In a footnote on page 69 of "Essays Philosophical and Psychological in Honor of William James," [this volume, p. 135] Professor Dewey says: "Of course on the theory I am interested in expounding, the so-called action of 'consciousness' means simply the organic releases in the way of behavior which are the conditions of awareness, and which also modify its content." If this is all that Professor Dewey means by the action of consciousness upon the existences which are the direct subject-matter of knowledge, there are several questions that I should like to have answered; for they have been bothering me ever since I have read the very interesting paper on "Reality as Practical."

First. How does such a theory bring about the evaporation of "the metaphysical puzzles regarding 'parallelism,' 'interaction,' 'automatism,' the relation of 'consciousness' to 'body'"? (p. 132, footnote). The organic releases in the way of behavior, we are told, are the conditions of awareness. Although elsewhere in this paper Professor Dewey defines awareness as attention, I presume that in this sentence he would mean to include consciousness in its inattentive forms also under awareness as conditioned by the organic releases. If these releases are the conditions of consciousness, they are thereby distinguished from consciousness; and they are at the same time asserted to be in a certain relation to consciousness: they are its conditions. Now the parallelist, the interactionist, the automatist, and the epiphenomenalist all agree in regarding the brain as in some sense the condition of consciousness. It is hard to see how the questions at issue between these different theorists are made to evaporate "when one ceases isolating the brain into a peculiar physical

[First published in *Journal of Philosophy, Psychology and Scientific Methods* 8 (1911): 458–60. For Dewey's article, see this volume, pp. 125–42; and for Dewey's rejoinder to this reply, see pp. 143–45.]

substrate of mind at large, and treats it simply as one portion of the body as the instrumentality of adaptive behavior,"
—unless what is meant be that any question evaporates when
it is ignored. It is true that if "the so-called action of consciousness means the organic releases in the way of behavior," there is no question as to the relation of the *action*
of consciousness to other physical things. We have here just
one physical thing in relation to other physical things. But if
consciousness is conditioned by the "action of consciousness"
(= organic releases in the way of behavior), there is a question as to the nature of this relation.

Second. In what sense can it be said that "a certain
promoting, a certain carrying forward of the vital impulse,
importing certain differences in things, *is* the aim of knowledge"? (p. 133). Knowledge is one kind of consciousness, presumably. Then, when we are told that the aim of knowledge
is the promotion of vital impulse, are we expected to take
this as meaning that the aim of the *organic releases* is to
promote vital impulse? This is the most natural interpretation; for the aim of consciousness is naturally the aim of the
action of consciousness. If this be the interpretation that
we are expected to put upon this assertion, the instrumental
theory of knowledge seems to be an instrumental theory of
the brain; and if this be what it is, I suppose that all of us
would subscribe to it. But after we have done so, there is
still the further question, What is the aim of knowledge *as
distinct from* and conditioned by these organic releases? This
leads to the third question.

Third. If it is the organic releases that change the environment in the act of knowing, does knowing as distinct
from these organic releases make any changes in the environment on its own account? If it does not, how does Professor
Dewey's theory on this point differ *in principle* from that of
the "program realists"? If it does, what further change does
knowing make, and how is he to find out what changes are
made? The method he seems to pursue is to set down the
difference made by "that organic adaptation involved in all
knowing" (p. 135) to the credit of knowing. Why to the credit
of *knowing* rather than to the credit of *that organic adaptation*, if these two things are distinct?

Fourth. If the action of consciousness is not the action

of *consciousness* but that of the *organic releases* that condition consciousness, why may not things be known as they were *when* they brought about the organic discharges, as well as be known as they become *after* these discharges have in turn reacted upon these things? In other words, once distinguish between consciousness and organic releases, what justification have we for asserting that knowledge can be only of the *effects* of the conditions of knowledge? If knowledge be distinct from its conditions, should we not study it as we study anything else, not confining ourselves entirely to the functions of its conditions, but extending our view to take in any possible functions it may itself have?

Appendix 3

THE CHICAGO "IDEA" AND IDEALISM
by Evander Bradley McGilvary

Every fundamentally new attempt at reconstruction in science involves, to some extent at least, a new terminology. The old words of a language may still be employed, but they are made to carry new meanings, and it is the task of the attentive reader to keep from slipping back into the old meanings when he would understand the new message. This commonplace reflection is suggested by the present status of the pragmatistic controversy. Professor Dewey has repeatedly complained that his critics have failed to understand him because they have interpreted what he says as if he were employing old words in their old meanings. The complaint is amply justified, and, of course, this misunderstanding is a bar to any true appreciation of his instrumental logic. There is no word which is apt to give more trouble to Professor Dewey's readers than the word "idea." The fault is not Professor Dewey's, for he has taken great pains to make clear just what he means by the term. But what he means is so different from what is ordinarily meant that it is no wonder that his critics have failed to remain true to his definition when they try to appraise the value of his statements about ideas. For instance, when one finds this challenge thrown down by Professor Dewey: "Do ideas present themselves except in situations which are doubtful and inquired into?"[1] one is apt to take up the gauntlet with confident heart, for does not every one know that ideas do present themselves constantly in situations which are untroubled by any doubt? But the cautious reader knows that the gauntlet has a string attached to it and may not be lightly taken up.

In this paper I shall try to state as best I may the new

1. This Journal, Vol. V., p. 378. [*Middle Works* 4:93.]

[First published in *Journal of Philosophy, Psychology and Scientific Methods* 5 (1908): 589–97. For Dewey's reply, see this volume, pp. 146–55.]

meaning of idea in Professor Dewey's writings, and then ask
some questions which this new meaning suggests. But before
doing this, let us take a brief survey of the current meanings
of the term. The word idea has at least two quite different
types of meaning in common use. These two meanings can
be traced back in English to Locke and Hume. They may
be called the inclusive and the exclusive significations of
the word. Locke used the word of everything of which we
are conscious when we think; Hume used it in antithesis to
"impression." And since their days, not to go farther back,
both these usages have been classic. Of course, the particular nuance which the term has in either sense is determined
by the views which are held in regard to the genesis and the
function or reference of ideas; and these views are various.
For instance, Lotze, like Locke, set over against the world of
ideas, used inclusively, a world of reality outside of ideas,
which ideas are to deal with as well as they can: Professor
Dewey has shown with masterly skill how Sisyphean is the
task which is set for ideas in this scheme of things. The idealist, also using idea in the inclusive sense, denies that there
is any reality that is not idea; he has, therefore, no need to
make ideas adjust themselves to a reality which is not ideal:
the only adjustment necessary is among the ideas themselves.
Hume, taking the term in an exclusive sense, finds, however, no work cut out for ideas in the fact that they are not
exhaustive of reality. They carry no reference to the other
class of realities. All they have to do is to be more or less
lively, and the laws of association manage this business for
them. The psychologist of the present day is apt to use the
word in the exclusive sense fixed by Hume, but, following
the hint given by Hume himself, although not developed by
him, the psychologist regards ideas as those elements in experience that are due to central stimulations of the cortex,
as opposed to sensations which are due to peripheral stimulations. The "plain man" uses the term in a manner similar
to that adopted by the psychologist, although, of course, he
has very vague notions of the basis of the distinction between idea and sensation. I think that it can properly be
said that the psychological employment of the term is merely
a refined and critical adaptation of the vulgar use. Now, when

ideas are used in this way in antithesis to sensation, it may
be recognized that they not only are occurrences accounted
for by their connection with brain-processes, but also are
in some way the vehicles of knowledge. They have not only
a structure and a genesis, but also a function and a value
determined by the success with which they perform their
function. This function is knowing. The examination of this
function and of the value of ideas in this functional process
is generally turned over by the psychologist to the epistemologist. If the latter takes up the problem on its own account
and ignores the psychological problems of structure and genesis, we have then two abstract sciences standing side by
side, much to the scandal of pragmatists and humanists. The
division of labor is regarded as an ultimate and hopeless
scission of the material taken in hand. The living unity of
experience is dissected into dead members, and where is the
Isis to gather up the scattered anatomy of experience, and
where is the Ezekiel to prophesy upon the dead bones that
they may live? There is no goddess in Egypt and no prophet
in Israel in these days.

But we have the pragmatist who can see to it that the
default of supernatural beings shall not be fatal to natural
human knowing. He employs an ounce of prevention where
they would have resorted to tons and tons of miraculous
cure. He would have no division of labor between psychology
and epistemology, for, of course, division of labor is division
of what you labor on, and this is to be avoided at all hazards.
One unspecialized type of laborer is to be employed on the
work, and this secures unity of finished product. Assembling
is an impossibility in manufacture; hence do nothing that
will make it necessary. The logician can do all the work and
keep the parts together from start to finish.

This, of course, necessitates a new terminology in the
factory. The real trouble with the antiquated method is found
in the kind of distinction that is made between "ideas, meanings, thoughts, ways of conceiving, comprehending, interpreting facts," "suggestions, guesses, theories, estimates," etc.,
on the one hand, and "facts," "objects," "data," and what not,
on the other. These are not forever fixed in their eternal
state; else they have done with things below. They are simply

instrumental distinctions, functional variants, and are just
what at any time you take them to be. Of course, even thus,
you can not get rid of the distinctions, and so can not get
rid of division of labor; but you have a different kind of division of labor. The division here falls upon the material
which the logician studies, not upon the students of the material. As this material is living reflective experience, it can
temporarily endure all sorts of tensions and distractions, taking these up and working them over till it effects a reorganization. Indeed, without this tension and distraction, there
would be no thinking life. But the student of this life must
not divide what in life is connected even in its division. So
that, while in this new way of ideas "datum and ideatum are
divisions of labor, cooperative instrumentalities, for economical dealing with the problem of the maintenance of the integrity of experience," the logician must recognize that either
"is a sheer abstraction from the standpoint either of the organized experience left behind, or of the reorganized experience which is the end—the objective."[2] "Thus the distinction
between subjectivity and objectivity is not one between
meaning as such and datum as such. It is a specification
that emerges, correspondently, in *both* datum and ideatum,
as affairs of the direction of logical movement. That which
is left behind in the evolution of accepted meaning is characterized as real, but only in a psychical sense; that which
is moved toward is regarded as real in an objective, cosmic
sense."[3] The psychic, the ideal, on the one hand, the cosmic,
the objective, on the other, are thus nothing but shifting
values in the ever growing unity of experience. Just what
shift is made is determined by the problem and its solution
in any definite concrete situation. When an intellectual problem is taken up in experience, there is always something that
for the time being is accepted as fact—this is the datum;
there is something else which is suggested as somehow ap-

2. "Studies in Logical Theory," p. 52. [*Middle Works* 2:339.] The
second quotation is taken out of its narrower context, where the
subject of the sentence is a particular datum, namely, "Mere
change of apparent position of sun, which is absolutely unquestioned as datum." But the larger context, I think, justifies the
use to which I have put this clause.
3. *Op. cit.*, pp. 53–54. [*Middle Works* 2:341.]

pertaining to this fact—this is idea. The idea may be subsequently rejected in the outcome of thought's travail—it is then definitively for this occasion characterized as merely psychic. On the contrary, the suggestion may be accepted; it then merges with the datum, after the latter has been correspondingly changed to receive the suggested content, and it ceases to be an idea for the occasion and becomes objective cosmic fact.

Not only is this shifting according to the concrete emergencies and the concrete achievements of the logical process a fate which befalls ideas and data, it likewise draws into its kaleidoscopic field even the terms sensation and image. "One of the aims of the 'Studies in Logical Theory' was to show . . . that . . . such distinctions as sensation, image, etc., mark instruments and crises in the development of controlled judgment, *i.e.*, of inferential conclusions."[4] Whether any experience is to be considered sensational is not determined then by resort to psychophysical investigation—except, perhaps, where the problem is psychophysical and not logical? —but by consideration of the harmonious outcome of the previously disturbed situation. We are not told whether sensation is synonymous with accepted fact, but we are at any rate warned not to consider it "in terms of the psychology which obtained in the *critic's* mind."[5]

Now these are perfectly clear distinctions, and although I may not have done justice to the clean-cut thought in which this view is worked out, still I hope that I have blocked the distinctions out sufficiently for recognition by their author and by others. But what follows? I think that we must agree that one thing follows; namely, the necessity of giving just the kind of answer that Professor Dewey gives to the five sets of questions which he asks on page 378 of this JOURNAL [this volume, pp. 93–94]. According to this new definition of ideas and of facts, ideas do *not* present themselves except in situations which are doubtful and inquired into. They do *not* exist side by side with the facts to which they refer *when* these facts are themselves known. They do *not* exist except

4. This Journal, Vol. V., p. 376. [*Middle Works* 4:92–93.]
5. *Ibid.*, p. 377. [*Middle Works* 4:93.]

when judgment is in suspense. They are *nothing but* the suggestions, conjectures, hypotheses, theories, tentatively entertained during a suspended conclusion, and so forth and so forth. *These answers are determined by the definitions already given of fact and idea,* and no examination of actual thinking experience is necessary for making the appropriate reply. All one has to do is to examine the definitions of the terms used, just as in Euclidean geometry all that one has to do in determining whether parallel lines meet is to consult the definition of parallel lines. The scheme is beautifully simple, and if you adhere to it, you get rid of some very disagreeable questions which force themselves on you if you refuse to adopt it. But if the questions referred to are asked with a view to determining whether the new way of ideas comports with facts, then we have a different matter on our hands. Into this question I can not go at present.

However, there are some questions which force themselves on me when I try to accept the new scheme on which the definitions rest. Is not the scheme a thoroughgoing idealism, and a subjective idealism at that? But to guard against misunderstanding in putting the question, let me hasten to say at once that I do not conceive the point of view underlying these definitions to be idealistic, if the connotation of "idealistic" is adapted to that of "idea" in the scheme. The "Studies in Logical Theory" admits the existence of facts as well as of ideas, each defined in a special way. Professor Dewey, therefore, has a perfect right to repel the suggestion that his scheme is idealistic, if idealism is defined according to "idea" in that scheme. We all remember how mildly indignant Bishop Berkeley used to get when the suggestion arose that his way of ideas did away with matter. He easily showed that it did no such thing. Did not the whole choir of heaven and furniture of earth find its place in his idealism, and what is meant by matter anyway but just such things as make heaven vocal and earth comfortable? But I believe that it is fairly settled these days, if it were ever doubted, that the fact that Berkeley's views admitted these material things did not make his doctrine non-idealistic. There is a *current* definition of idealism according to which we gauge systems as idealistic or not. Is Professor Dewey's system idealistic *according to this definition*? Idealism seems to be generally applied to any theory which regards all reality as embraced within experiences or within Experience. It is the view that recognizes no residual reality uncatalogued after the inventory of all experience is taken. The thinker called idealistic may not even use the term experience; but we can see from his writings whether, if he had used that term as it is now generally used, he would have been willing to say with Mr. Bradley: "I am driven to the conclusion that for me experience is the same as reality. The fact that falls else-where seems, in my mind, to be a mere word and a failure, or else an attempt at self-contradiction. It is a vicious abstraction whose existence is meaningless nonsense, and is therefore not possible."[6] If any thinker endorses these words, he is an idealist. Now when any of Professor Dewey's critics calls him idealistic, the critic uses the term in this current sense. When Professor Dewey repudiates the epithet, does he use the term in another sense? If so, are they not both right, each in his own way? Professor Dewey hardly refutes the claim of his opponent by failing to meet the claim on its own grounds. A clear unambiguous answer from Professor Dewey to the question whether he is an idealist in the current sense of idealism as defined above would, I am sure, make his view much more intelligible. Most of his readers have found him idealistic, only to be told that they are miserably mistaken. This has left them miserably nonplussed. If Professor Dewey thinks that it is too much of an accommodation to the weakness of his readers to answer the above question, he can at least tell us what *he* means by idealism, when he denies that he is an idealist. And if in the definition he employs the term idea, he can tell us whether that term is to be taken in the sense of the "Studies in Logical Theory."[7]

6. "Appearance and Reality," 2d edition, p. 145.
7. While I am asking questions, I should like to put another: What does Professor Dewey mean by "rationalism" and "rationalistic"? The rationalism of the *Aufklärung* we think we know, and we know that we are not rationalists of that sort; but we do not know whether we are rationalists in this seemingly new and derogatory sense in which the term is frequently used in his recent writings. It is natural that we do not like to be charged with being rationalists without being allowed to plead guilty or not guilty with the law of the term before us.

But, of course, when experience is used in the definition of idealism, we have another difficulty. What is meant by experience? The ordinary man in his ordinariness uses this term as in the first instance not inclusive of all reality. For he seems to find experience a very shifting thing. What is part of experience at one time is not part of it at another. Even if experience be used in the most inclusive sense as embracing ideas, guesses, hypotheses, theories, as well as facts, still these, of course, are in constant flux, as pragmatism tells us. Not only do these unstable beings chassé backwards and forwards in the figures they describe, but they often chassé incontinently out of these figures altogether. When this evanishment occurs, the ordinary man is apt to say that the wayward beings are no longer parts of the experience. Experience goes along without them. Yesterday I saw a certain stone by a brookside. To-day I remember that I saw it. In the interval I neither saw it nor remembered seeing it, nor had the least inkling of its presence. *Abiit, excessit, evasit, erupit.* Its eruption was clean out of experience. Experience, thus used, is a most labile thing; but this very slipperiness and instability is a part of its essence in ordinary thought. But there is another meaning of the term, an extraordinary meaning, but nevertheless prevalent in philosophical writings. Out of this Experience there is no exit, not even by way of fire-escape. It does even more for what we in our finitude and mutability lose from time to time than what the Grecian Urn does for the lover and his lady. The urn stereotypes just one moment of their lives. "Forever wilt thou love and she be fair." But Experience stereotypes all the moments of all lives, everything that was or is or ever shall be, upon the bosom of a flowing river, where it is both fixed and fluid. Either kind of experience has its difficulties for experience, although we are told that neither kind has any for Experience. But either kind is just what it is, not what it is not; it contains just what it contains, not what it does not. Professor Dewey will have none of the capitalized sort, yet he will have nothing that is not experience. But as we have seen, lower-case experience has no room for vanished stones, except as memories which themselves vanish most of the time; and this seems to be the reason why the humanistic pragmatist turns stones into self-supporting experiences. In this Professor Dewey disdains to follow the humanist. Now, the question is whether Professor Dewey uses experience in some other sense than one of those above mentioned. If he does not, is he not a subjective idealist? He is full of admiration for the "miracle" which the epistemologist works in getting his ideas united with fact; the epistemologist would feel justified in retorting the admiration if the pragmatist should attempt to make fragmentary and elusive experience, without a purchase in something more permanent, bring out of non-existence just what it always needs for the solution of its logical puzzles. But if what has disappeared from experience still lives on in spite of its disappearance, and yet does so in no eternal Experience, then how does this way of taking experience and its needed complement differ from strictly objectivistic realism? But how, according to the "Studies," can what vanishes from experience continue to exist except as a sheer (unwarranted?) abstraction from the standpoint of organized or reorganized experience?

There is one further difficulty that I wish to lay before Professor Dewey in connection with his new distinction between fact and idea. I suppose that most of us accept the other side of the moon as a fact, on a par *as fact* with this side of it. If we do not accept it, there seems to be considerable disturbance in experience, which, I believe, will continue in most of us till the other side gets accepted. Then it becomes "fact." This fact, while as accepted fact it is on a parity with this side of the moon, yet as experienced fact seems to differ considerably from it. I can see the one; I can not see the other. Grant that the term sensation should lose its ordinary acceptation and become merely a term to mark an instrument or crisis in the development of inferential conclusions. Still there is, after the conclusion is reached that the moon has two hemispheres, a considerable difference in our experience between the two hemispheres, and this difference does not seem to budge however we may pry upon it with changed meanings of terms. The realist, following the ordinary usage, says that while there are two lunar hemispheres, only one can be immediately experienced, and the other is accessible to us only by means of idea. If he is forced to accept the Chicago lexicography he finds himself at a loss to express himself on this point, but unfortunately he does not find any loss of the fact to be expressed. What is pragmatism going to do with this difference? If it ignores it, can it keep peace with science—a peace it is proud of proclaiming as one of its achievements? Science makes a thoroughgoing distinction between observation and inference, between empirical facts and scientific constructions upon the basis of facts. Now it is one of the great merits of the "Studies" that it has pointed out the ambiguous nature of much of what is taken by science to be fact and what is taken to be theory. But may not the ambiguity be pressed just a little too far? What we take to be a satellite, 240,000 miles distant from the planetary earth, may after all not prove to be what we think it is. But suppose that such a change in scientific construction should ever take place? All is not lost from present scientific fact; there remains the fact that there is a bright something occasionally in experience, growing from slender crescent to full orb. This fact antedated Ptolemy and has long survived Copernicus, and will, I think, survive Copernicanism if the latter, having had its day, should ever cease to be. This fact may come to be interpreted as anything you please, and get accepted as that thing; but it will be there to be accepted somehow whenever any one constituted like us opens his eyes and turns them in the right direction at an opportune time. This kind of fact, and there are many of them, forms the inexpugnable datum of thought. It is the givenest of givens, *datissimum datorum.* Thought does not seem to have anything to do with the making of it—although the idealist has another account of the matter. Nor can thought do much[8] in the way of changing these *datissima.* Not only do they constitute the prime starting-point of all scientific problems, but they retain their pristine character throughout the thought process and after thought has done its perfect work. While ideas and data of a secondary order play their game of hide-and-seek with each other, these data of the first order are in the game, but not

8. How much thought can do in this matter is an interesting question which we can not enter into here.

of it. They give to one lunar hemisphere a primacy which no terrestrial thought-reorganization can give to the other. Now a philosophy which keeps close to experience can not well ignore this distinction between the two kinds of data. Bow the difference out of the front door by refusing to recognize it under its old style of difference between sensation and idea, and it will come in at the back door unnamed, but no less obtrusive. Can logic afford to ignore it? If it does not ignore it, can pragmatic logic fix it somewhere, mid this dance of plastic circumstance which it portrays so well, but which the old logic would fain arrest; can it fix it there without giving up the thorough plasticity of circumstance?

Appendix 4

Editor's INTRODUCTION to *Moral Principles in Education*
by Henry Suzzallo

Education as a Public Business

It is one of the complaints of the schoolmaster that the public does not defer to his professional opinion as completely as it does to that of practitioners in other professions. At first sight it might seem as though this indicated a defect either in the public or in the profession; and yet a wider view of the situation would suggest that such a conclusion is not a necessary one. The relations of education to the public are different from those of any other professional work. Education is a public business with us, in a sense that the protection and restoration of personal health or legal rights are not. To an extent characteristic of no other institution, save that of the state itself, the school has power to modify the social order. And under our political system, it is the right of each individual to have a voice in the making of social policies as, indeed, he has a vote in the determination of political affairs. If this be true, education is primarily a public business, and only secondarily a specialized vocation. The layman, then, will always have his right to some utterance on the operation of the public schools.

Education as Expert Service

I have said "some utterance," but not "all"; for schoolmastering has its own special mysteries, its own knowledge and skill into which the untrained layman cannot penetrate. We are just beginning to recognize that the school and the government have a common problem in this respect. Educa-

[First published in *Moral Principles in Education* (Boston: Houghton Mifflin Co., 1909), pp. v–x.]

tion and politics are two functions fundamentally controlled by public opinion. Yet the conspicuous lack of efficiency and economy in the school and in the state has quickened our recognition of a larger need for expert service. But just where shall public opinion justly express itself, and what shall properly be left to expert judgment?

The Relations of Expert Opinion and Public Opinion

In so far as broad policies and ultimate ends affecting the welfare of all are to be determined, the public may well claim its right to settle issues by the vote or voice of majorities. But the selection and prosecution of the detailed ways and means by which the public will is to be executed efficiently must remain largely a matter of specialized and expert service. To the superior knowledge and technique required here, the public may well defer.

In the conduct of the schools, it is well for the citizens to determine the ends proper to them, and it is their privilege to judge of the efficacy of results. Upon questions that concern all the manifold details by which children are to be converted into desirable types of men and women, the expert schoolmaster should be authoritative, at least to a degree commensurate with his superior knowledge of this very complex problem. The administration of the schools, the making of the course of study, the selection of texts, the prescription of methods of teaching, these are matters with which the people, or their representatives upon boards of education, cannot deal save with danger of becoming mere meddlers.

The Discussion of Moral Education an Illustration of Mistaken Views of Laymen

Nowhere is the validity of this distinction between education as a public business and education as an expert professional service brought out more clearly than in an analysis of the public discussion of the moral work of the school. How frequently of late have those unacquainted with the special nature of the school proclaimed the moral ends of education and at the same time demanded direct ethical instruction as the particular method by which they were to be realized! This, too, in spite of the fact that those who know best the powers and limitations of instruction as an instrument have repeatedly pointed out the futility of assuming that knowledge of right constitutes a guarantee of right doing. How common it is for those who assert that education is for social efficiency to assume that the school should return to the barren discipline of the traditional formal subjects, reading, writing, and the rest! This, too, regardless of the fact that it has taken a century of educational evolution to make the course of study varied and rich enough to call for those impulses and activities of social life which need training in the child. And how many who speak glowingly of the large services of the public schools to a democracy of free and self-reliant men affect a cynical and even vehement opposition to the "self-government of schools"! These would not have the children learn to govern themselves and one another, but would have the masters rule them, ignoring the fact that this common practice in childhood may be a foundation for that evil condition in adult society where the citizens are arbitrarily ruled by political bosses.

One need not cite further cases of the incompetence of the lay public to deal with technical questions of school methods. Instances are plentiful to show that well-meaning people, competent enough to judge of the aims and results of school work, make a mistake in insisting upon the prerogative of directing the technical aspects of education with a dogmatism that would not characterize their statements regarding any other special field of knowledge or action.

A Fundamental Understanding of Moral Principles in Education

Nothing can be more useful than for the public and the teaching profession to understand their respective functions. The teacher needs to understand public opinion and the social order, as much as the public needs to comprehend the nature of expert educational service. It will take time to draw the boundary lines that will be conducive to respect, restraint, and efficiency in those concerned; but a beginning can be made upon fundamental matters, and nothing so touches the foundations of our educational thought as a discussion of the moral principles in education.

It is our pleasure to present a treatment of them by a thinker whose vital influence upon the reform of school methods is greater than that of any of his contemporaries. In his discussion of the social and psychological factors in moral education, there is much that will suggest what social opinion should determine, and much that will indicate what must be left to the trained teacher and school official.

Appendix 5

OUTLINE of *Moral Principles in Education*

I. The Moral Purpose of the School

1. Moral ideas and ideas about morality
2. Moral education and direct moral instruction

II. The Moral Training Given by the School Community

1. The unity of social ethics and school ethics
2. A narrow and formal training for citizenship
3. School life should train for many social relations
4. It should train for self-direction and leadership
5. There is no harmonious development of powers apart from social situations
6. School activities should be typical of social life
7. Moral training in the schools tends to be pathological and formal

III. The Moral Training from Methods of Instruction

1. Active social service as opposed to passive individual absorption
2. The positive inculcation of individualistic motives and standards
3. The evils of competition for external standing
4. The moral waste of remote success as an end
5. The worth of active and social modes of learning

[First published in *Moral Principles in Education* (Boston: Houghton Mifflin Co., 1909), pp. 59–61.]

IV. *The Social Nature of the Course of Study*

1. The nature of the course of study influences the conduct of the school
2. School studies as means of realizing social situations
3. School subjects are merely phases of a unified social life
4. The meaning of subjects is controlled by social considerations
5. Geography deals with the scenes of social interaction
6. Its various forms represent increasing stages of abstraction
7. History is a means for interpreting existing social relations
8. It presents type phases of social development
9. It offers contrasts, and consequently perspective
10. It teaches the methods of social progress
11. The failure of certain methods of teaching history
12. Mathematics is a means to social ends
13. The sociological nature of business arithmetic
14. Summary: The moral trinity of the school

V. *The Psychological Aspect of Moral Education*

1. Conduct as a mode of individual performance
2. Native instincts and impulses are the sources of conduct
3. Moral ideals must be realized in persons
4. Character as a system of working forces
5. Force as a necessary constituent of character
6. The importance of intellectual judgment or good sense
7. The capacity for delicate emotional responsiveness
8. Summary: The ethical standards for testing the school
9. Conclusion: The practicality of moral principles

TEXTUAL APPARATUS

INDEX

TEXTUAL COMMENTARY

On 28 April 1904, John Dewey had accepted a position in the philosophy department at Columbia University to start teaching in February of 1905 but not to be committed past one year; he wrote his friend James McKeen Cattell to tell him he had an understanding to that effect with Columbia president Nicholas Murray Butler because he wanted to be sure that "a decision to accept the present offer did not bind me irrevocably in case I wished later on to consider the desirability of administrative work."[1] Although he resigned from the University of Chicago in April 1904, his official connection there continued up to 1 January 1905; he and his family spent the intervening time in Europe. Upon returning from Europe, he started his work at Columbia on 1 February 1905. Apparently his experiences in 1905 and 1906, just before the start of the period represented by the present volume, were satisfying and challenging enough to convince him he had chosen well: he never again mentioned the possibility of going into administrative work.

These first years of settling into his teaching and of forming stimulating relationships with his colleagues mark the beginning of the most intensely polemical period in all of Dewey's career. Dykhuizen has pointed out that "between 1905 and 1914 Dewey wrote more than thirty major articles expounding and clarifying his ideas and defending them against his critics."[2] An important example of the discussions of that time, which one philosopher was later to call "a time

1. John Dewey to James McKeen Cattell, 28 April 1904, Cattell Papers, Manuscript Division, Library of Congress. For additional discussion of Dewey's reluctance to give up the idea of becoming an administrator, see the Textual Commentary for Volume 3, *The Middle Works of John Dewey, 1899–1924*, ed. Jo Ann Boydston (Carbondale: Southern Illinois University Press, 1977).
2. George Dykhuizen, *The Life and Mind of John Dewey* (Carbondale: Southern Illinois University Press, 1973), p. 124.

blessed (or cursed) with so many currents and cross-currents,"[3] is the extended exchange between Dewey and Evander Bradley McGilvary in this volume. "A Reply to Professor McGilvary's Questions," Dewey's culminating article in that part of the discussion that started in 1907, has been included in the present volume, although it was not published until 1912. As the exchange illustrates, the *Journal of Philosophy, Psychology and Scientific Methods*, edited by Dewey's colleagues, F. J. E. Woodbridge and, starting in 1906, by Wendell T. Bush also, was the arena for much of that debate. Of the twenty-six essays and reviews in this volume, the largest number in a single journal—seven—appeared in the *Journal of Philosophy*.

But Dewey's essays during the three years 1907–9 were not limited to philosophical debate or to the *Journal of Philosophy, Psychology and Scientific Methods*; he published on a wide range of topics and in a wide range of journals as well. The concentration of articles in the *Journal of Philosophy* was followed, although not too closely, by the four that were in the *Philosophical Review*, but only two other journals account for more than one article: three appeared in *Progressive Journal of Education* and two in the *Hibbert Journal*. One article, *Ethics* ("Intelligence and Morals") was issued as a monograph by Columbia University; another, "Does Reality Possess Practical Character?" appeared in a volume of collected essays in honor of William James, *Essays, Philosophical and Psychological* (New York: Longmans, Green, and Co., 1908), 53–80; still another, Dewey's address to the 1909 National Negro Conference, was published in the *Proceedings* of the conference. The remaining seven were contributions to seven journals: *Columbia University Quarterly*; *Educational Review*; *Mind*; *Political Science Quarterly*; *Popular Science Monthly*; the proceedings of the 1909 meeting of the Northern Illinois Teachers' Association, *Topics for General Sessions: Moral and Religious Training in the Public Schools*; and *School Science and Mathematics*.

3. Wilmon Henry Sheldon, "The Vice of Modern Philosophy," *Journal of Philosophy, Psychology and Scientific Methods* 12 (1915): 5–16.

Besides these twenty-six essays and reviews, the present
volume includes Dewey's syllabus, *The Pragmatic Movement
of Contemporary Thought,* and his small book, *Moral Principles in Education,* a contribution to the series of *Riverside
Educational Monographs* edited by his Teachers College colleague, Henry Suzzallo. Not included in this volume, but
written and published during these same years, is Dewey's
part of the Dewey and Tufts *Ethics* (New York: Henry Holt
and Company, 1908), Volume 5 of the *Middle Works.*

Another review-article that Dewey agreed to do during
this period was apparently never completed. In 1907, Cattell
had asked him to review William James's *Pragmatism* for the
journal *Science;* Dewey demurred, saying he was in Hyannis,
Massachusetts, and had no copy with him, and "besides I
told Woodbridge I'd review it for the Journal [of Philoso-
phy]."[4] That "review," "What Does Pragmatism Mean by
Practical?"[5] turned out to be, as Dewey said, not a review of
"Mr. James's book, but rather [of] the present status of the
pragmatic movement as expressed in the book."[6] After
Dewey's article appeared in the *Journal,* Cattell renewed his
request and this time Dewey responded, "Yes, I will do the
James for Science if you wish."[7] Such a review was, however,
not published.

Three series of outside lectures that Dewey gave during
this period also were not published, although the notes for
one series survive: Lectures in Greek Philosophy at The Johns
Hopkins University, fall 1906.[8] The others were those at the
Normal School at Hyannis, Massachusetts, and a group of
five at the University of Illinois, which are discussed in part
in the *Daily Illini* for 8, 10, 12, and 13 December 1907. The
titles of only the first four of these five lectures are known:
"Chief Places of Contact between Philosophical and Educational Problems," "The Individual and the Universal, or
Social," "The Relation of the Individual to Society as Con-

4. Dewey to Cattell, 11 July 1907, Library of Congress.
5. *Journal of Philosophy, Psychology and Scientific Methods* 5
   (1908): 85–99.
6. "What Does Pragmatism Mean?" p. 98.
7. Dewey to Cattell, 7 July 1909, Library of Congress.
8. John Dewey Papers, Special Collections, Morris Library, Southern Illinois University at Carbondale.

ceived in Modern Educational Practice," and "Culture versus Nature in Education."[9] In addition to the syllabus printed in the present volume, from Dewey's classes for the years 1907–9 a set of transcribed lecture notes has survived: "Advanced Logic," 1906–7, 60 pp., in the H. Heath Bawden Collection, St. Louis University.

Eighteen of the twenty-six essays and reviews in the present volume were printed only once during Dewey's lifetime; he revised eight for inclusion in collective volumes of essays. One of these, "Does Reality Possess Practical Character?" was not revised until 1931; a special list of those revisions is included in the present volume. For one of the remaining seven, "Nature and Its Good: A Conversation," the carbon copy of a typescript exists; as described later in this Commentary, however, the first appearance of that paper in the *Hibbert Journal* has been preferred as copy-text. For these seven articles, then, the first printed version of each has served as copy-text.

In revised articles for which journal publication is copy-text, except in the one *Hibbert Journal* instance mentioned, the house-styling and regularization imposed on Dewey's material by the journal was obscured and sometimes apparently reversed in wholesale by the book-publisher's subsequent house-styling and regularization. Where Dewey's characteristic practice with respect to accidentals is not known, or is known to vary, the general approach to emending accidentals here has been to accept as authoritative those changes occurring within or integral to a substantive revision, as well as changes in accidentals occurring in the same sentence with substantive revisions. Additionally, accidental changes which in themselves represent identifiable Dewey revisions have been accepted as emendations of the copy-text, e.g., his addition of italics or quotation marks to call attention to a word or to a special use of a word. Outside of these cases, the approach has been conservative: only for desirable correction, as noted in the commentary sections

9. A number of other public lectures and addresses that Dewey gave during these years are known by title only and were not published. See Dykhuizen, pp. 147–48, for a detailed compilation of the titles and locations of these speeches.

that follow, has the revised accidental reading been preferred to that of the copy-text.[10]

Problems of copy-text and editorial method for the seven revised articles are discussed in the sections that follow.

The Influence of Darwin on Philosophy

Four articles in this volume—"The Influence of Darwinism on Philosophy," "Nature and Its Good: A Conversation," "Intelligence and Morals," and "The Intellectualist Criterion for Truth"—were revised by Dewey before they were published in D: *The Influence of Darwin on Philosophy and Other Essays in Contemporary Thought* (New York: Henry Holt and Company, 1910). Each essay is discussed separately in sections that follow; the publishing history of *The Influence of Darwin* appears here, rather than in its proper chronological place, so that reference may be made to it in the sections about the four essays included in that book.

Except the paper "A Short Catechism concerning Truth," all the essays in *The Influence of Darwin* had been previously published in various journals between 1897 and 1909. Because, as Dewey wrote in his "Preface," they seemed to him to have a kind of unity,[11] he collected them as a "contribution" to the tentative and piecemeal "reconstruction of our stock notions."[12] The republication of the articles provided an opportunity for substantive revision, which was, as discussed in connection with each article, in some cases extensive.[13]

The book was registered for copyright 23 April 1910

10. Textual principles and procedures used in editing the *Middle Works* are discussed in detail by Fredson Bowers in his essay, "Textual Principles and Procedures," *Middle Works of Dewey*, 1:347–60.
11. *The Influence of Darwin on Philosophy and Other Essays in Contemporary Thought* (New York: Henry Holt and Co., 1910), p. iii.
12. *Influence of Darwin*, p. vi.
13. For a discussion of the six other articles republished in *The Influence of Darwin*, see *The Early Works of John Dewey, 1882–1898*, 5:cxxxii; *Middle Works of Dewey*, Textual Commentaries to Volumes 1 and 3.

with the number A26141. All copies located of the book carry the notice "Published April, 1910" on the copyright page. Some copies examined also have "1910" on the title page; others do not. A partial inventory record among the Holt Publishing Company records at Princeton University indicates that a second printing of the book was made between 1916 and 1920, probably in 1917. Machine collation of two copies of the book[14] against the Library of Congress copyright deposit copy reveals no variants in the texts of the articles that appear in the present volume.

Attention should be directed to the editorial treatment in the present edition of three kinds of regularization imposed on the several texts at the time they were collected in *The Influence of Darwin*. The frequent and consistent substitution of "that" for "which" in restrictive clauses (31 instances in four articles) is not demonstrably Dewey's change; he was far from consistent in this practice, whether in original composition or in revision, and no regular pattern of occurrence on which editorial decision can be based exists. Thus, although it is possible that some of these changes were instituted by an editor at Holt, it is also true that many of these changes are embedded in or associated with substantive revision that is clearly Dewey's. These changes have been accepted as emendations of the copy-text in the present edition; in three such instances, however, the *Darwin* change coincided with the original typescript for "Nature and Its Good: A Conversation," which had been house-styled by the *Hibbert Journal*. Thus these three *Darwin* readings are not emendations but rather restorations. Not adopted as emendations, however, are the commas invariably added before "and" and "or" in series. In this matter, too, Dewey's practice varied and, following the principle of divided authority, the copy-text reading has been preferred. The standard American conventions with respect to the relative position of punctuation marks have been followed, as have American spellings, in the three articles first published in the English journals *Mind* and the *Hibbert Journal*.

---

14. Dewey Center (a), which has "1910" on the title page; Dewey Center (b), which does not have the date.

Otherwise, except in cases of known Dewey spelling preferences, copy-text has also been followed in spelling.

"The Influence of Darwinism on Philosophy"

Dewey participated in a series of lectures at Columbia University on "Charles Darwin and His Influence on Science," in the spring of 1909. On 13 April of that year, he sent a copy of the lecture—presumably a typescript—entitled "Darwin's Influence upon Philosophy" to James McKeen Cattell, editor of the *Popular Science Monthly*, saying, "Doubtless you are more than full of Darwin matter for the Pop. Science Mo. However, I tho't I would send you the enclosed on spec."[15] The article was published in the July number of PSM: *Popular Science Monthly* 75 (1909): 90–98; PSM serves here as copy-text.

The article was revised by Dewey, probably using an offprint, and appeared the following year with a new title as the keynote essay in D: *Influence of Darwin*, pp. 1–19. In addition to Dewey's changes in substantives adopted for the present edition as emendations of the copy-text, ten changes in punctuation that occurred in connection with substantive changes—either caused by or in proximity to such changes—have been accepted as his intention for the text. These are: the addition of commas at 4.24, 4.34, 5.15, 7.33, 8.2(2), 12.31, and 12.37; the deletion of a comma at 14.14; and the addition of a semicolon at 7.36. Following Dewey's characteristic usage, the hyphen in "half-instinctive" at 8.14 was also accepted.

"Nature and Its Good: A Conversation"

In December 1908, John Dewey read a paper entitled "The Good, Nature and Intelligence: A Conversation" to the New York Philosophical Club, a small organization with usually twelve to eighteen members from New York and its

15. Dewey to Cattell, 13 April 1909, Library of Congress.

environs that met regularly at Columbia University for many years.[16]

A 23-page carbon copy of the typescript of the address, not typed by Dewey, is preserved in the papers of the Philosophical Club in Special Collections at Columbia University. Across the top of the first page is the notation apparently made by a secretary: "These copies need not be returned. Members are reminded that they may be anotated [sic] and brought to the meeting Dec. 10th, at 5 P.M." One member, as yet not identified, did so annotate a carbon copy; the extant document is his, not Dewey's. After the title, he has written, "by John Dewey—Read at meeting of N. Y. Philosophical Club, Dec. 17th 08." Sprinkled through the paper are corrections in the same hand, not recorded here because they have no authority. As the original version of the document, however, the carbon copy does have authority, even though it was professionally typed.

The ribbon copy of this paper probably served Dewey as the medium for reworking it for publication in HJ: *Hibbert Journal* 7 (1909): 827–43, with the title "Is Nature Good? A Conversation." In revising the material, Dewey made extensive substantive changes and additions that necessarily incorporated variations in accidentals. Moreover, he thoroughly altered accidentals throughout the paper in ways demonstrably characteristic of his own corrections and changes rather than of typical *Hibbert Journal* house-styling. For this reason, HJ has served as copy-text for the present edition. The accidental corrections and changes that Dewey made for HJ consisted of the following: thirty instances of the capitalization of a term—Nature (24), Science (2), Real, Reality, Appearance, Being; numerous corrections of punctuation, typographical, or spelling errors; modifications of punctuation to set off parenthetical expressions or otherwise clarify meaning. The HJ English spellings have been silently restored here to their original American form in TS; otherwise, only the TS addition of "s" to make "Grimes's" has been preferred over the HJ copy-text form, which was prob-

16. See Dykhuizen, *Life and Mind of Dewey*, p. 297; Jane Dewey, ed., "Biography of John Dewey," in *The Philosophy of John Dewey*, ed. Paul Schilpp (Evanston: Northwestern University Press, 1939), pp. 37–38.

ably house-styled along with the spelling. The numerous differences in both substantives and accidentals between TS and HJ are recorded in the Historical Collation.

The year after its publication in HJ, Dewey prepared the article for publication in the collective volume D: *Influence of Darwin*, pp. 20–45. Of the four articles in the present volume revised for D, "Nature and Its Good" was least changed substantively, D reflecting in almost every case the substantive readings of HJ. In fact, as the Emendations List shows, only twelve substantive differences occurred between the two versions, most of them minor changes in expression rather than in thought, as for example, the addition of "to" in the expression "and to make" at 18.27, and the change of "to" to "in" at 21.24. The remaining substantive emendations are in the title, and at 21.25, 23.8, 23.13, 23.29, 27.4, 29.14, 29.18, 29.37(2), and 29.38.

That relatively few changes in HJ accidentals were made in D points to Dewey's having used an offprint of HJ as printer's-copy, and confirms the desirability of using HJ as copy-text. Besides restoring American spellings and using American conventions on the relative position of punctuation marks, D regularly added an "s" to make the possessive form of "Grimes'" thus returning to the TS form which had been editorially changed by HJ. Ten additional accidental changes have been adopted as emendations from D. One of these changes was the addition of "s" to "Grimes'" in a passage not present in TS (21.20). The addition of quotation marks for a passage of indirect discourse at 16.37 and 17.5, and the removal of italics at 23.37 are changes deemed to have been made by the author rather than an editor. Found desirable for clarification of Dewey's meaning were the commas added at 16.34,35, to set off a parenthetical expression; the addition of a comma at 23.16; the substitution of a colon for a semicolon at 25.13; and the substitution of parentheses for commas at 29.37,38.

"Intelligence and Morals"

On 24 March 1908, Dewey presented a lecture at Columbia University in a series on science, philosophy, and art; his address was published that spring by the University as a monograph entitled *Ethics* (New York: Columbia University Press, 1908), 26 pp. That first publication has served as copy-text for the article in the present edition.

Ethics was revised and republished in *The Influence of Darwin* two years later, where it appeared with the new title "Intelligence and Morals," pp. 46–76. Dewey's substantive revisions in the article have been adopted as emendations of the copy-text, along with a number of changes in accidentals judged to be desirable corrections made by Dewey in the process of revision. These are: capitalization of "fate" at 34.12 and of "middle ages" at 37.8; setting off "however" with commas at 33.16; use of a comma to complete setting off a parenthetical expression at 42.38; deletion of commas at 32.16,17; 34.11; 36.39; 37.2; 46.15; the addition of hyphens to reflect Dewey's characteristic usage in "all-embracing", 43.31, and "all-inclusive", 46.33; addition of a comma at 31.18; change of a semicolon to a comma, 31.18; and the addition of an overlooked hyphen at 49.7 in "class-approvals", to complete the series "class-codes, class-standards".

"The Intellectualist Criterion for Truth"

Copy-text for this article is M: its first appearance with the title "Reality and the Criterion for the Truth of Ideas," in the British journal *Mind*, n.s. 16 (1907): 317–42. Emendations have been adopted from the revised version published in D: *Influence of Darwin*, pp. 112–53, with the new title used here.

Dewey's note on the first page of the article in D refers to "many changes . . . made to render the article less technical." He adds, however, that "it still remains, I fear, too technical to be intelligible to those not familiar with recent discussions of logical theory." Dewey's efforts to make the material less technical, which he seems to have considered largely unsuccessful, consisted of radical revision of the article both by internal rewriting and by rearrangement of the passages. All the excised passages appear in the Emendations List but it has not been possible to devise a table to reflect the original arrangement of the material.

In addition to changes in accidentals that Dewey made in connection with this substantive revision, five other emendations of accidentals have been made for the present edition: lower-casing "the" at 65.39; adding commas at 56.6, 67.1, 71.23; and changing commas to parentheses at 72.12–13.

Essays in Experimental Logic

After their initial journal appearance, three essays in this volume—"The Control of Ideas by Facts," "The Logical Character of Ideas," and "What Pragmatism Means by Practical"—were revised and republished in EE: *Essays in Experimental Logic* (Chicago: University of Chicago Press, 1916).[17] The three essays are discussed individually in succeeding sections of this Commentary; the collective volume *Essays in Experimental Logic* is described first so that reference may be made to it in those later sections.

Essays was initially seen by the University of Chicago Press as an almost routine republication of Dewey's contributions to the *Studies in Logical Theory* (Chicago: University of Chicago Press, 1903), "with corrections and some minor additions."[18] The Press apparently thought of the "minor additions" in terms of a few paragraphs or even pages to be added to the previously published *Studies*; Dewey, however, responding to the repeated invitation to make such additions, doubled the size of the projected book by adding nine essays published earlier in various journals.

Three printings of *Essays* were made from a single set of plates, in 1916, 1918, and 1920; the book went out of print in December 1925. Machine collation of copies of the three impressions[19] of the book against the copyright deposit

17. The genesis and history of *Essays in Experimental Logic* are discussed more fully in the Textual Commentary to Volume 2, *Middle Works of Dewey*. The account in the present volume is a summary of that material.
18. Memorandum from A .C. McFarland to Newman Miller, Director of the Press, 24 February 1916. Publishing records and correspondence cited here are, unless noted otherwise, among University of Chicago Press records at the Langley office and are quoted with the permission of the Press.
19. First impression, Dewey Center; second impression, University of Minnesota, 1329092; third impression, University of Chicago Press Collection of Record Copies.

copy (A433372) shows that in the three articles in the present volume only one line was reset; for the third impression, type was reset to eliminate a line-end break in the word "arrangements" in the article "What Pragmatism Means by Practical."

"The Control of Ideas by Facts"

The first publication of this article in three parts in JP: *Journal of Philosophy, Psychology and Scientific Methods* 4 (1907): 197–203, 253–59, 309–19, serves as copy-text. Emendations have been drawn from Dewey's revisions of the essay for its republication in EE: *Essays in Experimental Logic*, pp. 230–49.

One of the approaches that Dewey used in revising this article was to reduce the amount of material in the three sections. The original first section was divided into two parts, I and II, for EE; the second section as first published was omitted, as were the opening pages of the third section, thereby considerably reducing the length of the article.

Dewey's changes in substantives have been incorporated into the copy-text as emendations, as have revisions of accidentals made by him in the process of changing those substantives. In this article, a number of emendations of accidentals have clear substantive implications: for example, the hyphenated compounds Dewey made in all "relation" words—"meaning-relation", 81.12–13, 82.2–3, 89.18; "*meaning-relations*", 89.29; "*fact-relations*", 89.29; and "signification-relation", 88.34. Similarly, Dewey used italics and quotation marks to alter meaning and emphasis: in EE, he added italics at 83.40–84.1, 86.25, and 87.29 and removed them at 84.23 and 84.39, and he added quotation marks at 85.31 and 90.1. Other changes in accidentals also affecting meaning, adopted as emendations of the copy-text, were the deletion of commas at 81.16, 82.17, 84.8; elimination of commas between subject and verb at 82.6 and 83.8; substitution of a colon for a question mark at 83.21 and of a comma for a semicolon between clauses of a complex sentence at 86.18. Four additional accidental changes were accepted as desirable: the addition of a comma to set off a parenthetical expression at 86.36, the substitution of a colon for a comma at 80.18, and the deletion of two unnecessary commas preceding dashes at 90.32.

"The Logical Character of Ideas"

The first appearance of this essay in JP: *Journal of Philosophy, Psychology and Scientific Methods* 5 (1908): 375–81, is copy-text for the present edition. Emendations have been adopted from its revision for publication in EE: *Essays in Experimental Logic*, pp. 220–29.

Besides Dewey's substantive revisions of the text that have been used as emendations, four changes in accidentals, judged to have been Dewey's intentions in revising the material, have been adopted here. They are: the addition of a comma at 96.11; the addition of quotation marks to "knowledge" at 92.24; use of Dewey's characteristic spelling "practice" at 92.33; and the substitution of a dash for a semicolon at 94.22.

"What Pragmatism Means by Practical"

Dewey's "non-review" of William James's *Pragmatism* was first published in JP: *Journal of Philosophy, Psychology and Scientific Methods* 5 (1908): 85–99, with the title, "What Does Pragmatism Mean by Practical?" which serves as copy-text. The essay was revised for inclusion in EE: *Essays in Experimental Logic*, pp. 303–29, from which both substantive and accidental emendations have been adopted.

Supporting Dewey's statement that he did not consider this article a review in the usual sense of the word were his careful revision of it and his use of it in *Essays*. His substantive changes have been adopted as emendations of the copy-text as have the changes in accidentals made in con-

nection with those substantive revisions. The largest group
of accidental changes comprises Dewey's shifts in emphasis
in EE: he added italics four times and removed italics forty-
nine times, making fifty-three such shifts. In three instances
(101.33, 103.28 [2]) he added quotation marks and in three
other instances (104.9–10, 111.31, 113.6) deleted them. Another large group of changes in accidentals between JP and
EE occur in material quoted from the James volume. EE
incorporates changes of ten accidentals and one substantive
in these quotations. Dewey himself may have noted the substantive error at 110n.8, where "banded" had appeared instead of the correct "funded"; it is possible he checked
through all the quotations for correction of accidentals, but
failed to change his misquotation at 113.32 where he quoted
James's "potentest" as "most potential." Some support for
that hypothesis is found in the introduction of new errors in
the James material by EE, which would argue against a careful complete correction by the University of Chicago Press.
Routine styling at the Press accounts for changing "practise"
at 102.6 to "practice", a spelling that happened to coincide
with James's own; substitution of "anyone" for "any one" at
103.9 and 110n.11, however, was not in accord with the
Pragmatism in print at the time, although by chance "anyone" actually restored James's *own* usage that had been
house-styled for *Pragmatism*. The newly-established text of
Pragmatism (*Works of William James*. [Cambridge: Harvard
University Press, 1975]) restores James's original spelling;
the EE spelling within the quotation has therefore been
adopted here as an emendation. Further, the revision or
compositorial slip, changing "that fact" to "the fact" at
103.15 is an error, corrected here.

Other changes in accidentals accepted as emendations
are: Dewey's characteristic hyphenation of "never-failing" at
101.38; substitution of a semicolon for a dash at 98.8; addition of commas to set off parenthetical expressions at 101.8
and 102.37; use of a comma to complete setting off a series
at 106.26; substitution of a semicolon for a colon at 103.31,
32; addition of quotation marks to James's title at 114.15;
deletion of commas separating the subject from the verb at
109.7 and 115.15.

Syllabus: The Pragmatic Movement
of Contemporary Thought

Privately printed for use by Dewey's classes, this eleven-page syllabus is, as he pointed out in a note, "synoptic rather than analytic." The single previous impression has been used as copy-text. Because it was not a document published for general use, the four-page bibliography at the end of the syllabus was made up of suggested readings listed in sketchy form. For the present edition, a certain amount of correction and regularization of formal matters has been necessary to complete and clarify the references: names of articles have been supplied where only publication information was present; abbreviations have been spelled out; volume numbers of journals have been listed and the year of publication supplied; volume numbers are roman, chapter numbers are arabic; the beginning page numbers of articles, inadvertently omitted in some cases, have been added; following Dewey's pattern, only the last name of the author appears, except that when two authors with the same surname are listed, the initial(s) have also been given; and the punctuation in only this section has been regularized.

Moral Principles in Education

This small book, which Dewey said drew "freely" on his earlier *Ethical Principles Underlying Education*,[20] enjoyed a long and successful publishing history:[21] sixteen printings over a period of twenty-one years and sales of almost 20,000 volumes.[22] A single set of plates, melted in 1942, served for

20. *Third Yearbook of the National Herbart Society* (Chicago: The Society 1897); *Early Works of Dewey*, 5:54–83. See "A Note on the Texts," *Early Works* 5:cxxxiii, for a discussion of the relation between the material in *Ethical Principles* and *Moral Principles*.
21. Houghton Mifflin graciously made available copies, and in some cases originals, of all existing records related to *Moral Principles*.
22. If the publishing history is extended up to the time the book went out of print in 1956, it spans forty-seven years. A paper-back edition has recently been published with a new introduc-

all sixteen printings. Although none of the printings bears a publication date, visible deterioration of the type makes it possible to distinguish later printings. Machine collation of the last printing located (University of Michigan 26306) against the Library of Congress copyright deposit copy (A241723) reveals no variants in the text. Changes in the front and end matter were made, however, for most reprintings of the book, to reflect differences in the position of the editor, Henry Suzzallo, to update advertising material, and to add new locations of the publisher. These listings of locations verify the evidence of the broken and worn type and enable identification of the University of Michigan copy as the most recent: on that copy, five cities, including Dallas, appear; on Houghton Mifflin inventory records, Dallas is first listed as an outlet in 1928. A sixth location, Atlanta, is on the inventory tabulation in 1930, the year the last printing of *Moral Principles* was made, but no copy has been located with Atlanta on the title page.

No emendations have been made in the first-printing copy-text. In the present edition, Henry Suzzallo's introduction has been moved from its original position preceding the book to the end of this volume, where it appears as an appendix; similarly, the outline of contents, which was probably prepared also by Suzzallo rather than Dewey, has been made an appendix here.

Although *Moral Principles* was in large part a reworking of the 1897 *Ethical Principles*, that the latter work was reprinted by the University of Chicago Press through 1916 is a clear indication of a continuing demand for both books. *Moral Principles* was recognized at once as a distinct and important statement; reviewers were unanimous in their praise.[23] Carl Seashore wrote a brief analysis of "the argument in this forceful and sound little manual . . . which is an interpretation of consistent psychology, ethics and so-

---

tion by Sidney Hook (Carbondale: Southern Illinois University Press, 1975, Arcturus Books).
23. [*Proceedings of the*] *Second International Moral Education Congress*, 1912, 184–87; Frank A. Manny, *Elementary School Teacher* 10 (1909): 204; C. E. Seashore, *Journal of Educational Psychology* 1 (1910): 117–18; *Booklist* 6 (1909): 39.

ciology with reference to moral education in the school."[24]
Booklist called it "a forceful statement,"[25] and Frank Manny
said it was "the most important work we have upon the subject of moral education."[26]

24. *Journal of Educational Psychology,* 1:118.
25. p. 39.
26. *Elementary School Teacher,* 10:204.

LIST OF SYMBOLS

Page-line number at left is from present edition; all lines of print except running heads are counted.

The abbreviation *et seq.* following a page-line number means that all subsequent appearances of the reading in that section are identical with the one noted.

Reading before bracket is from present edition.

Square bracket signals end of reading from present edition, followed by the symbol identifying the first appearance of reading.

W means Works—the present edition—and is used for emendations made here for the first time.

The abbreviation [*om.*] means the reading before the bracket was omitted in the editions and impressions identified after the abbreviation; [*not present*] is used where appropriate to signal material not appearing in identified sources.

The abbreviation [*rom.*] means roman type and is used to signal the omission of italics.

Stet used with an edition or impression number indicates a substantive reading retained from an edition or impression subsequently revised; the rejected variant follows the semicolon.

The asterisk before an emendation page-line number indicates the reading is discussed in the Textual Notes.

The plus sign ⁺ means that the same reading appears in all collated printings and editions later than the one noted.

For emendations restricted to punctuation, the curved dash ∼ means the same word(s) as before the bracket, and the inferior caret ∧ indicates the absence of a punctuation mark.

EMENDATIONS LIST

All emendations in both substantives and accidentals introduced into the copy-texts are recorded in the list that follows, with the exception of certain regularizations described and listed in this introductory explanation. The reading to the left of the square bracket is from the present edition. The bracket is followed by the abbreviation for the source of the emendation's first appearance and by abbreviations for subsequent editions and printings collated that had the same reading. After the source abbreviations comes a semicolon, followed by the copy-text reading. Substantive variants in all texts collated are also recorded here; the list thus serves as a historical collation as well as a record of emendations, except for "Nature and Its Good: A Conversation," for which pre-copy-text readings appear in a separate list.

The copy-text for each item is identified at the beginning of the list of emendations in that item; for items that had a single previous printing, no abbreviation for the copy-text appears in the list itself.

The following formal changes have been made throughout:

1. Book and journal titles are in italic type; articles and sections of books are in quotation marks. Book titles have been supplied and expanded where necessary.

2. Superior numbers have been assigned consecutively throughout an item to Dewey's footnotes; the asterisk is used only for editorial footnotes.

3. Single quotation marks have been changed to double when not inside quoted material; opening or closing quotation marks have been supplied where necessary.

The following spellings have been editorially regularized to the known Dewey usage appearing before the brackets:

although] altho 241.14–15
centre] center 100.22, 218.16; (-s) 160.33, 163.39, 164.17
clues] clews 192.20
cooperation] coöperation 117.11, 278.21, 279.9
cooperative] coöperative 218.33, 219.6
coordinate] coördinate 225.19; (-ed) 272.7; (-tion) 245.33
demarcation] demarkation 279.33
expressed] exprest 231.1, 236.22
looked] lookt 233.15
mold] mould 164.6
program] programme 131.13; (-s) 268.11
sceptic] skeptic 235.1; (-al) 291.11
self-enclosed] self-inclosed 62.23
thorough] thoro 230.27; (-ly) 230.29
though] tho 206.12, 229.32, 230.9
through] thru 206.31, 210.30, 210.40, 213.15, 229.16, 230.33,
    234.14, 236.14, 238.35, 239.18, 241.4, 241.7, 241.8

The following instances of word-division and hyphenation have been editorially altered to the known Dewey forms appearing before the brackets:

all-important] all important 279.11
anyone] any one 65.36, 69n.11
black-smithing] blacksmithing 59.4–5, 62.20
common-sense (adj.)] common sense 129.29
cooperate] co-operate 191.8, 193.11; (-tion) 187.4, 191.6, 192.25;
    (-tive) 136.13–14, 184.2
coordinated] co-ordinated 183.12
coordinations] co-ordinations 183.19
eighteenth-century (adj.)] eighteenth century 169.3
everyone] every one 221.25, 267.32
half-century] half century 3.22
high-school (adj.)] high school 199.12–13
ostrich-wise] ostrich wise 133.10
other-worldly] other worldly 37.35
public-school (adj.)] public school 269.20–21
quotation marks] quotation-marks 143.18
ready-made] ready made 37.30
self-evident] self evident 199.39
someone] some one 25.16, 69.5, 232.32; (-'s) 76.16
subject-matter] subject matter 185.28, 188.36–37, 198.17, 202.33,
    205.6

"The Influence of Darwinism on Philosophy"

Copy-text is PSM: "Darwin's Influence upon Philosophy," *Popular Science Monthly* 75 (1909): 90–98. Emendations have been adopted from D: *The Influence of Darwin on Philosophy* (New York: Henry Holt and Co., 1910), pp. 1–19.

3.1–2	THE INFLUENCE OF DARWINISM ON PHILOSOPHY[1] . . . [1]A lecture . . . July, 1909.] D; DARWIN'S INFLUENCE UPON PHILOSOPHY
4.17	Although] D; However much
4.20–21	sought in . . . religion.] D; sought elsewhere.
4.24	as much as does] D; as does
4.24	Greeks,] D; ∼∧
4.34	species,] D; ∼∧
4.34	and it] D; and
4.37; 7.8	is] D; was
5.15	beings,] D; ∼∧
5.16	happen elsewhere] D; elsewhere
5.32; 9.30	which] D; that
5.35	distant] D; in spite of their being distant
5.38; 6.11	εἶδος] W; εἶδος
6.11	a] D; the
6.21	does not] D; can not
6.22	is] D; is also
7.11	as well as] D; and
7.17	Earth] D; earth
7.33	arrested,] D; ∼∧
7.33	because] D; for the most part, because
7.34	intervened] D; there intervened
7.36	ideas;] D; ∼∧
7.36	and] D; while
7.38–40	having conquered . . . thereby freed] D; having freed
7.40–8.1	morals and life] D; morals by conquering the phenomena of life
8.2	si] W; se
8.2	emancipated,] D; ∼∧
8.2	all,] D; ∼∧
8.4	explanations.] D; explanations in philosophy.
8.14	half-instinctive] D; ∼∧∼
8.16	vague] D; vaguer
8.17	a problem] D; one problem
8.17	long] D; great
8.17	currency] D; significance
8.20	or] D; and
8.30	inferences] D; two inferences
9.14	operated as] D; made
9.16	marvelous] D; marvellous
9.24	approved] D; proved
9.30; 13.6,16	that] D; which

9.37	installment] D; instalment
10n.2	pp. 283–84.] D; 283–84.
11.9	then] D; further
11.12	truth] D; truths
11.22	or] D; or in
11.34	how] D; how these
12.2	*must*] D; *must* really
12.4	goal.] D; goal, while the logic of the new science frees philosophy from this apologetic habit and temper.
12.6	that] D; that lies
12.7	all lies] D; all
12.11–12	not as yet] D; not yet
12.18	within] D; without
12.24–25	in comparison with the demonstrations] D; in behalf of the daily demonstrations
12.31	yet the] D; the
12.31	tired,] D; ∼∧
12.35–36	none the less truth] D; truth
12.37	concrete,] D; ∼∧
12.37	remain] D; remain none the less
13.5	it naturally] D; naturally it
13.16	to] D; into
13.23	practice] D; practise
13.25	seem] D; may seem
13.29	any] D; any changes
13.30	those] D; those wrought in those
13.32	are] D; are evident
13.38	one which] D; which
13.40–14.1	essentially goes beyond experience] D; radically transcends experiences
14.2	The] D; In other words, the
14.4	proclaim an] D; effect a more
14.14	questions∧] D; such questions,
14.14	their decreasing] D; decreasing
14.16	and a change of urgent interest.] D; and interest in their point of view.
14.20–21	dissolvent in contemporary thought] D; dissolvent
14.23–24	that found its climax in] D; completed in

"Nature and Its Good: A Conversation"

Copy-text is the first publication of the article in HJ: *Hibbert Journal* 7 (1909): 827–43, where it appeared with the title "Is Nature Good? A Conversation." Four readings have been restored from TS: a carbon copy of the typescript

of Dewey's address to the New York Philosophical Club, 17
December 1908, in Special Collections, Butler Library, Columbia University, 23 pp. All other variants between HJ and
TS are recorded in the Historical Collation. Emendations
have been adopted from the article's revision and republication in *The Influence of Darwin on Philosophy* (New York:
Henry Holt and Co., 1910), pp. 20–45.

15.1–2	NATURE . . . CONVERSATION] W; NATURE . . . CONVERSATION¹ . . . ¹Reprinted from the *Hibbert Journal*, Vol. VII., No. 4, July, 1909. D; IS NATURE GOOD? A CONVERSATION./ PROFESSOR JOHN DEWEY.
16.34	which, . . . search,] D; ~ʌ ~ʌ
16.37	"Modern] D; ʌ~
17.5	emit."] D; ~.ʌ
18.27	and to make] D; and make
19.17; 25.38; 29.36	that] TS, D; which
20.28	imagined] D; imagine
21.20	Grimes's] D; Grimes'
21.24	in] D; to
21.25	idealism] D; it
23.8	without] D; with
23.13	be correct] D; is correct
23.16	what is,] D; ~ʌ
23.29	to effect] D; to have effected
23.37	is the] D; *is* the
24.13	Grimes's] TS, D; Grimes'
25.13	Arthur:] D; ~;
27.4	since] D; as
29.14	possible] D; possible for its aims,
29.18	an] D; of the
29.37	valuation (] D; ~,
29.37	which defines] D; which should define
29.37	describes] D; describe
29.38	classifies] D; classify
29.38	knowledge,)] D; ~,ʌ

"Intelligence and Morals"

Copy-text is the first publication of this article with the
title *Ethics* (New York: Columbia University Press, 1908),
26 pp. Emendations have been adopted from the revision of

the article for its inclusion in *The Influence of Darwin* (New York: Henry Holt and Co., 1910), pp. 46–76.

31.1   INTELLIGENCE AND MORALS[1] . . . [1]A public . . .
            Art."] D;   ETHICS
31.18   character,] D;   ~;
31.19–20   consideration . . . on social] D;   the valuation of
            the functions of individuals with respect to their effect
            upon social
[1]31.26; 36.30; 43.6;   that] D;   which
45.4; 47.22; 48.31
31.28   analysis] D;   keen analysis
32.2   one: namely, a] D;   one:—the
32.4   focused] D;   focussed
32.5   perception] D;   adequate perception
32.6   materials] D;   methods
32.6   method] D;   vital method
32.7   conditions] D;   materials
32.13   inevitably] D;   as inevitably
32.16   customs‸] D;   ~,
32.17   without‸] D;   ~,
32.17   the friction of] D;   disintegration from
32.20   were fascinated] D;   were themselves fascinated
32.27   assertions] D;   assertion
33.16   theory,] D;   ~‸
33.16   however,] D;   ~‸
34.2–3   which aims at] D;   which is
34.6   customs] D;   custom
34.11   and‸] D;   ~,
34.12   Fate] D;   fate
34.35   remotely] D;   remote
35.3   barbarism] D;   barbarian
35.5   none] D;   no one
35.13   circumstances] D;   circumstance
35.16; 42.32   connection] D;   connexion
35.32–33   between divine] D;   the divine
35.33   corrupt] D;   the corrupt
35.35   were] D;   became
35.37   sure] D;   certain
35.38   for which] D;   which
35.38   fostered care] D;   much fostered
36.7–9   consideration . . . into] D;   consideration of differ-
            ences of better and worse in their natural sources and
            social consequences, into
36.11–12   Philosophy . . . erect] D;   Philosophy it was which
            bound the erect
36.19   more] D;   even more
36.28   to] D;   in order to

36.34	connections] D; connexions
36.36	a notion] D; an idea
36.39	own$_\wedge$] D; ~,
37.2	use$_\wedge$] D; ~,
37.8	Middle Ages] D; middle ages
37.9	association] D; associations
37.18	chemistry, occult] D; chemistry and occult
37.19	exalted] D; claimed
37.23	many] D; many others
37.23	stripping] D; stripping off
37.28–29	science . . . ; because] D; science; because
37.32	specific] D; better
38.1	single mother] D; common mother
38.1	experimental] D; the development of experimental
38.31	inevitable$_\wedge$] D; ~,
39.15	is also] D; is
39.26–27	is . . . the changed] D; was conceivable only with a changed
39.27	intelligence,] D; the intelligence$_\wedge$
39.28	science,] D; ~$_\wedge$
39.28	of want,] D; the want$_\wedge$
40.9	petrifaction] D; petrification
41.3–4	was returned] D; returned
41.10	such a] D; that
41.11	civil] D; civic
41.12	as] D; which
41.13	interests] D; interest
41.13	conducing] D; which conduce
41.28	that looked] D; that if looked
42.11	social] D; sociable
42.16	application . . . interests.] D; application.
42.17	saw] D; clearly saw
42.23	of] D; from
42.28	is] D; was
42.30	injunction issued] D; injunction
42.31	not] D; never
42.38	which,] D; ~$_\wedge$
43.3	sentimental] D; the sentimental
43.4	practical] D; the practical
43.22	apologetic] D; apologetics
43.31	all-embracing] D; ~$_\wedge$~
43.33	because] D; that
43.34	a] D; the
43.35,36	perfect] D; a perfect
43.36–37	contemporary, Green, is] D; contemporary is
43.38	this] D; it
43.39–40	is . . . known] D; is known
44.8	agreed] D; agree

44.10–11	that moves] D; which moves
44.18	implied] D; imply
44.27	but is] D; but that it is
44.31	impostures] D; imposture
44.34	theoretical] D; reflective
44.36	past] D; these past
45.2	undertake: study of] D; do: to study
45.4	developing] D; to develop
45.4	testing] D; test
45.6	to buttress] D; buttress
45.37	a universe] D; the universe
46.9	the] D; all the
46.15	amiss‸] D; ~,
46.19	nor] D; or
46.33	all-inclusive] D; ~‸~
47.7–8	to . . . read] D; then to turn about and read
47.22	statistical] D; those statistical
47.27–28	which, . . . interesting] D; which, in concealing their origin and structure, interesting
47.37	through] D; by
48.23	is] D; is itself
48.36	devising] D; the task of devising
49.7	class-approvals] D; ~‸~
49.12–13	pretense] D; pretence
49.25	members] D; it will be because members
49.25	must] D; can
49.27	be] D; are

"The Intellectualist Criterion for Truth"

This article was first published in M: *Mind*, n.s. 16 (1907): 317–42, with the title "Reality and the Criterion for the Truth of Ideas," which serves as copy-text. Emendations have been adopted from the revised version which was published in *The Influence of Darwin* (New York: Henry Holt and Co., 1910), pp. 112–53.

50.1	THE INTELLECTUALIST CRITERION FOR TRUTH[1] . . . [1]Reprinted, . . . logical theory.] D; I.—REALITY AND THE CRITERION FOR THE TRUTH OF IDEAS.
50.3	I] D; BY PROF. JOHN DEWEY.
50.12	is one in kind with] D; is essentially one with
50.14	atmosphere. Much] D; atmosphere, and to call to mind how much

50.16   to] D;   with
50.18   be based] D;   be wholly based
50.20   situation that] D;   situation as perplexing as it
50.23   *method*] D;   [*rom.*]
50.24   "reality,"] D;   ∧~,∧
50.24–60.5   reality reached . . . moment. Yet] D;   reality thus
         reached is itself no more rational in character than it
         is volitional (or an affair of purpose) or than it is a
         case of pure and immediate sentiency: or, more strictly,
         that the intellectual, affectional and volitional features
         are, in 'ultimate' reality, qualitatively transformed by
         some process of mutual absorption and reciprocal fu-
         sion. This, then, is the curious character of the situa-
         tion: Reality is an 'absolute experience' in which the
         intellectual as such is simply one transmuted moment;
         yet
51.15–24   experience. This paradox . . . reaching implications.
         First, let us] D;   experience. In any case the thesis I
         wish to maintain is that Mr. Bradley's Absolute Experi-
         ence, resting ultimately upon a rationalistic conception
         of the criterion of truth, is a temporary half-way house
         into which travellers from the territory of Kantian
         epistemology may temporarily turn aside in their jour-
         ney towards the land of a philosophy of every-day ex-
         perience. [¶] First∧ let us
51.26   thought; it] D;   thought. It
51.27; 69.23; 70.6,16   existence] D;   reality
51.37   to the modern idealist] D;   to Mr. Bradley
52.7   judgment, moreover,] D;   judgment,
52.8   judgment] D;   the judgment's
52.14   while] D;   but
52.27   which is] D;   which I take it is
52.31   whole.] D;   whole.[1] . . . [1]Possibly added interest at-
         taches to this last dilemma because Bradley seems to
         conceive of this act as essentially psychical in nature.
         It would be interesting to have more explicit details as
         to just how judgment as psychical act manages to keep
         house with judgment as logical content. We appear to
         have here either the postulate of a miracle, namely that
         a purely psychical somewhat gets outside of itself to
         perform an act which takes effect entirely in the region
         beyond itself, or else we have a position which logically
         developed leads to pure subjectivism. It would be in-
         teresting to know just how Mr. Bradley conceives this
         result of pure scepticism to be avoided.
52.32–53.32   These   considerations . . . thought   itself.]   D;
         [*not present*]
53.33   view] D;   view, then,

53.34–35   (and . . . judgment,)] D; ∧~,∧
53.35; 59.13,17;   that] D;   which
62.35; 63.30;
66.19,33; 67.14,34;
²70.2,11,36; 72.28;
73.4,34,39,40; 74.38
53.39   "Reality"] D;   ∧reality∧
54.3–4   truth . . . word.] D;   truth (as fulfilment of the spe-
           cific function of knowledge) are matters of appearance.
54.19–26   truth. We . . . thought. [¶] Speaking of thought] D;
           truth. [¶] Moreover there is ground for holding not
           merely that knowledge itself is inherently discrepant
           and thus in the realm of 'appearance,' but that the
           existence anywhere of self-contradiction and thus of
           appearance, is always due to the process of knowing:
           that the burden of the very existence of appearance as
           distinct from reality has to be borne by the intellectual
           function. Speaking of thought
54.31   aspects] D;   de facto aspects
54.32–33   qualities, . . . elements] D;   qualities, the relation of
           substance to its properties, the matter of relation to
           qualitative elements
54.37   seems] D;   seems to be
54.37   that the] D;   that it is the
54.38   thought is] D;   thought which is
54.39   mentioned precisely] D;   mentioned realised in con-
           creto precisely
54.40   situation in concreto] D;   situation
55.1   resolved] D;   resolvable
55.2   relations and elements related.] D;   relation and the
           elements which are related.
55.4–5   the nature of relation is such as to] D;   the elements
           and the relation are so related as to
55.15   pp. 485–86] W;   p. 486
55.15–23   original). It is not . . . thoughtless experience. [¶]
           On the one] D;   original). [¶] I have no respect for
           proof-text methods, and I should certainly not quote
           these selected passages did they not seem to be con-
           spicuously representative of the tenor—and the funda-
           mental difficulty—of the whole position. On the one
55.23   hand∧] D;   ~,
55.23   there] D;   as I have said, there
55.27   hand,] D;   ~∧
55.27   a strictly] D;   we find the strictly
55.28   criterion . . . adopted]   D;   criterion   deliberately
           stated
55.33; 68.29   things] D;   reality
55.35   character] D;   general character

55.36   I take] D;   I shall take
55.37   side,] D;   ~∧
55.38   Reality] D;   reality
55.38   reached by] D;   reached on the basis of
55n.2   "General Nature of Reality."] D;   ∧~·∧
56.6   say,] D;   ~∧
56.9   it follows] D;   this implies
56.24   here] D;   at first
56.34   discrepancy. Yes] D;   discrepancy. The further obser-
         vation that a method, involving inherent self-contradic-
         tion, has a certain postulate involves, logically, the self-
         contradictory character of that postulate. It can only
         sum up the contradiction scattered through concrete
         thinkings. Accordingly the fact that thought as such
         has an absolute criterion is just one proof the more of
         thought's zealous and unremitting activity in the cause
         of evolving mere ideality—disruption of meaning from
         existence. Yes
56.34–35 say (speaking formally), the] D;   say, the
56.40–57.1 falls . . . situation.] D;   falls in its import wholly
         within these limits.
57.2   special] D; [rom.]
57.2   alter] D;   alter radically
57.5–7   juncture . . . the Absolute.] D;   juncture can trans-
         form its fallen character.
57.14   short, whatever is finally] D;   short, finally
57.22–27 Mr. Bradley . . . position.] D;   Mr. Bradley, it may
         be said, has recognised this difficulty and adequately
         disposed of it. [¶] Consider, for example, the nature of
         the collision, incompatibility, etc., which, according to
         Mr. Bradley, supplies the immediate and empirical
         antecedent materials over against which thought gives
         us the conception of a completely harmonised reality.
57.27   He] D;   Mr. Bradley
57.28   far as] D;   far away from intellectualism as
57.28   an] D;   the
57.34   p. 151] D;   p. 51
58.4–14 The retort . . . practice?] D;   Now as against this
         pragmatic statement (which, with the exception of one
         phrase to which I shall momentarily return, could
         hardly be bettered) Mr. Bradley has seemingly nothing
         to offer save that the intellect is "a movement of a very
         special kind". "Thinking is an attempt to satisfy a
         special impulse, and the attempt implies an assump-
         tion about reality" (p. 153). And then comes the sen-
         tence which we have quoted above to the effect that all
         thinking involves the assumption of the standard of
         consistency which is absolute for it.

58.14–15   Why is] D;   He takes up, for example, this question:
           "Why is
58.19   pp. 152–53] W;   p. 153 D, M
58.24–25   satisfied"). [¶] Grant that] D;   satisfied"). Once more,
           very well; but if the incapacity of theory to reach any-
           thing beyond the realm of appearance has already been
           established, how does the supremacy of the theoretical
           standard within theory, prove anything more than that
           the standard of thought is infected with the same self-
           contradictory nature that troubles thought itself? The
           elaborate structure of absolute experience, perfect, un-
           changing, all-inclusive, is, from the logical point of
           view, simply another example of the appearance-char-
           acter of knowledge products; it simply shows how far
           thought can go in the perpetuation of internal discrep-
           ancies. . . .

               The transition from the purely formal to the ma-
           terial side of the discussion is made by realising that
           while Mr. Bradley declares that the standard of con-
           sistency in itself is "but formal and abstract" (p. 144);
           that in itself it is "mere theoretical consistency" (p.
           147), yet it is this "theoretical consistency" which
           "guarantees that reality is a self-consistent system" (p.
           148). The gist of the argument is that since thought
           demands self-consistency, absolute reality must be
           something in which all the discrepancies, deficiencies,
           loose ends, etc., of actual experience are found built
           into perfect unity. The argument is from the formal
           consistency of thinking to the material consistency of
           all the constituents of reality.[1]

    1. I am relieved from dealing with this problem in itself by the
    thoroughness with which it has already been considered in
    MIND by Prof. Sidgwick and Mr. Knox, see Nos. 53 and 54, N.S.

               Now if we remember the prior declarations that
           thought is and must be self-discrepant in its work-
           ings, we find a highly suggestive situation presented to
           us. Reality, in Mr. Bradley's philosophy, appears twice
           over; it enacts different rôles. On the one hand, it
           presents itself as an Absolute, ultimate reality, an
           eternal and all-inclusive experience; on the other hand,
           it presents itself as "our experience," as something
           riddled with discrepancies, everywhere at odds with
           itself, or as Appearance. Recall that this Jekyl-Hyde
           conception of reality is the result of the attempt to
           define reality on the basis of a purely theoretical stand-
           ard, "the intellect alone," and the situation seems
           made to order as an illustration of the theory of the

self-contradictory character of thought, *viz.*, the persistent alienating of existence and meaning in the very effort to unite them. What is reality in its absolute character except the meaning-function taken *in toto*, once for all? What is the appearance-character except the existence aspect taken in an equally wholesale way? [¶] Granted that

58.26   grant] D;   granted
58.28   and the] D;   the
58.37   give it] D;   say it has
58.39   "independent∧"] D;   '~,'
59.1–7   "special" . . . [¶] His underlying] D;   "special" be interpreted in this sense, it is no more an answer to the contention that thinking is essentially a practical activity to say that it is a *special* mode of activity, than it would be to say that black-smithing is not an industrial activity because its end is the *special* one of making horseshoes. His underlying
59.3–4   context] W;   contest
59.12   thinking∧] D;   ~,
59.16   testability] W;   testibility
59.23–24   Admit, however, . . . the result.] D;   [*not present*]
59n.4   it enters] D;   this is
59n.8–9   intellect] D;   the intellect
59n.11   itself as] D;   itself and of its purport as
60.6–13   II [¶] Let us, . . . criterion?] D;   [*not present*]
· 60.13   The intellectualism] D;   [¶] ~
60.14   represented] D;   well represented
60.16   148). But] D;   148). It is the use of a strictly theoretical criterion as a basis for ascribing in guaranteed fashion a certain character to reality which is the point at issue. But
60.18   of its object] D;   in question
60.20   of reality which] D;   in reality to which
60.21   necessitates] D;   refers
60.22   this] D;   that
60.28   intellectualism will] D;   intellectualism in all its forms will
60.29   urge that,] D;   urge
60.29   of the] D;   of
60.30   basis of] D;   basis in
60.30; 63.21,30;   "reality"] D;   ∧~∧
65.2; 70.28
60.31   process the] D;   process that the
61.1   experiences? The] D;   experiences? They will claim that to use the requirement of non-contradiction in thought as a basis for inferring the non-contradictory nature of reality, while the character of reality is then

	employed in order to make thought something more than merely formal, to give it a content of its own independent of other functions of life, is to offer us a begging of the question in lieu of its solution. The
61.5	*is* the material] D; is the real
61.7	Take the instance of a man] D; As an illustration of the specific as distinct from the 'at large' way of defining consistency, let us take the example of the man
61.19	make in] D; do with
61.26	imposed by] D; which
61.26	aim] D; aim imposes
61.27	to consistency] D; consistency
61.28	with the] D; and
61.28	of] D; in
61.28	appeal] D; appeal to
61.29	Try] D; Try on
61.31	and] D; while
61.31	deliberately introducing] D; you deliberately introduce
61n.4	intelligence.] D; intelligence and of intellectual statements, positions, ideas, etc.
61n.10	thought] D; thought and ideas
61n.11	intelligence, the] D; intelligence, it is clear the
61n.12	question] D; whole question
62.2–3	purpose . . . purpose] D; purpose is always to harmonise the conflicting elements of some situation through their own reorganisation, that purpose
62.9	type] D; character
62.11	heart, then, the] D; heart, the
62.12	thinking.] D; ~,
62.12	But] D; but
62.16	like] D; larger
62.18	shod. The] D; shod; and that the
62.19–26	shoe, but . . . footing?] D; shoe. In this case, it is easily seen that the ultimate character of the end for the operation is proper evidence that the operation itself is not ultimate, but relative and instrumental. Is there anything in the logic of the case which excludes analogous ideas holding good for the function of thinking and hence for its criterion, consistency? It may be that the contradictions which, according to Mr. Bradley, inhere in thought, do not belong to it in its proper character, taken in its real connexions with other functions of experience; but are found in it because it has been looked at wrongly; because it has been made unreal by isolation.

It is then the positive object of this paper to show the interpretation to be put upon the ideas of inconsistency, harmony, etc., with respect to thought, when this is not isolated, but taken in its nature, place and workings within experience. Since the difficulty of Mr. Bradley has turned out to be that thought can be made supreme only by isolating it, and that when isolated all its processes and results are found to be infected, tainted, with self-contradictions, it would seem, even on formal grounds, to be the part of wisdom to change the point of view, the underlying hypothesis, and to see what becomes of its work and of the criterion for the well doing of that work, when thought is regarded as serviceable, and hence as organically linked with other modes of practice.

62.27   then,] D; $\sim_\wedge$
62.27–28   by way . . . suggestion.] D;   start from another sup-
             position.
62.33–34   of good] D;   of the good
62.34   accidentally$_\wedge$] D; $\sim$,
62.34–35   essentially,] D; $\sim_\wedge$
62.36   that being] D;   that, in short, being
62.36–37   difficulty, is] D;   difficulties, *is*
62.38   when] D;   that
62.39   an] D;   that
62.40   happiness, that the] D;   happiness. This state of things
             would clearly mean harmony. Suppose, once more, the
63.1–2   peace . . . effort] D;   peace were to fail; and there
             were then effort
63.5   like were it reduced] D;   like if it were reduced
63.6   is worked] D;   to be worked
63.7   plan,] D; $\sim_\wedge$
63.7   effect,] D; $\sim_\wedge$
63.7–8   succeeds] D;   succeeded
63.14–15   inconsistent. [¶] But] D;   inconsistent, and in secur-
             ing fulfilment? [¶] This conception of thinking and its
             test may not be valid; that is not the point here at is-
             sue. The question is whether it is not a possible, rea-
             sonable alternative hypothesis concerning the nature,
             the criterion and correct precedure of thinking. Is there
             anything in the fact that consistency is a final criterion
             for thinking which renders self-contradictory such an
             interpretation of the meaning of consistency? Until
             otherwise informed, one must insist that the fact that
             the criterion of thinking is consistency cannot be em-
             ployed to validate one special definition of consistency
             and to rule out another special definition. [¶] But
63.16   reality,] D; $\sim$;
63.17–21   This statement . . . Why should] D;   This state-
             ment, to my mind, involves a subtle confusion of two
             different ideas. Thinking in the concrete is certainly an

assumption regarding reality; thinking in the concrete
also assumes consistency as its own criterion. But why
should

63.22   that] D;   that the

63.27   illusory. Why put upon] D;   illusory; it puts upon

63.29   them?] D;   ∼.

63.31   things just . . . *activity*,] D;   reality in its achieved
         form is such that, *through activity*∧

63.32   *thinking*, a] D;   *thinking*, it may *acquire* a

63.33   them] D;   it

63.37   also makes] D;   makes

63.38   *viz*.,] W;   viz., D;   to the effect

63.40   horseshoe. The] D;   horseshoe. What stands out here
         is that the

64.1   thing] D;   reality

64.2   The test, moreover, of] D;   Moreover, the test of

64.3   practical; it consists in] D;   practical, consisting in

64.4   namely,] D;   ∼∧

64.4   guide activities] D;   guide the activities

64.7–36 some assumption . . . I confess] D;   the assumption
         about reality *is* the idea and this assumption is that
         reality may through certain activities secure its own
         harmonisation.

         These remarks have a two-fold purpose. They are
intended to show that the fact that consistency is a
criterion of thinking does not solve but poses the problem of its nature, and to suggest that recourse to the
concrete facts of experience indicates that consistency
is practical in nature.[1] . . .

1. Mr. Bradley has very properly attacked the conception of 'mere
practice' or "the abstraction of activity and of function from the
quality of its object" (MIND "On Truth and Practice," vol. xiii.,
p. 25). Very properly, that is, if there be any one anywhere
who entertains any such notion of "practice" and "practical". It
appears, however, to be such a thoroughly intellectualistic construction, such an obvious abstraction, that I cannot believe any
empiricist has ever entertained it. As an indication of what I
understand by the term "practical," and as an indication also
that I have not modified my views simply in order to meet
criticisms, I may venture to quote from myself: "By practical
I mean only regulated change in experienced values" (*Logical
Conditions of a Scientific Treatment of Morality*, p. 10).

         What is the use of insisting that thought takes its
logical departure from resting back on reality as already an eternal, all-inclusive harmony, when at the
same time it has to be asserted that thinking takes its
actual departure from the fact that elements in our
experience collide and struggle with each other? Suppose that instead of starting from a purely theoretical

presumption we start from the experienced facts, namely, their collision and struggle. How is this to be understood? Is it something purely objective in either a physical or a logical sense? If so, who are the "we" who cannot rest satisfied with this state but endeavour to alter it? ("*We* cannot rest satisfied, *our* impulse," etc.) What has this "we" to do with the matter; how did it get implicated in a purely physical or intellectual collision? And even if it were implicated, how could it successfully interfere so as to induce peace and rest? If the collision is objective, in the physical sense, can an ego take any part in the matter? If the collision is of logical contents, is the ego also to be logically interpreted? If so, how can an extraneous logical factor interfere to any advantage? And if it is not intellectual, and the intellectual is always, logically, merely independent, how can this "we" intervene save to the undoing of the logical?

It is perhaps suggestive of caricature to suppose that the intellectualist regards the collision in question as of a physical nature—something like the eruption of Vesuvius, the explosion of a powder magazine on board ship, or the beating of hail-stones on a wheat-field. Yet the intellectualist's aversion to all change—his insistence that the temporal and transitive are not metaphysically real; his assumption that "fleeting and untrue character is perpetually forced upon our notice by the hard fact of change" (p. 460) and that "the absolute has no history of its own, for nothing perfect, nothing genuinely real can move" (pp. 499–500), seem to bear out that supposition. If such be the case, theory, of course, cannot practically intervene; it is condemned to the impotence of a merely theoretical intervention: that is, it can only proclaim the supreme reality of an Absolute Experience which we can neither experience nor employ as a criterion of specific thoughts and beliefs. It can only indulge itself in a purely metaphysical theory of what reality would be if it were totally different from what it is, consoling itself for its impotency with the reflection that this totally different reality is eternal and absolute.

If the collision be not objective in the physical sense, possibly it is such in the logical sense. But this alternative is open to grave difficulties. How can logical contents as such collide? Not as truths, for it is the very nature of truths to be consistent with each other; not as falsities, for recognised or detected falsities certainly do not collide, the fact that a certain thing is

false being obviously consistent with the proposition
that something else is true. Nor can falsities collide as
unrecognised; if they did, we should from the start be
aware of all errors and mistakes, instead of only in
retrospect. Just as the "collisions" of physical things
have significance for thought only as these things are
so involved in a system of practical activities that their
maladjustments mean disturbance and defeat of purpose, so theoretic collision is impossible save as the
contents defined as logical lead to inconsistent and
ambiguous responses. In short, on the face of the facts,
the one intelligible theory about the struggles which
induce theoretical activity is that they are practical;
disturbances in the activities which sustain a system
of values, involving disruption and instability in the
experiencing of those values.[1]

1. The difficulties usually brought against this view on the ground
of 'science,' have their source, I think, in the following conditions: (1) The objector puts himself at the standpoint of the
final results of scientific inquiry, instead of calling up cases of
the stress and strain of scientific procedure still in the throes of
development; (2) he overlooks the fact that every branch of
science means highly specialised and refined modes of response,
associated with specific types of value which the 'plain man'
does not entertain; (3) he overlooks the fact that these highly
refined types of reaction mean a new sensitiveness, and hence
increased awareness of disturbance, of menaced organisation,
where the 'plain man' is aware only of stability—in short, that
problems multiply with development of scientific aim and technique; (4) he overlooks the fact that such highly specialised
recognition of discrepancy on the basis of highly specialised
modes of technical reaction have a final usufruct even for the
plain man in making more secure, more fruitful, and, especially,
more liberal and free, his responses to the ordinary things of his
experience.

Reference to the concrete situation also serves to
explain the nature of the consistency in which is found
the test of the validity of an idea. This consistency is
the agreeing together of the exact or specific elements
which in their collision with one another set the problem of thinking. As attained harmony, it is proof of
the value of the idea; for it proves that the idea 'knows
what it is about,' that it is 'on to its job'. It is in no
way a harmony at large or *überhaupt*, a miscellaneous
altogetherness, but a harmonising of just the elements
that is needed to be brought into agreement, a harmonising through the capacity of the idea to instigate
and guide a mode of behaviour calculated to complete
the incomplete. Strictly speaking, it is this reorganising
capacity which is the criterion of the truth of the ideas.

> Since, however, that faculty is demonstrated in the
> final harmony achieved, this last term may be fairly
> enough regarded as the criterion of the worth of an
> idea, provided we bear in mind just what we mean.
> I confess

64.37   intellectualists] D;   intellectualist
65.1   conceive] D;   conceives
65.3   describe] D;   describe and define
65.8   truth$_\wedge$] D;   ~,
65.10   anything] D;   that is anything
65.10   involving] D;   so far as involving
65.14   an intelligible] D;   an intelligible and to me the only
         intelligible
65.16   apart] D;   prior to, apart
65.16   Truth] D;   truth
65.16–17 that *this* Truth is] D;   that it is *this* Truth or Reality
         which is
65.18   that may] D;   which can
65.21   ideas,] D;   ideas$_\wedge$ however valid,
65.22   of *their* truth] D;   of such truth as intellectual state-
         ments may aspire to
65.29   or] D;   nor
65.30   sense$_\wedge$ truth] W;   ~, ~ D;   sense, common, yet dif-
         ferent, truth
65.35   to be] D;   is
65.39   the] D;   The
66.7   is,] D;   ~$_\wedge$
66.9   Truth,] D;   ~$_\wedge$
66.10   intelligence as such] D;   intelligence
66.22   belief] D;   idea
66.24   an] D;   the
66.32–33 character . . . tested] D;   character that defines an
         idea so far as it is tested
66.33   action] D;   the action
66.33   it to] D;   to
66.33–34 completion.] D;   completion its own intent.
66.35   reaches this successful outcome] D;   can stand this
         test
66.36   initiates] D;   can initiate
66.37   the method] D;   the intention and the method
66.38   meaning] D;   idea
66.38   constantly] D;   constant
66.39   it,] D;   its meaning,
67.1   view,] D;   ~$_\wedge$
67.8   idea] D;   idea as it stood in some one's head
67.13   all of] D;   all
67.19   *such*] D;   [*rom.*]
67.19   an] D;   wholly an

67.20–21   a condition that] D;   the condition of affairs which
67.21   requirements] D;   requirement
67.21   the case] D;   the idea
67.28–30   situation . . . disconnected. In this] D;   situation
            previously disconnected, yet *hypothetically* connected,
            elements of existence and meaning. In this
67.31   a proposal] D;   proposition
67.35   always have] D;   have always
67.38   interpretation] D;   idea
68.3   reduplicated] D;   viewed and characterised in every
            conceivable respect from every conceivable point of
            view
68.4   have retained, so] D;   have so
68.5   concerned, its] D;   concerned retained its
68.7–16   any *intellectual* . . . have also to] D;   any intellectual
            ground which compelled it to be identified as just this
            definite thing—namely, a noisy street-car? If so, why
            should it not also have to
68.19   bearing] D;   its bearing
68.21   new] D;   a new
68.21   events] D;   fact
68.21–22   treatment of things? [¶] It is perhaps] D;   develop-
            ment of reality? [¶] Excepting then where the situation
            itself suggests some aim or intent beyond itself as ex-
            istence, is there ever an idea? Is it just existence as
            existence which determines the further presence of
            ideas, or is it the occurrence and maintenance of an
            end transcending the already existent? And even if it
            be supposed that all existences in all their incon-
            ceivable complexity *have* to mirror themselves in ideas,
            what is truth? Is it reality apart from its ideational
            version? If so, what has truth to do with ideas and
            ideas with truth? Or if it is a property of ideas in rela-
            tion to reality, is it their property so far as mirroring?
            Or does it belong to them with respect to changes they
            intend introducing into reality? Is not truth something
            to be achieved by an idea and something which can be
            achieved only through an activity which is neither a
            part of reality already existent nor a part of the idea
            conceived merely as intellectual? [¶] It is perhaps
68.29   ideas] D;   idea
69.11   be] D;   were
69.14   a statement] D;   interpretation
69.15   if acted] D;   acted
69.31   could] D;   would
69.32   far.[6]] W;   far.[1] D;   far. The conception may be false,
            but it cannot be refuted by manipulation of phrase-
            ology.[1]

69n.2   p. 311] W;   p. 3
69n.2   "Truth and Practice"] D;   ∧~∧
69n.9   criticism] D;   criterion
70.1   On the side of things, *reality*] D;   Such tautology is the
           argument by which the intellectualist persuades himself
           that truth is a character of ideas just as ideas—apart
           from the practical necessity they are under to issue
           in behaviour. On the other hand, there is the argument
           by which *reality*
70.2   then] D;   so that
70.11   such] D;   this
70.23   that embody] D;   which set forth
70.31   beliefs] D;   ideas
70.41   a function] D;   this function
71.1   corroboration] D;   corroboration of the truth
71.6   not ever] D;   never
71.12   truth might] D;   case might
71.16   as *proved*] D;   *as* proved
71.23   therefore,] D;   ~∧
71.25–27   and employment. . . . minded persons.] D;   and em-
           ployment.
71.28   IV] D;   [*not present*]
71.31   specific. I conclude with] D;   specific, and which to
           some will doubtless seem irrelevant or trivial. I con-
           clude then with
71.35–36   discrepancy] D;   discrepancies
72.2   or subjective, or] D;   nor subjective, nor
72.12–13   clash (an accompaniment of all desire)] D;   ~, ~,
72.17–18   judgment. . . . wholesale, but] D;   judgment. Taken
           on its own merits it is not irrational—a proof that we
           are dealing with mere appearance not with genuine
           reality; but
72.19   affair] D;   reality
72.25   Action] D;   It
72.32   the object] D;   the nature of the object
72.33   material] D;   the material
72.35   fact] D;   subject
73.4   a reality] D;   reality
73.8   through] D;   from
73.17–18   in terms of what is] D;   sought in a way
73.23,25   object] D;   reality
73.24   we so] D;   we do so
73.26–27   fulfilment . . . existence.] D;   fulfilment of plan
           through relevant response, and not as sheer objectively
           present reality.
73.29   treatment they] D;   resource they seem to
74.17   values] D;   values which are
74.20   may] D;   must

74.22   relatively] D;   relatively speaking
74.23   used as] D;   as
74.37   perception stands] D;   stands
75.4   character] D;   real character

"The Control of Ideas by Facts"

Copy-text is JP: first publication of the article in *Journal of Philosophy, Psychology and Scientific Methods* 4 (1907): 197–203, 253–59, 309–19. Emendations have been adopted from the article as revised and republished in EE: *Essays in Experimental Logic* (Chicago: University of Chicago Press, 1916), pp. 230–49.

78.1–2   THE CONTROL OF IDEAS BY FACTS / I] W; VIII /
           THE CONTROL OF IDEAS BY FACTS / I EE;   THE
           CONTROL OF IDEAS BY FACTS. I / I
78.8–9   the instrumental logician] EE;   in which the function-
           alist logician
78.12   unity] EE;   complete unity
78.13   due partly] EE;   partly due
78.15   view^1] EE;   view,
78.16   view] EE;   view^1
78.18   pragmatism. I wish here to] EE;   pragmatism, which
           resulted in interpreting the logic partly in terms of ad-
           ditional misconceptions of these philosophies, and partly
           in terms which, even if pertinent with reference to
           them, were not exactly relevant to the less ambitious
           logical theory. In the hope that the atmosphere is now
           more favorable, I wish to
78.21   place it was] EE;   place
78.21   frightful] EE;   present frightful
78.22   theories)$_\wedge$] EE;   theories), it was
79.2   judgment] EE;   ideas
79.4   judgment] EE;   idea
79.6   dualism, rendering] EE;   dualism$_\wedge$ which renders
79.9   consciousness] EE;   or consciousness
79.9   objects,] EE;   objects, or
79.15–16   agreement] EE;   consistency
79.20   any specific judgment] EE;   any idea qua idea
79.22   practice] EE;   practise
79.23   or *superior*,] EE;   the *superior*$_\wedge$
79.27–29   working adjustment persist? [¶] Putting] EE;   work-
           ing criterion of their correct adjustment persist? Putting
79.37   be?] EE;   be real?

79.37   it] EE;   then it
79.40   and while] EE;   and to common sense and science while
80.2   does not] EE;   can not
80.2   idea is] EE;   idea simply *as* an idea is
80.4   the] EE;   once more the
80.5   once more] EE;   again
80.6–7   there is by definition] EE;   by definition there is
80.11   gulf] EE;   gulf supposed to exist
80.16   one of a group] EE;   one group
80.18   up:] EE;   ~,
80.23   If it means simply] EE;   If simply
80.25   On the] EE;   What we still have on the
80.26   there is still] EE;   is
80.29   which is asserted] EE;   asserted
80.30   be true] EE;   true
80.31   any] EE;   the
80.32   holds] EE;   holds good
80.33   proposition.] EE;   conjunction.
81.5   own characters] EE;   qualitative character
81.10   it states] EE;   it only states
81.12–13; 82.2–3; 89.18   meaning-relation] EE;   ~$_\wedge$~
81.15   them, like] EE;   them as do
81.16   qualitative$_\wedge$] EE;   ~,
81.19   "thinking,"] EE;   the continuance of 'thinking,'
81.27   return later.] EE;   return in the last paper of this series.
81.30   will not] EE;   won't physically
81n.12   of little] EE;   of them as little
81n.12–13   entities or psychical stuffs.] EE;   entities.
82.3   being not] EE;   not being
82.4   ascertained] EE;   asserted
82.6   logical$_\wedge$] EE;   ~,
82.6   done; we have] EE;   done. In other words, we have
82.10   of valid] EE;   of its nature and valid
82.11–12   knowing . . . truth.] EE;   thinking and its relation to facts and to truth—that is, of any logic.
82.13   II] EE;   [*not present*]
82.17   *prima facie*$_\wedge$] W;   prima facie$_\wedge$ EE;   *prima facie,*
82.19   nor] EE;   and
82.20   facts.] EE;   facts, if there is to be any question of truth and error.
82.22   problem of the terms] EE;   problem and of the familiar terms
82.23   reality and value] EE;   value
82.23   interpretation] EE;   intellectualistic interpretation
82.23–24   What is insisted] EE;   What it insists
82.32   solved.] EE;   solved.[6] . . . [¶] [6]See Professor Russell's

article, in this JOURNAL, Vol. III., p. 599, entitled 'The Pragmatist's Meaning of Truth.' (It should perhaps be added that this article was in manuscript before I saw the comment of Mr. Schiller on Professor Russell's article, in this JOURNAL, Vol. IV., p. 42.)

83.4	presentative] EE; intellectual
83.6	given] EE; actual
83.8	true$_\wedge$] EE; ~,
83.10–11	acceptance$_\wedge$] EE; acceptance, in a general way,
83.14–15	which are possessed by other writers] EE; as have most writers
83.17	nor] EE; or
83.21	formed:] EE; ~?
83.25	them;] EE; them when the genuine article is at hand;
83.27	were] EE; was
83.33–34	unperceived] EE; the unperceived
83.34–35	perceived. Otherwise the] EE; perceived, or else the
83.37	or else to *conceive*] EE; or to conceive
83.38	is meant] EE; we here mean
83.40–84.1	*the interpretation . . . absent*] EE; [*rom.*]
84.1	*portion*] EE; portions
84.4	one's] EE; his
84.4–8	know. For . . . given. It is] EE; know. It is
84.8	constructed$_\wedge$] EE; ~,
84.14	Then comes the test of *agreement*] EE; As to the *agreement*
84.20	for] EE; for that
84.20–21	proceedings . . . theory.] EE; proceedings is the idea itself.
84.23	as a plan] EE; *as* a plan
84.39	such] EE; [*ital.*]
84.40–85.1	success? / III] EE; success? [¶] I can hardly hope that this brief account will be as convincing to others as it is to me; its very simplicity and brevity will— such is the reputation philosophy has made for itself— be odorous with the suggestion of hocus-pocus. But before entering upon a more detailed analysis, let me summarize the situation as a whole. The import of the discussion is that the terms environment, idea and agreement are all of them essentially *practical* terms, denoting distinctive functions or operations, the term 'practical' having no reference to any *fixed* utility, but simply to certain values to be sustained or transformed through an operation.

Every reflective situation has the problem of discovering the intent or meaning appropriate to the management or development of a troubled situation, its pertinency being proved by its capacity to administer the difficulty through the use of the idea as a method or plan. The woods of the scientist and the philosopher, his paths and sign-boards and miscues, the unfamiliar surroundings into which he wanders, his home, his schemes for getting there—all of these differ infinitely in local color and setting from those of the wayfarer in question. But the situation in its diagrammatic features remains the same. Types of agency and response differ according to the different sorts of disturbed organizations, interrupted universes of value, that present themselves; but the category of the problematic; the contrast of the given and the intended; the use of the given to form a conception or hypothetical view of an inclusive situation in which both it and the wanted are contained; the use of this conception as guide to experimental activity in transforming, through degrees, the given into the intended; the use of the results thus obtained to confirm and revise the guiding idea; final verification (if at all) through actively instituting or bringing about a condition of affairs which 'agrees with' the intent of the situation because it fulfills it— these characteristics are found in every reflective process and are found only in a reflective process.

JOHN DEWEY
COLUMBIA UNIVERSITY.

85.0   [*section om.*]] EE; Vol. IV. No. 10. May 9, 1907. / THE JOURNAL OF PHILOSOPHY / PSYCHOLOGY AND SCIENTIFIC METHODS / THE CONTROL OF IDEAS BY FACTS. II [¶] In a previous portion of this paper I endeavored to show, first, that every situation of reflective knowledge involves a discrimination and a reference of existence and meaning, of datum and ideatum; and secondly, that the significance to be assigned to these categories, as well as to their correspondence, is thoroughly instrumental or 'pragmatic,' being relative to the problem of reorganizing a situation of disturbed values. In this portion of the article I propose to go over the ground in more detail, dealing with some explicitness with each phase of the situation. Before taking up the interpretation of the logical categories of fact, meaning and agreement, it may be well to say a few words on the nature of the disturbed and disordered situation for the sake of rectifying which the reflective process takes place. A quotation from a recent critic affords a convenient point of departure. I quote from the first volume of Baldwin's 'Thought and Things': "In the writings of Dewey and his colleagues the case made much of is that of embarrassment and confusion, due to failure of habitual dispositional processes to establish themselves; this is made the starting-point of all new constructions, which come as the establishment of new equilibrium after these crises. But I am pointing out the further case that often such embarrassment or disintegration is not the extreme case; for it often happens that a new and unwelcome object simply forces itself upon us. It is not content with knocking down our fortifications and necessitating our building new ones; it rides full-armed through our walls, and compels its recognition in certain of its characters, *for what it is*—say, for example, a round stone which a child takes for an apple and attempts to bite" (p. 50, note).

I do not profess wholly to understand the supposed bearings of this, but it is clear enough that Baldwin takes the instance of the child's performance as in some way presenting the sort of fact before which the theory breaks down. Since it is precisely this unwelcome fact that Chapter III. of 'Studies in Logical Theory' (on the 'Datum') deals with, it is clear that Baldwin must have totally misapprehended its point. I accordingly append the following remarks in the hope that they may prevent, for some readers, the perpetuation of misapprehension.

1. 'Confusion and embarrassment' are not terms characteristic of the 'Studies.' Stress, tension, interruption *in* the organized system of value (or in the functions which sustain this value) are the usual phrases. If the terms 'confusion and embarrassment' are employed as equivalents, they must be taken in the same sense; *i. e.*, they must *not* be interpreted as emotions or states of consciousness of any sort, but as applying to a system of action and its values—as when we say the *affairs* of a banker are embarrassed. The emotional perturbations that may accompany this in the banker's personal history are not conceived as primary, but as the organic reverberations of the 'confused' state of a system of activities, in which all sorts of things and persons are involved; prior to reflective analysis, the emotions belong to the conflicting situation, but they never make it up.

2. The system of activities so far as organized or harmonious (having its various elements mutually reinforcing each other) both underlies and overlies the dualism between thought and datum. It is in the conflicting situation that they get set over against each

other, the thought being purpose and the object obstacle to realization of purpose. It is child-reaching-and-putting-object-in-mouth that is the total situation in the instance cited—an operation including a variety of values in themselves characterized prior to conflict neither as ideative nor as factual. But when *in* this activity various factors actively conflict with each other, then some stand out as purpose, intent, end: others as data, obstacles, which *through* thinking—through the ideational—are to be reinterpreted and readjusted.

If the child does not interpret the 'hard stone' with reference to an incompatible purpose, end, plan of action, there is no overriding object at all—many a child puts hard stones in his mouth for the sake of doing so. On the other hand, it is only as he sets some result conceived as desirable or intended over against the thing, that he goes on to perform those testing activities, *guided by the intent*, that will result in giving any intellectual content, any character, to that which at first is just interruption in the activity, so that finally the interruption is delimited and defined as round stone. Let the reader put this question to himself: *At what stage of proceedings and how* does the child determine that which forbids his purpose (which *is* purpose once more only in the conflict of activity) to be round hard stone? Not by hypothesis, at the outset; and in the degree that the purpose does not function as a plan of action in directing exploring (experimental) activities with reference to the nature of the interruption, the thing is not intellectualized at all, but is merely practically rejected—spewed out of the mouth. The normal conclusion of this investigating tentative process is the formation of a new total situation of harmonized values on the basis of mutually reinforcing, instead of conflicting, activities. When one wishes to eat an apple, it is not an overriding but a fulfillment of purpose to throw away what one has found out to be a stone.

3. The references to 'habitual dispositional processes' and to 'forcing itself upon *us*' seem to give the clue to the source of the misunderstanding. Strictly speaking, the 'us' is irrelevant to the logical problem, which is the problem of the relation of fact and idea. But if one chooses to *shift the issue* from the logical question to the question of the relation of 'external object' and 'me,' the mode of analysis just indicated serves. In any organized system, *qua organized*, there is no dualism of self and world. The emergence of this

duality is within the conflicting and strained situation
of action; the activities which subtend purpose and intent define the 'me' of that situation, those which constitute the interruptive factor define its 'external world.'
The relation *prima facie* is purely practical; its transformation into a reflective or intellectual duality of
fact—with described character—and purpose—of characteristic content—is precisely the process of rational-
ization by which a brute practical acceptance-rejection
gets transformed into a *controlled directed evaluated
system of action*, in which the duality of me and object is again overcome.

I should like here to refer to what is said in the
'Logical Studies' (pp. 16–17) about the evil of confusing the dualities of different types of situation, the
technological, the intellectual, the esthetic, the affectional, with one another. The moment, for example, it
is recognized that the logical fact-meaning duality is
not to be identified with the technological object-agent
duality, a large part of the present confusion of logic
and of psychological epistemology clears itself up—it
simply evaporates. It is this confusion which is, I believe, responsible for what Woodbridge in the article
already referred to[1] calls the end-term conception of

1. 'The Problem of Consciousness,' in 'Studies in Philosophy and
Psychology,' p. 140 ff.

mind—which I may paraphrase as the putty-magical-
faculty conception; putty, in so far as 'consciousness'
is regarded as receptive of impressions; magical-faculty,
in so far as it is supplied with a Lockean or Kantian
or Lotzean machinery for synthesizing, ordering and
objectifying these impressions. The significance, in the
scheme of reality, of an active and centered self or
agent or 'me' is a precious product of modern as
against ancient life and philosophy. But the offhand
identification of this practical agent with 'consciousness' is the source of endless woes. There is, as intimated above, a real point of connection, indeed,
between the 'object-me' and the 'fact-meaning' relationships. Through the intellectual function, the 'me'
becomes a rationalized, a truly purposive and investigating activity. From something just brutely accepting
or brutely rejecting, it becomes something which is
directed and put into action on the basis of relevantly
conceived aims and relevantly characterized facts. It is
precisely this intermediary power, inhering in the reflective, fact-meaning situation, which is meant by the

instrumental function of knowledge. In my conception the whole matter reduces itself to this: Is it with respect to reality as inert objects that intelligence functions, so that its duty is simply to copy or repeat them in another realm, or does it exercise its office in respect to reality as activity, so that its duty is to develop this activity in the direction of increased discriminations of value, into more complex and richer situations? If the condition in which reflective knowledge appears is already adequately real, thinking is futilely gratuitous; if it is real so far as it goes, if its lack is simply quantitative, the appearance of thinking, of significance relations, is miraculous and there is no possible test of the validity of any extension or amplification of the given narrow reality which they may happen to effect. Finally the activities that do, as undeniable fact, result from intelligence are on this basis mere tailpieces, deforming rather than ornamental in character, hitched on to reality as accidental by-products of knowledge. But if reflective thought presents itself as a developing phase of a situation inherently lacking in full reality and has for its purpose to delimit and interpret this situation, transforming its practical conflicts first into recognition of ambiguities and then into a clear conception of alternative possibilities—of intents— which may be experimentally tested, reflective knowing is natural in its origin, verifiable as to its contentions and contents, and fruitful in issue of reality. It lies, at every stage, within the processes of reality itself.

From this sketch of the disturbed or disordered situation within which and for the sake of which knowing occurs, I turn to the various terms of this knowing function as it energizes. The nature of 'fact' or 'existence' first presents itself. Since it is a not uncommon assumption that the theory which interprets knowing pragmatically supplies only a changed phraseology for a Berkeleian idealism, let the point be emphasized that we are dealing here with an intellectual or logical matter, the determination of a true description or delimitation, the assignment of a correct τὸ τί ἦν εἶναι of a given environment or set of facts. It is not the nature of existence or reality *ueberhaupt* which is under consideration, but of *that* reality of which, by assumption, there is an idea, and with respect to which there is to be a true idea. There may be, if you please, hundreds of realities both existing and existing in experience which are of any sort you please, and which are just what they are and just as they are. But we are not discussing such presences, for with respect to them we have and need to have no idea; as to them there *is* no problem of a true or valid idea; they do not at all come within the scope of reflection as such, or of logic or of any theory of knowledge as an intellectual operation.

Hence, however it may be in psychology and epistemology (I throw this concession in for the benefit of those whom it may concern, rather than on my own account, since I believe that any 'ology at least pretends to be logical), in logic there *is* no idea so long as there are nothing but realities as such, for logic does not demand the absurdity of duplicating in idea what we already have in reality. But, on the other hand, as soon as there is question of anything which is to be passed upon as true or false, of knowledge in the intellectual sense of that term, there is a reality which is not full reality, since it requires its own supplementation—which is not outward and quantitative, but inward and qualitative—through fulfillment of its intent. If the universe as complete reality is exhaustively present at one time to God or man, then neither God nor man has an idea or thought of it—and this even if the universe itself be only an idea. But if one has an idea of something which is there, then what is there is precisely that which needs for its own reality first interpretation and then transformation through that idea. Any given set of facts of which there is an idea is not yet fully real in itself, but is something which is to be made real through the transformation it receives in the process of fulfilling its own meaning or intent on the deliberate basis of that intent. On the other hand, so far as any one has a portion of reality present to him at any time in such fashion that this portion is adequate or self-included in value, there is no idea or thought of that thing—no knowledge in any reflective sense of the term knowledge. One has then to be constantly on one's guard against slipping the category of reality first in and then out of the reflective situation, not noting the different imports that the term inevitably receives according as it falls within or without reflective knowledge.[2]

2. In the hope that constant dripping may wear down the stony-hearted, I repeat once more that the idealistic fallacy is the assumption that 'real' reality, *the* 'Truth,' is just what reality is in and for the thought situation; while that of realism is that it is just the same in and for thought as it is outside. The central contention of the account I am presenting is that it is in the reflective situation, and there alone, that reality receives requali-

fication and development of values in a directed way, and that the criterion of knowledge-validity is not accurate reproduction of reality already there—the common assumption of both the idealistic and realistic epistemologies—but the effectual rendering of a value-transformation office. Labels are dubious matters, but it is in this sense that pragmatism is to be understood, if pragmatism is to develop into an acceptable theory of knowledge.

So long as one is not dealing with the knowledge-situation at all, one may have perfectly good realistic systems—realities which are what they are entirely apart from any relationship to the function of intelligence; but an intellectualistic realism—that is to say, a realism which conceives facts within the reflective situation as identical with reality irrespective of it—totally ignores the fact that it is only because independent reality has lost something of its full characteristic of reality that it enters into reflection at all; and that in being set over against its own meaning or intent it is inevitably modified from what it is when it is in complete possession of its value, and that in its reference to this meaning it demands precisely its own further requalification. It ought, I should say, to be axiomatic in logic that the reality concerned in any intellectual situation, in so far as intellectual, is not true and good reality in a final objective sense, but is a sign with respect to it, a sign whose significance still requires to be made out, and whose value (as in the case of any sign) is in the value of the consequences to which it may direct one.

When, accordingly, it is said that fact and meaning, environment and conception, are functional distinctions, it is meant that they are divisions of labor or discriminations of status with respect to the problem of control of activity. Once more any strictly intellectualistic view of the relation of fact and idea is in this dilemma. Idea is either an idea of present fact, in which case it is superfluous, or else it is an idea of some fact not present, with respect to which it is idle to talk of agreement. There is no epistemological straddle by which one can compare an idea with an unknown reality so as to pass upon its truth; while if the fact is already known, it is silly fooling to invent an idea and go through the form of comparing it. But if we take the matter practically, an idea may be formed on the basis of presented fact (which is not the reality of which there is the idea) which may succeed in transforming the given fact, the fact *there*, into a complete reality, the reality in which the idea is true.

The environment is, as we have already noted,

not identical with presented fact. If it were, the individual in the woods would not be lost. Or, generically, if
the facts, the truths, which the scientist already owns,
were *the* fact, *the* truth, he would not be a scientist;
there would be no inquiry, no reflection. Presented facts
define the lost traveller; the scientist perplexed. They
directly determine a problem, not a solution. Moreover,
the contrast with the total reality is a part of the internal content of the given facts, not something external or additional. If it is not a part of them, as
given, then at once they monopolize the whole field;
the man is no longer a lost soul seeking salvation
through reflection. He may esthetically enjoy what is
before him. It is as good as anything else. But if there
is thinking, aiming at 'making good,' then environment
involves the absent as well as the present; and this not
externally, say from our standpoint as distinct from
that of the traveller (we recognizing that what he sees
has to be pieced together with what he does not see),
but internally, since relation to the absent is an inherent part of the very quality of that which is present.
In other words, that which is present or given is inherently self-discrepant, self-irreconcilable, or actively
ambiguous, meaning differing things by turns. That
which is most positive or unquestionable is set in a
context, and this context colors through and through
what is set in it. The absent may determine the presented fact, as presented, either from the standpoint
of ground which has been traversed, with which the
present territory is continuous—a *Hinterland*—or from
that which the traveller wishes to traverse, a foreground. The given, the 'local environment,' so to say, is
apprehended as a portion of a larger whole in which,
however, it is disjointed. It is given as an element in a
disordered reality. And such is the character of all
'facts' about which we think. They are pragmatic,
'things done,' but, as yet, badly done.

JOHN DEWEY.

COLUMBIA UNIVERSITY.

85.0   [pp. *om.*]] EE; Vol. IV. No. 12. June 6, 1907. / THE
JOURNAL OF PHILOSOPHY / PSYCHOLOGY AND
SCIENTIFIC METHODS / THE CONTROL OF IDEAS
BY FACTS. III [¶] In the preceding paper, under this
title, I gave a sketch of the situation within which the
distinction of fact and meaning is instituted, and an
interpretation of the category of 'fact.' I shall conclude,
in this portion, with an account of the categories of
meaning and of agreement, or correspondence.

The 'facts,' as we have seen, refer to something absent. This, of course, is the ideal or ideative aspect of the situation. Now this absent, which is intended by the presented or factual, is asserted to be just as real as the presented itself. This assertion, moreover, is not a declaration on the part of an outsider who has the entire reality before him; it is the assertion of the given qua given, since it *is* given only *as* pointing to, intending, something beyond itself.[1]

1. The 'given' is an ambiguous term. It means sometimes the whole situation, *not* as taken reflectively or for knowledge at the time, but just as it is in the total experience of it—what I have elsewhere termed the immediate. (See this JOURNAL, Vol. II., p. 393.) But it also means this total experience as contemporaneously intellectualized or delimited, as setting the terms for thought, the data, the 'facts.' It is, of course, in the latter sense that the term is here consistently used.

The reality of the absent can be questioned only by questioning the reality of the presented. This is present, then, *in idea* or *as idea*. As such it is contrasted with the given facts of disordered system. But as realities, the reality of presented fact and of idea stand on exactly the same level.[2]

2. The fallacy of orthodox logical empiricism is right here. It supposes there can be 'givens,' sensations, percepts, etc., prior to and independent of thought or ideas, and that thought or ideas may be had by some kind of compounding or separating of the givens. But it is the very nature of sensation or perception (supposing these terms to have any knowledge-force at all, such as Lockean empiricism ascribed to them) already to be, in and of itself, something which is so internally fractionized or perplexed as to suggest and to require an idea, a meaning.

What we call idea denotes the way in which the *entire* reality, to which the local self-discrepant fact is referred for its own reality, is present[3]

3. Hence, to return, in passing, to the statement in terms of the discrimination and reference to one another of physical relations and significance relations (see Vol. IV., p. 200), it is not strictly true that, in the first instance, or from the standpoint of the reflective situation itself, the meaning relation is one relation among or along with others. Rather the *thing meant* is that inclusive whole in which *physical* relations would realize coherently, instead of expressing ambiguously, their *physical* relations to one another: water-quenching-thirst, ice-cooling-water are just integrated situations of physical elements, which mean *it* only by meaning to modify one another so as to abrogate their discrepancies as given. The discrimination of a meaning relation along with and over against the physical relations as another relation of the same elements takes place not in the situation itself, but in that situation in which the logician reflects upon a reflective situation: a new and interesting type of situation, the implications of which can not be followed out here.

(it isn't, once for all, a bit of sublimated psychical stuff); while what we call facts denotes this entire situation presented in its disrupted, fragmentary elements.

While, however, the entire reality as entire can be present, under such circumstances, only in idea, it does not follow, of course, that the idea is real in the same mode as are the presented facts. When we say the idea stands on the same level of reality as the given facts, we refer only to the idea as idea, as existent, not to the details of its content. These *may* be false; at best, they are hypothetical. We have, then, a very pretty situation. The presented facts are brutely, unquestionably, stubbornly, there,[4]

4. It may turn out, of course, that something taken to be *there* was in truth suggested or intended, and hence this may be transferred to the ideal side. But this affects only the specific contents; something immediately *there*, and hence not idea, there must be in order that something may be meant, or be ideative.

but they present themselves as *not* the whole and genuine reality, but as a distorted and perverse portion of it, requiring absent portions in order to be made sound and whole. On the other hand, this total reality, or environment, is present only as an idea—an intention, suggestion or meaning. In claim, it is *the* real; in performance, it is the doubtful, problematic, hypothetic; just as the 'given' facts are real in execution, but uncertain in value and unstable in pretension. Yet the idea, while it may be contrasted with brute, given fact, can not be set over against the total reality, for it *is* that total in the only way in which, *under the circumstances*, it can be realized. The relationship of given fact and idea stands, then, as follows. Neither is real in the sense that it can be cut off from the other and *then* taken to be the total reality, since this latter is precisely the tension in which one stands out against and yet for the other. Both are real in the sense that they present that reality as a condition of disturbed or disordered values. *Both present one and the same reality: but, as distinguished from one another, present it from different standpoints, or in different functions.* The 'given' facts are the reality in its *existent* disorganized state of value. The 'idea' or intended is this same reality in its *projected* rectification. In this practical sense, fact and idea necessarily have a certain agreement or correspondence with one another from the start. They correspond as a disease and its diagnosis, or as the diagnosed disease and its proposed

remedy, or as a statement of a problem and the suggested method of its solution, as an obstacle and an
end which functions that obstacle. To correspond is to
respond to one another—to incite and answer one another.

Here, then, we have two aspects of control. On the
one hand, the total situation, postulated as fundamentally real in form, but now present only as intended
or suggested (and hence hypothetical in content), controls the determination of the 'given' facts. It sets the
limits of what shall be taken as given and what not; of
what is a relevant and proper element in the determination of presented fact and what not. The given or fact
of the lost traveler is obviously different in constitution from that of a botanist, or lumberman, or hunter,
or astronomer, whom we might put into his boots.
Apart from reference to the kind of total reality which
is demanded as the rectification of the troubled or internally discrepant situation, there is no control over
the τὸ τι ἦν εἶναι or intellectual content of the facts. If
reference to this demanded total reality is dropped out,
then the given becomes self-sufficient, an object of
esthetic admiration or curious elaboration. Or, when
it is forgotten that the function of observation is to
define the facts that describe the problem of a situation, we get an indefinite accumulation of detail which
intellectually is totally insignificant, save *per accidens*.
It is the idea then as purpose, as end in view, which
prescribes the selective determination of the constitution of the 'given' facts.[5]

5. This, once more, is the truth omitted by the rigid or structural
type of empiricism. It is, of course, also the truth emphasized by
idealistic logics. (See, for example, Royce, 'The World and the
Individual,' Vol. I., Ch. VII.)

The environment varies, in intellectual definition, as
the organism, character or agent varies. If this be
taken to mean that the world is the sport of the organism, merely subject to its whims, or only a collection of its own states, this overlooks, first, the fact that
the constitution of the agent is itself a correlative determination in the same system of values that is
undergoing reorganization through internal dissension;
and secondly, the point already mentioned that what
we mean by fact is just that which, as problem, controls the correct formation of the idea as intent and
method of action. It is not some indifferently existing
world totally irrelevant to the development of the true
idea of *this* situation. An indiscriminate universe, one

without selective determination, one, that is, not arranged for the sake of building up and testing an idea,
could never be an object of knowledge; at its worst, it
would be total reminiscence on a vast scale, a vast
mirage or pointless anecdote; at its best, something
better, perhaps, than any knowledge—an esthetic delight and free play.[6]

6. Once more, the total absolutely completed, unified, harmonious
reality, the absolute fact which is also absolute meaning, is a
case of esthetic fallacy when treated as the reality which is involved in knowledge. Esthesis may be 'better' than gnosis, but to
substitute it for gnosis is to translate, from the esthetic side, a
delight into an illusion, and from the cognitive, a possible good
intent into a certain self-imposture.

The other aspect of control is that exercised by
the given facts over the formation of the *content* of
the end, purpose or intent. The fact of being lost is the
fundamental given fact; that which simply can not be
got rid of. This may suggest a blind struggle, aimless
wandering. But in the degree in which the aim of
finding home is used to define the problem set by being
lost, there is study, investigation, accurate observation;
the content of 'being lost' is more or less reconstructed;
certain features drop out as irrelevant and misleading
—especially the grossly emotional ones; others are emphasized, new features are brought to light. *That*
'given' is gradually determined which shall be most
likely to suggest the total situation, or rearranged harmonized whole of discrepant details, in the way most
likely to be effectual as standpoint and method of action. The end first operates, so far as the situation is
rationalized, as a basis of inspection and analysis of
the situation in its given or disturbed form. The result
of this analysis states the obstacles of which the end
must take account, if it is to be realized. Thus the end
is intellectualized in its content; for it assumes detail
in accordance with the needs of the situation defined
as obstacles. From mere end, it becomes a systematic
plan of action, a method of procedure in overcoming
obstacles by utilizing them. The disturbed values constitute the brute, the obdurate, the stubborn[7] factors,

7. This involuntary stubborn character as reality-exponent is valid
when taken in relation to succeeding reactions—as that which
must be reckoned with; when interpreted in an intellectualistic,
ontological fashion, it always gives rise to the end-term or putty
conception of mind.

because they evidence the obstructive factors which
must be reckoned with if success—harmonization of
elements—is to occur. In this practical sense, they are

coercive as regards the idea, and control its formation as to specific content. As the method of action is put into effect, it, so far as successful, changes the obstacles into resources; they lose their obtrusively coercive practical quality, and become cues, signboards and real means to the end. In this change of practical function, the brute character of the given is transformed into luminous or significant character —it not merely *means* to signify, but it *does* signify. In the same degree, of course (because it is the same process), the idea ceases to be just an intention of the given and becomes an inherent, constituent value of reality. The individual who is really finding his way sees his original givens, or data, assuming new and positive imports as they cease to be evidences of being lost and become evidences of being found; as they cease to be obstacles and become effectual and energizing conditions in a total situation. When the situation which has been represented in its disrupted character by facts as given, and in its total character by the idea or meaning, is realized as an effectively harmonized situation, the original brute datum is transformed through the acquisition of the meaning which it had previously simply pointed to, while the guessed-at meaning is verified by becoming a structural value of the facts. This reciprocal transformation is the signal and seal of their agreement or correspondence. It is possible that one and the same reality should be brute and inconsistent in fact while harmonized and one in idea, precisely because the situation, being an active one, is reality in transition, and, so far as reflective, is in process of *directed* transformation. Moreover, we escape wholly from the intellectualistic dilemma of having to compare an idea with a fact which is present, or having to compare the idea with a fact which is merely absent, because their correspondence is witnessed in the eventual construction of a harmonized scheme of meanings. The objective reality which tests the truth of the idea is not one which externally antecedes or temporally coexists with the idea, but one which succeeds it, being its fulfillment as intent and method: *its* success, in short.

In these last remarks we have, of course, passed on to the subject of agreement.

85.3   intellectualistic] EE;   strictly intellectualistic
85.9–10   conception of . . . experimental] EE;   conception is
            there of agreement save the experimental
85.24   an opportunity] EE;   a fresh opportunity

85.27   improvement] EE;   reinterpretation
85.30   self-rectification] EE;   constant self-rectification
85.30–31   content through acting upon it in] EE;   content and
           intent through the modification introduced by acting
           upon them in
85.31   "absolute"] EE;   ∧~∧
85.31   knowledge] EE;   reflective knowledge
85.36   Facts] EE;   The facts
85.36–37   and meanings exist as] EE;   and so the meanings
           exist just as
86.1   compulsive. . . . existence] EE;   compulsive, but on
           this basis, as just existences
86.1–2   element in] EE;   element of content in
86.3   brute] EE;   most brute
86.4   form. What is] EE;   form. The moment we recognize
           the element of uncertainty in the contents unreflectively
           supplied for facts and meanings and set to work to
           redefine those contents with reference to the require-
           ments of their adequate functioning in the transforma-
           tion of the situation, reflective knowledge, rationaliza-
           tion, begin. What is
86.6   made.] EE;   made in determining them.
86.10–11   every . . . unquestioned] EE;   every introduction of
           unquestioned
86.11   objectivity, compromises] EE;   objectivity∧ into the
           structure compromises
86.12   work.] EE;   work, save accidentally.
86.13   taken] EE;   conceived
86.14–15   reconsideration. Any] EE;   reconsideration and re-
           qualification at the bidding of the needs of the develop-
           ing situation. Since the logical force and function of
           the facts are not ultimate and self-determined, but
           relative to suggesting an intent in the form of an ap-
           proved method of action, the reflective situation is
           adequately reflective only in so far as the thought of
           the purpose to be attained is consistently utilized to
           recharacterize the fact. Any
86.17   themselves (all being equally real)] EE;   themselves,
           since all are equally real,
86.18   weight,] EE;   ~;
86.18   that their] EE;   their
86.19   must be] EE;   be
86.20   worthlessness] EE;   complete worthlessness
86.22   proofs] EE;   proof
86.23   facts] EE;   fact
86.24–25   a situation. [¶] The more] EE;   a practical situation.
           Supply an end to be reached, a purpose to be fulfilled,
           and at once there is a basis for supplying internal in-

dividuality and external restriction to the facts in question, while so long as the end is tentative the character, inherent and external, assigned to facts must also be provisional.

It has been suggested that the controlled development through reflection of a disordered situation into a harmonized one is compromised and hindered in just the degree in which the facts and meaning are permitted to assert, as fixed and final within the reflective situation, the contents which they bring to it from without. The more

86.25   full] EE;   [rom.]
86.30   meaning] EE;   intent
86.31   fact] EE;   facts
86.32   its] EE;   their
86.33   with reference to control of the] EE;   with deliberate reference to the control and reordering of the
86.36   meaning,] EE;   ~∧
86.40   phenomena] EE;   both phenomena
86.40–87.1   conceptions . . . forms) with] EE;   conceptions (Platonic ideas, Aristotelian forms) in Greek thought with
87.3   hypotheses] EE;   ideas
87.6   theories] EE;   hypotheses
87.9   That realities] EE;   That, indeed, realities
87.10   meanings] EE;   values and meanings
87.13   existence is to be] EE;   existence is of the intellectualistic type, *i.e.*, is to be
87.16   imperfect] EE;   frustrate
87.17   modern. Science] EE;   modern. Waiving the question whether this existence of independent realities and meanings signifies anything at all apart from participation and position in systems of well-ordered activity, it is certain that science
87.21   to this . . . realized] EE;   to it; in which it is realized
87.24   of the new situation] EE;   of the needs and intent of just the new situation
87.25   IV] EE;   [*not present*]
87.27   there is] EE;   there need be
87.29   such comprises something] EE;   such involves within itself something
87.29   meant] EE;   [*rom.*]
87.30–33   there. But . . . accentuated.] EE;   there. None the less, since every reflective situation is a specific situation (one having its own disturbance and problematic elements and its own demanded fulfillment in the way of a restored harmony), it is true that the contents carried over from one reflective situation into another

are at the outset non-reflectional with reference to the
new reflective situation, entering primarily as *practically* determining or alogical elements; and this remains true of the outcome of the most comprehensive
thought so far as that becomes datum for another intent. Because the stated condition of fact or meaning is
a satisfactory solution with respect to the concrete
problem of one concrete situation, its functioning as
the disturbing and uncertain element in some other
concrete situation is not thereby prevented. Hence the
requirement of requalification within each new specific
intellectual process. In the second place, there are many
situations into which the rational factor—the mutual
distinction and mutual reference of fact and meaning
—enters only incidentally and is slurred, not delibera-
tively accentuated.

87.33–34   disturbances are] EE;   disturbances of value systems
           are
87.36   meaning] EE;   their meaning
87.37   of meaningful] EE;   of inherently valuable and mean-
           ingful
88.1   problem.] EE;   problem and to the specific purpose
           now entertained, and which accordingly require no
           redefinition.
88.4   of slight] EE;   of relative and slight
88.7   not] EE;   not in the least
88.10   the main business.] EE;   the central problem.
88.10   speak of] EE;   call
88.13   highway as knowledge] EE;   highway while his main
           attention is elsewhere, knowledge
88.13   sense] EE;   logical sense
88.16   denial to it of] EE;   denial of
88.17   factor.] EE;   factor in the former.
88.22   the great . . . scientific] EE;   the primary difficulty
           of critical or scientific
88.24–25   from other situations.] EE;   from situations which, in
           their contrast with the requirements of reflection in
           this case, may be fairly termed non-reflective; so that
           the essential problem of intelligence so far forth as
           intelligence, is precisely the reassignment of content
           in accordance with the needs and purposes of this
           situation: it is just this resurvey and revaluation which
           constitutes rationality.
88.28   paper.] EE;   paper (Vol. IV., pp. 199–200).
88.30   another relation is added] EE;   there is another rela-
           tion added
88.33   may signify] EE;   may suggest or signify
88.34   signification-relation] EE;   ~∧~

89.6   it] EE;   so it
89.23–24   element. [¶] It is quite] EE;   element. It is quite
89.24   that a thing] EE;   the fact
89.29   *fact-relations*] EE;   ~ₐ~
89.29   *meaning-relations*] EE;   ~ₐ~
89.37   an] EE;   the
89.38   it becomes] EE;   it ceases to be just reality as such
            and becomes
89.38   thing,] EE;   realityₐ
90.1   "reality"] EE;   ₐ~ₐ
90.2   it] EE;   reality
90.3   practical] EE;   the practical
90.16   active] EE;   practical
90.16   operative] EE;   already operative
90.19   and giving direction] EE;   and control
90.20–21   function. [¶] In conclusion] EE;   function.

            Reality in its characterization as fact, in the logical
       force which it has in the regulation of the formation
       and testing of ideas, is not, then, something outside of
       or given to the reflective situation, but is given or
       determined *in* it. Reality as such is the entire situation,
       while fact is a specific determination of it. If the re-
       flective situation were purely intellectualistic, then the
       objective idealist would have logic on his side; but
       since it is a focusing of a disturbed system of activities
       and divided values on their way to a unified situation
       of harmonized values, we have a dynamic realism.
       Similarly the idea is not a fixed thing, an entity exist-
       ing in some ontological psychical region, and then hap-
       pening to get caught in a reflective situation. If it were,
       either the subjective idealist would be right, or else the
       determination of truth would by its nature be impos-
       sible. But idea is a logical determination, ultimately
       practical in origin and function. What on one side is a
       name for operative realism, names on the other an
       experimental idealism.
            In conclusion
90.24   organic] EE;   thoroughly organic
90.24–25   incarnate] EE;   already incarnate
90.28   something because,] EE;   a certain reality, becauseₐ
90.29–30   feature of . . . light. Such confusion] EE;   feature
            of that reality which previously had not been stated
            but assumed, he puts the affair in such a strange light
            as to appear arbitrarily to change its character. Such
            a confusion
90.31–32   psychologicalₐ—] EE;   ~,—
90.32   adjustmentₐ—] EE;   ~,—
90.33–34   by our getting] EE;   by getting

90.34   viewpoint, rather] EE;   view-point, so as to see things
            from it, rather
90.35   argument.] EE;   argument. Meanwhile the argument
            of this paper is proffered in the hope that it may, with
            some, facilitate the process of habituation.

"The Logical Character of Ideas"

Copy-text is the first appearance of the article in JP:
Journal of Philosophy, Psychology and Scientific Methods 5
(1908): 375–81. Emendations have been adopted from the
revised version published in EE: *Essays in Experimental
Logic* (Chicago: University of Chicago Press, 1916), pp.
220–29.

91.0   [*om.*]] W;   VII EE;   Discussion
91.9   is a substance] EE;   is itself a substance
91.11   he would] EE;   would
91.15   occupied by them] EE;   occupied
91.16   an account of] EE;   that which regards
91.17   from treating] EE;   and which treats
91.17   making up] EE;   marking
92.7   equaling] EE;   equalling
92.24   "knowledge"] EE;   ∧∼∧
92.30   than] EE;   than at most
92.31   makes] EE;   has to make
92.33   conceptions] EE;   conception
92.33   practice] EE;   practise
92.37   structures involved] EE;   the structures which are in-
            volved
92.38   acts] EE;   functions
93.8   was perhaps] EE;   perhaps was
93.14–15   process. [¶] These] EE;   process. Thus when Dr. Pratt,
            in a recent discussion,[3] says that the aforesaid "Essays"

     3. This JOURNAL, Vol. V., p. 131, note.

            "might well have been written from the standpoint of
            solipsism," I accordingly find an unintended compli-
            ment. Not that they were written, I hasten to add,
            from the solipsistic standpoint, but that they were
            written from a *logical* standpoint, to which the solip-
            sistic controversy is irrelevant;—since a logical in-
            quiry is concerned only with inferential relations
            among things, not with preconceptions about a lonely
            consciousness, or soul, or self. The assumption of a
            separate ontological world of consciousness which

either *is* the self or is the possession of some self simply does not enter into the discussion.

When Dr. Pratt speaks of a "private stream of consciousness," of "outer realities that never come within one's own private stream of consciousness," and of a relation between "these realities and our judgments about them, a relation which from the nature of the case one can never experience," and "puts a dilemma" on the basis of these assumptions (p. 131), he puts, indeed, a dilemma to those who hold to these assumptions, but he misses the point of the "Logical Studies." Whether with such assumptions Dr. Pratt and others who hold to them can logically escape solipsism—except by saying they escape it—is also a matter for them to consider.

In the earlier part of his article, however, Dr. Pratt seems to admit that logical inquiry may be carried on in its own terms, without being compromised by the necessity of accommodating it to foregone epistemological assumptions. He accepts the position of the "concrete situation" (p. 123), and emphasizes the notion that the center of the problem of the truth of ideas is found in the problem of judgment (p. 130).[4] He gives an illustration, moreover, on the basis

4. Just how this doctrine is to be reconciled with the other assertion that the problem of knowledge is concerned with the relation (which "by the nature of the case can not be experienced") between judgments *in* a private stream of consciousness and unexperienced objects *outside* the stream, it would be interesting to find out.

of which points at issue may be logically, not epistemologically, discussed. Dr. Pratt says: "Thus I believe my friend *B* is in Constantinople. If *B* really is in Constantinople, my thought is true. I confess it is impossible for me to see how anything could be simpler than this" (p. 124). In short, "a thought is true if the object of thought is as you think it." Just before this (p. 123), however, Dr. Pratt has discriminated another sense of truth which marks a current, a correct, and an intelligible usage. This is the identification of truth "with *known fact*" (italics in original). What is the relation of these two meanings? Dr. Pratt insists (quite correctly, as it seems to me) that truth or falsity is a character of ideas only when ideas are in judgment: only, that is, as I understand it, when they intend a certain objective reference. The men who denied the existence of the antipodes presumably had the idea (or they could not have denied

its truth), and the object was "as" they thought it
when they "had" the idea. But their idea was not
"true" because their judgments denied a certain *objective* connection. And when I "believe" my friend
is in Constantinople, I do not merely entertain the
idea as a floating image; I intend a factual reference.
In short, the question of truth is not whether an
object is "as you think it," unless the term "think"
means as you *judge* it to be. The logical idea is short
for a certain *judgment* about a thing. It states the
way an object is *judged to be*, the way we *take it* in
the inference process, as distinct from the way it
actually may be.

If we compare this conception of truth with
that of "identification with known fact," we get some
striking results and some even more striking questions. When there is a *known fact*, there *is* a known
fact and no judgment, and no idea. The known fact
may very well be the *outcome* of a judgment, but it
can not be part of any judgment that involves a
thought of *B's* whereabouts. Or (since it is not the
word judgment we are concerned with) the *kind* of
judgment occurring when it is a *known* fact where
B is, is radically different from that occurring when,
his whereabouts *not* being certain, we inferentially
judge him to be at Constantinople. Since the latter
involves inference, consideration of evidence, it involves some doubt. Do we have any *thought* (as a
part of an intended objective reference) of *B's* presence in Constantinople, save as we have also the
thought of his *possible* presence somewhere else, plus
the conviction that the weight of evidence is in favor
of his being in Constantinople? [¶] These

93.15	considerations] EE; questions
93.15–16	intelligently raise] EE; raise intelligently
93.16–17	consider] EE; consider the question of
93.21	facts when the facts] EE; facts to which they refer *when* these facts
93.22	"ideas"] EE; the "ideas"
94.2	validity] EE; this matter of validity
94.2	with truth] EE; with the question of truth
94.5	judging] EE; it
94.7–8	known fact,] EE; [*ital.*]
94.21	There] EE; These
94.21	things.] EE; things in their factual relations.
94.22	objects—] EE; ~;
94.28–29	as effectively as accredited] EE; more effectively even than accredited

94.30   situation.] EE; situation.⁶ . . . ⁶Such a use differs
          from that of Perry, who would employ the term to con-
          note formerly accepted, but now definitely discredited,
          objects: recognized errors, illusions, etc.
94.31   to be valid] EE; valid
95.4   value] EE; [*ital.*]
95.5   character:] EE; ∼;
95.6; 96.22   that] EE; which
95.7   which‸] EE; ∼,
95.7   operations‸] EE; ∼,
95.8   would not be so] EE; be as
95.10   for regarding] EE; of entertaining
95.10–11 for employing] EE; of employing
95.13   and also] EE; and
95.20   our own.] EE; *our own* states.
95.21   are not] EE; would not be
95.28   with reference to one another] EE; simply as events
          on their own account
95.31   *is*] EE; [*rom.*]
95.32   is tentatively] EE; is being tentatively
95.38   are] EE; were
96.4   personal] EE; purely private
96.4   have,] EE; ∼‸
96.5   temporarily,] EE; ∼‸
96.9   serve as means] EE; serve
96.11   different] EE; new
96.11   treated,] EE; ∼‸
96.14   which] EE; and they
96.17   recognition] EE; distinct perception
96.17–18 which are not] EE; not as
96.18   or] *stet* JP; nor EE
96.19   inchoate] EE; as inchoate
96.19   experimental] EE; empirical
96.20   resolves] EE; solves
96.21   that] EE; which yet
96.23   which] EE; that
96.24   say: This] EE; say this
96.24–25 nor the picture nor] EE; or the picture or
96.25–26 an event . . . system] EE; *my* color
96.27   *reference—*] EE; ∼,
96.29–30 inquiry.] EE; inquiry which may lead to the dis-
          covery of a previously unexperienced thing, and pos-
          sibly to a thing of a qualitatively different order from
          anything previously experienced.
96.33   with pointing] EE; to point
96.34   a] EE; the
96.34   critic‸] EE; ∼,
96.36–37 interprets . . . theory] EE; interprets

97.1   distinction.] EE; distinction, in terms of his own
          theory.
97.4   apprehension] EE; sympathetic apprehension
97.4   it . . . conception.] EE; it.

"What Pragmatism Means by Practical"

Copy-text is the first publication of the article with the
title "What Does Pragmatism Mean by Practical?" in JP:
Journal of Philosophy, Psychology and Scientific Methods 5
(1908): 85–99. Emendations have been adopted from the
revision and republication of the article in EE: *Essays in
Experimental Logic* (New York: Henry Holt and Co., 1916),
pp. 303–29.

98.0   [*om.*]] W; XII EE; [*not present*]
98.1   WHAT PRAGMATISM MEANS BY PRACTICAL] EE;
          WHAT DOES PRAGMATISM MEAN BY PRACTICAL?[1]
98.6   thinking."[1]] EE; ~." ∧
98.8   mind;] EE; ~—
98.19   is] EE; is also
98n.3   Green, & Co.,] EE; ~∧ ~∧
99.21–22 the *Journal of Philosophy, Psychology*∧ *and Scientific
          Methods,*] W; ~, ~, ~, EE; this JOURNAL
99.27   I] EE; [*not present*]
100.2   "cash in"] EE; "cash" in
100.15   science] EE; modern science
100.17   would] EE; should
100.27   pp. 122–23] W; p. 123
100.36   controversy∧] EE; ~,
100.36   exists∧] EE; ~,
101.8   them,] EE; ~∧
101.8   stand,] EE; ~∧
101.10   controversies] EE; [*ital.*]
101.13   *conceiving*] EE; [*rom.*]
101.13; 102.8 objects] EE; [*ital.*]
101.24   *the specific last*] EE; *last*
101.28   will mean in] EE; will in
101.29   from] EE; than in the case of
101.32   distinct] EE; [*ital.*]
101.33   "practical"] EE; ∧~∧
101.35   1. When] EE; When
101.38   never-failing] EE; ~∧~
101.39   object:] EE; [*ital.*]
102.2,3   object] EE; [*ital.*]

102.10–11   What is . . . object?] EE;   what do *objects* mean.
102.16   confused with them] EE;   confused
102.18   When, then, it] EE;   When it
102.18–19   question of] EE;   question, then, of
102.19   signifies its] EE;   signifies
102.22   2. But] EE;   But
102.26   an idea] EE;   the idea
102.35   an] *stet* JP;   and EE
102.37   actions,] EE;   ~∧
102.40   itself] EE;   [*ital.*]
103.3–4   it, as our attitude,] EE;   it∧ *as* attitude∧
103.5   3. Then] EE;   Then
103.6   or] *stet* JP;   nor EE
103.9   anyone] EE;   any one
103.9   were true?] EE;   [*ital.*]
103.15   that fact] *stet* JP;   the fact EE
103.22   means] EE;   is
103.28   "meaning"] EE;   ∧~∧
103.28   "practical"] EE;   ∧~∧
103.31   conception] EE;   conceptual cannotation
103.31   *object*;] EE;   object:
103.32   *idea*;] EE;   idea:
103.33   *importance*] EE;   [*rom.*]
103.34   the attitudes] EE;   attitudes
103n.1   are] *stet* JP;   have EE
103n.5   text] EE;   test
104.8   anyway] EE;   any way
104.9–10   ∧misunderstanding∧∧] EE;   "~,"
104.17   II] EE;   [*not present*]
104.22(2),23,30   world-formula] EE;   ~∧~
104.25   import] EE;   value
104.26   hypothesis] EE;   hypotheses
104.32   regards] EE;   to
104.35; 106.4,17,32,40   value] EE;   [*ital.*]
104.36–37   its logical content already] EE;   its content, its
             logical meaning, already
105.1   constitute the meaning] EE;   *constitute* the proper in-
             tellectual meaning
105.6   old] EE;   the old
105.11–12   a "seeing] EE;   "a seeing
105.16   a seeing] EE;   seeing
105.21   runs] EE;   run
105.23   *discernible*] EE;   *descernible*
105.29   belief in it] EE;   [*ital.*]
105.30   interpretation.] EE;   interpetation, but I do not think
             that is what Mr. James intends.
105.40   substitute] EE;   [*ital.*]
106.5   does] EE;   is it

106.6   effect] EE;   which effects
106.8   meaning] EE;   [*ital.*]
106.13–14 existence] EE;   [*ital.*]
106.14   themselves] EE;   [*ital.*]
106.17–18 meaning of the terms] EE;   [*ital.*]
106.19   entire] EE;   [*ital.*]
106.21   abolish] EE;   [*ital.*]
106.23   that] EE;   [*ital.*]
106.26   design,] EE;   ~‸
107.1   significance] EE;   intellectual significance
107.1–2   determined;   a fact . . . simply] EE;   determined by
           treating it not as *a truth*, but simply
107.3   hypothesis.] EE;   hypothesis and method.
107.6   never] EE;   [*ital.*]
107.7; 109.20; 110.23   any] EE;   [*ital.*]
107.16   thereby] EE;   that
107.17–19 a passage . . . the truth] EE;   a classic passage
           concerning Centaurs, and yet the determination of its
           true sense does not establish the truth
107.31   the meaning of] EE;   meaning of
108.1   is not given] EE;   it is not
108.7   valuable] EE;   [*ital.*]
108.7   leads] EE;   [*ital.*]
108.13   duty] EE;   [*ital.*]
108.18   foregoing] EE;   above
108.22   certain] EE;   [*ital.*]
108.23   good for] EE;   good *for*
108.24   for what] EE;   what
108.24   claim] EE;   [*ital.*]
108.25   idea] EE;   [*ital.*]
108.29   Then arises] EE;   Now we have
108.31   the attaining of] EE;   attaining
108.35–36 *existences*] EE;   *realities*
109.5–6   statements] EE;   statements from him
109.7   consequences‸ was] EE;   ~, ~
109.16   consequences] EE;   these consequences
109n.4   supreme value] EE;   [*ital.*]
109n.13   truth] EE;   truths
110.3   many.] EE;   many who are not rationalists.
110.6   criterion of the truth of ideas] EE;   criterion for ideas
           as ideas
110.15–16 the antecedent] EE;   antecedent
110n.5   backward] EE;   backwards
110n.7   anyone] W;   any one
110n.8   funded] EE;   banded
110n.11   anyone] EE;   any one
110n.18   idea as] EE;   [*ital.*]
110n.18   as *true*] EE;   *as true*

110n.21   absolute] EE;   [ital.]
110n.21   if true] EE;   [ital.]
111.30–31   pragmatists . . . sense, because] EE;   pragmatists
          or not, because
111.31   ∧practical,∧] EE;   "∼,"
111n.5–6   not as distinct from] EE;   as distinct, not from
112.1–2   knowing . . . passage.] EE;   knowing what pragma-
          tism means by practical. And since Mr. James first in-
          troduced the term into print, and since he is chiefly
          responsible for its currency, he can speak with an
          authority possessed by no one else.
112.4   doctrine] EE;   doctrine, I think,
112.5   both] EE;   [ital.]
112.5   and] EE;   [ital.]
112.12   pp. 63–64] W;   p. 64
112.19   one] EE;   [ital.]
112.23   the charge] EE;   charges
112.23   which] EE;   that
112.28   III] EE;   [not present]
112.37   aspects–] EE;   ∼,
113.1   reality–] EE;   ∼,
113.2   synthetic pragmatism] EE;   [ital.]
113.6   ∧personal.∧] EE;   "∼."
113.16–17   enters into judgments passed] EE;   enters in passing
113.19   with encouraging] EE;   of encouraging
113.32   potentest] W;   most potential EE, JP
113.37   influence us unconsciously] EE;   unconsciously influ-
          ence us
113.39   a responsibility for judging] EE;   for judging
114.1   it] EE;   [rom.]
114.13,14   special] EE;   [ital.]
114.15   "Will to Believe"] EE;   ∧will to believe∧
114.23   define . . . responsibility] EE;   define it, and to ac-
          cept moral responsibility
114.24   "will∧"] E;   "∼,"
114.27   seems] EE;   would seem
114.27–28   matter correctly.] EE;   matter.
114.29   attempted] EE;   not attempted
114.29   review not so much] EE;   review
114.30   book∧] EE;   ∼,
114.30   as the] EE;   but rather the
114.30–31   which is] EE;   as
114.31   I have] EE;   have
114.34   James,] EE;   ∼∧
114.36–37   expect . . . which] EE;   expect the kind of clear-
          ness and explicitness in such lectures which
114.38   that] EE;   which
115.13–14   philosophical] EE;   philosophic

115.15   it~] EE;   ~,
115.19   facts,] EE;   facts and
115.29   pragmatism.] EE;   pragmatism. [¶] As for the thing
           pragmatism, moreover, Mr. James has performed so
           uniquely the composing of different elements into a
           single pictorial or artistic whole, that it is probable
           that progress in the immediate future will come from
           a more analytic clearing up and development of these
           independent elements. It will then be possible to pass
           upon their differential traits, and the possibility of their
           consistent, logical combination. After a period of pools
           and mergers, the tendency is to return to the advan-
           tages of individual effort and responsibility. Possibly
           "pragmatism" as a holding company for allied, yet
           separate interests and problems, might be dissolved and
           revert to its original constituents.

"Discussion on Realism and Idealism"

The only previous appearance of this article, PR:
Philosophical Review 18 (1909): 182–83, serves as copy-
text.

116.1   DISCUSSION ON REALISM AND IDEALISM] W;
           Discussion: Realism and Idealism.
117.13   knowledge] W;   knowlege

"Pure Experience and Reality: A Disclaimer"

Copy-text for this article is its only previous publication
in PR: *Philosophical Review* 16 (1907): 419–22.

122.39   anachronism] W;   ananachronism
123.8   thought-relations] W;   ~~~
123.32   transsubjective] W;   transubjective

"Does Reality Possess Practical Character?"

The first publication of this article in *Essays, Philosophical and Psychological*, in Honor of William James (New
York: Longmans, Green, and Co., 1908), pp. 53–80, serves
as copy-text. Dewey's substantive changes made for the ar-

ticle's appearance in PC: *Philosophy and Civilization* (New York: Minton, Balch and Co., 1931), pp. 36–55, appear in the "List of 1931 Variants" in this volume. One such change that would have been made editorially here appears below.

138n.4   *another*] PC;   *other*

"Objects, Data, and Existences: A Reply to Professor McGilvary"

Copy-text for this article is its only previous publication in JP: *Journal of Philosophy, Psychology and Scientific Methods* 6 (1909): 13–21.

148n.3   *Studies in*] W;   Contributions to
152.6   orb" . . . datum.ᴧ] W;   orbᴧ . . . datum."
153n.2   misapprehension] W;   misapprenhension

"Address to National Negro Conference"

Copy-text for this address is its only previous publication during Dewey's lifetime, in *Proceedings of the National Negro Conference 1909* (New York: National Negro Conference Headquarters, n.d.), pp. 71–73.

156.4   two;] W;   ~,

"The Bearings of Pragmatism upon Education"

Copy-text for this article is its first publication in *Progressive Journal of Education* 1 (Dec. 1908): 1–3; 1 (Jan. 1909): 5–8; 1 (Feb. 1909): 6–7. The reprinting in R: Louis Win Rapeer, *Teaching Elementary School Subjects* (New York: Charles Scribner's Sons, 1917), pp. 552–69, is cited as the first appearance of emendations that would have been made editorially.

178.16   judgment of] R;   of judgment
178.25   biological] R;   bioligical
179.24,   a priori] R;   aprion
180.29
180.19   successful] R;   successive
180.26   issue] R;   isssue
180.29   They are] R;   It is
183.5   natural] R;   neutral
183.34   multiplying] R;   multipliyng
184.30   and] R;   or
184.30   obstacles,] R;   ~∧
185.14   light] R;   height
186.7–8   instinctive eagerness] R;   instructive tenderness
186.13–14   activity—an] W;   activity. An
186.33   senses] R;   sense
186.35   and is not set] R;   and not to set
187.3   was] R;   were
187.23–24   researchers] R;   researches
189.21   meagre] R;   meager
189.28   centres] R;   centers
189.30   natural] W;   neutral
190.33   tends] R;   tend

"The Purpose and Organization of Physics Teaching in Secondary Schools"

Copy-text for this contribution by Dewey to a Symposium on Physics Teaching is its only previous publication, in *School Science and Mathematics* 9 (1909): 291–92.

199.5   period] W;   peroid

"Teaching That Does Not Educate"

Copy-text for this article is its only previous appearance, in *Progressive Journal of Education* 1 (June 1909): 1–3.

202.39   attention,] W;   ~.

"The Moral Significance of the Common School Studies"

Copy-text for Dewey's address is its only previous publication, in Northern Illinois Teachers' Association, *Topics*

for *General Sessions: Moral and Religious Training in the*
Public Schools, November 5th and 6th, 1909, Elgin, Illinois
(n.p., n.d.), pp. 21–27.

205.14	represents] W;	represent
207.31	spectator] W;	speectator
210.30	instilling,] W;	~ₐ
213.10	absorption] W;	absorbtion

Review of Studies in Philosophy and Psychology

Copy-text is the only previous publication of this review,
in *Philosophical Review* 16 (1907): 312–21.

218.8	results."] W;	~.ₐ
218n.4	philosophizes] W;	philosophisizes
224.7	enfolding] W;	unfolding

Review of The Life of Reason

Copy-text is the only previous publication of this review,
in *Educational Review* 34 (1907): 116–29.

234.19	inspiration] W;	aspiration
236.9	good] W;	goods
238.31	sensuous] W;	senusous

Review of Henry Sidgwick: A Memoir

Copy-text for this review is its only previous publication,
in *Political Science Quarterly* 22 (1907): 133–35.

242.3	London] W;	Landon

LIST OF 1931 VARIANTS IN "DOES REALITY POSSESS PRACTICAL CHARACTER?"

"Does Reality Possess Practical Character?" in *Essays, Philosophical and Psychological*, in Honor of William James (New York: Longmans, Green, and Co., 1908), pp. 53–80, was revised and printed in the collective volume *Philosophy and Civilization* (New York: Minton, Balch and Co., 1931), pp. 36–55, with the title "The Practical Character of Reality." Substantive changes made in the article for that later edition appear below to the right of the bracket.

125.1–2	DOES REALITY POSSESS PRACTICAL CHARACTER?] The Practical Character of Reality
125.9	postulate:] postulates:
125.11–12	and requiring accordingly some] and which accordingly needed some
125.18	grounds at] ground at
125.25	knowing were] knowing had been
126.12	doctrine if] doctrine were it
126.13	Yet surely as] Yet as
126.13	is] is surely
126.25–26	things, but] things. But
126.29	so far as] as far as
126.31–32	science, . . . phenomenalism,] science is led by the idea of evolution to introduce into the nalism,
126.33	carried] led
126.34	into introducing] to introduce
127.10	An imagination bound] Imagination when bound
127.15	doing well this business,] doing this business well,
127.16	right difference∧] *right* difference,
127.32–33	those . . . accepting the] those perfectly free to feel the
128n.6	which it *is* used] which *is* is used
129.19	moral historian] historian
129.22	which itself] which
129.36	was only] was
130.6	offices] office
130.11	Our] One
130.21	that all knowledge issues] that knowledge *issues*

131.17   of his traditional] of one's traditional
131.22–23   procedures] active procedures
132.6   of moral] to moral
132.15   scientific] specific
132n.5   body as] body which is
133.18   No one] [¶] No one
133.32–33   involve] involves
134.17   fulfilment of its end.] fulfillment of its office.
134.18   whether the] whether
134.36   character] quality
134.37   matter] content
135.4   existences] existence
135.19   solution. It] solution according to which it
135.19   that] the
135.21   difference, any] or
135.30   such harmony] harmony
135.31   as to reinforce] and re-inforcing
135.32   enlarge its functioning] enlarging its function
136.2   *because*] since
136.24   at large] [*ital.*]
136.29   so taken] taken
136.29   response] response so
136.33   that] one
137.3   pretend] lay claim
137.4   that] which
137.12   differences] consequences
137.19   this] a
138.25   a state] that
138n.4   *other*] *another*
139.5   that] it
139.10   the awareness] awareness
139.23   involved also] also involved
139.30   by] [*ital.*]
139.40   these] there
140.3   quale] quality
140.19   so] as
141.1   make] introduce
141.1   other and more] other
142.5   as] to be

"Nature and Its Good: A Conversation"

In the following list appear all variants in substantives and accidentals between the copy-text first publication of this article, HJ: *Hibbert Journal* 7 (1909): 827–43, and TS: a carbon copy of the typescript for Dewey's paper "The Good, Nature and Intelligence: A Conversation" housed in Butler Library, Columbia University, in the papers of the New York Philosophical Club, as well as variants between the present edition and TS. Omitted from the tabulation are the instances of faulty spacing, chiefly words run together, and obvious typographical errors that do not make words. The reading to the left of the bracket is from the present edition and will not coincide with the copy-text reading if an emendation has been made. The reading following the bracket is, in all cases, that of TS.

15.1–2   NATURE . . . CONVERSATION] The Good, Nature and Intelligence: A Conversation.
15.3   scattered$_\wedge$] ~,
15.5   day's] days
15.7   *Various voices.*] ~:
15.8 *et seq.* *Eaton.*] ~:
15.11   gone;] ~:
15.13 *et seq.* *Grimes.*] ~:
15.14   well-fed] ~$_\wedge$~
15.14   well-read] ~$_\wedge$~
15.14–15 of wealth and of knowledge] and their leisure
15.17 *et seq.* Nature] nature
15.25   discussion] affair
15.26   work] work up
15.26   limit$_\wedge$] ~,
15.27   beyond] beyond that limit
16.10   world;$_\wedge$] ~:-
16.10–11 and even] and
16.11   you philosophers] you
16.12 $_\wedge$advanced$_\wedge$] "~"

16.19–20   affairs—which] affairs; and these
16.20   analysis‸] ~,
16.20   the business] always questions
16.21   living.] ~‸
16.22   Yes;] ~,
16.24   life‸] ~,
16.24   more] is more
16.24   insane,] ~‸
16.26   found] decided
16.30   sea-sands] sands
16.33   results;] ~,
16.34–35   which . . . found.] which proper means may be
           found by intelligently directed search.
16.40   but also] but
16.40   regard] regard for
16.40–17.1 preference,] ~‸
17.2   redistribution] redistributions
17.2–3   motion;‸] ~;-
17.4   screeching,] ~‸
17.5   This is . . . but] [*not present*]
17.5–6   suppose it were] Suppose this is
17.6   so,] ~:
17.12   Insist‸] ~,
17.12   please‸] ~,
17.14   partial,] ~‸
17.16   specific] particular
17.17   values that] values
17.18   madness;‸] ~;-
17.20   still,] ~‸
17.21   in] when in
17.22   no.] ~—
17.23   "go . . . returns."] ‸~.‸
17.24   knowledge. Examine] knowledge—examine
17.24,25   find] you find
17.30   all-embracing] ~‸~
17.33   No;] ~,
17.33   accept it;] ~,
17.33   its face value] that
17.34   value more concretely] more value concretely
17.34   securely] actually
17.35   than it] than
17.35   was] was there
17.36   mis-step] misstep
17.37   all-inclusive] ~‸~
17.38   disease? Does] disease, does
17.40   No;] ~,
17.40   ‸Never] "never
17.40   for] that

18.2   really Real.₍∧₎] real."
18.3   pain, which the] pain, the
18.6   nth] [rom.]
18.8 et seq.   Moore.] ~:
18.9   which, . . . not] which is, as certainly, not
18.10   however,] ~₍∧₎
18.11   an inkling] a lurking suspicion
18.11   question;] entire question,
18.13   wit,] ~₍∧₎
18.13   false logic] logic
18.16   waves,] ~.
18.19   with!] ~.
18.21   cynical] a form of cynical
18.22   But it] It has
18.23   drowning of sorrow] process of drowning sorrow
18.25   wilful restlessness] it
18.32–33   cultivation,] ~₍∧₎
18.33   the nurture,] and nurture₍∧₎
18.36   Reality] reality
18.36   values;] ~:
18.38   absolute] absolute reality
18.40   say: Accept] say, accept
19.2   obscure even] obscures
19.3   say: Perhaps] ~₍∧₎ perhaps
19.5   realities; and a] realities. I say that a
19.6   materialist,] ~₍∧₎
19.7   standard,] ~₍∧₎
19.8   one₍∧₎] ~,
19.17   Drop the] Drop that
19.17   presupposition] presupposition of yours
19.18   everything] everything which
19.18   the idea] namely
19.21   are, a multitude] are. A multitude
19.22   both] both exist
19.27   reduce] lessen
19.28   reality] Reality
19.30   trouble and] trouble
19.30   that] [rom.]
19.33   we (I] ~, ~
19.33   pragmatists)] ~,
19.34   ends₍∧₎] ~,
19.36–37   indeed, not merely that] indeed that
19.37–38   intelligence . . . is.] intelligence is.
19.39   how₍∧₎] ~,
19.40   conditions₍∧₎] ~,
20.1   intelligence₍∧₎] ~,
20.10   a transcendent] the transcendental
20.13   between, say, the] between the

20.14-15   slander, . . . valetudinarianism.] slander.
20.18   concrete] specific
20.20   side of experience, and] side and
20.21-22   wish . . . drop] wish you would both drop
20.23   a struggle] a matter of the struggle
20.23   existence—] ~∧
20.26   struggle,] ~—
20.28   eighteenth] 18th
20.28   imagined] thought
20.28   are at least] at least are
20.29   for the needs of all] for all
20.29-30   monopolization] monopoly
20.30   few persons] few
20.32   things, then to be] things and then again be
20.40   monopolists∧] ~,
21.4   rebellious. That] rebellious—that
21.4-5   would know] know
21.5   the ideal] your ideal
21.6   beyond. When] beyond; when
21.6   will perceive] perceive
21.9   about] [rom.]
21.9   different] which is different
21.11-30   Moore . . . for all.] [not present]
21.31 et seq. Arthur.] ~:
21.31   in respect] with respect
21.32-33   in this peculiarity] in it
21.38   some] something
21.38   different Reality beyond] different, beyond
21.40-22.1 give . . . in the] give us results in the
22.1,3   Science] science
22.1-2   yields in her direct application.] yields.
22.6,12,14 fulfilment] fulfillment
22.11   directly obtained] already known
22.13   then, and] ~∧ ~
22.13   then, can] ~∧ ~
22.13   consciousness] mans consciousness
22.15   to sound] in sound
22.15   thinking—] ~;
22.15   save, historically,] ~∧ ~∧
22.22   Nature,] ~∧
22.27   detail, and] ~∧ ~
22.27   detail, as] ~∧ ~
22.28   existence,] ~∧
22.29   results,] ~;
22.32   reflection),] ~)∧
22.33   importance— . . . exercise] importance, which more-
           over exercise
22.38-39   not obiter dicta] obiter dicta

23.10   naïve] naive
23.12   of our] our
23.12   of our "contemplation,"] our 'contemplation,∧
23.15   variation,] ∼∧
23.15–16   is an] is merely an
23.16   eyes to what is,] eyes∧
23.19   is just—not true] just is not true
23.22   shows,] ∼∧
23.22   design,] ∼∧
23.22–23   but tendency and purpose;] but purpose:
23.23   not indeed of] not of
23.27   true as far as it goes,] true it is—
23.29–30   ends— . . . know.] ends.
23.32   I do] We do
23.34   I only] We only
23.35   be told,] shall be told:
23.35   be noted] shall be noted
23.36   namely,] ∼∧
24.4   good:∧] ∼;—
24.15   gain,] ∼∧
24.19   at least it is] is at least
24.20   error,] ∼∧
24.24   giving] which gave
24.24–25.27 Nature's] nature's
24.25   the existing] this
24.29   in saying] which says
24.30   others] others are
24.31   *some*body] [*rom.*]
24.37   deserve∧] ∼,
24.37   moment's] moments
24.39   these] the
24.40   capable∧] ∼,
24.40   insight∧] ∼,
25.1   incapable∧] ∼,
25.2–3   how . . . Aristotle?] the difference from Aristotle is
           purely verbal.
25.7   Grimes,] ∼;
25.7   *are*] [*rom.*]
25.8   desire is] desire
25.12   *Grimes*∧(] ∼: (
25.12   shoulders∧] ∼,
25.13   says):] ∼)∧
25.15   believe—] ∼:
25.18–19   (as *he* well knew)] ∧∼∧
25.24–25   despises. Doesn't] despises;   doesn't
25.31   end∧] ∼,
25.34–35   (one . . . are)] [*not present*]
25.39   passage—] ∼,

25.40   Nature (all] nature, which is all
26.1   us)] ~,
26.1   problem,] ~ₐ
26.1   contradictionₐ] ~,
26.1–2   originally in question?] in question.
26.6–7   Not . . . but] [*not present*]
26.7   precisely] Precisely
26.9   Appearance,] appearance.
26.9–10   and . . . Reality.] [*not present*]
26.11; 27.28 *Stair.*] *Rose:*
26.16   had] has
26.21   unity,] ~ₐ
26.22   truth,] ~ₐ
26.24–25 Being] being
26.28   inevitably] mentally
26.29   intelligence] all intelligence
26.29–30 must dwell] dwells
26.31   These] So these
26.31   words,] ~ₐ of
26.32   to woo] to
26.32   yourselves into] yourself in
26.34   beatific] ecstatic
26.36–37 self-impartation] self-realization
26.37   ultimate] alternate
26.39   empiricism,] ~;
27.1   than] than it is
27.1   The] For the
27.1   mystical] mystic
27.1   marks] measures
27.2–3   hence measures] hence
27.13   being] Being
27.15   not] which is not
27.16–18 Who . . . communications.] [*not present*]
27.23   efforts] these efforts
27.25   from] with
27.26; 28.9 Stair] Rose
27.28   This] It
27.28   not so true as] no truer
27.28   that in] that than to say that
27.29   you are] are
27.33   mindₐ] ~,
27.39   a sporadic reminder and] a sort of
28.3   are] are better
28.7   to be solved only] only to be solved
28.14   wonderful—as Arthur does—that] wonderful that
28.15   values] them
28.15   trivial,] ~-
28.17   Beingₐ] Bring,

28.25   indeed, as you say,] indeed,
28.28   bestowed;] ~,
28.29–30   and because, in] and in
28.29   conscious] deliberate
28.31   results,] ~—
28.33   occur] occur as
28.34   Nature∧] nature,
28.35   results,] ~∧
28.36–37   that, . . . as well] that kills man with malaria in
           achieving itself as well
28.38   fulness] fullness
28.38   germ-fulfilment] germ-fulfillment
28.40   types] sorts
28.40   value,] ~∧
29.1–18   Nature, . . . intelligence.] To nature till a conscious
           being is produced all things are alike valuable and
           valueless. Only when a sentient organism says I want
           this, I like this and dislike that, does value appear—in
           producing sentiency nature for the first time shows it-
           self capable of effecting good. And for the organism to
           identify by affection its own fortunes with the career
           of a natural process, to prefer *its* result to that of an-
           other process, generates intelligence.
29.19   selecting] selection
29.19   organizing∧] organization,
29.19–21   out of . . . *is* intelligence] on the basis of this end of
           certain conditions as means out of the natural flux, is
           intelligence
29.21   Not, then, when] Not when
29.23   it] she
29.23   organism that has settled] organism as an organic fac-
           tor, does nature show any settled
29.24   preferences] preference for good over evil, or for one
           good above another good.
29.24   and endeavors] [*not present*]
29.24–25   complexity, health, adjustment,] these things
29.30–31   partial. Because] partial; because
29.31   an] one
29.31   preferred, is selected] preferred and selected
29.32   because intelligence] intelligence
29.32   not a world,] not the impartial world
29.33   just . . . the conditions] but the conditions
29.37–38   valuation . . . is] valuation is
29.40   solved] really solved
30.6   wide-viewing∧] wide-viewed,
30.10   life *is*] life
30.10–11   philosophy] *is* philosophy
30.12   loyally] seriously and loyally

LINE-END HYPHENATION

I. Copy-text list.

The following are the editorially established forms of possible compounds which were hyphenated at the ends of lines in the copy-text.

5.22	self-fulfilling	162.1	quasi-magic
9.9	outbursts	164.21	subject-matter
16.29	beefsteaks	167.22	supernaturalism
18.8	tender-mindedness	172.40	show-down
26.3	self-contradictions	176.8	supernatural
30.9	farsighted	183.16	cooperation
41.38	re-edited	189.40	shop-work
47.30	bugaboos	190.24	cooperate
62.14	[1]black-smithing	198.13	non-physicist
68.28	twofold	205.24	long-continued
69n.8	question-begging	205.29	subject-matter
71.3	street-car	210.21	second-rate
83.26	wayfaring	213.4	subject-matter
111.22	overrides	213.9	cooperation
121.15	pre-existent	248.2	forerunners
130.17	subject-matter	267.31	character-forming
135.11	subject-matter	268.16	school-teachers
136.32	hall-mark	272.5	black-smithing
137.13	subject-matter	272.35	undergoing
139.39	subject-matter	277.4	cooperation
143.17	prefixed	279.12	subject-matter
152.22	subject-matter	287.24	wishy-washy
159.8	tax-payers	287.38	override
160.9	township	290.32	all-important
161.13	subject-matter		

II. Critical-text list.

In transcriptions from the present edition, no line-end hyphens in ambiguously broken possible compounds are to be retained except the following:

CORRECTION OF QUOTATIONS

Dewey represented source material in varying ways, from memorial paraphrase to verbatim copy, sometimes citing his source fully, in others mentioning only authors' names, and in still others, omitting documentation altogether.

To prepare the critical text, all material inside quotation marks, except that obviously being emphasized or restated, has been searched out and the documentation has been verified and emended when necessary. Steps regularly used to emend documentation are described in Textual Principles and Procedures (*Middle Works of John Dewey*, 1:347–60), but Dewey's substantive variations from the original in his quotations have been considered important enough to warrant a special list.

All quotations have been retained within the texts as they were first published, except for corrections required by special circumstances and noted in the Emendations List. Substantive changes that restore original readings in case of possible compositorial or typographical errors are similarly noted as "W" emendations. The variable form of quotation suggests that Dewey, like many scholars of the period, was unconcerned about precision in matters of form, but many of the changes in cited materials may have arisen in the printing process. For example, comparing Dewey's quotations with the originals reveals that some journals house-styled the quoted materials as well as Dewey's own. In the present edition, the spelling and capitalization of the source have been reproduced.

Dewey's most frequent alteration in quoted material was changing or omitting punctuation. He also often failed to use ellipses or to separate quotations to show that material had been left out. No citation of the Dewey material or of the original appears here if the changes were only of this kind—

omitted or changed punctuation, including ellipses. In the case of omitted ellipses, attention is called to short phrases; if, however, a line or more has been left out, no attention has been called to the omission.

Italics in source material have been treated as accidentals. When Dewey omitted those italics, the omission is not noted, though Dewey's added italics are listed. If changed or omitted accidentals have substantive implications, as in the capitalization of some concept words, the quotation is noted. The form of listing the quotations, from Dewey as well as from his source, is designed to assist the reader in determining whether Dewey had the book open before him or was relying on his memory.

Notations in this section follow the formula: page-line numbers from the present text, followed by the text condensed to first and last words or such as make for sufficient clarity, then a square bracket followed by the symbol identifying the Dewey item. After a semicolon comes the necessary correction, whether of one word or a longer passage, as required. Finally, in parentheses, the author's surname and shortened source-title from the Checklist of Dewey's References are followed by a comma and the page-line reference to the source.

"The Influence of Darwinism on Philosophy"

7.18–19   alterations and generations] PS;   alterations, mutations, generations, etc. (Galileo, *System of the World*, 45.3–4)
7.22   The nature of physical things] PS;   nature is (Veitch, *Philosophy of Descartes*, 180.29)
7.23–24   coming gradually] PS;   coming in this manner gradually (Veitch, *Philosophy of Descartes*, 180.30–31)

"The Intellectualist Criterion for Truth"

52.25   act] M;   [*rom.*] (Bradley, *Principles of Logic*, 10.34)
52.25   refers the] M;   refers an (Bradley, *Principles of Logic*, 10.34)
52.26   to the] M;   to a (Bradley, *Principles of Logic*, 10.35)

54.8   but] M;   and (Bradley, *Appearance and Reality*, 167.7)
55.10   *that it becomes one as soon as we judge it*] M;   [*rom.*]
        (Bradley, *Appearance and Reality*, 486.2–3)
56.1   must be] M;   is (Bradley, *Appearance and Reality*,
        136.36)
56.13   the] M;   a (Bradley, *Appearance and Reality*, 153.8)
57.39   such shape] M;   such a shape (Bradley, *Appearance
        and Reality*, 152.17)
58.2   *when reflected upon and made explicit*] M;   [*rom.*]
        (Bradley, *Appearance and Reality*, 152.20–21)
58.2   upon] M;   on (Bradley, *Appearance and Reality*,
        152.20)
58.10   to a movement] M;   to movement (Bradley, *Appear-
        ance and Reality*, 152.31)
58.11   *very special kind*] M;   [*rom.*] (Bradley, *Appearance
        and Reality*, 152.32)
58.12   *special*] M;   [*rom.*] (Bradley, *Appearance and Reality*,
        153.3)
58.16   *here*] M;   [*rom.*] (Bradley, *Appearance and Reality*,
        153.22)
58.16   *metaphysics*] M;   [*rom.*] (Bradley, *Appearance and
        Reality*, 153.23)
58.24   which is] M;   which has (Bradley, *Appearance and
        Reality*, 154.36)
59.10–11 its contents into peaceable unity.] M;   the content to
        such a shape that the variety remains peaceably in one.
        (Bradley, *Appearance and Reality*, 152.16–18)

"The Logical Character of Ideas"

91n.3   heap, a] JP;   heap or (Hume, *Treatise*, 495.24)

"What Pragmatism Means by Practical"

99.7   of] JP;   of our (James, *Pragmatism*, 58.14–15)
99.24   in the] JP;   in (James, "The Absolute," 547.7)
100.25–26 in ₐthe 'seat] JP;   ~ '~ ₐ~ (James, *Pragmatism*,
        123.9)
101.1   many] JP;   many different (James, *Pragmatism*, vii.15)
105.36 our] JP;   our concrete (James, *Pragmatism*, 107.6)
106.26 freeₐwill] JP;   ~-~ (James, *Pragmatism*, 121.12)
106.28 on to] JP;   into (James, *Pragmatism*, 121.14)
106.29 then] JP;   *there* (James, *Pragmatism*, 121.15)
108.9   home] JP;   house (James, *Pragmatism*, 203.13)
110n.7 one,] JP;   one else (James, *Pragmatism*, 233.18)

110n.12   commandments] JP;   commandment (James, *Pragma-*
           tism, 234.1)
111.2   Ideas] JP;   *ideas (which themselves are but parts of*
           our experience) (James, *Pragmatism,* 58.5–7)
112.11–12 *our double urgency*] JP;   [*rom.*] (James, *Pragma-*
           tism, 64.2–3)

"Pure Experience and Reality: A Disclaimer"

120.21   *no*]   PR;   [*rom.*]   (McGilvary,   "Pure   Experience,"
           274.13)

"Objects, Data, and Existences: A Reply to Professor McGilvary"

149.13   as an] JP;   as (McGilvary, "The Chicago Idea," 596.10)
149.13   *experienced*] JP;   [*rom.*] (McGilvary, "The Chicago
           Idea," 596.10)
149.15   as an] JP;   as (McGilvary, "The Chicago Idea," 596.9)
149.15   *accepted*] JP;   [*rom.*] (McGilvary, "The Chicago Idea,"
           596.9)
149.16   one side] JP;   one (McGilvary, "The Chicago Idea,"
           596.20)
150.8   *omnibus*] JP;   [*rom.*] (McGilvary, "The Chicago Idea,"
           458.35)
153.5   whenever] JP;   whenever any (McGilvary, "The Chi-
           cago Idea," 596.42–43)
154.29–30 sense] JP;   sense of idealism (McGilvary, "The Chi-
           cago Idea," 594.19)

"*Review of* Studies in Philosophy and Psychology"

219.19   association, instead] PR;   association is itself a vast
           plasma of human interests. Instead (Woods, *Studies in*
           Philosophy, 96.13–14)
221.20   desires, considered] PR;   desires, in so far as they are
           called for by a given situation, considered (Sharp,
           Studies in Philosophy, 108.23–24)
221.27   when] PR;   when it is such that, (Sharp, *Studies in*
           Philosophy, 116.28)
221.27–28 ourselves in] PR;   ourselves in imagination in
           (Sharp, *Studies in Philosophy,* 116.29)

221.28–29 member of it] PR; member (Sharp, *Studies in Philosophy*, 116.30)
224.2 that by] PR; that from (Woodbridge, *Studies in Philosophy*, 149.25)

"*Review of* The Life of Reason"

231.10 force which] ER; force" pompously appealed to (Santayana, *Life*, 5:57.24)
231.34 writings] ER; writing (Santayana, *Life*, 5:133.20–21)
234.3–4 standard,] ER; standard, action at the same time veering in harmony with estimation, (Santayana, *Life*, 1:47.8–10)
235.20 substantial] ER; substantial physical (Santayana, *Life*, 1:25.16)
236.16 altogether;] ER; altogether. Here the ideal interests themselves take possession of the mind; (Santayana, *Life*, 2:205.11–13)
237.2 about] ER; about experience or (Santayana, *Life*, 3:11.13)
239n.3 interests brought] ER; interest to bring it (Santayana, *Life*, 5:177.12)
240n.2 and] ER; and is (Santayana, *Life*, 5:315.22)

"*Review of* Henry Sidgwick, A Memoir"

243.21 them resemble] PSQ; men [resemble] (Sidgwick, *Henry Sidgwick*, 395.31)
243.23 instinctively] PSQ; naturally (Sidgwick, *Henry Sidgwick*, 395.32)

CHECKLIST OF DEWEY'S REFERENCES

Titles and authors' names in Dewey references have been corrected and expanded to conform accurately and consistently to the original works; all corrections appear in the Emendations List.

This section gives full publication information for each work cited by Dewey. When Dewey gave page numbers for a reference, the edition he used was identified exactly by locating the citation. Similarly, the books in Dewey's personal library have been used to verify his use of a particular edition. For other references, the edition listed here is the one from among the various editions possibly available to him that was his most likely source by reason of place or date of publication, or on the evidence from correspondence and other materials, and its general accessibility during the period.

Aliotta, Antonio. "Il pragmatismo anglo-americano." *La Cultura Filosofica* 3 (1909): 104–34.

Amiel, Henri-Frédéric. *Amiel's Journal: The Journal Intime of Henri-Frédéric Amiel.* Translated by Mrs. Humphrey Ward. London: Macmillan and Co., 1893.

Armstrong, Andrew Campbell. "The Evolution of Pragmatism." *Journal of Philosophy, Psychology and Scientific Methods* 5 (1908): 645–50.

Bakewell, Charles Montague. *Latter-Day Flowing-Philosophy.* University of California Publications in Philosophy, vol. 1, no. 5. Berkeley: University Press, 1904.

———. "On the Meaning of Truth." *Philosophical Review* 17 (1908): 579–91.

Baldwin, James Mark, ed. *Dictionary of Philosophy and Psychology.* Vol. 1. New York: Macmillan Co., 1901.

———. "The Limits of Pragmatism." *Psychological Review* 11 (1904): 30–60.

———. "On Truth." *Psychological Review* 14 (1907): 264–87.

Bawden, H. Heath. "The New Philosophy Called Pragmatism." *Popular Science Monthly* 73 (1908): 61–72.

Benn, Alfred William. *The History of English Rationalism in the*

Nineteenth Century. London: Longmans, Green, and Co., 1906.

Bode, Boyd Henry. "The Concept of Pure Experience." *Philosophical Review* 14 (1905): 684–95.

Borrell, Philippe. "La notion de pragmatisme." *Revue de Philosophie* 11 (1907): 587–90.

Boutroux, Pierre Léon. "L'objectivité intrinsèque des mathématiques." *Revue de metaphysique et de morale* 11 (1903): 573–92.

Bradley, Francis Herbert. *Appearance and Reality: A Metaphysical Essay.* London: Swan Sonnenschein and Co., 1893.

———. *The Principles of Logic.* London: Kegan Paul, Trench and Co., 1883.

———. "On the Ambiguity of Pragmatism." *Mind,* n.s. 17 (1908): 226–37.

———. "On Truth and Copying." *Mind,* n.s. 16 (1907): 165–80.

———. "On Truth and Practice." *Mind,* n.s. 13 (1904): 309–35.

Brown, William Adams. "The Pragmatic Value of the Absolute." *Journal of Philosophy, Psychology and Scientific Methods* 4 (1907): 459–64.

Bush, Wendell T. "A Factor in the Genesis of Idealism." In *Essays, Philosophical and Psychological,* pp. 81–102. New York: Longmans, Green, and Co., 1908.

———. "Provisional and Eternal Truth." *Journal of Philosophy, Psychology and Scientific Methods* 5 (1908): 181–84.

Carus, Paul. "A German Critic of Pragmatism." *Monist* 19 (1909): 136–48.

———. Letter from Professor James. *Monist* 19 (1909): 156.

———. "Pragmatism." *Monist* 18 (1908): 321–62.

Chiappelli, Alessandro. "Philosophie des valeurs." *Revue philosophique* 67 (1909): 225–55.

Chide, Alphonse. "Pragmatisme et intellectualisme." *Revue philosophique* 65 (1908): 367–88.

Colvin, Stephen S. "Pragmatism, Old and New." *Monist* 16 (1906): 547–61.

Cox, Rev. Ignatius W. "Pragmatism." *American Catholic Quarterly* 34 (1909): 139–65.

Creighton, James Edwin. "The Nature and Criterion of Truth." *Philosophical Review* 17 (1908): 592–605.

———. "Purpose as Logical Category." *Philosophical Review* 13 (1904): 284–97.

Darwin, Charles Robert. *The Life and Letters of Charles Darwin.* Edited by Francis Darwin. New York: D. Appleton and Co., 1897.

———. *On the Origin of the Species by Means of Natural Selection.* London: John Murray, 1859.

———. *The Variations of Animals and Plants under Domestication.* New York: D. Appleton and Co., 1876.

Defoe, Daniel. *Robinson Crusoe*. Edited by Edward R. Shaw. Standard Literature Series, no. 25. New York: University Publishing Co., 1897.

Dewey, John. *Moral Principles in Education*. Boston: Houghton Mifflin Co., 1909. [*The Middle Works of John Dewey, 1899–1924*, edited by Jo Ann Boydston, 4:265–333. Carbondale: Southern Illinois University Press, 1977.]

———. *The Significance of the Problem of Knowledge*. University of Chicago Contributions to Philosophy, vol. 1, no. 3. Chicago: University of Chicago Press, 1897. [*The Early Works of John Dewey, 1882–1898*, edited by Jo Ann Boydston, 5:3–24. Carbondale: Southern Illinois University Press, 1972.]

———. *Studies in Logical Theory*. Chicago: University of Chicago Press, 1903. [*Middle Works* 2:292–375.]

———. "Beliefs and Realities." *Philosophical Review* 15 (1906): 113–19. [*Middle Works* 3:83–100.]

———. "The Control of Ideas by Facts. I." *Journal of Philosophy, Psychology and Scientific Methods* 4 (1907): 197–203; II., ibid., pp. 253–59; III., ibid., pp. 309–19.

———. "Does Reality Possess Practical Character?" In *Essays, Philosophical and Psychological*, pp. 53–80. New York: Longmans, Green, and Co., 1908. [*Middle Works* 4:125–42.]

———. "Experience and Objective Idealism." *Philosophical Review* 15 (1906): 465–81. [*Middle Works* 3:126–44.]

———. "The Experimental Theory of Knowledge." *Mind*, n.s. 15 (1906): 293–307. [*Middle Works* 3:107–27.]

———. "Logical Conditions of a Scientific Treatment of Morality." In *Investigations Representing the Departments*. University of Chicago, The Decennial Publications, first series, 3:115–39. Chicago: University of Chicago Press, 1903.

———. "The Logical Character of Ideas." *Journal of Philosophy, Psychology and Scientific Methods* 5 (1908): 378–81. [*Middle Works* 4:91–97.]

———. "Psychology and Philosophic Method." *University* [of California] *Chronicle* 2 (1899): 159–79. [*Middle Works* 1:113–30.]

———. "Reality and the Criterion for the Truth of Ideas." *Mind*, n.s. 16 (1907): 317–42. [*Middle Works* 4:50–75.]

———. "Some Stages of Logical Thought." *Philosophical Review* 9 (1900): 465–89. [*Middle Works* 1:151–74.]

———. "What Does Pragmatism Mean by Practical?" *Journal of Philosophy, Psychology and Scientific Methods* 5 (1908): 85–99. [*Middle Works* 4:98–115.]

Galileo, Galilei. *The Systeme of the World: In Four Dialogues*. London: William Leybourne, 1661.

Gardiner, Harry Norman. "The Problem of Truth." *Philosophical Review* 17 (1908): 113–37.

Garman, Charles Edward. Letter. *American Journal of Psychology* 9 (1897–98): 600–606.

Gordon, Kate. "Pragmatism in Aesthetics." In *Essays, Philosophical and Psychological*, pp. 459–82. New York: Longmans, Green, and Co., 1908.

Hébert, Marcel. *Le pragmatisme et ses diverses formes anglo-américaines.* Paris: Librairie critique Emile Nourry, 1908.

Hibben, Grier. "The Test of Pragmatism." *Philosophical Review* 17 (1908): 365–82.

Hume, David. *A Treatise of Human Nature.* Edited by T. H. Green and T. H. Grose. 2 vols. New York: Longmans, Green, and Co., 1898.

James, William. *A Pluralistic Universe.* New York: Longmans, Green, and Co., 1909.

———. *Pragmatism: A New Name for Some Old Ways of Thinking: Popular Lectures on Philosophy.* New York: Longmans, Green, and Co., 1907.

———. *The Varieties of Religious Experience: A Study in Human Nature.* New York: Longmans, Green, and Co., 1902.

———. *The Will to Believe and Other Essays in Popular Philosophy.* London: Longmans, Green, and Co., 1896.

———. "The Absolute and the Strenuous Life." *Journal of Philosophy, Psychology and Scientific Methods* 4 (1907): 546–48.

———. "Does 'Consciousness' Exist?" *Journal of Philosophy, Psychology and Scientific Methods* 1 (1904): 477–91.

———. "The Essence of Humanism." *Journal of Philosophy, Psychology and Scientific Methods* 2 (1905): 113–18.

———. "Humanism and Truth." *Mind*, n.s. 13 (1904): 457–75.

———. Letter. *Monist* 19 (1909): 56.

———. "The Place of Affectional Facts in a World of Pure Experience." *Journal of Philosophy, Psychology and Scientific Methods* 2 (1905): 281–87.

———. "The Pragmatic Method." *Journal of Philosophy, Psychology and Scientific Methods* 1 (1904): 673–87.

———. "Pragmatism's Conception of Truth." *Journal of Philosophy, Psychology and Scientific Methods* 4 (1907): 141–55.

———. "The Pragmatist Account of Truth and Its Misunderstanders." *Philosophical Review* 17 (1908): 1–17.

———. "Professor Pratt on Truth." *Journal of Philosophy, Psychology and Scientific Methods* 4 (1907): 464–67.

———. Review of *Le pragmatisme et ses diverses formes anglo-américaines*, by Marcel Hébert. *Journal of Philosophy, Psychology and Scientific Methods* 5 (1908): 689–94.

———. "The Thing and Its Relations." *Journal of Philosophy, Psychology and Scientific Methods* 2 (1905): 29–41.

————. "A Word More about Truth." *Journal of Philosophy, Psychology and Scientific Methods* 4 (1907): 396–406.

————. "A World of Pure Experience. I." *Journal of Philosophy, Psychology and Scientific Methods* 1 (1904): 533–43; II., ibid., pp. 561–70.

————, and Russell, John E. "Controversy about Truth." *Journal of Philosophy, Psychology and Scientific Methods* 4 (1907): 289–96.

Janet, Paul. *Final Causes*. Translated by William Affleck. Edinburgh: T. & T. Clark, 1878.

Joachim, Harold H. *The Nature of Truth: An Essay*. Oxford: Clarendon Press, 1906.

Knox, Howard V. "Pragmatism: The Evolution of Truth." *Quarterly Review* 210 (1909): 379–407.

Lalande, André. "Pragmatisme, humanisme et verité." *Revue philosophique* 65 (1908): 1–26.

Leighton, Joseph Alexander. "Pragmatism." *Journal of Philosophy, Psychology and Scientific Methods* 1 (1904): 148–56.

Le Roy, Edouard. "De la valeur objective des lois physiques." *Bulletin de la société française de philosophie* 1 (1901): 5–6.

Lorenz-Ightham, Von Theodor. "Das Verhältnis des Pragmatismus zu Kant." *Kant Studien* 14 (1909): 8–44.

————. "Der pragmatismus." *Internationale Wochenschrift* (1908).

Lovejoy, Arthur O. "The Thirteen Pragmatisms: II." *Journal of Philosophy, Psychology and Scientific Methods* 5 (1908): 29–39.

Lyman, Eugene William. "The Influence of Pragmatism upon the Status of Theology." In *Studies in Philosophy and Psychology*, pp. 219–36. Boston: Houghton Mifflin Co., 1906.

McGilvary, Evander Bradley. "The Chicago 'Idea' and Idealism." *Journal of Philosophy, Psychology and Scientific Methods* 5 (1908): 589–97. [*Middle Works* 4:317–27.]

————. "Prolegomena to a Tentative Realism." *Journal of Philosophy, Psychology and Scientific Methods* 4 (1907): 449–58.

————. "Pure Experience and Reality." *Philosophical Review* 16 (1907): 266–84.

Maine, Sir Henry Sumner. *Village-Communities in the East and West*. New York: Henry Holt and Co., 1876.

Mill, John Stuart. *A System of Logic, Ratiocinative and Inductive*. 5th ed. London: Parker, Son, and Bourn, 1862.

Mead, George Herbert. "The Definition of the Psychical." In *Investigations Representing the Departments*. University of Chicago, The Decennial Publications, first series, 3:75–112. Chicago: University of Chicago Press, 1903.

Mentré, François. "Note sur la valeur pragmatique du pragmatisme." *Revue de philosophie* 11 (1907): 5–22.

———. "Complément à la note sur la valeur pragmatique du pragmatisme." *Revue de philosophie* 11 (1907): 591–94.

Moore, Addison Webster. *The Functional versus the Representational Theories of Knowledge in Locke's Essay.* Chicago: University of Chicago Press, 1902.

———. "Absolutism and Teleology." *Philosophical Review* 18 (1909): 309–18.

———. "Existence, Meaning, and Reality in Locke's Essay and in Present Epistemology." In *Investigations Representing the Departments.* University of Chicago, The Decennial Publications, first series, 2:29–51. Chicago: University of Chicago Press, 1903.

———. "Pragmatism and Its Critics." *Philosophical Review* 14 (1905): 322–43.

———. "Professor Perry on Pragmatism." *Journal of Philosophy, Psychology and Scientific Methods* 4 (1907): 567–77.

———. "Truth Value." *Journal of Philosophy, Psychology and Scientific Methods* 5 (1908): 429–36.

Norton, Edwin Lee. "The Intellectual Element in Music." In *Studies in Philosophy and Psychology,* pp. 167–201. Boston: Houghton Mifflin Co., 1906.

Nunn, Sir Thomas Percy. *The Aim and Achievements of Scientific Method: An Epistemological Essay.* London: Macmillan and Co., 1907.

Parodi, M. "La signification du Pragmatisme." *Bulletin de la société française de philosophie* 8 (1908).

Peirce, Charles Santiago Sanders. "How to Make Our Ideas Clear." *Popular Science Monthly* 12 (1878): 286–302.

———. "Issues of Pragmatism." *Monist* 15 (1905): 481–99.

———. "Prolegomena to an Apology for Pragmatism." *Monist* 16 (1906): 492–546.

———. "What Pragmatism Is." *Monist* 15 (1905): 161–81.

Perry, Ralph Barton. "A Review of Pragmatism as a Philosophical Generalization." *Journal of Philosophy, Psychology and Scientific Methods* 4 (1907): 421–28.

———. "A Review of Pragmatism as a Theory of Knowledge." *Journal of Philosophy, Psychology and Scientific Methods* 4 (1907): 365–74.

Pierce, Arthur Henry. "An Appeal from the Prevailing Doctrine of a Detached Subconsciousness." In *Studies in Philosophy and Psychology,* pp. 315–49. Boston: Houghton Mifflin Co., 1906.

Poincaré, Henri. "Sur la valeur objective de la science." *Revue de metaphysique et de morale* 10 (1902): 263–93.

Pratt, James Bisset. *What Is Pragmatism?* New York: Macmillan Co., 1909.

———. "Truth and Ideas." *Journal of Philosophy, Psychology and Scientific Methods* 5 (1908): 122–31.

———. "Truth and Its Verification." *Journal of Philosophy, Psychology and Scientific Methods* 4 (1907): 320–24.

Raub, William Longstreth. "Pragmatism and Kantianism." In *Studies in Philosophy and Psychology*, pp. 203–17. Boston: Houghton Mifflin Co., 1906.

Rey, Abel. "Vers le positivisme absolu." *Revue philosophique de la France et de l'étranger* 68 (1909): 461–79.

Rieber, Charles Henry. *Pragmatism and the "a priori."* University of California Publications in Philosophy, vol. 1, no. 4. Berkeley: University Press, 1904.

Rogers, Arthur Kenyon. "Professor James's Theory of Knowledge." *Philosophical Review* 15 (1906): 577–96.

Royce, Josiah. "The Eternal and the Practical." *Philosophical Review* 13 (1904): 113–42.

Russell, Bertrand. "The Nature of Truth." *Mind*, n.s. 15 (1906): 528–33.

Russell, John E. "Pragmatism as the Salvation from Philosophic Doubt." *Journal of Philosophy, Psychology and Scientific Methods* 4 (1907): 57–64.

———. "The Pragmatist's Meaning of Truth." *Journal of Philosophy, Psychology and Scientific Methods* 3 (1906): 599–601.

———. "Some Difficulties with the Epistemology of Pragmatism and Radical Empiricism." *Philosophical Review* 15 (1906): 406–13.

———, and James, William. "Controversy about Truth." *Journal of Philosophy, Psychology and Scientific Methods* 4 (1907): 289–96.

Santayana, George. *The Life of Reason, or the Phases of Human Progress.* 5 vols. New York: Charles Scribner's Sons, 1905–6.

Schiller, Ferdinand Canning Scott. *Humanism.* New York: Macmillan Co., 1903.

———. *Studies in Humanism.* London: Macmillan and Co., 1907.

———. "Axioms as Postulates." In *Personal Idealism*, edited by Henry Sturt, pp. 47–133. London: Macmillan and Co., 1902.

———. "In Defence of Humanism." *Mind*, n.s. 13 (1904): 525–42.

———. "Is Mr. Bradley Becoming a Pragmatist?" *Mind*, n.s. 17 (1908): 370–83.

———. "Mr. Bradley's Theory of Truth." *Mind*, n.s. 16 (1907): 401–9.

———. "Plato or Protagoras." *Mind*, n.s. 17 (1908): 518–26.

———. "A Pragmatic Babe in the Wood." *Journal of Philosophy, Psychology and Scientific Methods* 4 (1907): 42–44.

————. "The Pragmatic Cure of Doubt." *Journal of Philosophy, Psychology and Scientific Methods* 4 (1907): 235–38.
————. "Pragmatism and Pseudo-Pragmatism." *Mind,* n.s. 15 (1906): 375–90.
————. "Pragmatism versus Skepticism." *Journal of Philosophy, Psychology and Scientific Methods* 4 (1907): 482–87.
Schinz, Albert. *Anti-pragmatisme: Examen des droits respectifs de l'aristocratie intellectuelle et de la démocratie sociale.* Paris: F. Alcan, 1909.
Shakespeare, William. *Shakespeare's Comedy of The Merchant of Venice.* 12th ed. London: J. M. Dent and Co., 1904.
Sharp, Frank Chapman. "An Analysis of the Moral Judgment." In *Studies in Philosophy and Psychology,* pp. 101–35. Boston: Houghton Mifflin Co., 1906.
Sidgwick, Alfred. "The Ambiguity of Pragmatism." *Mind,* n.s. 17 (1908): 368–69.
Sidgwick, Arthur, and Sidgwick, Eleanor M. *Henry Sidgwick.* New York: Macmillan Co., 1906.
Stein, Ludwig. "Der Pragmatismus." *Archiv für systematische Philosophie,* n.s. 14 (1908): 1–9, 143–88.
Studies in Philosophy and Psychology. By Former Students of Charles Edward Garman, in Commemoration of Twenty-five Years of Service as Teacher of Philosophy in Amherst College. Boston: Houghton Mifflin Co., 1906.
Stout, George Frederick. "Error." In *Personal Idealism,* edited by Henry Sturt, pp. 1–46. New York: Macmillan Co., 1902.
Strong, Charles Augustus. "Pragmatism and Its Definition of Truth." *Journal of Philosophy, Psychology and Scientific Methods* 5 (1908): 256–64.
Sturt, Henry. "Mr. Bradley on Truth and Copying." *Mind,* n.s. 16 (1907): 416–17.
Tausch, Edwin. "William James, The Pragmatist—A Psychological Analysis." *Monist* 19 (1909): 1–26.
Taylor, Alfred Edward. "Truth and Consequences." *Mind,* n.s. 15 (1906): 81–93.
————. "Truth and Practice." *Philosophical Review* 14 (1905): 265–89.
Tufts, James Hayden. "On Moral Evolution." In *Studies in Philosophy and Psychology,* pp. 3–39. Boston: Houghton Mifflin Co., 1906.
Vailati, Giovanni. "A Pragmatic Zoologist." *Monist* 18 (1908): 142–51.
————. "Pragmatism and Mathematical Logic." *Monist* 16 (1906): 481–91.
Veitch, John. *The Method, Meditations and Philosophy of Descartes.* New York: Tudor Publishing Co., 1901.
Willcox, Walter Francis. "The Expansion of Europe in Its Influence upon Population." In *Studies in Philosophy and Psy-*

chology, pp. 41–70. Boston: Houghton Mifflin Co., 1906.

Woodbridge, Frederick J. E. "The Field of Logic." In *Congress of Arts and Science*, Universal Exposition, St. Louis, 1904, edited by Howard J. Rogers. Boston: Houghton Mifflin Co., 1905.

———. "Pragmatism and Education." *Educational Review* 34 (1907): 227–40.

———. "The Problem of Consciousness." In *Studies in Philosophy and Psychology*, pp. 137–66. Boston: Houghton Mifflin Co., 1906.

Woods, Robert Archey. "Democracy a New Unfolding of Human Power." In *Studies in Philosophy and Psychology*, pp. 71–100. Boston: Houghton Mifflin Co., 1906.

Woodworth, Robert Sessions. "The Cause of a Voluntary Movement." In *Studies in Philosophy and Psychology*, pp. 351–92. Boston: Houghton Mifflin Co., 1906.

INDEX

Absolute: Bradley on, 55–58
Amiel, Henri-Frédéric, 44, 242
Appearance: Bradley on, 54–55
Aristotle: on species, 5; on the state and individual, 32–33; on class distinctions, 33–34; mentioned, 24
Art: teaching of, overworked as moral force, 206–8
Attention: non-voluntary, voluntary, and reflective, 201–3
Awareness: as a fact, 125–37; as attention, 138–42, 314

Bacon, Francis, 254
Bentham, Jeremy: on morals, 40
Berkeley, George, 255
Bosanquet, Bernard, 304, 312
Bossuet, Jacques Bénigne: on truth, 77
Bradley, F. H.: on reality, 50–75; on intellectualism, 51–75; on appearance, 54–55; on truth, 54, 64–70; on "absolute," 55–58; on "special," 58–59; on thinking, 60–64; mentioned, xiv, 254
Butler, Nicholas Murray, xvii

Cambridge, University of: as reflected in Sidgwick biography, 242
Character: necessary constituents of, 287–91
Chicago, University of: pragmatic spirit of, x
Chicago School, 113
Cicero, 42

Columbia University: non-pragmatic philosophy of, x
Consciousness: as a natural good, 23–24; Dewey's conception of, 91–94; McGilvary's misunderstanding of Dewey's view of, 143–45; Woodbridge on, 222–27; McGilvary on Dewey on, 314–16; mentioned, 255
Copernicus, 7, 305–7

Darwinian logic: its bearing upon philosophy, 10–14
Democracy: its conception of intelligence, 39–40; Woods on, 218–19
Democritus, 38
Descartes, René, 254
Design, principle of: *versus* chance, as causal principle of life, 8–10; undercut by Darwin's natural selection, 9
Dualistic epistemology, 82n

Education: history of, 161; methods of, 161–62; philosophy of, 162–63; as purveyor of religion, 165–66; as separate from religious instruction, 167–70; several theories of mind applied to, 181–91; as public business, 328
Emerson, Ralph Waldo, xxxiii, 241
Environment: related to idea, 83–84
Everett, Edward, 159

Evolution, moral: Tufts on,
219–21
Experience: as central concept
in Dewey's mature philosophy, xv–xvi; and reality,
120–24; McGilvary on, 151–
55; McGilvary on James on,
295–96; McGilvary on Dewey
on, 295–313

Fact and idea: McGilvary's
criticism of Dewey's view of,
146–57
Feudalism: Greek philosophy
used to justify, 35

Galileo, 7
Geography: social significance
of, 211; moral bearing of,
211–12; used to teach social
progress, 280–81
Good: related to nature, 15–30
Gray, Asa: attempted to reconcile design with natural
selection, 9–10
Green, Thomas Hill: on morals
in nature, 43–44; on reality,
50; mentioned, 227
Grotius, Hugo: on natural law,
41

Hamilton, William, 309–10
Happiness, 45
Hegel, Georg Wilhelm Friedrich: on reason, 43
Herbart, Johann Friedrich, 52
Heredity, cultural, xxx, 156–57
History: as dynamic account
of social life, 192–93; study
of, gives more interest to
nature study, 194; biographic
element in, 194–95; chronological order not desirable
in teaching, 195–96; teaching of, divided into three
phases, 196–97; teaching of,
as moral force, 208–10; used

to teach social progress,
282–83
Hobbes, Thomas, 254
Hook, Sidney, xxxii
Hooker, William Jackson, 4
Hume, David: on morals, 40;
on mind, 91n; on idea, 318;
mentioned, 254
Huxley, Thomas Henry, 4

Idea: defined, 83–84; agreement of, with environment,
84; fact and, 146–57; Mc-
Gilvary on Dewey on, 317–
26; Hume on, 318; Locke on,
318; Lotze on, 318
Idealism, 116–17
Individualism, 256–57
Intellectualism: Bradley on,
51–75; mentioned, xvi
Intelligence: related to nature,
15–30; as an active life
force, 36; democracy's conception of, 39–40; pragmatism's theory of the nature of,
181–91

James, William: Dewey's interpretation of, xx–xxii; on
pragmatism, 98–115; on
significance of object, 101–
2; on idea, 102–3; on truth,
103, 107–12; on function of
philosophy, 104; on design,
105–6; Schinz on pragma-
tism of, 248–49; on pure experience, 295–96
Janet, Paul, 77
Johns Hopkins University,
The, xi

Kant, Immanuel, 42, 52, 248,
254
Kepler, Johannes, 7
Knowledge: pragmatism's
theory of the nature of, 181–
91, 255–56

The Collected Works of John Dewey, 1882–1953

The Later Works, 1925–1953